Aloysius Sabetti

The decree 'Quemadmodum'

Aloysius Sabetti

The decree 'Quemadmodum'

ISBN/EAN: 9783741103858

Manufactured in Europe, USA, Canada, Australia, Japa

Cover: Foto ©ninafisch / pixelio.de

Manufactured and distributed by brebook publishing software (www.brebook.com)

Aloysius Sabetti

The decree 'Quemadmodum'

THE DECREE "QUEMADMODUM,"

WITH EXPLANATIONS.

BY

REV. A. SABETTI, S. J.,

Professor of Moral Theology at Woodstock College, Md.

BALTIMORE:
JOHN MURPHY & CO.
(METROPOLITAN PRESS.)
1892.

APPROBATIO.

Cum opusculum cui titulus est "The Decree *Quemadmodum*," etc. aliqui nostrae Societatis revisores, quibus id commissum fuit, recognoverint et in lucem edi posse probaverint, facultatem concedimus, ut typis mandetur, si iis, ad quos pertinet, ita videbitur.

THOMAS J. CAMPBELL, S. J.,
Praep. Prov. Maryl., Neo-Ebor.

NEO-EBORACI, *die 15 Martii*, 1892.

IMPRIMATUR.

JACOBUS CARD. GIBBONS,
Archiep. Baltimorensis.

BALTIMORAE, *die 2 Apr.*, 1892.

THE DECREE "QUEMADMODUM."

The Decree " *Quemadmodum* " was promulgated the 17th Dec., 1890, in order to suppress abuses that had arisen in certain religious communities. It is our purpose to make a few notes and remarks on its bearings and meaning, and to solve some difficulties that may arise as to its interpretation. In doing so we shall present the text by paragraphs, making use of the official translation sent by our Ordinaries to the superiors of those religious communities that are concerned with it. The text of the Decree is italicised.

Just as it is the fate of human things, how praiseworthy and holy soever they may be in themselves, even so is it of laws wisely enacted, to be liable to be misused and perverted to purposes opposed and foreign to their nature. Wherefore it sometimes happens that they no longer serve the purposes which the lawmakers had in view; nay, they sometimes even produce quite a contrary result.

1. In this first paragraph a general reason for the promulgation of the Decree is presented, and the mind is prepared for its dutiful acceptance. Moreover, an objection which would seem to present itself most readily to us, is anticipated; for we are reminded of what experience teaches us; that, what has been established for the general good, is very often turned to evil. Consequently, what had been wisely sanctioned or granted by the supreme authority is now prudently taken away, and that, too, without the least suspicion of contradiction or fickleness. Therefore there is no question here of a law, new in all its bearings, but only of certain arrangements and limitations for suppressing the abuses that have evidently crept in, and of restoring to usefulness what has become fraught with danger.

Much it is to be deplored that such has proved to be the case with the laws of several Congregations, Societies, and Institutes, both of women who emit simple or solemn vows, and of men who by their profession and discipline are merely laymen. For, inasmuch as occasionally their Constitutions permitted the making a manifestation of conscience, in order that thereby the members might the more easily learn, in their doubts, from experienced Superiors, how to walk in the path of perfection, it has happened, on the contrary, that some of the latter have introduced the practice of thoroughly inquiring into the state of their subjects' conscience, which is a thing reserved exclusively to the Sacrament of Penance. In like manner, and in conformity with the prescriptions of the Sacred Canons, it was ordered that Sacramental Confession in all such communities should be made to the respective Ordinary and Extraordinary Confessors; while, on the other hand, the arbitrary conduct of some Superiors has gone so far as to refuse to their subjects an Extraordinary Confessor, even in cases where the conscience of the persons so refused stood greatly in need of such privilege. These Superiors were given a rule of discretion and prudence for the purpose of enabling them to direct their subjects in a proper and right use of peculiar penitential exercises and other practices of piety; but this very rule, also, was so perverted by abuse that they [the Superiors] took it on themselves to permit, at their pleasure, their subjects to approach the Holy Table, or even sometimes to forbid them Communion altogether. Hence it has happened that such regulations as these, established for the salutary and wise purpose of promoting the spiritual progress of members and fostering in communities the union growing out of peace and concord, have not unfrequently resulted in imperilling the salvation of souls, in deeply disturbing consciences, and, moreover, in the disturbance of exterior peace,—as it is most evidently proved by the appeals and complaints frequently made to the Holy See.

2. Here we come more closely to the object of the Decree; and our attention is called more particularly to those points in which the abuses to be corrected may occur.

These points are three—*a*, the manifestation of conscience; *b*, the recourse to Extraordinary Confessors; and *c*, the frequency of Holy Communion. A few words on each.

a.—Manifestation of conscience, which is called in other places in this Decree "a close searching of the conscience," "an intimate manifestation of heart and conscience," is described by Father Lehmkuhl, S. J., in his annotations on this Decree as "a communication made to a Superior, of the thoughts and affections, temptations and interior struggles of one's soul." Father S. Franco, S. J., in a letter to a certain Superioress, a letter which is a full and excellent commentary on the Decree itself, expresses the same opinion; for he says that "by manifestation of conscience as it is commonly understood in religious communities, is meant a knowledge of the state of one's soul, imparted by a subject to a Superior, not indeed freely or voluntarily, but because the rule requires it, and so given that one's dispositions and desires for doing good, the obstacles and difficulties met with, the passions and temptations which move or harass the soul, the faults that are more frequently committed, are sincerely and unreservedly made known."

That this and no other manifestation of conscience is the object of this Decree is evident, not only from the very tenor of the words, but from the reason which is added; namely, on account of the abuses and dangers which arise from it; the abuses, we know, come from the arbitrary severity exercised by some Superiors; the dangers from this, that women and lay persons undertake to manage matters which belong strictly to the Sacrament of Penance, and meddle with the business of Confessors.

Wherefore with respect to the manifestation of exterior actions nothing is changed. Superiors still have the right to inquire about external faults, that they may take measures against the guilty, so too Masters and Mistresses of Novices may inquire if their instructions on the different works of piety and the exercises of the spiritual life were rightly understood. And here it should be observed that, as far as our own knowledge goes, hardly anything more than this is done in the convents of this country. Yet it must by no means be inferred, from this statement, either that there is some exaggeration in the terms of the Decree, or that there is no need to be solicitous in these matters. For, although, on the one hand, no one imagines, for a moment, that all the abuses referred to in the Decree have place in each and every religious community, or in every part of the Lord's vineyard; yet on the other, we cannot close our eyes to the frailties of our human nature, to that inborn curiosity, which has such a hold on all, especially on women, to find out all that can be known about everything.

b.—With respect to an Extraordinary Confessor, we know that one is not only allowed, but even required by the laws of the Church, for those religious who live under rule, and this for the purpose of more effectively protecting liberty of conscience. Recourse to him may be considered a necessary consequence of that law, by reason of which, not all Confessors, but only those specially appointed, can validly and licitly hear the confessions of nuns and of religious in general.

On this point two essentials may be noted : the first is that nuns should have a special and suitable Confessor, who can lead them safely and prudently, on the way to perfection ; the other, that this seeming restriction should not degenerate into absolute subjection, that so the danger of sacrilege or despair may be avoided. To this two-fold necessity corresponds the two-fold head of ecclesiastical legislation, in consequence of which both the Ordinary Confessor of nuns ought to be specially approved, and besides an Extraordinary Confessor granted to them several times during the year.

These provisions, which were sanctioned by the Council of Trent, sess. 25, De Reg. c. x., and by many Roman Pontiffs, especially by Gregory XV. and Clement X., were, with even more explicitness, confirmed and urged by Benedict XIV. in the Bull "*Pastoralis Curae,*" August 5, 1748. In it that Holy Pontiff complains of the rigorous severity which some Prelates and Superiors use in granting Extraordinary Confessors. This same severity is the reason for the fatherly complaint of Leo XIII. ; and it is the very thing that once for all should be crushed as an abuse of power.

Here perhaps it may be asked whether this point of the Decree has any practical application in this country ; and the reason for the question is that here with us, with very few exceptions, we have no nuns in the strict sense, such as were meant by the Council of Trent and by Benedict XIV. And yet the Decree does apply to us, because, from the very words of the Pontiff, the privilege of having recourse to an Extraordinary Confessor should be conceded to all those religious to whom the Decree is directed, and the Decree is directed to all congregations, societies, and institutes of women and merely lay-men, and that independently of the kind of vows they make, whether they be simple or solemn. But apart from this, is it true that the legislation enacted by Trent and by Benedict XIV. has no application to our nuns for the reason that, for the most part, they are not such in the strict sense, that is, according to the strict standard of canon law? Such would indeed be the case, if we are to understand that this legislation was not *made* for them; but not, if we meant that the legislation is not *applicable* and, in fact, *applied* to them. Not only the statutes of the two last Councils of Baltimore require this application, but also the intention of the Church, frequently made known to us in these later days, and, besides, a parallel reason; for when once the law of having one Special Confessor has been admitted, the liberty of having recourse to an Extraordinary Confessor must follow as a consequence. Here are the words of the Third Plenary Council of Baltimore, n. 96: "And with regard to the Sisters who make only simple vows, our Bishops should not neglect to follow out the prescription of Holy Church which provides not only for an Ordinary Confessor appointed by the Ordinary or other Superiors, but also that an Extraordinary one should be delegated several times during the year. Reason itself and the Rules and the practice of these new Institutes approved and commended by the Apostolic See, demand both."

There is, however, one case in which this obligation of providing for an Extraordinary Confessor ceases. It is when, in any diocese, whether from the expressed or tacit consent of the Ordinary, nuns have permission to go to any Confessor, as they please; and though an Ordinary Confessor has been named for them, he is not considered as such because he alone can validly and licitly hear their confessions, but only because they can go to him with more freedom and convenience.

c.—The third abuse the Holy Father complains of is that some Superiors of these several congregations and institutes have taken upon themselves to decide who, among their subjects, may go more frequently, and who more rarely, to Holy Communion.

Now decisions like these belong to that tribunal in which the Confessor alone is judge, and so it is easy to see how arbitrary is such a manner of acting, how liable to abuse and danger.

The Holy See through different Congregations has often made known its mind on this very subject as well as on that which relates to the manifestation of conscience. Passing over more ancient decrees I mention now but two of recent date. And first we have a reply given by the S. Poenitentiaria on the 19th of November, 1885. It was asked, "to whom it belonged to allow nuns to go more frequently to Holy Communion," and the answer was, "it belongs to Confessors to grant permission to individuals, according to the rules laid down by approved authors, and especially by St. Alphonsus Liguori."

Again when the S. Congr. Conc. was asked concerning the meaning in which those statutes of religious communities were approved, which constitute certain days as Communion-days for all, the S. Congr. on the 4th of August, 1888, answered that—"the faculty of going frequently to Holy Communion must be left, with the right of denying it, to the judgment of the Confessor, independent of the consent of the Superior or Superioress."

Wherefore our Most Holy Father, Leo XII., impelled by the peculiar solicitude for which he is distinguished toward the most select portion of his flock, in the audience which he gave me, the Cardinal-Prefect of the Sacred Congregation of Bishops and Regulars, on the 14th day of December, 1890, after carefully and diligently considering everything, has willed, determined, and decreed as follows:

3. From these words we can clearly conclude how great is the judicial authority of the Decree, what too is the force of its obligation. True, many are the opinions of Canonists on the judicial value of decisions, declarations, and answers coming from the Roman Congregations, and to arrive at the truth in those questions we must have in mind many nice points and fine distinctions. But there is one thing which all agree in regarding as beyond the sphere of doubt or controversy; it is the supreme judicial value and binding force of any document formulated by a Congregation and emanating in a special manner from the Sovereign Pontiff. The reason is given by Lehmkuhl, namely, that since the Roman Congregations have not by their own right legislative power, it follows that if ever they do formulate a true law, as in the case we are now dealing with, it is not the Congregation that acts, properly speaking, but the Holy Father himself, who, in the exercise of his supreme power, makes use of the same Congregation

as a means to promulgate it. The binding power of this Decree is then supreme; to disobey it would be a sin.

His Holiness annuls, abrogates, and declares of no force whatever, hereafter, all regulations whatsoever in the Constitutions of Pious Societies and Institutes of women who emit either simple or solemn vows, as well as in those of men of the purely lay order (even though the said constitutions should have received from the Holy See approbation in any form soever, even that which is termed most special), in this one point, in which these Constitutions regard the secret manifestation of conscience in whatsoever manner or under what name soever. He therefore seriously enjoins on all the Superiors, Male and Female, of such Institutes, Congregations, and Societies to absolutely cancel and expunge altogether from their respective Constitutions, Directories, and Manuals all the aforesaid regulations. Likewise he declares whatsoever usages and customs in this matter, even such as are from time out of mind, to be null and void and to be abolished.

4. In this part of the Decree three things must be noted—*a*, the statute; *b*, the precept; *c*, who they are, to whom statute and precept apply. We will touch upon these three points briefly:

a.—The statute consists in this—that the Pope in the fulness of his power takes away from the rules and constitutions of the religious to be specified below, any approbation ever given with regard to the manifestation of heart and conscience. The juridical effect of this Pontifical enactment is that whatever has been written on this subject now becomes a dead letter, whatever custom has established ceases to be. Consequently, even supposing that no precepts were given, from this statute alone it would follow, that a Superior who should exact such an account of conscience would act arbitrarily, and the subject who should refuse to make such a manifestation would be guilty of no fault.

We must notice also that the force and extension of this law reaches not only to the repealing of any approbation given in specific form, which embraces any special approbation given spontaneously, from certain knowledge and personally by the Roman Pontiff himself, but, that it also embraces the annulment of any law whatsoever, even unwritten and coming from long established customs.

b.—It would seem that the above enactment would suffice of itself to gain the end in view. But, because human nature like history, repeats itself, and to avoid any danger of the old abuses cropping up again, the Holy Father commands all whom it concerns, to cut out from their rules, constitutions and directories whatever refers to or in any way whatever explains this same manifestation of conscience. This eradication may be done in many ways, provided it be thorough and effective. And at the same time it is clear that this is the duty not of each and every Superior, but only of general Superiors who have the charge and care of the whole congregation or institute.

c.—And now we must enquire who are the religious to whom this law and precept apply? In the case of women there can be no doubt or difficulty; for it is clearly stated that the law binds all institutes and all congregations of women, no matter whether their vows be simple or solemn. But the case of men is not so clear. For it is so expressed, " that these only are bound by the law who are of the *purely lay-order*, or who by their profession and discipline are merely *lay-men.*"

Let us see now which are the religious communities of men, so called.

According to Canon Law a *lay-man* is so styled in distinction to a cleric; consequently, men of the *purely lay-order* are those who do not receive even the first tonsure; consequently, again, those congregations of men are here meant from which the clerical state is excluded whether by their profession or form of government; such are, for instance, the Christian Brothers.

But a difficulty is suggested by the letter which Cardinal Verga, Prefect of the Congregation of Bishops and Regulars, sent to all the Metropolitans when he published this very Decree. In that letter, it is said, that "only those institutes of men are excepted, which, by nature and rule, are purely ecclesiastical." These words certainly have a wider meaning than those of the Decree, for they seem to embrace even those institutes in which non-clerics are admitted as members; these institutes may perhaps be said, at least in some sense, not to be *purely*, that is in all their members, *ecclesiastical.* The point at issue was brought to the Congregation of

Bishops and Regulars and the doubt was proposed thus : " Whether the Decree comprised, besides the institutes of women, only those institutes of men of purely lay character as the Brothers of the Christian Schools, etc., or embraces also ecclesiastical congregations like the Salesians, founded by Don Bosco, the Rosminians, Lazarists and the like, in which, besides Priests, many lay brothers are numbered?" The Congregation on the 15th of April, 1891, answered *affirmatively* to the first part, *negatively* to the second.

He, moreover, forbids absolutely such Superiors, male and female, no matter what may be their rank and eminence, from endeavoring, directly or indirectly, by command, counsel, fear, threats, or blandishments, to induce their subjects to make to them any such manifestation of conscience; and he commands these subjects on their part to denounce to the higher Superiors such as dare to induce them to make such manifestation; and if the guilty one be the Superior-General the denunciation should by them be made to this Sacred Congregation.

5. The precept mentioned in the preceding paragraph would lose its efficacy and fall short of its object were it not supplemented by another. For it is not beyond the range of possibility that some Superiors, whilst acknowledging that they have no right to oblige their subjects to an account of conscience, might nevertheless, by means of blandishments, or by counsel and exhortation, draw their subjects to a full manifestation of their interior. Such subtle ingenuity had to be guarded against by a new precept which carries with it its own sanction. And so in this paragraph two other precepts are imposed : one absolute, prohibiting any recourse to blandishments, counsels, and the like; the other hypothetical, commanding that those Superiors who are guilty of such conduct be denounced to the proper authorities. The first precept applies to all Superiors no matter what may be their rank and eminence ; the second is directed to inferiors. Both may be called, and in point of fact are, auxiliary precepts ; for just as the precept which binds one to denounce Superiors is given to sanction and confirm the one which forbids all use of persuasive arts, of coaxing or urgent counsel, so the other which binds Superiors is imposed to concur with the one mentioned in the preceding paragraph, the object of which is the total abolition of the manifestations of conscience.

If it were asked whether both oblige under pain of mortal sin; it must be answered that beyond all doubt, the first does; so that those Superiors who have recourse to such counsels and blandishments to gain their end sin grievously. And the reason is drawn not only from the very tenor of the words, especially from that term, "*districte*," that is *absolutely*, but also from the serious penalty imposed; for, to be denounced for punishment is certainly not a light thing, but something very serious; and, besides all this, we must consider also the very matter of the precept and the end proposed, and draw our conclusions from both; for if this precept had not been imposed the whole force and efficacy of the Decree itself would be weakened and in a very short time would be utterly destroyed.

On the other hand, it seems probable that the precept obliging inferiors to denounce the guilty Superiors does not bind under pain of grievous sin, although Father Lehmkuhl says that its violation ought to be deemed a sin "*grave ex genere suo*," that is, mortal of itself, but whose matter admits of extenuating circumstances, in consideration of which it may or may not remain mortal.

This, however, in nowise hinders subjects from freely and of their own accord opening their hearts to their Superiors, for the purpose of obtaining from their prudence, counsel and direction, in doubts and perplexities, in order to aid them in acquiring virtues and advancing in perfection.

6. In this part of the Decree we have an explicit statement of what could be already inferred, namely, the right and lawfulness of that particular manifestation which is called "amicable," which might be made by reason of intimate friendship and confidence. Consequently, inferiors can still lay open the state of their souls to Superiors and seek from their prudence consolation and direction.

But all suggestions to this, all counsels from Superiors and exhortations with this in view, must be avoided; because in that case such a manifestation would cease to be given *freely* and, consequently, would by no means be confidential. In a word, it is strictly required that the manifestation should be given by inferiors "*freely*" and "*of their own accord*."

Another restriction, which, though not expressed, is certainly understood, is to abstain, whilst manifesting doubts and perplexities of soul, from such frailties of our fallen nature as are so naturally connected with danger and shame that they should be manifested only to the Confessor in the sacred privacy of the tribunal of Penance.

But besides these two conditions, namely, that this manifestation of conscience should be voluntary and unasked, and not touching upon the vow of chastity, is there not another one required? Is not that which is permitted in this paragraph so to be understood that it may fully agree with that clause so often, even in our own times, affixed by the Sacred Congregation to the approbation of the rules of nuns, namely, that one may freely manifest her conscience but only in regard to external faults and to her progress in the acquisition of virtues and perfection?

To this it must be answered that there is no foundation whatever for such an interpretation; because "to lay open the soul in doubts and perplexities," means a great deal more than "to tell how much progress each one is making." Even before the promulgation of this Decree many were of the opinion that "progress in virtue" signified "the internal difficulties of the soul." But now, as Father Lehmkuhl says, "there is no longer any question of *opinion* in this matter, since the words of the Decree are so clear, by which this manifestation of one's progress in virtue is permitted to subjects according to their own discretion."

Moreover, while the prescriptions of the Holy Council of Trent, Sess. 25, Cap. 10, de Regul., retain their full vigor, as well as the decrees of Benedict XIV. of holy memory in the Constitution Pastoralis Curœ, His Holiness admonishes Prelates and Superiors not to deny their subjects an Extraordinary Confessor as often as the need of their conscience requires it, and without seeking to find out in any way the reason why their subjects make such a demand, or without showing that they resent it. And, lest so provident a disposition as this should be made illusory, he exhorts the Ordinaries to name, in all localities of their diocese, in which there are communities of women, well-qualified priests with the necessary faculties, to whom such Religious may easily have recourse to receive the Sacrament of Penance.

7. In this paragraph there are four points: 1. The injunction of Trent and that of Benedict XIV. about the Ordinary and Extraordinary Confessors of nuns are confirmed, or rather, their confirmation is taken for granted. 2. "*Prelates*," that is to say Bishops or the Ordinaries of the places and "*Superiors*," by whom are meant the local or General Superiors, are admonished not to deny an Extraordinary Confessor to their subjects. This admonition applies to the Prelates in granting the necessary faculties: to Superiors where they would prevent recourse to the Confessor as often as he is reasonably called for. 3. These same Superiors are warned not to inquire into the reason why an Extraordinary Confessor is asked for. 4. The Bishops are exhorted to appoint suitable priests and to grant them all faculties so that the nuns may have easy recourse to one of them as to an Extraordinary Confessor.

On each of these points a few words must be added in explanation.

a.—The words of Trent concerning the Extraordinary Confessors of nuns are the following: "Besides the Ordinary one an Extraordinary Confessor shall be appointed twice or three times during the year who ought to hear the confessions of all."

At first sight a difficulty arises from these very words, for they seem to impose an obligation rather than grant a privilege. But Benedict XIV. explains their meaning to be that the Extraordinary Confessor must hear the confessions of only those nuns who wish to confess to him. They are not, however, obliged to make a confession to him, although each and every one is bound to present herself before him to receive spiritual advice and direction.

b.—With regard to the caution given to Prelates and Superiors not to deny an Extraordinary Confessor to their subjects as often as the needs of their conscience require one, it must be remarked that the sense does not seem to be that Superiors must have *positive* knowledge of the particular need of their subjects, because this would imply that they should know why the Extraordinary Confessor is asked for, an inquiry which they are by no means allowed to make. The meaning, therefore, seems to be this: taking it for granted that the request is reasonable, which must always be done according to that rule of canon law—*nemo malus nisi probetur*—namely, that no one is to be deemed guilty unless evident facts prove him to be so, then the Extraordinary Confessor ought to be granted in all those cases in which it is not evident that the request is unreasonable. And if it be asked when or how we can be sure of the reasonableness of the demand, the obvious answer is that this must depend very much upon circumstances; that is, upon the person who makes the request, upon the manner in which it is made—and, above all, upon the greater or less frequency of the petition.

c.—The prohibition that stops all inquiry into the reasons why the Extraordinary Confessor is called for, is a dictate of the natural law. Such prying curiosity is of itself sinful, and perhaps this is the reason why the caution is not expressed in more sharp and more solemn words. Such inquisitiveness would soon sound the depths of the soul and would fetter and destroy all liberty. And this brings us face to face with the very abuses and disorders which the Holy Father wishes to crush out of existence by the present Decree. Therefore such over-curious questioning is of itself a serious fault, and only on account of mitigating circumstances could it be deemed a light one.

d.—In the exhortation given to Ordinaries for the appointment of *suitable priests* observe that the plural is used, that so the privilege of having recourse to an Extraordinary Confessor, when necessary, may meet with no difficulty. The intention of the Holy Father is that there should be, if possible, not one but several priests having faculties for each community; and this provision should not be confounded with the admonition given above to *Prelates* not to deny Extraordinary Confessors, for that admonition carries with it an obligation; it is meant to provide for cases of need and to meet the request of any nun in particular, whilst the measure now before us provides for an ample privilege and for the greater convenience of all concerned.

As to what regards either permission or prohibition to receive Holy Communion, His Holiness also decrees that such permission or prohibition belongs solely to the Ordinary or Extraordinary Confessor, the Superiors having no right whatever to interfere in the matter, save only the case in which any one of their subjects had given scandal to the community since his or her last confession, or had been guilty of some grievous public fault, and this only until the guilty one had once more received the Sacrament of Penance.

8. Almost all that is contained in this and the following sections, about going to Holy Communion, may be said to belong already to common law; but here we have a forcible and solemn statement of the fact.

In note No. 3 (c.) certain documents were cited, but there yet remain many answers and decrees of Roman Congregations from which we could easily infer even before the promulgation of this Decree that the established rule of common law is that the confessor may give permission to go frequently to Holy Communion, and that the consent of the Superior or Superioress is not necessary, but merely that they should be informed of the matter. There are, however, two points here to which our attention is called. First, that whereas before in particular decrees only the Ordinary Confessor was named as the one who could give this permission, now it may be granted also by the Extraordinary Confessor. Second, that there are cases in which the Superior can prohibit the subject from going to Holy Communion for a time only, that is, until the subject goes to confession again.

This can have place when the subject has given scandal to the community or is guilty of some serious public fault.

We must now examine more closely into the meaning of this. How are we to understand this little word *or*? Does it connect the two clauses between which it lies, or does it separate them? For if it is taken in the copulative sense, then the scandal and the serious public fault must go together, and in that case the Superior can forbid the inferior to go to Holy Communion only when the guilty one has scandalized the community by some culpable external misbehavior. But if the *or* is taken in the disjunctive sense, then we would have, strictly speaking, two cases, and Holy Communion would be forbidden, either when some serious external fault had been committed, but not before the community, or when the community has been shocked, seriously shocked, but not necessarily by extraordinary public guilt.

It seems certain that this last meaning is a true one; and the reason is, not only that it is the obvious meaning of the conjunction *or* and of the whole sentence, but also that, if we would take the first interpretation, we should have to conclude that the Decree is inaccurate in its wording, that it says more than it intends, for it would have been sufficient, if the first meaning were the true one, to say "if anyone has scandalized the community," without adding "or is guilty of some grievous public fault."

All are hereby admonished to prepare themselves diligently and to approach Holy Communion on the days prescribed in their respective Rules; and when the Confessor may judge conducive to the spiritual advancement of any member to receive more frequently, he may give the needful permission. But whoever receives from the Confessor the permission to receive more frequent or daily Communion is bound to inform the Superior of the same; should the latter think that he has just and serious reasons to oppose such frequent Communion, he is bound to make them known to the Confessor, in whose judgment he must absolutely acquiesce.

9. Excepting the admonition to prepare themselves diligently and to approach Holy Communion on the days prescribed in their respective rules, the first part of this section does not pertain to the religious but to their Confessors. To these also belongs the exercise of that right which, as noted in the preceding paragraph, has been exclusively vested in them.

Let these Confessors, then, examine and consider the rules given by doctors and theologians to guide them in granting frequent or daily Communion. They may be found in the Praxis Confessarii of St. Alphonsus No. 152, and, in the Philothea of St. Francis of Sales, part ii., cap. 20. The scope of these rules and directions is that daily or very frequent Communion is to be granted only to those who besides an ardent desire to receive the Blessed Sacrament have acquired a certain freedom from deliberate venial sins and with earnest endeavor are tending ever onward to greater perfection.

Here the attention of Confessors is called to two suggestions. The first is that since there is question now of persons living in community, who are often fatigued and worn out by all kinds of occupations, due consideration must be had for the numberless distractions and obstacles which arise from these different duties and offices, and very great prudence and discretion should be exercised in granting privileges which might give rise to some jealousy and so disturb the peace and harmony which ought to reign in religious communities.

The second suggestion is intended for those who, to say the least, are more than willing to grant daily Communion. They draw a parity from the example of priests who celebrate Mass daily. But the cases are entirely different, and the reason of the disparity is well put by F. Lehmkuhl; for the priest in celebrating Mass is no longer a mere individual, but is invested with a public character and acts for the faithful, and so he is permitted more readily, nay even counseled, to offer the Divine Sacrifice each day, notwithstanding his many imperfections. As a practical rule, if there is question of persons living in community, it is seldom advisable to grant Communion on days on which the rule does not prescribe it; more rarely still daily communion.

In the second part of this paragraph there is question of the information to be given to Superiors by the subjects who have obtained permission from their Confessors for frequent Communion.

Is this a question of real obligation, and must Superiors be informed each and every time? It would seem that here we have a case of real obligation, even though it binds but venially, as appears from the words "is bound," which certainly mean more than mere advice or direction, and besides, if this information were withheld, not a little disorder and confusion in domestic discipline would follow.

To the second query it may be answered that it is not necessary to inform Superiors each particular time one obtains permission for an extraordinary Communion, but only when one has been allowed to communicate daily, or, for a certain fixed time, more frequently, than is common. The whole intent and purpose of the words seems to favor this opinion, and besides it was so declared by the Congr. S. Of., 2 July, 1890, with the approval of the Holy Father; and although this was a declaration made for a particular case, with reference to the Confessors of the Sisters of Charity, yet it can, with safety, be taken as a general rule.

On the last part of this paragraph it is well to note that the just and serious reasons which the Superior may have in opposition to such frequent Communions, may come not only from the general and particular conduct of the person who has obtained this permission, but from the general rule and discipline of the house and from any other source that has direct bearing on the individuals or on the whole community. Hence there seems to be sufficient reason for dissenting from the opinion of some commentators on this

Decree, who seem to hold that the just and serious reasons must be drawn only from the conduct of the subject to whom the permission for more frequent Communion has been granted.

His Holiness, furthermore, commands all Superiors General, Provincials and Local Superiors of the Institutes aforementioned, whether of men or of women, to observe zealously and accurately the regulations prescribed in this Decree under pain of incurring ipso facto the penalties decreed against Superiors who violate the mandates of the Holy See.

10. The command here given has been mentioned already; now we have its explicit statement and its sanction in ecclesiastical penalties.

A word on the command and its sanction:

a.—The persons who are bound by the regulations of this Decree are of different orders or conditions. We have the Bishops or Ordinaries, the Confessors, the Religious and their Superiors; and yet this particular command is not given to all these persons, but only to Superiors; and we must further notice that this same order does not direct them to take all possible measures for the observance of all the regulations of the Decree, but it simply says that "they should observe them;" and this means that the object of the command is merely that Superiors observe such regulations as directly pertain to themselves.

These regulations are reduced to the five following:

1. That Superiors expunge from their rules, be they written or only sanctioned by custom, whatever bears upon the secret manifestation of conscience.

2. That they never induce their subjects to make such manifestation, whether by counsel, by threats, by blandishments or any other such persuasive methods.

3. That they never refuse their subjects recourse to an Extraordinary Confessor, when they reasonably ask for one, nor give any sign of displeasure at such a request.

4. That they never in any way inquire into the reason for this request.

5. That they do not meddle with the permissions or the prohibitions made by the Confessors of their subjects with regard to Holy Communion.

b.—To the question, what are the penalties fixed in sanction of this Decree, some commentators reply that they vary, and are in proportion to the gravity of the transgression; they may be censures, deposition from office, loss of active and passive voice, and whatever else may be determined by the proper authorities.

But this answer cannot be accepted because it is contrary to the very words of the Decree, which declare that the punishments are not *ferendae*, but *latae sententiae;* that is, the guilty do not wait for judgment, but incur the penalties by the very violation of the Decree.

The true answer is given by Father Lehmkuhl, who quotes the Apostolic Constitutions, "*Officii nostri Debitum,*" promulgated by Innoc. VIII, Jan. 25th, 1491, and "*Romanus Pontifex,*" published by Clem. VII, Dec. 29th, 1533, by force of which excommunication is incurred by those who impede the execution of Apostolic Letters.

And if this interference is abetted by the support of lay-power, an excommunication is incurred, which is in a special manner reserved to the Pope, in the Constitution "*Apostolicae Sedis,*" promulgated by Pius IX.

He lastly commands that copies of this present Decree, translated into the vernacular, shall be inserted in the Constitutions of the said pious Institutes, and that at least once in a twelvemonth, at a stated time in each House, either in the public Refectory, or in Chapter assembled for this special purpose, this Decree shall be read in a loud and intelligible voice.

11. What is here ordained refers to the future inviolable observance of this Decree. These several regulations rightly fulfilled, no plea can be made on the ground of ignorance or desuetude.

And thus hath His Holiness determined and decreed, notwithstanding all things to the contrary, even such as are worthy of special and individual mention.

12. The seal of authority is stamped upon the Decree by these words, and whatever objection might be made against it is anticipated and set aside.

DECRETUM

S. C. EPISCOPORUM ET REGULARIUM

DE APERITIONE CONSCIENTIÆ HAUD EXIGENDA, DEQUE
JURIBUS CONFESSARII QUOAD MONIALES ET
INSTITUTA VIRORUM LAICORUM.

Quemadmodum omnium rerum humanarum, quantumvis honestæ sanctæque in se sint; ita et legum sapienter conditarum ea conditio est, ut ab hominibus ad impropria et aliena ex abusu traduci ac pertrahi valeant; ac propterea quandoque fit, ut intentum a legislatoribus finem haud amplius assequantur : imo et aliquando, ut contrarium sortiantur effectum.

Idque dolendum vel maxime est obtigisse quoad leges plurium Congregationum, Societatum aut Institutorum sive mulierum quæ vota simplicia aut solemnia nuncupant, sive virorum professione ac regimine penitus laicorum; quandoquidem aliquoties in illorum Constitutionibus conscientiæ manifestatio permissa fuerat, ut facilius alumni arduam perfectionis viam ab expertis Superioribus in dubiis addiscerent; e contra a nonnullis ex his intima conscientiæ scrutatio, quæ unice Sacramento Pœnitentiæ reservata est, inducta fuit. Itidem in Constitutionibus ad tramitem SS. Canonum præscriptum fuit, ut Sacramentalis Confessio in hujusmodi Communitatibus fieret respectivis Confessariis ordinariis et extraordinariis; aliunde Superiorum arbitrium eo usque devenit, ut subditis aliquem extraordinarium Confessarium denegaverint, etiam in casu quo, ut propriæ conscientiæ consulerent, eo valde indigebant. Indita denique eis fuit discretionis ac prudentiæ norma, ut suos subditos rite recteque quoad peculiares pœnitentias ac alia pietatis opera dirigerent; sed et hæc per abusionem extensa in id etiam extitit, ut eis ad Sacram Synaxim accedere vel pro lubitu permiserint, vel omnino interdum prohibuerint. Hinc factum est, ut hujusmodi dispositiones, quæ ad spiritualem alumnorum profectum, et ad unitatis pacem et concordiam in Communitatibus servandam fovendamque salutariter ac sapienter constitutæ jam fuerant, haud raro in animarum discrimen, in conscientiarum anxietatem, ac insuper in externæ pacis turbationem versæ fuerint, ceu subditorum recursus et querimoniæ passim ad S. Sedem interjectæ evidentissime comprobant.

Quare SSmus D. N. Leo divina providentia Papa XIII, pro ea qua præstat erga lectissimam hanc sui gregis portionem peculiari sollicitudine, in Audientia habita a me Cardinali Præfecto S. Congregationis Episcoporum et Regularium negotiis et consultationibus præpositæ, die decima quarta Decembris 1890, omnibus sedulo diligenterque perpensis, hæc quæ sequuntur voluit, constituit atque decrevit.

I. Sanctitas Sua irritat, abrogat, et nullius in posterum roboris declarat quascumque dispositiones Constitutionum piarum Societatum, Institutorum mulierum sive votorum simplicium sive solemnium, nec non virorum omnimode laicorum, etsi dictæ Constitutiones approbationem ab Apostolica Sede retulerint in forma quacumque etiam quam aiunt specialissimam, in eo scilicet, quod cordis et conscientiæ intimam manifestationem quovis modo ac nomine respiciunt. Ita propterea serio injungit Moderatricibus hujusmodi Institutorum, Congregationum ac Societatum, ut ex propriis Constitutionibus, Directoriis, ac Manualibus præfatæ dispositiones omnino deleantur penitusque expungantur. Irritat pariter ac delet quoslibet ea de re usus et consuetudines etiam immemorabiles.

II. Districte insuper prohibet memoratis Superioribus ac Superiorissis, cujuscumque gradus et præeminentiæ sint, ne personas sibi subditas inducere pertentent directe aut indirecte, præcepto, consilio, timore, minis, aut blanditiis ad hujusmodi manifestationem conscientiæ sibi peragendam; subditisque converso præcipit, ut Superioribus majoribus denuncient Superiores minores, qui eos ad id inducere audeant; et, si agatur de Moderatore vel Moderatrice Generali, denunciatio huic S. Congregationi ab iis fieri debeat.

III. Hoc autem minime impedit, quominus subditi libere ac ultro aperire suum animum Superioribus valeant, ad effectum ab illorum prudentia in dubiis ac anxietatibus consilium et directionem obtinendi pro virtutum acquisitione ac perfectionis progressu.

IV. Præterea, firmo remanente quoad Confessarios ordinarios et extraordinarios Communitatum, quod a Sacrosancto Concilio Tridentino præscribitur in *Sess. 25, Cap. 10 de Regul.*, et a *S. M. Benedicti XIV.* statuitur in Constitutione quæ incipit " Pastoralis curæ :" Sanctitas Sua Præsules Superioresque admonet, ne extraordinarium denegent subditis Confessarium quoties ut propriæ conscientiæ consulant ad id subditi adigantur, quin iidem Superiores ullo modo petitionis rationem inquirant, aut ægre id ferre demonstrent. Ac ne evanida tam provida dispositio fiat, Ordinarios exhortatur, ut in locis propriæ Diœceseos, in quibus Mulierum Communitates existunt, idoneos Sacerdotes facultatibus instructos designent, ad quos pro Sacramento Pœnitentiæ recurrere eæ facile queant.

V. Quod vero attinet ad permissionem vel prohibitionem ad sacram Synaxim accedendi, Eadem Sanctitas Sua decernit, hujusmodi permissiones vel prohibitiones dumtaxat ad Confessarium ordinarium vel extraordinarium spectare, quin Superiores ullam habeant auctoritatem hac in re sese ingerendi, excepto casu quo aliquis ex eorum subditis post ultimam Sacramentalem Confessionem Communitati scandalo fuerit, aut gravem externam culpam patraverit, donec ad Pœnitentiæ sacramentum denuo accesserit.

VI. Monentur hinc omnes, ut ad Sacram Synaxim curent diligenter se præparare et accedere diebus in propriis regulis statutis ; et quoties ob fervorem et spiritualem alicujus profectum Confessarius expedire judicaverit ut frequentius accedat, id ei ab ipso Confessario permitti poterit. Verum qui licentiam a Confessario obtinuerit frequentioris ac etiam quotidianæ Communionis, de hoc certiorem reddere Superiorem teneatur ; quod si hic justas gravesque causas se habere reputet contra frequentiores hujusmodi Communiones, eas Confessario manifestare teneatur, cujus judicio acquiescendum omnino erit.

VII. Eadem Sanctitas Sua insuper mandat omnibus et singulis Superioribus Generalibus, Provincialibus et localibus Institutionibus de quibus supra sive virorum sive mulierum, ut studiose accurateque hujus Decreti dispositiones observent, sub pœnis contra Superiores Apostolicæ Sedis mandata violantes ipso facto incurrendis.

VIII. Denique mandatur, ut præsentis Decreti exemplaria in vernaculum sermonem versa inserantur Constitutionibus prædictorum piorum Institutorum, et saltem semel in anno, stato tempore in unaquaque Domo, sive in publica mensa, sive in Capitulo ad hoc specialiter convocato, alta et intelligibili voce legantur.

Et ita Sanctitas Sua constituit atque decrevit, contrariis quibuscumque etiam speciali et individua mentione dignis minime obstantibus.

Datum Romæ ex Secretaria momoratæ S. Congregationis Episcoporum et Regularium die 17 Decembris 1890.

I. Card. VERGA, *Præfectus*,
Fr. ALOYSIUS EPISC. CALLINICEN. *Secret.*

CHRISTIAN EDUCATION

IN

AMERICA

A LECTURE

BY

JOHN J. KEANE,

BISHOP OF AJASSO,

RECTOR OF THE CATHOLIC UNIVERSITY OF AMERICA

WASHINGTON, D. C.
THE CHURCH NEWS PUBLISHING COMPANY
1892

COPIES CAN BE PROCURED, PRICE 10 CENTS, BY ADDRESSING
"CHURCH NEWS," WASHINGTON, D. C.

CHRISTIAN EDUCATION IN AMERICA

BRETHREN: Your hearts are filled with joy to-day because years of faithful and generous labor have at last been crowned by the dedication of this beautiful church* to the service of Almighty God. But in your joy I am sure you do not lose sight of the fact that during those years of endeavor and of hope our dear Lord and His adoring flock found welcome and fitting shelter in the hall of the parish school-house. Your prudent and zealous pastor, knowing well that "the child is father of the man," and that the way to make a parish of good Christians is to see to the Christian training of the children, erected the school-house before laying a stone of the church; he invited Our Lord and the people of the parish to be for awhile the guests of the children; and it is only after having for years blessed with His Real Presence that home of Christian education that our Divine Saviour has come to occupy this His beautiful dwelling place.

Friends, is not this an object-lesson of the relation between religion and education? It is putting in concrete and symbolic form the lesson so frequently inculcated by the word of God, that Our Lord is "the Light of the World," that He is "the true Light which enlighteneth every man that cometh into this world," that "God is Light and there is no darkness in Him," that Christians must be "children of the light."

It is the will of God that neither ignorance nor stupidity nor error shall rule His people, but the knowledge of the truth, which, He says, is to "make us free," breaking the fetters of ignorance, dispelling the illusions of error, developing and setting free all the powers which our Creator has bestowed on the human intelligence for His creatures' good. And before the opened eye of our intelligence God puts the book of nature, the book of humanity, and the book of rev-

---

*St. Elizabeth's Church, Chicago, dedicated June 19, 1892.

elation, that from all three we may drink in such measure as we can of the fulness of the truth, for our own welfare, and for our Heavenly Father's glory. Thus, in the nature of things, education and religion are inseparable.

Again, yonder school-house stands not in a desert solitude, as if the light imparted in it was only for the purposes of prayerful contemplation, only for the uses of the other world and not of this. Far from it. The school-house is planted on one of the thoroughfares of this busy city, to show that its training is meant not only for the other life, but also for this present life with all its myriad duties; not only for heaven, but also for earth with all its burdens and cares and toil; not only for God, but also for our fellow-men and all the multifarious relations which link human society together. Again, therefore, this is an object-lesson concerning the intimate relation between education and civilization. Men may differ in their definitions of civilization, but all must recognize that its essential conditions and its chief constituents are the intellectual development and the moral development of the people. Without intellectual development there is childhood of the race; whereas civilization is manhood or advance towards it. Without moral development there is no beauty nor symmetry nor soundness in their condition, whereas civilization implies all these. And since education means intellectual and moral development, we see that education and civilization are also inseparable.

This natural and inseparable relationship between religion and civilization, on the one hand, and education on the other, has in all ages been clearly understood by mankind. History shows that, among all civilized races, the prevalent notions concerning religion and civilization determined the character of the education given to the young, and that, on the other hand, the kind of education imparted was the chief agency in maintaining the national type of civilization and moral character. It is of the greatest importance that we should rightly grasp this lesson of history. A just appreciation of existing conditions and of the measures they demand can best be attained through a right understanding of the conditions which existed in preceding ages, the measures they called for, and the results which they led to. The lesson is written so plainly on the pages of history that a very brief glance will suffice to show us its meaning and its moral.

In the ages preceding Christianity, religion and civilization were universally dominated by one great idea and characteristic—that of absolute and exclusive nationalism. Civilization then meant the fitness of men for the duties of citizenship and for promoting the welfare of the nation. Religion was a department of national life; worship was a function of the State, and its ministers were State officials. Accordingly, education was a preparation for duty as citizen and soldier. In Sparta the child belonged to the State and was raised by the State from its birth. The child that was unfit for the duties of citizen and soldier was considered to have no right to live and was put to death. Children that gave promise of future usefulness were brought up by State officials in common barracks and received only such training as would fit them for the work which the State was to demand from them.

Athens had a broader notion of the purposes of life and the meaning of civilization. But Athens, too, held as a fundamental principle that the purpose and end of the individual was the State. From the age of seven years the child's training was conducted by the State, and even the great Plato taught that a child not fit to serve the State had no right to live.

Rome inherited the theories of Sparta and Athens; and while in the successive stages of her civilization we can discern at first the stern drill of the former and then the more liberal culture of the latter, still Rome held throughout to the idea dominant in both—that civilization means fitness for the duties of citizenship, and that education must have this for its almost exclusive aim.

Thence followed two great consequences, which may be regarded as the chief characteristics of the ancient civilizations. The first was the heathen estimate of man. The individual was absorbed in the State, was considered to exist only for the State, had worth or dignity only through his relation with the State. The Roman citizen could everywhere boast of the dignity that invested him; but it was not the dignity of personal worth, but of the great empire to which he belonged. This estimate of man's nature and end is the real foundation of the heathen civilizations.

The second consequence was that education was restricted to the governing classes only. They alone had the rights of citizenship, and education was only to fit for citizenship. All other classes of the community had only to obey the governing classes and to work for them They were held as serfs or slaves. Education was withheld from them, because, it was said, it would be useless to them, nay, it would even be dangerous to the State, since education would naturally inspire them with higher aspirations. Thus the great mass of the people were systematically cut off from education and kept in ignorance, as shown by the fact that in the palmy days of Athens the citizens are said to have numbered 20,000 and the serfs who toiled for them 400,000. If here and there we remark that slaves were used by their masters as school teachers or even produced literary works of note, these were only rare and singular exceptions, serving but to prove the rule. And the rule was that human worth was made identical with citizenship, and that the ideal of politics and education among the ancients was a handful of strong and cultured men ruling a world of ignorant beings, who live only for their masters' aggrandizement and who are ready even to slay one another for their masters' pastime.

Against this shocking system, the only noteworthy efforts at reaction were that of the Sophists and that of Socrates.

The Sophists leaped to the opposite extreme, and instead of absolute nationalism taught absolute individualism. Their ideal was a world of individuals absolutely independent of one another, each living according to the light of his own notions or the prompting of his own caprices. Its logical outcome was Epicureanism, whose tendency was, as Horace said, to turn men into "swine of Epicurus' pig-sty." The remedy was worse than the disease.

Socrates rose in honest protest against both these extremes. His fundamental ideas were the immortality of the soul and moral accountability to God. These two great truths he taught with all the earnestness of his noble soul. His teaching was a condemnation of both the systems then in vogue. On the one hand it put to shame the flippancy of the Sophists and the moral corruption which their theories fostered. On the other hand it was an assertion of the worth and the rights, as well as the duties of every human being, which was quite inconsistent with the all-absorbing nationalism of what was then considered the civilized world. We know the result. Athens commanded him to desist from his teachings; and because he could not in conscience desist from saying the truth, he was put to death. His noble teachings may, alas! be said to have died with him. Even his great disciples, Plato and Aristole, failed to grasp the full import of his ideas or to lead them to the conclusions which he evidently had in mind.

And so there was left no hope for heathen civilization. It was founded on a wrong idea of man; it ignored what truly constitutes the worth and dignity of humanity; it logically aimed at making human life absolutely intolerable to the great bulk of mankind; it made education a mere instrument for the perpetuation of this false system, and used religion to uphold it by her temporal and eternal sanctions. Any attempt at protest or reform was treason. Hence the old system had in itself no power for its own cure. For the good of mankind it necessarily had to pass utterly away, to be supplanted by a system totally different in its principles and its aims. That system was Christianity.

Our Lord Jesus Christ sent forth His Church to electrify the world and to startle the old Cæsarism by proclaiming the dignity and the inalienable rights of every human being—dignity and rights based, not on the power and glory of empire, but on the immortality of the individual soul and its relation to the Infinite and Eternal God. The proclamation was a battle-cry; and heathen Rome tried to deal with Christianity as Athens had dealt with Socrates. The Roman Empire, the empire of the then known world, was the battlefield on which the contest was fought out for three centuries. Christianity prevailed at last, not through force of arms, for arms she wielded not, but by the power of truth, against which all weapons of violence are in vain. She prevailed, and the great colossus of pagan might crumbled to pieces at her feet. It was a contest and a victory for all ages and all nations. It was the dawn of a new civilization, the civilization of Christendom.

Christian civilization gave a new direction to social ideas and civil polity. Its initial idea is the worth, the dignity, the welfare and destiny of the individual. Its fundamental principle is that right is superior to might—that might exists only for the assertion and defence of right. It is no longer the individual that belongs to the State, but the State—yes, and the Church, too—belongs to the individual. "All things are yours," writes St. Paul to the Christians of his day, "all things are yours, whether it be Paul or Apollo or Cephas, or the world, or life or death, or things present or things to come; all are yours, and you are Christ's, and Christ is God's." Rulers are taught that they hold power, not for their own aggrandizement, but for the good of the people; that the only legitimate end of government is the welfare of the governed. They are reminded, moreover, that the humblest human being has rights which are absolutely inalienable, because bestowed by his Creator, rights which the State did not give and which the State dare not violate or ignore. Plato taught the State that it might slay any child that did not give promise of civil usefulness; Christ teaches that to slay that child would be murder, and that the mightiest empire on earth dare not do it. Thus the individualism of Jesus Christ was substituted for the nationalism, the Cæsarism of old.

But the individualism taught by Christ was totally different from the individualism taught by the Sophists. She did not, like them, put a gulf between the man and the citizen. She did not aim at disintegrating humanity into individual atoms without social links and obligations. On the contrary, she taught that every individual is born into society, is meant by the Creator to be a social being, is by his very nature a member of civil society, and is bound to become by regeneration a member also of the spiritual society of Jesus Christ.

Thus Christianity avoided both of the one-sided extremes into which the old schools of philosophy and civilization fell. Its teaching was marked by that well-balanced symmetry which is the characteristic of truth and which alone can insure a lasting civilization. It not only told man of his heaven-bestowed rights; it also reminded him of his heaven-imposed duties thence resulting—duties to himself, duties to his family, duties to his country, duties to God. Religion showed him the sacred foundations of his rights; she also held ever before him the sacred and awful sanctions which enforced his duties. Education was henceforth to have as its aim to make him appreciate more worthily the moral dignity with which his natural rights invest him, to show him the pathway of upright living in which his character as man and as Christian demands that he should walk, and to give all his faculties the development and the direction which will best fit him for the fufillment of all his duties, both to this world and to the world to come.

In the heathen systems education was usually almost entirely in the hands of the State, because education had no other end in view than the duties of a citizen, duties to this world alone. In the Christian system the State was still to have some influence over education, because Christianity, no less than heathenism, considered the duties of the citizen as of great importance and of bounden obligation; but the paramount influence and control naturally belonged to the family and the Church, because these represented interests and duties of a still more sacred character and a still more imperative and essential obligation. Thus all exclusiveness and one-sidedness is guarded against; thus all sides of human life and every kind of human relationships are taken into account; thus the broad and sure foundations are laid on which religion, civilization, and human welfare in all its forms of domestic felicity and civil prosperity may stand forever.

And now let us consider some consequences which follow immediately from the Christian principles which we have thus far been studying.

In the first place, the fundamental idea of Christian civilization is, as we have seen, the worth and the rights of every human being and the responsibility of governments towards every individual, even the least and humblest, over whom they rule. Now this theory must, in the very nature of things, gradually lead to the elevation of the individual citizen, gradually give him a larger share in the civil polity of his country. And such elevation of the individual citizen must logically lead up, step by step, to popular institutions and representative governments. That such has been the steady drift and influence of Christian civilization during all the ages of its existence no serious student of history can doubt. It would be easy and interesting, did time permit, to trace the progress from despotism and barbarism to feudalism and chivalry, and from these to the popular and representative institutions of modern times.

Again, let us remark that every step in the elevation of the individual citizen is an appeal to his intelligence; that every advance towards popular institutions is logically an advance towards general enlightenment and popular education. Where one governs, and the many have only to obey, the many can feel no great need of intellectual enlightenment. If they know enough to perform well their daily toil and to save their souls at last, this is apt to be considered quite sufficient for them. But in proportion as all become active factors in the social organism and are brought into competition for the first places in the race of life, each one is spurred to acquire for himself and to procure for his children all he can of that intelligence and enlightenment which best secure preeminence. From social conditions of that sort the school develops as a matter of course. It is not at home but in the school that youth must receive the instruction which such a social state demands. Home must supply them with food, clothing and shelter, and every rightly managed home ought to suffice to supply these without any co-operation on the part of others. But not every home, though ever so well managed, can suffice to supply the education which such social conditions require. Education is, by its nature, a matter of co-operation. The school is the natural outgrowth of a community which appreciates the demands of advancing civilization. And the character of the instruction given in the school will, of course, largely depend on the condition and needs and aspirations, both spiritual and temporal, of the community.

Here we have, as it were in germ, the whole philosophy and history of Christian civilization and Christian education. During the first four centuries and more, while the civilization and culture of heathen Rome still prevailed, Christian schools arose in all the great centres of learning, equal in every respect to the philosophic schools around them, and Christian sages were ready and able to maintain the truth against the subtleties of the ablest writers who assailed it. When barbarism had overflowed the continent with devastation, and every monument of civilization was submerged beneath the awful flood, and the dark ages began, then the Church carried her blessed light everywhere amid the darkness, shedding abroad both the moral and the intellectual influences which were to dispel the dense gloom of ignorance, to establish over the fierce barbarians the reign of the Prince of Peace, to build up Christendom.

Simple indeed was the store of learning, whether sacred or profane, which the wild tribesmen were able or willing to receive. The Church gave them what they could take. And when the chaotic confusion of barbarism was brought into some shape and order by feudalism, still the social conditions were so simple and rude that the Christian schools had, as a rule, but little to do beyond teaching the artless flock their duties towards God, and the merest rudiments of secular knowledge made needful by the elementary domestic and civic duties incumbent upon them. In proportion as social conditions improve we behold an increasing expansion of intellectual aspiration and activity. Then in the legislative assemblies, in which the Bishops and the nobles, the representatives of the Church and of the State, sat and voted side by side, we find educational matters receive more and more attention, and we see a Charlemagne and an Alfred vieing with the pontiffs and pastors of the Church in erecting and supporting schools and laying the foundations of the great universities which were to become the glory of Christendom.

Thus by slow but sure degrees Christianity was to work out in human society its grand and beneficent ideal. It found society in its childhood, the rude, impetuous, uncultured, and dependent childhood of barbarism. Through the influence of the ideas and spirit of Jesus Christ it was to lead society up to its enlightened, cultured, strong and self-governing manhood. Perhaps we may be tempted to wonder that the process has been so slow, and that even now the result, as a whole, has been so imperfectly attained. But should such a question occur to our minds, we have only to glance at the facts of the case in order to find a clear and sufficient answer.

In the first place, we behold this tendency of Christianity met and resisted, century after century, by a counter tendency to absolutism, to Cæsarism, on the part of rulers and governments. This was the spirit of the old Roman civilization; it was equally the character of the barbarian chieftians; and from both these sources it was transmitted to the princes and kings and emperors of later times. They have left the record of their proud, despotic self-assertion on every page of history since the beginning of Christendom. As a matter of course, they could only regard with aversion and hostility Christianity's declaration of the inalienable rights of individuals and of the people. Often in the course of history it has seemed as if Cæsarism would prevail and roll the world back into absolutism. Many an interesting chapter in the history of the emperors of Germany and the kings of France has just this for its meaning. And many a thrilling story of the resistance opposed to their assumptions by the Chief Pastors of the Church, meant simply the assertion of the inalienable rights of that civil and religious liberty which Christ had brought into the world, against the grasping Cæsarism that would fain ignore those rights or trample on them or use them as its tools.

Again, we have only to glance at a map of Europe in order to recognize a second hindrance which has constantly resisted the advance of true Christian civilization. We see the surface of the continent cut up by a multitude of boundary lines. These boundary lines not only mark, as at first, the division of clans and tribes and peoples; they have unfortunately come to indicate the separations of national rivalries, jealousies, and enmities. Century after century we behold the nations of Europe arrayed in armed hostility. This has necessitated military rule, and therefore tended to perpetuate Cæsarism. National narrowness, moreover, intensifies the clinging to old traditional ways and notions, and thus co-operates with Cæsarism in resisting the advance of ideas and the improvement of institutions; in a word, in opposing the reign of the Prince of Peace.

Against these two great hindrances Christian civilization was making its way as best it could, when a third obstacle was raised by the disastrous results of the great religious revolution which broke forth in the midst of Christendom three centuries ago. It divided Christians into conflicting and ever-multiplying sects. It arrayed creed against creed and church against church. To national animosities it added religious animosities still deeper and more bitter. It taught men, alas! to hate one another for the love of God, to persecute and kill one another for the sake of the Prince of Peace ! It not only set individuals against individuals and communities against communities, but plunged nations into disastrous wars. In a word, it resisted the unity and the universal brotherhood inculcated by Christ Our Lord, and put new and weighty obstacles in the way of the true reign of Christian civilization.

When we consider the power and the obstinacy of these three great hindrances, we may well cease to marvel that the advance of the spirit and aim of Christianity has been so slow. No wonder that human progress has so frequently had to make its way through violent upheavals, which usually leave much to deplore as well as something to be thankful for.

Such, then, was the condition of Christendom when Divine Providence opened up America as a refuge for humanity from all forms of oppression, as a fresh field for the development of Christian civilization, as a new world free from all the entanglements and hindrances which had so impeded Christianity in the old world.

Here in our own country, which Providence had destined to be pre-eminently the land of liberty, there lay open to the world a territory as large as the whole of Europe, with none of those national boundary lines which turned Europe into a vast camp of jealous rivals or open foes. Here men who had been enemies in the old world, because belonging to different nations, could meet as fellow-men, as brothers, and blend into one great people, fit symbol of the universal brotherhood of men.

Together with the curse of nationalism, Providence banished from our country the scourge of Cæsarism; and our Declaration of Independence based the rights of the man and the citizen, not on the gift of the State or the favor of Cæsar, but on the bestowal and ordinance of the Creator.

With these two great hindrances to Christian civilization, the third obstacle, sectarian animosity, was likewise banished from our country by the God of Nations. It was but natural that religious intolerance and resentments should have reigned among the early colonists. Most of them had smarted under religious persecution of one form or another in the old world, and no wonder that they carried the memories and the bitterness of religious strife to their new homes. But the providence of God could not allow such a spirit to reign here. Catholic Maryland was the first to unfurl the banner of religious liberty. Other colonies soon imitated the noble example. During the war of independence Churchman stood shoulder to shoulder with dissenter, and Catholic with Protestant, in equal devotedness to their country's cause. Catholic France and Puritan New England joined hands as they followed Washington to victory. Thus the hand of God broke down the barriers of religious hostility, and showed our people that the un-Christlike spirit of hatred and persecution was to have no home here; that Americans, while not yet united in religious belief, must agree to disagree in friendliness and charity; that while each one is free to follow his conscience fully, yet doctrinal differences must in no way hinder them from forming a thoroughly united and homogeneous people. While the harsh cry of bigotry is, alas! still occasionally heard, yet the voice which the American people above all love to hear is the voice of Him who said: "By this shall all men know that ye are my disciples if ye love one another."

The great hindrances to the full reign of Christian civilization in the old world being thus to so great an extent eliminated by the hand of Providence from our favored country, it was but natural that she should become, not only the grandest organization of popular and representative institutions that history has ever known, but also the nearest approach which the world has yet beheld to the universal brotherhood of men, to their universal equality, to the universal recognition of man's inalienable rights, in a word, to a national system practically based on the social principles of Christian civilization.

No wonder, then, that everyone who loves God and loves humanity should also love America. No wonder that from every corner of the earth the fettered and down-trodden of other climes flock to her with eagerness, or stretch out their arms to her with wistful yearning. No wonder that they who have elsewhere borne the galling yoke of oppression, or whose forefathers have smarted under its lash, should here rival and even surpass America's free-born sons in devotedness to the country of their adoption. No wonder that the old Church of Christ, whose only object is the glory of God and the welfare of humanity, and which has had and has to-day so much to suffer from persecution in other lands, should give thanks to God for this land of liberty, in which the rights of God and the rights of man blend so harmoniously together.

And now, from the principles whose practical application we have been studying, it logically follows that as America exhibits the fullest development of popular institutions which the world has ever beheld, so she must also be the field of the greatest activity for popular education. And so in fact she is. Without the slightest intention of disparaging the zeal for education now manifested in other countries, it can with truth be said that there is no country in the world in which such efforts are made for the education of all classes of the people. That it should be so is the natural outcome of the principle of universal suffrage. This universal right to take part in the life of the nation, this universal right to aspire to her highest honors and privileges, is naturally a spur to every individual citizen to fit himself for the best that he is capable of attaining to. And, on the other hand, the fact that such is the right of every citizen forces the nation to see that the people are provided with all the intellectual advantages which they desire and demand. Nay, the national interests demand it as much as the rights of the citizens do, for a country of univeral suffrage can less afford than any other country to have ignorant citizens. The people of America ought to be the best educated people in the world.

And this has reference not only to the quantity of education imparted, but also, and still more, to its quality. It must be an education which is adapted to make them not only intelligent men and citizens, but also good men and virtuous citizens. It is a universally received axiom that the success of a republic must depend on the virtue of its citizens. To secure this end must be the great aim of popular education. The youth of America are born into an inheritance of broader civil rights, and therefore of weightier civil responsibilities than the youth of any other country on earth. In the young life of the American child there lie dormant more capabilities, both for good and for evil to his fellow-men, than are within the reach of the child of any other nation. Hence, the people of America, and, in the last and truest analysis, the parents of America, have a greater responsibility than any others to use all possible means for hindering the development of bad capabilities and fostering the growth of good capabilities in the characters of their children.

In this great work three agencies must co-operate—the influence of home, the influence of the Church, and the influence of the school. It is not necessary to dwell here on the part which home and church must have in the formation of character. No one will think of calling in question the paramount importance of home influences. Nor will any parents, worthy of that sacred relationship, imagine that any amount of care bestowed on their children by other people could possibly dispense them from being the special agents of Divine Providence in the moral moulding of their offspring. Neither will any Christian doubt that children ought from their tenderest years to be brought close to Him who said : "Suffer little children to come to me, and forbid them not, for of such is the kingdom of heaven." If they appreciate what the Church of Christ is to themselves, they will not fail to desire that their children should, as soon as possible, become partakers in its treasures of truth and grace.

The only possibility of doubt among intelligent Christians is about the part which the school ought to have in moulding character as well as in imparting knowledge. Yet no lengthy reasoning is necessary for recognizing that the influence of the school is apt to be the most potent, and therefore the most important of the three.

From the time that children begin to go to school, they spend far more of their waking hours under the care and influence of their teachers than under that of parents or of pastors. During those hours the mind, the heart, the character of the child are in the teacher's hands. During school hours the child expects to have serious matters presented for his study, and applies himself to them as best he can. When set free from the restraint of the school he considers it his right to have all his time for rest and play, and if then the most serious of all matters be forced upon him, he is apt to rebel and to hate these matters instead of appreciating and loving them. He considers it quite enough that he should be compelled to devote some of his free time to preparing for his classes of the following day. Experience shows that this is almost universally the disposition of children, and that it is scarcely less so in the years of youth than in the years of childhood.

And not only does experience show that it is principally during school time that the young are to be trained to clear and deep and strong convictions; it also proves that the impressions received in school are, as a rule, more potent in forming convictions for life than the impressions of either home or Church. If the teacher succeeds, as all teachers should strive to do, in winning the esteem and confidence of his scholars, they will instinctively come to weigh in his scales all that they hear at home or in church, and the more the school trains them, as it is said, to think for themselves, the stronger does this instinct become. Practically speaking, therefore, the school is the most efficacious agency in the forming of convictions, and it is on convictions that the shaping of conduct and character must mainly depend. Any system of character-moulding which ignores this fact is short-sighted and foolish. Any system of training which does not aim at making the influence of the school as salutary as possible for the character of the scholars, is blind to palpable facts and to good sense, and must expect disastrous results from so serious an omission.

Mr. Gladstone has lately written with solemn significance that the all-important question now pressing, not only on America, but also on the nations of the world, over which America is sure to exercise a growing influence, is "not what manner of producer, but what manner of man the American of the future is to be." To this momentous question we can only answer, this must, in the nature of things, depend on what kind of schools the American of the future is trained in. The welfare of our country absolutely demands that the youth of America should be trained in schools which will form them not only as producers, but also, and above all, as men. The most important question, therefore, now demanding the attention of the American people is this: How shall the schools of America be best fitted for the moulding of American character?

Answers to this great question will vary chiefly according to each one's estimate of the necessity of the Christian religion for shaping character and regulating life. Should anyone consider the Christian religion not an essential element in character-moulding, then he will logically not be very anxious for its action in the school. He will be content that the moral training of the children should be effected by appealing to their honor, to their sense of propriety, to their respect for the rights of others—in a word, to the principles of natural ethics. Now these are good, as far as they go; but the experience of history has shown that they do not go far enough, that they need for their foundations a sense of duty, of obligation, of right and wrong in conscience and before God; and it has shown that these foundations are laid only by religion—nay, that they are solidly and efficaciously laid by the Christian religion alone. Heathenism had its teaching of ethical principles, but they were powerless, except in extraordinary cases, to control passion and mould character, and they utterly failed to form a sound civilization before the Christian religion entered the world. Just as powerless would they be to preserve it if the influence of the Christian religion were withdrawn. This is a point about which Christians, at any rate, can hardly differ. Nor can they fear that the influence of Our Lord and of His religion in the school-room would depress the children or stunt their energies, or put gloom into their young lives; for well they know that He who is truth and grace is also light and peace and joy, and that it will be well with the children in every way just in proportion as their minds and hearts and lives are shaped under His blessed influence. Hence the question practically resolves itself into this: How can the influence of the Christian religion be best brought to bear in the schools of America, in order to efficaciously mould the character of American youth?

But in facing the solution of this problem we are at once met by a very grave difficulty in the composite character of the American people. In our sixty-five millions every shade of religious creed and opinion is represented. If, then, the conscience and the rights of all are to be respected, how can any system of Christian schools be possible?

To some the difficulty seems insurmountable. Hence they are willing to accept as the only practicable solution a system of schools from which all religious teaching is excluded, contenting themselves with the hope that the religious influences of home and of the Church will be sufficient. But I hope that the arguments already advanced have made it clear that in the light both of logic and of history this conclusion is untenable. The action of Christian homes and of the Christian Church is indispensable; but without the co-operation of Christian schools they cannot suffice for the Christian moulding of the people. To shape characters and direct lives according to the principles of the Christian religion is no easy task; for it is a religion that is hard on flesh and blood, hard on the instincts and passions of the human heart. If religion does not control these, then its profession is only hypocrisy. And if it is to control them, if it is indeed to shape and direct all the conduct of life towards God, towards self, and towards one's fellow-men, then all the period of character-moulding and all the influences that can co-operate in it will not be found too much. In a word, if we are to have a practically Christian people, then we must have Christian schools, as well as the Christian Church and Christian homes.

A large proportion of the American people now recognize this truth, and are anxiously trying to devise some method for introducing the influences of the Christian religion into the public schools. Various plans have been suggested for devising a system of Christian teaching which would suit all classes of conscience and conviction, some sort of compromise Christianity, a minimized Christianity, containing so little of distinctively Christian dogma that no one could find anything in it to object to. But any such system of compromise and of minimizing cannot possibly succeed, and that for various reasons.

Unbelievers will not accept it, for they have shown themselves determined to accept for themselves and their children no Christian teaching whatsoever.

Christian believers cannot accept it, because this minimized Christianity, although made up of some excellent things culled from the Christian religion, can be no substitute for the Christian religion.

People of common sense will say : If you wish that Christianity should be an influence in the schools for your children's good, don't minimize it ; the more you minimize it, the more you minimize its influence on their character. Let it be what Christ made it. Christ has given us nothing in it that we do not need, and that the children do not need to be taught and moulded in ; then, in the name of consistency, either let Christianity be in the schools just what Christianity is, or make no pretense of introducing it at all.

Let us learn a lesson in regard to the arrangement of religious differences among our people from our method in regard to political differences. People come to our shores from all the nations of the world, from under all forms of government, with all kinds of political convictions and opinions. In this land of liberty we have no desire to tyrannize over any one's political convictions. What, then, do we do? Do we adopt a system of compromise, and minimize our political principles so as to suit all forms of political opinions? Not at all. We assert and uphold our American ideas of civil rights and duties, of governmental prerogatives and limitations, and we minimize them for no one. We trust in their evident truth and the advantages of their practical working; and to those who hold lower ideas we say : "Friends, come up higher." And they do come up, and we rejoice in a united and homogeneous people.

Now, this is as it should be. And will any one say that the method, though true and good as to political ideas, would be false and pernicious as to religious ideas? Let those say it who believe, with Locke, that a thing can be true in philosophy and false in religion, or *vice versa*. No; what is true and good in social philosophy is true and good in religion. We should neither minimize Christianity nor coerce people to accept it; we should teach it clearly and fully as we understand and believe it, and leave the result to the force of truth. He would have very poor confidence in Christianity who would fear to put it to this test, and he would do injustice to Christianity who would refuse it this much fair play.

But, it will be urged, how could we possibly teach any one form of Christianity clearly and fully in the schools, since our people would naturally differ as to which form of it should be taught? But, I would answer, do the religious differences among our people hinder them from teaching Christianity, as they understand it, clearly and fully in their churches? Would they ever dream of devising a compromise Christianity to be taught in all the churches of the land, so that all the people might go to churches of the same kind? Not at all. Bodies of Christian believers follow their conscience in having different churches, according to their convictions of Christian truth and duty. Nay, if they were capable of sacrificing conscience in regard to their religious convictions by making compromises of them to suit other people, what reliance could be placed on conscientiousness in any other respect, and what foundation would there be left for public trustfulness and prosperity? And if it is so in regard to the churches, and if its being so is to the advantage and not the detriment of the American people, why should it not be the same in regard to the schools, which may be considered to be for the little folk almost what the churches are to the grown people?

But, it will be objected, will not the unity and homogeneity of the American people be thus broken up, or at least seriously imperilled? Not a whit more than by their having separate churches. On the contrary, the surest guarantee of a thorough union of our people in mind and heart is each one's firm assurance that fullest justice is done, and shall be done, to his conscientious convictions, and that he has to make no compromise of them because his neighbor believes differently from himself. Were such compromise attempted it would not change convictions, and these would inevitably assert themselves sooner or later and lead to conflict. But now each follows his conscience towards God, rejoices that he is free to do it, and therefore loves his country and his fellow-citizens all the more for conscience' sake, for God's sake, and for freedom's sake. How much better this than the clashing, the suspicions, the accusations, the strife, sure to result from the contrary experiment. Has there not already been too much such clashing in regard to the schools? In vain should we seek the remedy in more compromise, in more minimizing. The remedy must be found in fullest fidelity to conscience, and in lovingly "agreeing to disagree." Let us put far from us the delusion that we will train the children to be better citizens by training them to be compromise Christians. It was not in neutral or compromise schools of the sort that Washington and Madison and all our great models in American patriotism were taught. There were no such schools in their day. All schools then aimed at being Christian schools. The neutral or compromise school is the invention of a later and far inferior epoch. Without the influence of Christian schools, in vain will we hope for a return of their spirit of unselfish patriotism.

There is indeed one class of churches and of schools which, while claiming to be Christian, would necessarily exercise a most detrimental influence on the unity of the American people. I mean churches and schools in which the people and the children would be taught religious bigotry and sectarian animosity. There are some such churches, and perhaps some such schools; but, thanks be to God, they do not belong to the Catholic Church. Our teaching is, and shall be, that of devoted and practical love of God, and that of universal love of our fellow-men without limit or exception. Let such be the teaching in all the churches and all the schools; let the contrary spirit be everywhere denounced and eliminated from among our people; and then between all the churches and all the schools there will only be a beautiful and beneficent rivalry as to which shall best teach the purest and fullest Christianity, and the purest and fullest patriotism.

But, it is insisted, would not this logically place all the schools under the exclusive control of the churches, so as to do away with the control of the State? Not at all. No such consequence as the exclusion of the State is involved in this idea. True, were the State determined that State schools could not be, or should not be, Christian schools, then indeed intelligent and conscientious Christians would be compelled to have for their children Christian schools which would not be State schools. And in the present state of public opinion this is really the existing condition of things; the State schools at present exclude the teaching of the Christian religion, therefore the land is covered with Christian schools, Catholic and non-Catholic, which do not belong to the State, and receive from the State neither aid nor direction. But this is a situation for which there is no necessity in the nature of things. There is no necessary incompatibility whatsoever between the idea of a State school and that of a Christian school. Let the State recognize the plain and palpable and all-important truth that the schools of the country will be all the better for being Christian schools, and that any school which is up to the required level in secular instruction is all the more deserving of State support if it imparts a Christian training also; let it be willing that, without any detriment to the secular teaching, Christian teaching and Christian influences should exercise their blessed action on the children without limitation or hindrance; then there would remain no good reason why every Christian school in the land should not be a State school also. There is no lack of good will, surely, on the part of any of the Christian churches; why need there be on the part of the State? Other nations have found this practicable and advantageous to their people. To suppose that America would find it either impracticable or undesirable would be to judge very meanly either of her ingenuity or of her Christianity. We have no desire to see any foreign system transplanted here, but we trust that American good sense recognizes that it is well to learn wisdom even from the experience of one's neighbors.

But, it is again objected, even were this arrangement possible in case the State had only one or two denominations to deal with, is it not evidently impracticable where there might be a multitude of varying sects asking for the same recognition? By no means. This would indeed be true if the State had to take the various forms of religion into account and superintend the religious side of the work done in the schools. But such would evidently not be the case. The State pays for and superintends the work done in teaching the ordinary school branches, with which alone the State is concerned, and without the slightest reference to the religion which the teacher might profess, or which he would teach to the children whose parents desired it, for with this the State has nothing to do. And thus, whether the religious denominations represented by the parents of the children in the various schools numbered two or three or two hundred would be a matter of no concern whatever to the State, since it is only the secular side of the instruction that the State is concerned with and would take note of.

But, it is still urged, why should any denomination be so sweeping in its expectations as to ask that its religion should have full sway in a school supported by the State? Has not the Catholic Church decided that religious instruction after school hours suffices, and ought not that to satisfy all claimants? It is true that the Holy See has decided that such an arrangement may be made where no better can be done for the children, and where the State will allow them no fuller and freer exercise of their religion. And in so deciding, the Church has again, as on innumerable previous occasions in history, shown the conciliatory spirit that animates her, shown how earnestly she desires that Church and State, though distinct and independent in their respective spheres, should co-operate harmoniously for the moral welfare of mankind, and how ready she is to adapt herself to circumstances, to make concessions and compromises when necessary, provided only that they involve no sacrifice of principle. But why need the State deal with religion in so ungenerous a spirit? Why should a nation of sensible people wish to limit and diminish to the utmost the beneficent influence of religion over the children? What good reason can the State possibly have for refusing them the fullest and freest exercise and influence of their religion? Does the State suppose that the children will be better American citizens for being influenced as little as possible by their religion? The idea is preposterous; such cannot be the mind of the American people. The State knows that the rising generation will need all the moral and religious influences which they are capable of receiving in order to be the kind of citizens they ought to be. Does America suppose it would be to her discredit in the eyes of the civilized world if she gave more liberty than that to religion in the schools? Far from it; she knows that the civilized world, now so anxiously asking, in the words of Gladstone, "What manner of man is the American of the future to be?" will bless America for bringing Christian influences to bear on the children of the land as fully as possible. Does she imagine that any denomination would thus gain power for the country's harm? Cursed be any denomination that could be capable of such treacherous ingratitude! The thought is simply monstrous. Only a mind blinded by fanaticism could harbor such a suspicion. The Catholic Church, at any rate, has so repeatedly and so unmistakably declared, by the mouths of her Bishops and even of the Pope himself, her admiration for America, for her principles and her institutions, that of her, at least, the suspicion cannot be with any shadow of reason entertained. Or does the State fear that injustice would be done to the conscience of any child or of its parents? But when the children in a particular school are all of one denomination, and sufficient provision is made in other schools for children of different religious convictions, no such injustice is to be apprehended. Or does the State fear that, if full freedom were given to religion in the schools, the time would be so taken up with religious instruction that secular instruction would suffer thereby? But this would be to mistake entirely the character of the constant influence which religion would fain exercise over the minds and hearts of the children. This influence does not consist in long and frequent doctrinal instructions. Such a system as that would only disgust and weary the children and thwart its own purpose. It consists principally in the gentle and almost imperceptible influence constantly exerted by the religious character of the teachers, by the nature of their answers to the questions the children ask, by the explanations and observations which they would naturally introduce wherever the study in hand has a moral aspect, by the tact with which a conscientious and skillful teacher will avail himself of the thousand opportunities occurring all through the day to imprint impressions of truth and duty and virtue on the susceptible young minds and hearts which Providence has entrusted to his care. Such a system as this detracts not in the least from the fulness and excellence of the secular instruction imparted, but breathes into it the living soul which makes it truly an education for the citizen and for the Christian. Why, then, should the State wish to hinder this, to banish these elevating and beneficent influences from the children or to minimize their humanizing and christianizing action. Where the State is thus minded and the support of a better system is found impracticable, then those children and their parents may perhaps be considered fortunate in having a half loaf, or even a very small crust, rather than no bread. But why should the State ever be thus minded? Let the State do full justice to herself and to her citizens by doing full justice to Christianity in the schools.

That America will one day do this we cannot for a moment doubt. We have the fullest confidence in the fulfillment of her Providential mission as a great Christian power in the world's future. We have fullest confidence in the good sense of the American people, and in their love of fair play. Therefore we cannot but feel certain that America will yet make sure the foundations of her Christian civilization by providing for the youth of the land a system of Christian education. For that day we pray and we wait in patient hope.

Meantime the duty of Christian parents, who love their children and their country as they ought, is manifest. They are bound to procure for their children, by their own exertions and with their own means, that greatest of all earthly blessings, the priceless boon of an education which, while thoroughly sound and thoroughly American, will also be thoroughly Christian. To this they are called by the voice of the Church, whose councils have repeatedly and emphatically declared that the spread of Christian education is the great work of the age, and that no parish is complete without a Christian school. To this they are called by the voice of nature, by the heaven-imposed obligations of parental duty and parental affection. Let them win their children's everlasting gratitude by giving them that best of all inheritances, an education fully fitting them for all their career, for all their duties to time and to eternity To this they are likewise called by the voice of patriotism. For a while their country may misunderstand their action and misjudge their motives. This we profoundly regret, but it cannot deter us from doing our duty. We will push on in our glorious work, on towards the noble aim of placing the advantages of an excellent Christian education within the reach of every Catholic child in the land. And the day will surely come when, all prejudices and misunderstandings being dispelled, our country will do us justice, and recognize that we have indeed been her best friends.

Brethren, the only sure foundation of both the Christian Church and the Christian State is Christian education. In God's name, let us redouble our energies, and make that foundation broad and solid and everlasting.

CHURCH AND STATE.

Mr. Chairman, Ladies and Gentlemen: It would be, indeed, a cold heart that would remain untouched by the warmth of this reception. I am sensible that the flattering words of the chairman in presenting me to you to-night places me somewhat at a disadvantage. I do not feel that I quite deserve his praise, but I know that I fully appreciate the warmth of sentiment which prompted him to lavish the kindly words upon me.

I have met you to-night to discuss a somewhat important subject, and one which, perhaps, as it is first stated to you, might be inclined to awaken apprehensions among the cautious. People are apt to level a reproach against the Catholic Church, and to declare that it attempts to interfere with the policy of the State. Now, I believe that, in a party sense, in the limited sense in which the word politics is used in our country, the Church has no part or concern. But I do believe that the Christian Church has founded Christian civilization, and that the civilization of this age and of the century upon which we are about to enter depends upon the fidelity of the Catholic Church to the mission which she has received at the hands of her divine founder.

If I were asked to-night to name the most important event of the last fifty years I would unhesitatingly answer, that it was the jubilee of the Pope, which has been celebrated within the last few weeks. Now, this may seem a startling and even an extravagant assertion. I know that the last fifty years have been crowded with events of momentous importance, and that they have followed each other with startling rapidity. I know that dynasties have been razed and thrones subverted and the boundaries of nations turned; that on this Continent we have seen the stain of slavery wiped from our constitutional system of the States, and an indestructible Union established forever; but nevertheless of these all momentous and important events, all these changes, the advance of Russian armies to the gates of Constantinople, the creation of new empires in the East, the changes in the map of France, the burning question between countries which threaten to plunge Europe yet into war, I repeat the assertion with which I opened, that the jubilee of Leo XIII. is the most important event, and that which far transcends them all in political as well as in religious importance.

This Pontiff of ours, who, in the closing days of the nineteenth century, beholds himself shorn of all the ancient possessions of his predecessors— this "prisoner of the Vatican" has proved that he possesses an empire which is bounded only by the confines of this earth. This Prince, who could not bestow a single reward to stimulate attachment or enthusiasm, is the object of a reverence that can be commanded by no temporal ruler.

In the vast throngs which were assembled in St. Peter's the other day, the enthusiasm with which the approach of the Pope was welcomed, the various uniforms, typifying all the countries of the world, concurring in this expression of reverence and affection to the head of the Christian Church, we behold the proof of the unquenched and unquenchable vigor of the Christian faith and a revival of the fervor of Catholic piety throughout the universe. Now, the spiritual aspect of this great manifestation, has been discussed and expounded by the venerable prelates to whom has been committed the government of the Christian Church throughout the world, and if we discuss its importance here to-night, it is from the standpoint of a layman and a citizen striving to find by the light of the experience of the human family in the past, an indication of the future influence of the Christian Church upon the institutions under which we live and upon the civilization of this age. I have heard it said that the mission of the Catholic Church is now accomplished; that an age of enlightenment and consequently of indifference has set in; that there is no function left for it to discharge which is of value to the citizen; and to that I answer that the whole story of the civilization of the last nineteen hundred years is a refutation of the assertion.

What has been the mission of the Christian Church since the very beginning of its foundation? It has been a mission of charity, a mission of enlightenment, a mission of peace and of good will among men, and the elevation of the social conditions of the human race. And it is a remarkable coincidence that in this nineteenth century of her existence she finds the condition of men almost touching the extreme of that condition which she beheld in the first century of her existence. The policy of the Roman Cæsars had been to make all men equal, but it was the degradation of the patrician, and not the elevation of the plebeian; it was the common equality of servility and of subjugation.

In the nineteenth century we behold the human race tending again towards equality—but it is the equality of liberty, of progress, and a recognition of human rights, and of the elevation of the human race to a higher plane of civilization, and I say that the Catholic Church—the Christian Church—has been the agency which has been the most active and the most important in producing this condition.

Let us look back for a moment over the history of the human race during the last eighteen hundred years. We know that when the barbarian tribes of the northern forests overwhelmed the ancient civilization of the Roman Empire, a period of darkness set in throughout Europe; that the monuments of ancient civilization, having been trampled under foot, a period of rapine, pillage and bloodshed ensued. Men knew no other law than the force of arms. There was no security for property except the defence of it in the open field. There was no security for human rights, because the whim of a lord controlled the life and the liberty of his vassal. And throughout that period, when no man could call his life secure; when civil strife was the constant and continual condition of humanity, the victims of civil war were immediately doomed to destruction and slaughter before the victorious armies of their conquerors.

But there was one spot inside which neither the writ of the king nor the retainer of the noble nor the *posse* of the sheriff could penetrate, and that was the sanctuary established by the Christian Church, inside which the pursued and the fugitives could always find a refuge that no foot could profane and that no hand would desecrate. And during all the years, all the centuries when men seemed plunged into a condition of degraded barbarism; when the thirst of conquest could be assuaged only in human blood; when no power could withstand the march of a victorious noble or a conquering king, we read again and again in history, that the priest or the bishop stood at the doorway, and the arms that no human agency could withstand, he braved and defied in the name of God, while the shivering victim stood behind in security and in peace.

I have often read of the splendors of the Pontificate in the age of the Renaissance, but I believe that the brightest page in human history is that which tells of Gregory of Tours refusing to surrender to King Chilperic his own son, who sought refuge among the priests, and though the monarch laid waste their fields and burned their buildings, and the monks could read their prayers at night by the light of their burning hay-stacks, that fugitive remained secure and the king was beaten back by the power of charity and love, wielded by a Church whose motto was "Peace and good will among men." Now, through all the Middle Ages, in every country of Europe the story was repeated. When the House of York or the House of Lancaster triumphed in the field they pursued their victims without quarter.

The idea of sparing human life was scouted. Women and children were the victims of their rage and vengeance, but the churches were always crowded. Bishops lost their lives; Archbishops were executed in cold blood, every violence was done to the men who were the soldiers standing guard over the pursued, but the sanctuaries were always respected, and those who sought their shelter found they were always secure. And it was not alone in the preservation of human life that the Church played this important part, but everywhere this influence was towards the preservation of civilized life and the development of the sentiments of humanity which are at the basis of our civilization to-day. When the barbarians had extinguished the light of learning; when the age of violence came over the world, and nothing was respected but prowess in the field; when the nobles boasted of ther ignorance and looked upon learning as a sign of effeminacy, the flame of learning was kept alive in the Christian monastery. There, and there alone were the arts of reading and writing preserved; and although that light of learning has now grown to be a flame that bathes the whole civilized world, when the steady march of progress, of the growth of science,—aye, when we are whirled from one side of this Continent to another by the steam engine which seizes the forces of nature and harnesses them to the needs of man; when intelligence is flashed under the ocean in an instant and we are placed in communication with the peoples of the most distant ends of this earth; when we behold the splendor of this civilization which we enjoy, we should remember that every bit of it emanates to-day from that small flame which was kept alive in the monasteries whose inmates were dedicated to the service of God and to the preservation of enlightenment. And when in that same rude age we find that those who were sick, those who were infirm, those who were crippled, those who were useless in the service of masters, whose time was dedicated to strife, were cast out as unworthy of shelter, the monasteries fed the hungry, gave a resting place to the footsore and shelter to the homeless. Now the march of progress and the growth of civilizing influences has established a system of jurisprudence based upon the natural laws of equity, and every man's life is secure unless he has committed an offense which properly forfeits it to the law. And, as the march of civilization has therefore rendered life secure, the sanctuary no longer shelters those who fly from the oppressions of man. The whole world is devoted to the spread of science, and the Church no longer claims to possess for herself a monopoly of all learning. The monasteries have been suppressed in many countries, but their work of charity survives and the State has been compelled to assume that duty from a sense of self-preservation which the monks discharged from a sense of duty to God. And thus we behold that in learning, in charity, in science and in law every step that human progress has made has been a step in the direction of spreading and making universal the function which the Church discharged in a period when the State denied these responsibilities or was unable to discharge them.

But it may be asked, now that the State has assumed all those functions, now that the necessity for the special devotion of the Church has passed away, what mission remains to the Church that is peculiarly hers and that unless she discharges, society itself is in danger? Have we indeed made such progress that we can afford to despise this divine institution which has held the light before the steps of man in the darkness and guided his tottering movements as he progressed towards the civilized state? Is there no function left her that she can discharge to-day and she alone can discharge fully and to the complete safety of society? The days of civil strife have passed. Men no longer butcher each other in the open field. The business of life is no longer the waging of war; but though these contests in the open fields of battle have passed, a contest for bread goes on around us every day, under conditions as cruel as those that prevailed in the fields of open strife. We see to-day, this very progress of ours sowing the seeds of difficulty all around us. Economical conditions have produced results which breed enormous fortunes on one side, and appalling poverty on the other. The fields are everywhere being deserted by the youth of the nation, and the cities are becoming crowded every day with a larger population. Our needs are becoming more urgent. Everywhere we hear the cry of distress going up in all lands, that tells us there is something wrong with the social order. In this country we have heard the appeals for aid from the General Government or from the State Governments. Out in the West, whole States have risen up and demanded that the Federal Government should go into the business of loaning money to the farmers to enable them to gain their bread. There is advocated a policy of the issue of something that would stand for money, in the vain hope that by increasing the circulation their own condition would be improved. All these are but the cry in the night of men who have lost their way. It is like the sound of the whistle on the ocean steamer in a fog, which is in itself a confession that the captain can no longer rely on the science of navigation, that he can but cry out in the night to avoid the danger, that the prow of his ship may pass in safety. Society cannot claim that it is on a sound and indestructible basis when all around we hear the cry of distress and of discontent. It will not do to turn our backs upon these conditions and to forget them, and in contemplating the prosperity which we enjoy, close our ears to the sounds that tell us that there are dangers that lurk in the pathway of the ship of State. That condition is not confined to this country. It exists in a more aggravated form in the countries of Europe. Those of us who observe how the resources of the world are being taxed for the consumption of luxury and the conditions of comfort, who see stately buildings in which commerce is prosecuted, in which the successful competitors in the race of life dwell in luxury and opulence, where these stately buildings dedicated to the worship of God cast a gentle shadow over the highway, must not believe that these and these alone are all that make up a city. We need to go but half a mile to find ourselves face to face with a poverty so awful, that the mind recoils from its contemplation. We know that in every city of the world there are men reduced to penury, whose penury and poverty are not the fruits of vice or of sloth. In every city thousands of honest men go every day into the public highway seeking an opportunity to sell their labor, and night after night they are driven back to their homes unsuccessful in their search—driven back to homes, whose sweating walls breed distemper and disease, through whose broken windows the winter wind can whistle at will, while the cry of wailing from children maddens the brain and is calculated to nerve his arm to destructive and mutinous deeds.

The barbarian who came from the North on to Europe was a hungry man. We read to-day—it seems almost yesterday—of a wonderful demonstration in the city of London, where a hundred thousand starving workmen, not idlers, not men who were reduced to penury through sloth or vice, but workmen—came to Trafalgar square, and there in the presence of the monuments of the greatness of the British Empire, called out for work that they might live; called out for bread and were willing to exchange for it the sweat of their brows, and no consoling answer came to them. Was the ancient barbarism any greater menace to civilization than these incidents of this progress of ours, and do we find in purely secular institutions the means of remedying this evil and curing and eradicating it? Where has it been suggested? What profane philosopher who tells us the mission of the Church is accomplished, tells us how this evil is to be met? Is it to be met by force? The white Czar, with five millions of trained soldiers who could have successfully defied the combined powers of the whole civilized world, riding through his own capital—a missile no larger than a billiard ball, thrown from a group of by-standers, explodes under his carriage; and this Czar, this head of the Church and State, ruler of eighty-five millions of human souls, in an instant is a quivering, mangled, bruised, dying mass of humanity upon the snows of St. Petersburg.

Is the remedy in education? If society is to be preserved by education, let the exploding bombs in Chicago, hurled by Anarchists who were themselves lettered and educated men, be answer to that statement. There is not in Europe an Anarchist or Socialist who is not a well-read, if not a well-educated, man. They are not the men who pine in cells or suffer their agonies and their wants without complaint. They are the men who read, and who find in these social conditions which produce these enormous accessions of wealth and this terrible and degrading condition of poverty, reason, not for submission, but for revolt; and their teachings, caught up by others who reflect and think as they do, constitute a danger to society of which we have had evidences in every capital of Europe as well as in the great city on our own Western Lakes. Where, then, is the secular institution that is going to provide for the safety of the State? When we exhaust force, when we see the hopelessness of purely secular education, what is left on which the reflecting man can build his hopes for the future? The institution that has always lasted. The institution which shed light in the darkness of the past and casts its light into the gloom of the future,— in faith we have the true system of civilization which was originally founded upon the Christian Church.

I remember, that some years ago, a person connected with the school system of New York told me that in one of the schools a boy who had shown great aptitude in his studies and who had become the favorite of his teacher, whose diligence had been remarkable for months, suddenly disappeared. Days having elapsed and he having given no sign of re-appearance, the truant officer was invoked to seek him out and ascertain the cause of his absence; and the officer returned and said that he went down into one of the districts on the East Side, close to the river front, and came to a tenement house and ascertained that the boy lived in a building constructed in the rear, and he entered this structure, into which no ray of sunlight ever penetrated, and he ascended six flights of stairs through Cimmerian darkness and came to a small room under the roof and there found an old man sitting in a chair, without fire, though it was the depth of winter, the walls sweating with the deadly sweat of disease and death, which is so frequent a feature of the abode of the poor. He was wrapped up in an old coverlet, which was the covering that he used at night on the wretched pallet which lay in the corner, and he sat there chained to that chair, a victim of a hopeless disease, and told the officer that he was compelled to send this boy out on the streets to sell papers for bread. Chained to that chair, he had no hope of ever leaving it. The hand of God was on him and he was doomed to death. The condition of poverty in which he was found was awful beyond conception, and yet it was the best condition that he could ever hope to see in this world, for each successive day meant a day of aggravated misery for him, and yet that man was resigned and happy because the priest of God had visited him that morning and he had received from his hands the same sacrament that a king would have received in the stateliest palace that had ever been constructed by the hand of man. Eliminate the element of faith from that man's condition, show me that man with rational beliefs founded upon human reason and irresistible systems of human logic and tell me why should not he be an Anarchist or a Socialist? What motive could control him to respect the laws which created wealth all around him and left him there hopeless from day to day? Tell me any reason founded upon logic, which would convince that man that a general convulsion of society would not be for his benefit, for in the confusion that would attend crumbling institutions he might at least be secure of one meal and that was more than he was secured of then. Yet society was in no danger from him. Aye, this helpless man was a bulwark of order, and whoever could have seen him would have read in the influence of the Church exercised on him the reasons why those who believe in the mission of the Church to-day are those who entertain no doubt about the future of our civilization even though they be alive to the dangers which confront it.

It was many years ago. That life has long since been snuffed out. The man who spent so many weary days upon his couch has seen that bed of pain converted into a chariot that led him to a glorious reward. But who shall say that that life is not without its fruits? Shall any man say that because this man vegetated, suffered and died in that back room that his influence is lost to civilization; that his influence on humanity is not far-reaching even now as I speak? When a thin ray of sunlight escapes from the dark clouds of a winter day, how many people pay attention to it? How many people think of the influence that is exercised, or remember it three seconds after it has disappeared? And yet who can tell how many roots have been saved from destruction and fertilized by it; how much life has been preserved throughout all the kingdom of God; what influence it bears on the glorious vegetation which will salute our eyes everywhere in the coming summer? So, each life animated by faith, interpreting the will of God is a ray of sunlight descending from Heaven, working its influence everywhere long after the life shall be extinguished, and it is in the multiplication of such influences as these that we see the glorious and full effects which the mission of the Church will exercise over the civilization of this age.

If we are told that the influence of the Church has waned at different times, that it is not fair to claim for this civilization of ours that it has been altogether the product of Christian faith and of that alone, let us look at the history of a country whose national festival we celebrate to-night. There for fourteen hundred years we can follow the unbroken, unchecked influence of the Catholic Church upon a people in every phase of vicissitude which would test their loyalty to faith and to their country. Conceive for a moment what is meant by that space of time. Why, this festival carries us back, as we look for its origin, to the time when on the plains of Tolbac the conquered arms of France were revived by God in answer to the prayer of Clotilde, and the whole Frankish nation embraced the Christian faith. This island was a century old when Mohammed penned the Koran, when Mecca rejected and Medina accepted him. It was three hundred years old when

Pepin beat back the Lombards from the gates of Rome and established the independence of the Republic of God. It was venerable with the celebration of a thousand years when the janizaries entered Constantinople and the Church of St. Sophia became the chief temple of the Mussulman faith. For if I have mentioned the length of this mission and the circumstances under which it began and the events which this celebration has witnessed, it has been but to invite your attention to the conditions that existed when St. Patrick began his mission of evangelization and of enlightenment. He began it at a period of rapine, at a period of violence, yet his mission was a mission of peace and good will. In an age of war he did not invade a country with drawn sword or with flaming torch. His sword was the crucifix which typified the sacrifice of immeasurable love by which the human race is redeemed. He came clothed in the vestments of Christian truth. He did not come to overturn thrones, or to found a dynasty amid the wreck of States, but to establish schools and temples in which the truth of God should be worshipped throughout the world. He lit the pure light of Christian truth upon the Irish hills, and that light to-day carried in the bosoms of Irishmen into the four quarters of the globe, is an evangelizing influence on which the future hope of the Church must largely rest. And during those fourteen centuries through which the Irish people remained faithful to the teachings of St. Patrick, it was no holiday manifestation of faith. Other countries are Catholic, other countries worship Christ according to the tenets of our Church, but in no other country has the Catholic faith survived the persecution, the long years of oppression over which she has triumphed on the Irish soil. I believe that any person who has ever visited the stately cathedrals of Continental Europe, who has ever seen the impressive ceremonies with which the Catholic worship is conducted in those favored countries, would cease to wonder that people should be Catholic. Who that has ever bowed his knee under the mighty Dome of St. Peter, or bent his head in prayer under the lofty spires of Notre Dame, who has smelled the incense which has burned before marble altars, whose eyes have been dimmed by the glory of innumerable candelabra, who has seen on the windows the life-like pictures of saints and confessors, of cherubim and seraphim move almost to life as the rays of the sun streamed into the windows while the praises of God swept through aisle and transept and sanctuary, reaching the ear of the listener on the wings of heavenly strains,— who that has ever heard or seen all this, can wonder that a people before whom all these ceremonials were conducted should remain steadfast and loyal to the Church of which they were exponents?

But the Irish people had no such outward incentives to maintain or stimulate their faith. Through long ages of oppression they worshipped God when their ceremony was denuded of everything that could attract the eye or appeal to mere lofty senses. Crowded in garrets, hiding in out-houses, driven from the cities and villages they sought the seclusion of the mountain glen, there to worship their God, and their priest was never faithless to his people, where flock and shepherd together worshipped their Creator, and if in these places of hiding they had no stately domes to shelter them from winter skies, they had over their heads the blue vault which had been constructed by their Father in Heaven. If they had no marble altars on which to conduct the service, they stretched a white cloth upon a narrow ledge of rock just large enough to support the sacred chalice. If they had no incense to burn before that lowly altar, the fires on the hillside and grass meadows yielded a perfume as sweet as if it rose from any of swinging censers. Kneeling in this desolation, they worshipped God, making up in fervor what they lacked in splendor, even though the words of the sacrifice might at any moment be interrupted by the crack of the Saxon rifle and the blood of the priest be mingled with the wine of the sacrificial offering.

Fourteen centuries have elapsed, seven centuries since the Norman invasion, three centuries of persecution, the like of which the history of no other country can show, of penal laws that sought to sap even the natural fountains of affection, to array father against son, brother against brother; the priests hunted down like wolves and a price placed on the head of whomsoever should celebrate mass yet that priest so persecuted became—with the bond of affection existing between him and the people, which has never existed in any other country on the globe—the hunted and persecuted fugitive of the law became the *soggarth aroon* of Irish song and story, whose sufferings have been one of the chief glories of Catholic history throughout the world.

And if I have mentioned these stories of persecution, if I have spoken of this feature of our celebration as illustrating the purpose of what I have to say to you to-night, it has only been to call your attention to this story of persecution and wrong, and then to point out the glorious results of the Catholic leadership of Irish patriotism. The penal laws have been abolished. Already we can see through the dark clouds of tyranny, almost riven by the hand of enlightened English statesmanship, the dawn of Irish liberty and of Irish independence. But while we stand upon the threshold of our emancipation, when we behold the day almost arrived when the Irish people shall enter again into the management of their affairs, nowhere do we hear one syllable breathed of a thirst for vengeance or of a desire for reprisal. Seven centuries of confiscation and of outrage; seven centuries of pillage and of wrong; seven centuries of persecution of a population, of injury to old and young, men and women, are forgotten in the hope that the Irish people will now press forward to accomplish the destiny of their race. Where can you find in the history of the globe a people pursued as this has been, on the very threshold of their deliverance addressing themselves to missions of peace and good will, stifling every suggestion of revenge or of bloodshed? Who to-night talks of revenging the wrongs of these seven hundred years? Everywhere we hear one voice, one word, one sentiment, and that is a sentiment of forgetfulness and forgiveness for the past and of hope and confidence for the future. The Irish people do not seek independence to slaughter a single life, or to confiscate one inch of property. They seek independence in order to establish the glory of their ancient race upon a firmer basis. They hope to see their country once more become the land of song, the home of literature, their schools sending out fires of enlightenment as in ancient days their missionaries preached the gospel of Christ from the Apenines to the Danube. They hope once more to see their schools attain that importance throughout Europe that they enjoyed a thousand years ago, while everywhere we hope to see such a development of the country, as will send ships from every quarter of the island, from the peaks of which will float the ancient flag bearing the harp and the sunburst proclaiming a new force in the civilization of the century. The emblem of our race, the emblem of St. Patrick, the emblem of this day which we celebrate, the emblem of Christian, Catholic leadership among this generous race is not the sword, is not the torch, is not the instrument of war or of oppression. It is not the creation of man. It is the creation of Heaven. It finds its bed in the green fields where the flocks find pasture. It spreads its green leaves by the rippling brooks, whose waters dance with gladness in God's sunlight. In peace it flourishes; under the cruel heel of war it droops and dies. The dews and the rains of Heaven nourish it. The blood of God's creatures chokes it. It is the herald of early spring. It typifies the valor of man and the virtue of woman. Emblem of a mighty race! Thy roots are no longer confined to thine own soil. Tender hands remove thee to-day from the earth; gentle hearts cherish thee. To-night in every quarter of the globe, the hearts of Irishmen swell with patriotic emotion, and the eyes of Irish women are moistened with tenderness and love as they contemplate the Shamrock of Erin.

The mission of the Christian Church as a civilizing force for fourteen hundred years is illustrated in the history of the Irish people. Without a break, without a suspension of a moment it has ever been the active influence which has kept alive the fires of Irish patriotism, and that has led the Irish race to their freedom along the pathway of self-denial and shows them to-day their hour of triumph without fear of seeing it stained by a single act of violence; and what it has accomplished among that people it has accomplished everywhere when it has been allowed an opportunity to freely discharge its functions. But I have heard it said that in this country there is a conflict between the Church and the State; that the Church is undemocratic; that it is an influence that is hostile to republican institutions; that in some way or other the Pope may send an influence across the sea— for I scarcely think they expect he will come himself—and turn around the heads of some gentlemen who fear that in some way or other they will lose their liberties if the Pope be given a chance to discharge his spiritual function. I would like to know where there is a democratic institution whose antiquity compares with that of the Catholic Church itself? Where has the world ever seen a republic as perfect as the Christian Church? What is this republic founded on except a recognition of the teachings of Catholicism? We have spoken of the growth of wealth, the march of progress, the better opportunities that are open to-day before the footsteps of Christian men and of civilized men. The free institutions which we enjoy in this country, towards which the customs of all men are now tending, are not the result of the invention of new principles but of the recognition of old ones. There is not in our Constitution to-day, so far as it concerns the right of the citizen, a single new discovery. There is a wider recognition of fundamental political truths, but these principles have been preached by the Church and illustrated in her practices for nineteen hundred years. We talk to-day and boast that our Constitution holds all men equal at the ballot box. For nineteen hundred years the Church has held all men equal at the communion rail. We boast that for a hundred years we have held all men equal before the law. For nineteen hundred years the Church has held all men equal in the sight of God. We say that every man can find his way to the highest office in this country to-day. For nineteen hundred years any son of the Church who entered the priesthood was eligible to the Supreme Pontificate. Our Constitution recognizes the right of all men to pursue health, wealth and happiness. The Christian Church has taught that for nineteen hundred years. Show me one single element which we possess as a fundamental feature of this government that has not been illustrated in the Church in her practices for nineteen centuries. In a period long anterior to the recognition of these principles in human affairs by any State or by any principality, when the known equality of men was scouted by all, the Church against the pomp and pride of privilege and rank preached the levelling democracy of the grave. She exacted from the king the same penance that she imposed on the subject. She had no sacrament to administer in palaces that she would not bring to the bedside of the humblest man who suffered throughout the land. She had no prayer to offer over the tomb of a king that she did not say at the bedside and grave of the pauper. Her mission has not been to the great ones of this earth. She is founded on the rock of the humble fisherman, and this Church, founded on those principles which are unalterable, has been the institution of the spirit of liberty through the ages when the rights of man were not even understood, when there were none to assert, much less to demand them. But the crowning service which the Church has rendered to the State, which gives her the right to claim that she is the author of this modern civilization, has been the creation of the Christian home, which is the distinguishing feature of the civilization in which we live. In the first century of her existence she found the world plunged either in a refined corruption or in the midst of degraded barbarism. In the barbaric state the woman was the property, the thing, the slave of the man. In the enlightened and civilized state, marriage was recognized as a civil contract, which might be dissolved at will by either of the parties. In the one case you had a degraded womanhood; in the other you had a corrupted womanhood in this civilized condition all over the world. In the midst of that corruption the Church preached the doctrine of pure morality. To the idea that marriage was a civil contract she opposed the doctrine that it was a sacrament instituted by God to last during the lives of those who received it. Amidst the barbaric state where the woman was trampled under the heel of man, she told the story of the redemption of the human race through the Immaculate Mother of God. She elevated the conception of womanhood by teaching to all the world that came to study her beliefs, that while men might be heroes in the field, while Cæsars might conquer provinces, while statesmen might frame laws, while travellers might brave the dangers of distant climes, while men alone were eligible to the honors of the triumph over the enemies of Rome, that the woman had accomplished a mission vaster and grander than all, that through one of her sex the whole human race had been redeemed. And that doctrine, preached in the teeth of persecution, preached in the teeth of the corrupt who reviled and of the kings who struck and maimed and killed the preachers, finally robbed love of all its grossness, elevated and dignified the conjugal condition, gave it a maternal and new glory which finally established and consecrated the Christian home, and the home is the corner-stone of the civilized State in which we live to-day.

What is the State? Why, it is a huge family composed of the aggregation of a number of small families. Everywhere modern civilization recognizes that if we are to have progress and security and wealth and prosperity we must preserve the home, and how is it to be preserved if we surrender the doctrine that the marriage state is a condition assumed by man and woman, not for the gratification of themselves, but to carry out the scheme of God for the peopling of His universe with Christian men and Christian women? There we find to-day, a danger that menaces the integrity of civilization and of the social system. Who shall protect it if we eliminate the influence of the Church from the social conditions? The law cannot recognize marriage as anything else but a civil state and a civil contract. The law of the State can only recognize in the coming together of men and women, an agreement, because the State has no concern with things spiritual. But here the Church steps in, as she always must step in, to supply that which every condition of mankind has lacked, to furnish the divine essence necessary to keep society together, and while giving full faith and credit to the system of jurisprudence, that recognizes the marriage state as the result of a civil contract, goes further and pronounces upon it a benediction and places upon it a permanency and a responsibility which no man who believes in God will violate.

Now, I have expressed my faith that the Church can solve the difficulties of the social condition by aiding the State in the work of improving the condition of mankind. I believe it as firmly as I believe anything that I have not yet seen; I believe it as firmly as anything which can be demonstrated by principles which are not conclusive. I am asked how? I answer I cannot tell. I cannot claim to explain the manner in which Providence will work out His wonders, but I do know that there is no peril which threatens the social system of this day that is one-half as pressing, as terrible or as apparently hopeless, as the condition which the Church confronted in the first century of her existence, when out of degradation and immorality she constructed the Christian home and revolutionized the face of the world. Wherever we find that the State assumes for itself a duty which it can discharge, it is the business of the Church to leave it to the State.

We have made our subject to-night, "Church and State," and the use of these words suggests the idea that the State owes a support to the Church. I have chosen it for the reason that I want to state here before you to-night, that that doctrine is exploded, and the duty is not from the State to the Church, but from the Church to the State. To pension priests of the Church, to pay them out of the treasury, would be to make them agents of the State, able perchance, properly to discharge any duties of the State just as any other officer could, but in assuming that relation they would surrender their independence, and in surrendering that, they would lose their usefulness. In the dark ages when the state of society was incapable of furnishing protection to the weak, the Church created and maintained the sanctuary. A system of jurisprudence was established, the sanctuary was reserved for the worship of God, and men were remitted the decrees of the laws because the laws were incapable of protecting them. And wherever the State can discharge a function and discharge it properly and fully, the Church will tell you to "render unto Cæsar, the things that are Cæsar's," and to render to God the things that are God's. The enforcement of the civil law, the protection of territory, the developments of our ports, harbors and rivers, the construction of highways—all these are functions of the State which the State must discharge. It has assumed the burden of supporting the poor, but the Church had discharged it so long and so well, and while I believe it is a fact that the alms given by the State have never been accepted by those who received them as the poor received the support of the Church in ancient years, still in accepting it as a part of its duty, the State confessed and confesses to-day, the magnitude of the service, which during long centuries the Church performed for the children of men. The State established hospitals, furnishes medicines, supplies all that the skill of surgery may do and in all these cases the State discharges a function which belongs to it, but there is something which the State cannot furnish to the sufferer on the bed of pain. The State may do for his body, all that science can suggest, but it needs the aid of the priest at the side of the dying to nerve him for the journey which he must take. There is a consolation in religion, there is a power which brings about a resignation to the gravest ills that can affect the flesh, which the State can never control. So the Church to-day finds a glorious mission which it discharges with a loyalty that commands the admiration even of those who reject her tenets.

We find in education that the State assumes the burden of that; and the Church welcomes it so far as it goes, but it reserves to itself the right to supplement that purely secular education by instruction on subjects that teach a man better than all else what are his duties to God, and from that to deduce the lesson that he must, as a good citizen, be submissive to the laws. The laws of the land are made to be the law of God by the teaching of the Church; and he who discharges his duty to her receives a lesson in citizenship better than anything that can be culled from profane literature. And so I believe that the mission of the Church to-day is one of salvation to the State,—that there never has been a condition of human society where she has not supplied everything that was lacking to the human family; and when to-night we are confronted with this question which perplexes the statesmen of the world, when men admit the dangers and cannot supply the remedy for them, when the statesmen of every age and of every country are appalled by the growth of poverty and misery in great cities, and no one can suggest a cure for it, I fall back on that unbroken record of nineteen hundred years; and I believe that the Church which kept the lamp of progress alive during periods far darker than this will ultimately, through the mysterious ways of Providence, find a means of reconciling men to their condition, and of ultimately improving it and bettering it—to emancipate the citizen from any difficulty that may confront him. I believe that I may say of her that she is and she always has been the light of progress, the bulwark of order, the temple of liberty, and that whoever labors in her service works to the benefit of mankind; that whoever is loyal to her teachings must be loyal to the laws; that whoever is a good Catholic must be a good citizen, loyal to good citizenship. And I believe as the influence of the Church spreads there will be an amelioration in the condition of man. Her mission has never been to the opulent, but to the fallen, the outcast, and the hopeless. The rich were never committed to her care, but the poor were made her wards; and it is among the poor that she means to continue her labors, which will be more important than in the past. And so as Catholics obey the rules and discipline of their Church, as they carry out the motto of this order, and work to the greater glory of God, everywhere they will be found to work for the spread of civilization, for the credit of the State, for the solution of these problems which have puzzled statesmen, and which must be solved by the wisdom of the Almighty, working through the instruments which he has chosen, which he has never abandoned for nineteen centuries, and by which he will abide to the end of time.

The Catholic Educational Exhibit in the Columbian Exposition.

ALL who think at all in our day, find their thoughts turn to the subject of education; for all men now understand that right education offers the best means to give being and life to our human ideals; since all efforts to develop, strengthen and perfect character are educational. The school, of course, is but one, though a most important one, of the agencies by which education is given. Its influence is constantly widening, and the tendency seems to be to have it supersede both the family and the church in the work of moulding men and women.

"Whatever we wish to see introduced into the life of a nation," says William von Humboldt, "must first be introduced into its schools." Now, what Catholics wish to see introduced into the national life, first of all is true religious faith and practice. Religion is God's presence in the soul, it is the revelation of life's goodness; it is the fountain of hope and joy; it is the impulse to a noble activity in which we are conscious that failure itself means success. In happy days, it is light and perfume; and when the waters of life are bitter it draws them heavenward, and again they are sweet. Through it the sense of duty—duty to ourselves, to others and to God—is awakened; and the caring for duty is the vital principle in the creation of character. Hence to introduce true religious faith and practice into the national life is to introduce that which is more important than material prosperity or intellectual activity; for religion is not merely the manifestation of our kinship with God, of the divine and imperishable nature of the soul; it is the only air in which mortality thrives, in which virtue becomes fervent, and goodness kindles with beauty's glow. Conduct rests upon a firm basis only when we believe in the infinite and godlike nature of the good; in a universe of moral ends in which the right is also for ever the best.

No school, therefore, is good which attempts to educate the body, or the mind, or the conscience without the aid of religion, for man is not a patchwork of parts, but a something whole and organic, which springs from God, and which can be developed into harmonious completeness only through vital union with the Author and End of its being.

Hence the church does not and cannot consent to the exclusion of religion from any educational process. As we live and move and have our being in God, the moral and intellectual atmosphere we breathe should be fragrant with the aroma of religious faith; and the inspiration to goodness and duty, which comes chiefly in early years, and is imparted with most power by a voice made persuasive by an open and enlightened mind, should be received in the schoolroom as well as in the home and in the house of worship. To forbid the teacher who holds the child's attention during those years when aspiration is purest, when conscience speaks most clearly, when reverence is most natural, when belief in the heroic and godlike is most spontaneous, to appeal to his pupil's religious nature, and thereby to strive to awaken in them a keener sense of the divine, a more living consciousness of the sacredness and worth of life, is to repress in him precisely that form of activity which is most salutary and most helpful from an educational point of view. What is education worth if the spiritual side of our nature be permitted to lie dormant? if the sense of modesty and purity, of single-mindedness and reverence, of faithfulness and diligence, of obedience and love, be not called forth? What kind of education can be given by the teacher who may not speak of the evil of sin, of the harm wrought by vanity, jealousy, envy, cowardice, hatred, and vulgarity of thought and word? If he be forbidden to enter the inner life of man, how shall his soul ever be brought into contact with the souls of his pupils? He becomes a machine, and his living personality, in which consists his power to educate, is condemned to inaction.

When our common-school system was finally organized as exclusively secular, nothing was left for Catholics to do but to build and maintain schools of their own, in which the will, the heart, and the conscience, as well as the intellect, should be educated. If Catholic children have a right to a Catholic education it follows that the duty devolves upon Catholics to provide the means whereby it may be received; and the Catholics of the United States have accepted the task thus imposed with a spirit of generous self-sacrifice which is above all praise. They have built three thousand and five hundred parochial schools, in which seven hundred thousand Catholic children now receive a Christian education.

They have also established and maintained a large number of universities, seminaries, colleges, academies, reformatories, and asylums, in which religious influence is made to interpenetrate all the processes of nurture and training. The development of this Catholic educational system is carried on from year to year with increasing zeal and energy. The beginnings were difficult; progress is now comparatively easy. What has been done shows us not only what we have still to do, but gives confidence that we shall be able to do it. The people take an interest in the work not less earnest than that of the bishops and priests, while the teaching orders make almost superhuman efforts to meet the ever-growing demands for their services. The indispensable need of religious schools, which thirty or forty years ago was proclaimed by but a few, is now conceded by all Catholics. The utterances of Pius IX. and Leo XIII. on this subject have no uncertain sound; and the bishops of the Catholic world, in pastorals and in councils, have raised their voices, in unison with that of the visible head of the church, to proclaim the vital importance, whether from a religious or a social point of view, of thoroughly Christian schools. They declare that a purely secular education is a bad education, that if our civilization is to remain Christian our schools must recognize the principles of Christianity. In the third Baltimore Council, held in 1884, the zeal of the American hierarchy in the cause of Catholic education glowed with greater warmth than in any previous assemblage of our bishops. The eighty prelates gathered in this national council decree that a parochial school shall exist close to every Catholic church, and that no ordinary difficulties shall be considered as an excuse for its non-existence. A pastor's serious neglect to build a school is declared to be a sufficient cause for his removal; and they affirm that it is a bishop's duty to provide schools which shall be Catholic, not in name alone, but which shall be thoroughly efficient. As a means to this end, they would have the pastor consider himself the principal of his school. He should watch over it and make it the object of his special care and devotion. To equip priests more fully for this office, the bishops urge that a course of pedagogics be made part of the curriculum of theological seminaries. Can we make our schools as good as the best of the public schools? Can we make them even better?

"Can we do this?" asks Bishop Hennessy, of Dubuque, and he answers: "If I had a voice that would resound from New York to San Francisco, with that voice I would say—We can!" He adds: "The parochial school as it should be, and as it will be, will not only guard the faith of the children and transfigure the church of God, but it will prove to be the most potent factor at our service for the conversion of our beloved country." Those who know with what earnestness and zeal the Catholic body of the United States is enlisted in the cause of Catholic education, will readily understand why the American bishops have determined to have a "Catholic Educational Exhibit" in the "World's Columbian Exposition."

Our school system is an organic part of our ecclesiastical constitution. It rests upon principles as wide as human nature, as immortal as Truth. We cannot if we would, we would not if we could, recede from the stand we have taken. We hold that the common-school system is radically defective, though we have no disposition to interfere with those to whom it commends itself. We concede to others, as we demand for ourselves, religious and educational freedom. Our convictions on this point are unalterable; and since here there is question of vital, temporal and eternal interests, there can be no compromise which conflicts with the principle of religious education.

The Catholic Church is irrevocably committed to the doctrine that education is essentially religious, that purely secular schools give instruction but do not properly educate. The commemoration of the discovery of America, by holding an Exposition which will attract the attention and awaken the interest of the entire world, offers an opportunity such as we cannot hope to have again in our day, or in that of our children, to give public evidence of the work we are doing. In the four hundred years which have flown by since the stars of heaven first saw reflected from these shores the white man's face, beside his white sail, there has been no such occasion for such an advertisement, and when the fifth centenary shall be here there will be no need, we may confidently trust, of special efforts to commend and uphold the cause of religious education. Catholics assuredly have a right to a prominent place in this great celebration. Juan Perez, Isabella and Columbus, to whose lofty views and generous courage the discovery of America is chiefly due, were not only devout Catholics, but they were upheld and strengthened in their great undertaking by religious zeal and enthusiasm. Their faith was an essential element in the success of their enterprise. There should be no desire to ignore or obscure this fact, even on the part of the foes of the church, and it is a duty which Catholics owe to the honor of the name they bear to see that the part which their religion played in opening to the Christian nations a new hemisphere, thereby extending and quickening the forces of civilization through the whole world, shall not be misunderstood or passed over in silence at this time, when the eyes of all men turn to America to behold the marvels which have been wrought here by strong hearts and awakened minds.

To this end the Catholic Educational Exhibit, if rightly made, cannot but contribute; and since it will be the only distinctively Catholic feature in the Columbian Exposition, every honorable motive should impel us to leave nothing undone to make it worthy of the event commemorated and of our own zeal in the cause of Christian Education. We shall thus place before the eyes of the millions who will visit the Exposition a clear demonstration of the great work the Church in the United States is doing to develop a civilization which is in great part the outgrowth of religious principles, and which depends for its continued existence upon the morality which religious faith alone can make strong and enduring. There can be little doubt that many are opposed to the Catholic school system from the fact that they have never given serious attention to the principles upon which it rests, or to the ends which it aims to reach. It is the fashion to praise education, and hence all declare themselves favorable to it; but those who love it enough to make it a matter of thoughtful and persevering meditation are, like the lovers of Truth, but few. But those who do not read seriously, or think deeply, may be got to open their eyes and look, and what they see may arouse interest and lead to investigation. Opinion rules the world, and the Catholic Exhibit offers a means to help mould opinion on the subject of education, which in importance is second to no other; and in an age in which the tendency is to take the school from the control of the church, to place it under that of the state in such a way as to weaken its religious character, nothing which may assist in directing opinion to true views upon this subject may be neglected by those who believe that education is essentially religious.

The exhibit will help also to enlighten and stimulate teachers, by diffusing among them a more real and practical knowledge of the various educational methods and appliances. It will arouse a new interest in pedagogics as a science and an art. We may easily become victims of the fallacy that a school is Catholic because this adjective is affixed to its name, or because in it prayers are said and catechism is taught. A poor school cannot exert a wholesome influence of any kind. Idle, inattentive, listless, and unpunctual children will not become religious, however much they are made to pray and recite catechism. In a truly religious character self-respect, truthfulness, a love of thoroughness and excellence, a disinterested ambition, are as important as a devotional spirit. Where the natural virtues are lacking, the supernatural have no proper soil in which to grow. A right school system does not necessarily make a good school.

An educational exhibit will help to impress these and similar truths more vividly upon the minds of educators; it will enable a very large number of Catholics to take a general survey of the educational work which the church in the United States is doing, of which most of us have but a very inadequate knowledge; it will bring into juxtaposition the methods and systems of the various Teaching Orders, and will make it possible for all to adopt whatever may be found excellent in any of them. There will, of course, be no unworthy rivalry, no thought of advertising this or that institution or teaching order. The aim is to advance the cause of Catholic education. We care little where or by whom good work is done; it is enough to know that it is done. In certain instances a bishop will prefer to make a separate exhibit of the work done in his diocese, because he believes that in this way the end will be attained more effectually. From a similar motive the Teaching Orders may choose to make collective exhibits of their work; and institutions of learning which stand alone and have an individuality of their own, will avail themselves of this opportunity to offer evidence of the kind of education they give. All our institutions of learning, from the university to the kindergarten, come within the scope of this display of educational work.

The third Plenary Council emphasizes the urgent need of a wider and more thorough training of the priesthood, and it is believed that the theological seminaries will make an exhibit which will be interesting and at the same time a valuable evidence of the progress we are making in fitting our priests for the special and arduous tasks which this age of unsettled opinions and weak moral convictions imposes upon them. It is not rash to hope that the Catholic Educational Exhibit will awaken new zeal, arouse a more generous spirit of sacrifice, inspire a deeper enthusiasm, in the cause of Christian education, which is the cause of our country and our religion.

The suggestion has been made that this exhibit will offer a favorable opportunity to hold a congress of Catholic teachers. The good results to be expected from such a meeting are numerous and manifest. Those who have paid any attention to the workings of the associations, whether county, state or national, of the public school teachers, are aware of the stimulating and illuminating effects which their discussions and deliberations produce. It is desirable that our Catholic educators should be brought together, that they should learn to know and appreciate one another, that they should enlighten and correct one another by a comparison of opinions and experiences. This, and much else, could be done in an educational congress. A regret is often expressed at the absence of lay action in Catholic affairs. Education is precisely the field in which Catholic laymen can most readily and most effectively bring their zeal and knowledge to bear upon the living issues and interests of the church. They build and maintain our schools, and there is no good reason why they should not take an active part in stimulating them to higher efficiency. A certain number of our teachers are of the laity, and their relative proportion will doubtless increase. One need not be a Brother or a Sister to be at the head of even the best of Catholic schools. Why should not the intelligent laymen or women of a parish be invited to visit the school and to examine the pupils? Their presence would have a good influence upon the children, and their knowledge of the school would enable them to counteract the apathy or opposition of indifferent and foolish parents.

Finally, it is not probable that the Catholic Educational Exhibit and the Congress of Catholic Teachers will lead to the founding of a Catholic Educational Magazine? Catholic newspapers we have—too many of them possibly. Catholic reviews and magazines we also have; but we have no periodical of any significance devoted to the cause of Catholic education. The establishing of a periodical of this kind, with competent editors, would certainly be a safe venture from a financial point of view. We have nearly four thousand schools, and the heads of a very large number of them, at least, would take such a magazine, and among its subscribers would be found all the priests who are really interested in education. As an advertising medium it would have special advantages. The directors of the Catholic University, at Washington, have decided not to have a general review of their own, but might they not consent to edit a purely educational magazine? Or if they do not see their way to this, might not the heads of the University of Georgetown or of Notre Dame be induced to undertake the work? What more interesting subject is there than education? It is a question of life, of religion of country; it is a question of science and art; it is a question of politics, of progress, of civilization; it is a question even of commerce, of production, of wealth. What could be more instructive than a series of articles on the history of education, on the great teachers and educational reformers, on pedagogics as a science and as an art; on educational methods; on the bearing of psychology upon questions of education; on hygiene in its relations to the health of teachers and pupils; on the educational values of the various branches of knowledge; on personal influence as a factor in education; on the best means of forming a true religious character?

An educational magazine would become the organ of the great and growing system of Catholic schools. In its pages the practical and speculative questions which are constantly suggesting themselves to teachers would be discussed, and thus the body of Catholic educators would be brought into active, intelligent communion with one another. At all events, to whatever practical results and undertakings the Educational Exhibit may lead, there can be no doubt that its influence will be for good. The bishops and Catholic educators have already shown their great interest and earnestness in the work, and as the time for holding the Exposition draws nearer an increasing enthusiasm in the success of the enterprise will manifest itself. The general expenses of the manager and his secretaries will be borne by the prelates; but it is well to call the attention of all true friends of Catholic education to the fact that the more money we have, the more creditable and effective will the Exhibit be made, and we confidently believe that an appeal to the priests and Catholic laymen of the United States will place in the hands of those who have control of the enterprise a sufficient sum to make the Catholic Educational Exhibit in the World's Columbian Exposition a memorable event in the history of religious education.

J. L. SPALDING.

Peoria, Ill.

AMERICAN CATHOLICS

AND THE

ROMAN QUESTION

BY

Monsignor JOSEPH SCHROEDER, D.D., Ph.D.

PROFESSOR OF DOGMATIC THEOLOGY IN THE CATHOLIC UNIVERSITY
OF AMERICA

Quam malae famae est, qui derelinquit patrem.
—*Ecclus.* iii. 18.

The whole Catholic world, very jealous of the independence of its head, will never rest until justice has been done to his most righteous demands. (Leo XIII., Letter to Cardinal Rampolla, June 15, 1887.)

NEW YORK, CINCINNATI, CHICAGO
BENZIGER BROTHERS
Printers to the Holy Apostolic See
1892

Imprimatur

MICHAEL AUGUSTINE

Archbishop of New York

NEW YORK, March 28, 1892

Copyright, 1892, by BENZIGER BROTHERS

To my Dear Friend

RIGHT REVEREND SEBASTIAN G. MESSMER, D.D., D.C.L.

Bishop of Green Bay

PREFACE

THE following pages are an expansion of an article published by me on the same subject in the *American Catholic Quarterly Review*, January 1892. Certain qualified judges, whose desire was for me a command, having urged me to publish it separately, I felt it my duty to somewhat enlarge its scope and reinforce its argument. It is unnecessary to say that I have by no means either the intention or the pretension of exhausting such a subject in no few pages. I have proposed to myself primarily to show clearly and frankly the Catholic point of view from which the Roman question should be regarded, indicating the principal considerations which should be taken into account in a true conception and solution of it, and thus to disengage it from those prejudices and ambiguities with which the best-intentioned people sometimes surround it.

I must touch upon questions no less delicate than important in theology, in philosophy, and particularly in international law. Moreover, the matter is one that more than any other depends exclusively upon the supreme teacher and ruler of the Church. It will not, then, be superfluous to say openly at the start what I believe to be the true Catholic attitude in this as in all other questions.

I profess, then, from the bottom of my heart, with Pius IX., that "the obligation by which Catholic teachers and writers are strictly bound is not restricted only to those doctrines which are proposed by the infallible judgment of the Church as dogmas of faith to be believed by all."

I declare, moreover, that here, as in all teaching, I look upon it as a sacred duty to avoid "the audacity of those who, not enduring sound doctrine, contend that 'without sin and without any sacrifice of the Catholic position, assent and obedience may be refused to those judgments and decrees of the Holy See whose object is declared to concern the Church's general good and her rights and discipline, provided only they do not touch the dogmas of faith and morals.'"

I am profoundly convinced that "this is grievously opposed to the Catholic dogma of the full power divinely given by Christ Our Lord to the Roman Pontiff of leading, ruling, and governing the Universal Church." [1]

To the Roman question in particular we would apply the words of Leo XIII.:

"Every one should rely upon the judgment of the Holy See, and conform to it his sentiments." [2]

The principles to be followed in the present

---

[1] Encyclical "Quanta cura."
[2] Oportet Apostolicæ Sedis stare iudicio, et quod ipsa senserit, sentire singulos. (Encyclical "Immortale Dei.")

question are given with a perfect lucidity in the letter of Leo XIII. to Cardinal Rampolla. This letter can justly be called a masterly résumé of the question in all its phases and in all its extent. It will serve us, then, as our principal guide and support.

Papa Beatissime, si minus perite, aut parum caute forte aliquid positum est, emendari cupimus a te, qui Petri et fidem et sedem tenes.[1]

J. S.

WASHINGTON, D. C.,
    Feast of St. Joseph, 1892.

[1] St. Jerome to St. Damasus.

LIST OF REFERENCES

WORKS TO BE CONSULTED

I destini di Roma. Father Brunengo, S.J.
The Independence of the Holy See. Cardinal Manning.
La Question romaine internationale et anglaise et non pas seulement italienne. Bishop Vaughan, of Salford, England. [To my regret, I have not within reach the English original of this beautiful little work, and am compelled to rely upon the French translation made by the Abbé Moreau.]
Les Relations entre le Saint Siège et le Royaume d'Italie. Marquis de la Vega de Armijo. Translated from the Spanish by the Abbé Moreau.
Etude sur la Question romaine. Abbé Vennekens, Brussels, 1890.
La verita nella soluzione della questione Romana. A work authorized by Leo XIII. himself (1888).

I would also call attention to the numerous essays of Orestes A. Brownson on the same question, as well as to the following remarkable articles which have appeared in two of our best American reviews: "Liberty and Independence of the Pope," Very

Rev. Isaac T. Hecker, *Catholic World*, April 1882; and "Nationalism, the Conclave and the next Pope," Rt. Rev. Mgr. Bernard O'Reilly, *American Catholic Quarterly Review*, January 1892.

The celebrated French economist Leroy-Beaulieu has written in the *Revue des Deux Mondes* three articles under the title of "Le Vatican et le Quirinal depuis 1878" which have justly attracted general attention. The author is not a Catholic believer, and treats the Roman question mainly from the international point of view.—See also "The Foreign Policy of Italy," by the well-known Belgian writer Emile de Laveleye, in the *Contemporary Review*, March 1892.

Special mention is due to the *Civiltà Cattolica*, which has always taken a front rank among Catholic periodicals in its able defence of the rights of the Holy See.

ANALYSIS

ANALYSIS

I. OPPORTUNENESS OF THE DISCUSSION.
    1. Recent patriotic objections.
    2. Unremitting papal claims.
        a. Assertions of right to temporal power.
        b. Catholics urged to second papal demands.
    3. Concurrence of the Universal Episcopate.

II. THE CATHOLIC POSITION.
    4. Origin of the temporal power.
    5. The perpetual primacy of the Roman bishop.
    6. Problem not soluble by transfer of the primacy.
    7. Doctrinal value of papal utterances on the temporal power.
        a. Intimate connection between papal independence and the temporal power.
        b. The obligation of religious assent to the decisions of the Holy See in the matter.

III. STATEMENT OF THE PROBLEM NOW BEFORE AMERICAN CATHOLICS.
  8. Reconciliation of the temporal power of the popes with—
    a. The sovereignty of the people.
    b. The principle Salus publica suprema lex.

IV. INDIRECT ANSWER TO OBJECTIONS AGAINST THE TEMPORAL POWER.
  9. True and perfect obedience due to the Pope.
  10. Obligation of obedience not dependent upon the conformity of authoritative utterances with private theories.
  11. Importance of a Catholic rather than a national standpoint.

V. EXAMINATION OF OBJECTIONS BASED UPON THE SOVEREIGNTY OF THE PEOPLE.
  12. Statement of objections.
  13. No popular sovereignty in the Church.
  14. Popular sovereignty as a political principle.
    a. Extreme theory untenable.
    b. Moderate theory tenable.
    c. Impropriety of imposing it upon other peoples.
    d. True basis of American liberties.
    e. Conclusions.
  15. General attitude of the American citizen.
  16. Political aspect of the spoliation of the Papal States.
    a. Legitimacy of the papal kingdom.

Analysis 17

  b. Sanction of papal claims by the European powers.
  c. Declaration of the Italian government.
  d. Law of guarantees not sanctioned by other powers.
  e. Different attitude of powers towards other Italian sovereigns.
  f. Recognition of the unique and international character of the Roman question.
17. Religious aspect of the same in the light of—
  a. Common-sense.
  b. History.
  c. Christian concept of the Church.
  d. Recent events.
  e. Utterances of the Popes.
18. Brownson's statement of the case.

VI. EXAMINATION OF OBJECTIONS BASED ON THE SUPREME IMPORTANCE OF THE PUBLIC WELFARE.
19. Elucidation of the principle.
20. Its applicability to the question of the relations between Church and State.
21. The welfare of the whole Church demands the re-establishment of the temporal power.
22. The temporal power a benefit to Italy itself.
  a. Its overthrow not the wish of the people.

  b. Its overthrow a source of **misery** to the Italian nation.
  c. Its existence the greatest glory of Italy.
  d. The occupation of Rome a detriment to Italy in her international relations.
  e. Importance of religious concord to the cause of Italian unity.
 23. The temporal power a benefit to the whole world.
  a. The Holy See as an international arbitrator.
  b. The Holy See as a conservative and progressive power.
 24. The Papal States compared with the District of Columbia.
  a. As Washington is politically to the United States,
  b. Rome is religiously to the world.
VII. WHAT SHOULD BE THE SOLUTION OF THE ROMAN QUESTION?
 25. The question still open.
 26. Necessity of co-operation with Providence.
 27. This duty devolves on the Italian government, other Christian governments, and the whole Catholic world.
 28. The temporal sovereignty must be re-established.
 29. The Pope alone must determine the conditions of its re-establishment.

Analysis 19

    30. The solution can and should be pacific.
    31. Sentiments of the Italian court.
    32. Advisability of its taking the initiative in the matter.

VIII. THE PRESENT DUTY OF CATHOLICS IN THE PREMISES.
    33. Existence of such a duty.
    34. How it should be fulfilled.
    35. Importance of popular action.
    36. Our responsibilities cannot be shifted upon the Italian Catholics.
    37. Appeal to the Catholics of America.

APPENDIX. Twenty theses on the Roman Question.

AMERICAN CATHOLICS AND THE ROMAN QUESTION

AMERICAN CATHOLICS

AND

THE ROMAN QUESTION

I. OPPORTUNENESS OF THE DISCUSSION

1. SOME time ago the *Catholic World* published an important article on the temporal sovereignty of the pope from the pen of one to whom we can apply a well-known phrase: *Cuius laus est in universa Americæ ecclesia.*[1] A distinguished Catholic priest, in his remarks on this article, incidentally called attention to an objection "which rises naturally in the minds of republican Catholics." He formulates this objection in the following words:

> There is no use trying to enlighten the Catholic laity, unless you place in the clearest light the consistency between the right of the pope to independence and the right of the people to self-government. That the pope ought to be free to treat with all the nations of the earth of course all admit, but how his temporal sovereignty consists with republican principles is the question to be treated in an article addressed to the people of these United States; and Catholic writers should devote their energies to making clear this aspect of the great

[1] Very Reverend A. J. Hewit, *Catholic World*, December 1890.

and important subject. We Catholics live in the midst of fifty-five millions of people estranged from the Church and holding, theoretically at least, this latter principle; we cleave to it ourselves as well; in order, therefore, that we may give to the pope "reasonable service" in this matter, and give also to our fellow-citizens "a reason for the faith that is in us," and answer their demand "why we meddle with the affairs of Italy," we must have more on the subject.[1]

We entirely agree with this conclusion. We are sincere Catholics and sincere patriots. A theoretical or practical consequence of Catholic doctrine can never conflict with true patriotism. Contradictions can therefore only be apparent; and objections on this score must be either inexact and grounded on a defective knowledge of Catholic teaching, or not to the point.

2. The appropriateness of treating the question is therefore manifest. Another consideration will prove its opportuneness and necessity. The pope, according to Catholic doctrine, is not only the infallible teacher, but also the supreme ruler of the Church. A Catholic owes the assent of faith to his doctrinal definitions, and perfect obedience to his orders and precepts. Entire docility in both cases is the characteristic of a true Catholic.[2]

[1] We may be allowed to mention that, before the above lines came to our notice, we referred to the difficulty, and answered it substantially, in an article in which we openly defended the application of the principles of self-government to France. See *American Catholic Quarterly Review*, January 1891, "Cardinal Lavigerie and the French Republic," p. 120, note.

[2] Summus autem est magister in Ecclesiâ Pontifex Romanus. Concordia igitur animorum sicut perfectum in una fide consensum requirit, ita voluntas es postulat Ecclesiæ Romanoque Pontifici perfecte subiectas atque obtemperantes, ut Deo. Perfecta autem esse obedientia debet, quia ab ipsâ fide præcipitur, et habet hoc commune cum fide, ut dividua esse non possit . . . . cuiusmodi perfectioni tantum christiana consuetudo tribuit, ut illa tanquam nota internoscendi catholicos et habita semper sit et habeatur. (Encyclical "Sapientiæ Christianæ," 1889.)

The following facts are undeniable: *First*, the pope himself does not cease advocating his claims to the temporal power. In the Encyclical "Inscrutabili," 21st April, 1878, he says: "Never shall we abstain from claiming that freedom be again restored to the Holy See by the recovery of the temporal power. Therefore we renew all the declarations and protestations of our predecessor, Pius IX., of blessed memory." Again: "It is our sacred duty," he says in an allocution to the College of Cardinals, March 2, 1880, "to preserve our right intact in spite of all opposition to the contrary, no matter whence it comes." This alone is enough to convince a Catholic that the "concordia animorum" forbids silence on this question; more especially at this time, when our Father in his distress and afflictions appeals to the hearts of his children for sympathy and redress.

Secondly, the Holy Father expressly calls upon the Catholics of the whole world to second his efforts in the defence of his rights and the restoration of his territorial independence, and thus prove themselves devoted and loyal Catholics. "The Catholics of the various States can never hold their peace until they see their chief, the teacher of their faith, the guide of their consciences, again possessed of true liberty and really independent."[1] Therefore the Holy Father doubts not "but that all Catholics all the world over will support, openly and unrestrained, these rights of the Holy See."[2]

---

[1] Letter to the Secretary of State, Cardinal Nina, August 27, 1878.
[2] Allocution, June 1, 1888.

Frequently he directs this admonition to the Catholics of Italy itself.¹ With an affectionate tenderness he reminds Catholic writers, and above all Catholic journalists, of this duty: "Therefore, my beloved sons, cease not, both by word of mouth and in your writings, to contend that the temporal sovereignty of the pope is necessary for the free exercise of his spiritual power." ²

3. Just one more fact. The canonization of the Japanese martyrs had brought more than three hundred bishops to the feet of the great Pius IX. in 1862. Before departing they presented His Holiness with an address in which they unanimously and in a most forcible manner gave expression to their approval of his solemn utterances concerning the necessity of the temporal power; they declared that "the Head of the Church could never be subject to any prince, or even depend upon the hospitality of one;" that "it is the duty of all Catholics to defend the temporal sovereignty and the patrimony of St. Peter," for the maintenance of which rights they should be prepared to go with him "to prison and to death." ³

Ever since the perpetration of the Piedmontese

---

¹ 3d January, 1888.
² Address to Catholic journalists, February 22, 1879.
³ Oportebat sane totius Ecclesiæ caput Romanum Pontificem nulli principi esse subiectum; immo nullius hospitem, sed in proprio domicilo ac regno sedentem suimet iuris esse. . . . Alto pariter et solemni eloquio declarasti, te civilem Romanæ Ecclesiæ principatum eius que temporales possessiones ac iura, quæ ad universum Catholicum orbem pertinent, integra et inviolata constanter tueri et servare velle; immo Sanctæ Sedis principatus Beatique Petri patrimonii tutelam ad omnes Catholicos pertinere; teque paratum esse animam potius ponere quam hanc Dei, Ecclesiæ et iustitiæ causam ullo modo deserere (Alloc. 16 Sept. 1859). Quibus præclaris verbis nos acclamantes ac plaudentes respondemus, nos tecum et ad carcerem et ad mortem ire paratos esse. (Declaratio episcoporum, 8 Jun. 1862.)

robbery in 1870, this accord of the entire episcopacy with the Holy See has been manifested even more clearly on divers occasions. A Catholic, therefore, can entertain no doubt about it: obedience to ecclesiastical authority, to the pope and the episcopacy, puts upon every Catholic the obligation to defend to the utmost of his ability the temporal sovereignty of the head of the Church. What is the fundamental reason of this obligation? Is it the maintenance of a possession to which both from an historical and juridicial standpoint the popes have an inviolable right? No; it is to be found in the intimate relation existing between the temporal power of the pope and the divinely ordained independence and freedom of the head of the Church, which is the freedom of the Church itself. Hence our position in the Roman question is prescribed by the inviolable rights of our father, of the Church, and of all the Catholics of the world.

II. THE CATHOLIC POSITION

4. A few preliminary remarks must be made in order to define exactly from what motives and in what sense Catholics declare the temporal power to be necessary.

We treat this question from the Catholic standpoint, as in it is involved that twofold obedience which the Catholic owes. Our non-Catholic fellow-citizens must likewise accept the same standpoint as the basis of their criticism. We need not prove to a child of the Church that the pope, by divine disposition, has the right and the duty to rule the Church in perfect independence of any earthly power, and that, by the same divine right, he is exempt from any secular jurisdiction whatsoever. He therefore is, as Leo XIII. expresses it, "by the express will of the Founder of the Church not subject to any secular power."[1]

The right to this independence is essential to the papacy. The exercise of that right, however, is not absolutely necessary to the existence of the Church (*ut Ecclesia sit*), but it is necessary for the perfect development of its social life (*ut bene sit*). Providence availed itself of the temporal power as a means to secure to the popes the free and undisturbed development of their sublime prerogative.

In the early ages, triumphant and victorious through all the many and bitter persecutions, the Church had the stamp of her divine origin set upon her. Those years might be called the Church's infancy. The time came, however, when she was to put forth the full vigor of life. The freedom and independence of the head of the Church was, by divine Providence, to foster its steady growth, and thus it came to pass that the popes acquired the temporal dominion over Rome, the seat of their pontificate.[2] No unbiassed historian has ever called into question the legitimacy of this temporal dominion, and that, too, considering only its historical origin. This, for us, is a

---

[1] Letter to Cardinal Rampolla, 15th June, 1887.
[2] *Idem.*

settled question in our present discussion. It is
equally unnecessary to prove that the pope, since the
spoliation of his States, September 20, 1870, no
longer enjoys that liberty and independence which
the nature and dignity of his office demand.
Verius in aliena potestate sumus quam nostra—" We
are more really in the power of another than our
own." We might refer to two facts which will
convince even the most ardent friend of Italian
unity of the truth of these words of Leo XIII.: the
outrageous scandals of which Rome was the scene
in the early part of October, 1891, when the city
echoed the cry "*Abasso il papa!*" and the infamous insult which was heaped upon the corpse of
the great Pius amid the demon-cries, "*Al fiume!*"
These two events in the history of New Italy speak
more than volumes.

A Catholic cannot rejoin : Let the pope look for
a free abode elsewhere.

This is not the language of a child towards its
father ; and every Catholic should know that such
a decision belongs to the pope alone, and that the
successor of St. Peter is responsible for it to God
and to no one else.

5. There is still another reason of much greater
importance. The Catholic dogma of the primacy
expressly teaches not only that it was instituted by
Christ in St. Peter, and must continue for all ages
in his successors, but also that from the beginning
of the Church the bishop of Rome alone was the
successor of St. Peter, and that to this day it is only
as bishop of Rome that the popes succeed St. Peter

and possess the plenitude of apostolic power. We may add that it is a theological truth drawn from the teaching of faith that the primacy *iure divino* belongs, until the end of time, to the bishop of Rome alone, and that it therefore cannot be transferred even by the pope himself to another see. This is not the place to enter more fully into the explanation of this doctrine. The theological basis for the temporal power is to be found in the dogma: The bishop of Rome and he alone always was and is up to the present day the successor of St. Peter. The immutability of this relation between the primacy and the see of Rome only serves to enforce the argument. As to this, it is sufficient to say that no other see can become the "apostolic see of Peter." It is only the see of Rome in which the pope is "the successor of Peter, prince of the apostles." It must always remain true, because it is defined, that "the Roman pontiff is the successor of St. Peter;" that "the Roman Church possesses by divine ordination the primacy over all churches." The profession of faith, "I acknowledge the Roman Church to be the mother and teacher of all churches," can never be changed; the Church of Christ must always remain the "*Roman* Catholic Church." The translation of the Apostolic See to another city, for instance to Cologne or Baltimore, would necessarily change those definitions and professions into these: "the Cologne Catholic Church," "the Baltimorian Catholic Church"! We will add that the apostolicity is a visible note of the true Church, and that no change could take place without shaking the stability of the apostolic succession and without serious detriment to the whole Church. All this goes to prove that not even the pope has a right to effect such a translation. As to any other ecclesiastical or popular power, it is a proposition censured in the apostolic letters of August 22, 1851, as well as in the Syllabus, "that the primacy may by a decree of a General Council or by the verdict of all nations be transferred from the Roman bishop and the city of Rome to another bishop or city."[1] Such teaching was only the logical outcome of the Gallican and Febronian theory respecting the sovereignty of the people in the Church. In our own days it was Nuytz, professor in Turin, whose writings have brought about the condemnation of the aforesaid proposition. Would it be too bold to say that the same doctrine can be logically deduced from the following words of the Vatican Council?—

The holy and blessed Peter to this day, *and always*, lives, presides, and judges in the persons of his successors the bishops of the Holy See of Rome, which he has founded and consecrated with his blood. *Whoever therefore succeeds him in this see* obtains his primacy over all the Church, according to the institution of Jesus Christ Himself.[2]

Leo XIII. has expressed the perpetuity of this privilege as follows: "What may be said generally

---

[1] Prop. 35. Nuytz meant a "General Council" without and even against the pope; "auctoritate Ecclesiæ," as Febronius expressed it.

[2] Sanctus beatissimusque Petrus . . . ad hoc usque tempus et *semper* in suis successoribus, Episcopis Sanctæ Romanæ Sedis ab ipso fundatæ eiusque consecratæ sanguine, vivit et præsidet et iudicium exercet. *Unde quicunque in hac cathedra Petro succedit*, is secundum Christi ipsius institutionem primatum Petri in universam Ecclesiam obtinet. (Constitution "Pastor æternus," cap. 2.)

of the temporal power of the popes holds still more strongly and in a special way of Rome. Its destinies are written large across all its history; that is to say, as in the designs of Providence all human events have been ordered with regard to Christ and His Church, so ancient Rome and its empire were founded for the sake of Christian Rome; and it was not without a special disposition of Providence that St. Peter, the prince of the apostles, turned his steps towards this metropolis of the pagan world, to become its pastor and to hand down to it forever the authority of the Supreme Apostolate. It is thus that *the fate of Rome has been bound in a sacred and indissoluble way with that of the vicar of Jesus Christ*."[1]

6. But suppose this translation were possible, still we cannot find therein a solution of the difficulty; for elsewhere the same questions may arise.[2] It therefore remains true that the pope as bishop of Rome, and according to the natural order of things in Rome and from Rome, governs and directs

---

[1] Letter to Card. Rampolla.

[2] We will mention as a matter of curiosity a book published in Paris in 1885, under the equivocal title of "*Le Rétablissement du Pouvoir temporel, par le Prince de Bismarck,*" in which the author, who is by no means a Catholic, undertakes to prove that the re-establishment of the temporal power of the popes is necessary from the point of view of international politics, that this question is very important especially for Germany, and that consequently the German and Austrian statesmen, and notably Prince Bismarck, are called to realize this desire of the Catholic world; that, finally, as Rome cannot be any longer the city of the papacy, it will be transferred to "a free, international, and neutral city." This city will be, according to the fantastic plans of the author, "the second eternal city, which is elevated like the first upon seven hills: Roma Nova—Constantinople, after the destruction of the Ottoman Empire"!

Two years ago a French Catholic author, the antipode of his compatriot Drumont by his predilection for the Jewish race, predicted to us the transition of the see of St. Peter to Jerusalem, and a series of great popes and great bishops of Semitic blood.

the affairs of the Church of God unmolested, and that in Rome at least he must not be subject to any secular authority, that is, the pope must also be the temporal ruler of Rome. In this sense Catholics in concert with the pope declare the necessity of the temporal power.

7. In the face of the many and luminous declarations in which the popes, and especially Pius IX. and Leo XIII., have affirmed the necessity of the temporal power for the free and independent exercise of their apostolic authority, a Catholic may raise the following questions: Are these declarations of the popes decisions or decrees of the Holy See to which Catholics are bound to give their religious assent (*assensus religiosus*), that internal and external obedience which the sacred authority of the Church demands, or do they exact more than this? That is, have the popes in their encyclicals and apostolic letters delivered a definitive and infallible judgment on this matter, and must Catholics respond to the infallible teacher by an act of faith?[1]

Certain Italian and Italianizing theologians, turning theology into politics, were, and still are, fond of the following style of argument: If the pope and all the bishops of a General Council should decide that, under present circumstances, the Sovereign Pontiff needs the temporal power, we should not be obliged to submit, because they would not speak

[1] Not, of course, an act of divine and Catholic faith (*fide immediate divina et catholica*), which can be given only to revealed dogma proposed by the Church, but the act of mediately divine faith (*fide mediate divina vel ecclesiastica*), with which we must accept the teaching of the Church when she pronounces definitively on doctrines or on facts connected with revealed truths.

as doctors of the Church (*come maestri della chiesa*), their judgment having for its object matters which have not been revealed. This is purely and simply the Jansenistic distinction between the *right* and the *fact*. They pretend to admit the infallibility of the Church, but repudiate it as soon as she would exercise it; and yet they boast themselves true Catholics—Catholics better and more enlightened than the pope and the episcopate! The reasoning quoted above destroys the infallibility of the Church. The first thing required, nay, the essential supposition for the action of the Church's *magisterium*, is that this teaching authority cannot deceive itself when judging concerning the range of its power and the extent of its object. Her competency, then, is defined by the very fact of the definition; *in actu exercito*, as is said in the schools.

The encyclical " Quanta cura," December 8, 1864, indicates clearly that the infallibility of the Church and of the pope extends also to " things which bear on the general good of the Church " (*res ad bonum generale ecclesiæ pertinentes*). If the faithful are bound to believe with divine faith the right and necessity of the full and entire freedom of the head of the Church, his complete independence of every human power, who does not see how important it is to know the means which in certain circumstances constitute the principal and even the only way of assuring it? But in our days the circumstances are such that the pope must necessarily be the subject of a secular prince, if he is not a temporal sovereign himself. Therefore this temporal sovereignty is intimately connected with the full liberty which belongs to the Holy See by divine right. Hence it can well be the subject of an infallible definition, even though it be a fact, because it has become and is a dogmatic fact. All Catholic theologians agree on this point. "No one has ever dreamt," says the *Civiltà Cattolica*, "that the temporal power is or could be the subject of a dogmatic definition, which is never issued except regarding revealed truths. But the sincere Catholic does not limit his obedience to the dogmas alone; he gives it to all the doctrines and teachings of the Church. This doctrine and teaching embraces, besides dogmas, many truths which are either dependent on dogmas, or connected with them by an interior or exterior bond.

"Now the necessity of the temporal power of the Roman Pontiff at the present time, although, as we have said, it is not and cannot be a dogma, is, however, contained in the doctrine and teaching of the Church, because it has been solemnly proclaimed by all the bishops of the Catholic world and by their head, the pope."[1]

In these words the *Civiltà* indicates that as a matter of fact the necessity of the temporal power is already defined. We openly declare that we share in this opinion. But this need not be insisted upon here. For our present subject the two following conclusions are of importance:

(*a*) **Every good Catholic must admit the intimate**

---

[1] *Civiltà Cattolica*, January 15, 1876. See our article "Theological Minimizing," in the *American Ecclesiastical Review*, February 1891.

connection between the independence of the Holy See and its temporal power.

(b) Every good Catholic owes assent and obedience, at least religious assent, to those judgments and decrees of the Holy See in which the temporal power is declared necessary in order to secure the true independence of the head of the Church; he is, as the Syllabus expresses it, "bound to hold most firmly" what the popes have taught (*proposita et asserta doctrina*) on the necessity of the temporal power in the documents cited explicitly by the Syllabus itself (prop. 25, 26), and " to conform his judgment to the judgment of the Holy See."

The singular political theology of which we have spoken above was chiefly proposed and upheld by the *Mediatore*, "*giornale politico, religioso, etc.*" The acts of the Vatican Council refer at length to this journal. It was against its arguments that the theologians of the Council had drawn up a plan for a conciliar definition on the temporal power in the following words:

> Renewing the decrees of the Apostolic See and of the Council, we condemn and proscribe the heretical doctrine of those who say that it is contrary to divine right that civil principality should be united to the spiritual power, and also the perverse opinion of those who pretend that the Church has no right to legislate with authority on the relations between this civil principality and the general welfare of the Church, and that, consequently, it is permissible for Catholics to depart from the decisions of the Church in this subject and to hold other sentiments.[1]

[1] Sacro approbante Concilio innovantes huius Apostolicæ Sedis ac præcedentium Conciliorum iussa ac decreta, *damnamus atque proscribimus* tum eorum *hæreticam* doctrinam, qui affirmant, repugnare iure divino ut cum spirituali potestate in Romanis Pontificibus principatus civilis coniun-

The *adnotationes* of the same theologians, after having explained the *Mediatore*'s theory, the substance of which is given above, add:

> But these doctrines are really detestable, altogether perverse and dangerous, full of sedition and of scandal, and offensive to pious ears.[1]

We know well enough that a plan for a conciliar definition is not a definition of a Council; but this scheme, elaborated by order of the pope, approved by him and by the Episcopal Committee, and submitted to the bishops of a Council, surely furnishes us at least with a new proof of the definability of the doctrine in question, viz., of its intimate connection with the Catholic dogma of the primacy of Peter.

Pius IX. declared in his encyclical of June 18, 1859:

> We openly affirm that the civil principality is necessary to the Holy See, in order that it may exert without any obstacle its sacred power for the good of religion.[2]

Again in the apostolic letter of the 26th of March, 1860:

> God has willed that the See of St. Peter should be possessed of the civil principality, in order to protect and preserve the liberty of the apostolic ministry.[3]

---

gatur, tum *perversam eorum sententiam*, qui contendunt, Ecclesiae non esse de huius principatus civilis ad generale christianae reipublicae bonum relatione quidpiam cum auctoritate constituere, adeoque licere catholicis hominibus, ab illius decisionibus hac de re editis recedere aliterque sentire. *Acta et Decreta Concil. Vatic.* (Coll. Lac. § vii, p. 572, 619 sqq.)

[1] Sed doctrinae sunt istae plane detestabiles, perversae penitus ac perniciosae seditionis ac scandali plenae, quasque piae aures non ferunt. (p. 622.)

[2] Necessarium esse palam edicimus Sanctae huic Sedi civilem principatum, ut in bonum religionis sacram potestatem sine ullo impedimento exercere voluit.

[3] Quo [civili principatu] Deus hanc Beati Petri sedem instructam voluit, ad apostolici ministerii libertatem tuendam atque servandam.

In the allocution "Maxima quidem," June 9th, 1862:

We take pleasure in recalling the unanimous consent with which you [the bishops] have not ceased to teach that this civil principality of the Holy See has been given to it by a special design of Providence, and that it is necessary in order that the Sovereign Pontiff may never be subjected to any other prince or to any civil power, that he may exercise his supreme power with perfect liberty for the greater good of the Church and of the faithful.[1]

In regard to these and other utterances on the same subject the Syllabus says after § IX:

Outside of those errors explicitly noted, several other errors are implicitly condemned by the doctrine expressly proposed and declared on the civil principality of the Roman pontiff, which should be firmly held by all Catholics. This doctrine is clearly taught in the allocution *Quibus quantisque* [here follows the citation of five other pontifical documents].[2]

See the "Declaratio Episcoporum" (June 8, 1862):

We recognize that the temporal sovereignty of the Holy See is necessary, and that it has been established by the manifest design of divine Providence; we do not hesitate to declare that in the present state of human affairs that temporal sovereignty is absolutely essential to the welfare of the Church and the free direction of souls.[3]

---

[1] Iuvat commemorare miram prorsus consensionem, qua . . . numquam intermisistis . . . . docere, hunc civilem Sanctæ Sedis principatum Romano Pontifici fuisse singulari divinæ Providentiæ consilio datum, illumque necessarium esse, ut idem Romanus Pontifex nulli unquam principi aut civili potestati subiectus supremam . . . potestatem . . . plenissima libertate exercere ac maiori eiusdem Ecclesiæ et fidelium bono, utilitati et indigentiis consulere possit.

Præter hos errores explicite notatos alii complures implicite reprobantur *proposita et asserta doctrina*, quam catholici omnes firmissime retinere debent, de civili Romani Pontificis principatu. Eiusmodi doctrina luculenter traditur in Allocutione '*Quibus quantisque*,' 20 Apr. 1849, etc.

[3] Civilem enim Sanctæ Sedis principatum ceu quiddam necessarium ac providente Deo manifeste institutum agnoscimus, nec declarare dubitamus, in presenti rerum humanarum statu, ipsum hunc principatum civilem pro bono ac libero Ecclesiæ animarumque regimine omnino requiri.

III. Statement of the Problem

8. We are now concerned with the task of reconciling this duty of Catholics with certain principles of modern and particularly of American public law.

We divide the objection into two parts, according to the two principles upon which it rests : *The people are sovereign;* and *Salus publica suprema lex*—private interest must be subordinated to the public good.

We must first agree on the terms we are to use. The harmony between the right of the pope to independence and the right of the people to self-government does not mean that the pope has a right to be the temporal ruler of Rome independently of the consent of the Roman people, and that at the same time the Roman people has actually a right to choose its own ruler.

Nor shall we prove that the temporal power is in harmony with republican principles in this sense, that the pope's right to monarchical government does not exclude the right of the Roman people to proclaim the republic.

We shall not strive to reconcile contradictions. The school of Fichte itself would find it difficult to do so; and surely no American principle demands it.

If two rights are contradictory, then one of them is no right, or, at least, one of them ceases to be a right because of this contradiction.

Our task is to prove that we give "reasonable service" to our Church and to our country.

Giving a reason for the liberty of thought and conscience guaranteed by our Constitution, we shall prove that as philosophers we admit, *in abstracto*, not only the republican principle, but also in a true sense a sovereignty of the people.

Giving a reason for our patriotism, we have only to prove that the Catholic view of the Roman question does not hinder us from being wholly and sincerely attached to our Constitution and from obeying the laws of our country. Freely giving a reason for the faith that is in us, we shall prove that neither the republican principle nor the right of the people to self-government has anything to do with the right of the pope to independence; in a word, that this right does not fall under any such principle.

The following words of Brownson are to the point: "Liberty is never to be understood as exemption from all restraints, nor from all restraints but those which are self-imposed, which are no restraints at all.... There is a strong tendency, and, I hold, a dangerous tendency, among us ... to extol and defer to the alleged wisdom and good sense of the mass.... The genuine people, if their voice could really be heard, would be loud and earnest in condemnation of this tendency.... In the name of science, of knowledge, of wisdom, of virtue, of the people, ... I for one solemnly protest against this servility to the mass, a servility to which a man never submits in good faith nor for

honest purposes. . . . Let us, then, cease our
adulation of the mass, cease our insane efforts to
adapt everything to the apprehension of the mass,
to gauge the amount of truth we may tell by the
amount the multitude can take in; and do our best
to gain all truth, to nourish and invigorate ourselves for wisely-directed and long-continued efforts
for the elevation of all men."

IV. INDIRECT ANSWER

9. We answer first: The objection is inadmissible in respect to the supreme authority of the
Church, and doubly inadmissible because it views a
Catholic question from an exclusively national standpoint. We will not pass over this reply, because
we desire to define our position openly and without
any equivocation. It is a distinguishing characteristic of Catholicity that both in doctrinal and practical teachings it is most logical. Every attempt to
weaken the principle of authority on which it rests
is objectively uncatholic and subjectively very
dangerous for genuine Catholic sentiment.

We owe the pope a perfect, undivided, and absolute obedience in religious matters, not a *simu-
lacrum obedientiæ*, which is contrary to the very
nature of the virtue, as Leo XIII. remarks in the

---

[1] Works of O. Brownson, vol. xv. p. 299 *seqq*. A careful study of the articles, "Origin and Ground of Government," "Demagogism," and "National Greatness," would answer the objection we are considering.

We use the words "self-government" and "sovereignty of the people," although they cannot be strictly taken in their literal meaning. Their true sense will be made clear as we proceed. Let us also note that "republican principle" and "the right of self-government" are very different things; the one does not imply the other.

encyclical "Sapientiæ Christianæ." But the Roman question is a religious one, because intimately connected with the independence of the head of the Church ; and the pope has declared in unmistakable terms how every faithful child of the Church must consider the question and shape his practical conduct in accordance therewith.

10. Whether the pope is acquainted with our objections or not is of no importance whatever. As supreme ruler of the Church, in his judgments and commands he is in no way dependent on our assent. We have not only to believe all that he as the infallible teacher of the Church defines to be of faith ; we must also obey him when as ruler of the Church he prescribes matters governing our practical conduct.

To act otherwise would be to make our individual views the rule of our actions ; it would be to follow our own mind and not that of the Church, which the pope represents juridically, i.e., possessing the plenitude of all ecclesiastical power. *Si quæ vult tenet, et quæ non vult non tenet, non iam inhæret Ecclesiæ . . . sed propriæ voluntati,* as Leo XIII. says in the same encyclical, following St. Thomas.

Therefore we might simply reply to our opponents : We do not need to enter into your theories respecting the sovereignty of the people, etc.; you owe the head of the Church the same childlike obedience as a simple peasant who has perhaps never heard anything of your philosophico-political principles, or, if he did, would not understand them. This is the true Catholic position, as it was taught by the divine Founder of the Church Himself, who has built it on Peter and on Peter alone.

11. In our religious duties we are not to look to nationalism as our guide, but to the Church's authority. As a matter of fact we know full well that the faithful performance of our duties as citizens of the United States does not bring us into conflict with any doctrinal or moral teaching of the Catholic religion. As Catholics, and precisely because we are Catholics, we should not allow any one to surpass us in that respect. But the objection supposes the opposite, which will explain our categorical answer.

If every nation of the world asserted its national standpoint as a condition *sine qua non* of its obedience to the pope, what would be the result? Have they not all the same right to hold their national traditions, customs, and regulations as we Americans? The Church, like a loving and just mother, always respects national peculiarities and all just claims founded on them. In this the Church gives us an example worthy of imitation. But just as she unites all in the unity of faith, she also desires all to be one in obedience to her visible head. *Ecclesia nationum, non vero nationalis!* This is the motto of the Catholic Church, which is contained in the apostolic dictum: "There is neither Jew nor Greek, there is neither bond nor free, there is neither male nor female; for you are all one in Christ Jesus."[1] Moreover history shows by sad examples to what

[1] Galatians iii. 28.

an uncatholic result nationalism leads. Photius brought about the most terrible schism in the name of Greek sentiment against the Latins; Luther disguised his apostasy by publishing in 1516 a "German theology" against "Romanism"; Gallicanism sought a support in the so-called "traditions of the Church of France"; Döllinger's lamentable desertion was already sealed when he set in 1863 the "German science" in opposition to the "Roman school." In short, all spurning of the authority of the Holy See must inevitably strengthen the hands of those whose battle-cry has ever been: Away from Rome! All nationalizing in Catholic questions has at all times weakened the true Catholic spirit, made room for a diluted and vapid Catholicism, and prepared the way to that ugliest excrescence of nationalism which is known in some countries as "State Catholicism."

V. The Sovereignty of the People

12. Now let us attempt a *direct* answer and a complete solution. Our opponents say: "We have positive reasons to reserve our judgment on the Roman question. For, as Americans, we recognize the principle of popular sovereignty; it is the ground-work of the Constitution of the United States, the support of our public and political life. But now, did not the Italian, or at least the Roman, people desire the fall of the temporal power of the pope? Is it not a contradiction, then, for us to extol the sovereign will of the people of this country

and at the same time to approve of the restoration of the territorial independence of the pope? Is that not virtually to deny the sovereignty of another people?"

13. We ask, has popular sovereignty any place *in the Church?* The answer of Catholic doctrine is *No.* To enter deeply into a confirmation of this answer here would be out of place, but a concise explanation is necessary to illustrate the religious aspect of our question.

The Church is an institution essentially supernatural, to which all men, by the decree of God, must look for salvation. The Incarnate Son of God founded it immediately and in His own person, and gave it that authority which was to bring about that happy and blessed union here below whose highest ideal and archetype is in heaven, "that they all may be one as Thou, Father, in Me and I in Thee." But more than this. The divine Founder of the Church not only defined the spiritual power His Church was to exercise for that end, but He also designated in particular who were to exercise it. Upon St. Peter and his successors He bestowed the plenitude of pastoral power; to the successors of the other apostles—the bishops—He entrusted the direction of particular churches "in which the Holy Ghost had placed them." Every pope receives immediately from Christ the entire apostolic authority with which Peter, the first pope, was endowed. This authority is, therefore, neither in its origin nor in its exercise, dependent on the approbation of the Church, the bishops, priests, or laity. The episcopacy, no less than the papacy, is of divine institution; it is an essential institution of the Church. Nevertheless it remains true that only one rules the whole Church; that only one possesses the fulness of power; that all others are subject to him; that he can judge all, but cannot be judged by any one; that he is the centre of unity about which all must gather to be partakers of the kingdom of God.

The constitution of the Church is, therefore, truly monarchical, though tempered to a certain extent with the aristocracy of the divinely instituted episcopacy, but not mixed with it. The rest of the faithful are the *ecclesia discens*. The authority of the Church does not proceed from them, nor does it depend on them, either immediately or mediately. Still, all the offices of the Church, the highest included, are within the reach of the humblest of its members. In this sense, and only in this sense, can we speak of a democratic element in the constitution of the Church.

Efforts to introduce the principle of popular sovereignty into the Church have not been wanting. The court theologian of Louis the Bavarian, Marsilius Patavinus, inaugurated the movement in the thirteenth century. He claimed that, according to the will of Christ, all ecclesiastical power is vested in the people. Gerson and Peter D'Ailly enunciated similar principles during the Great Schism of the West. The apostate, Mark Anthony de Dominis, sought to spread them in the seventeenth century. From his works the Gallicans, especially Richer, drew their arguments; Jansenism, Febronianism and Josephism had recourse to the same theological arsenal for their weapons. At the time of the Vatican Council Döllinger renewed this theory, inasmuch as he claimed that the bishops at the Council are only mandataries of the people. The clear decisions of this Council dealt the death-blow to all these attempts. If, in spite of this, Catholics dare to assert, or write, that "the Church desires a non-Italian pope, who will grant the people a greater share in the government of the Church," we can only say that such an assertion is the untheological offspring of a narrow-minded nationalism.

Protestantism, to be consistent with its denial of the ecclesiastical principle of authority, was forced to place all ecclesiastical power in the hands of the people. It rejected the divine origin of the ecclesiastical hierarchy, transferred all power to the congregations, and degraded the "ministers of the word" to mere representatives of the people. Secular princes, whose aid could not be dispensed with, were made the highest representatives of the community. This was practically to convert the sovereignty of the people with regard to ecclesiastical matters into Cæsaro-papism.

14. We have now to consider the sovereignty of the people from a political, and especially from an American, standpoint. Is it a general principle? Is it an American principle, and in what sense?

Popular sovereignty can be understood to mean that the ultimate ground and original source of all authority is the common consent of all; the will of the people, and not God, of whom all paternity, all authority, is named in heaven and earth.[1] This principle is totally false, or rather no principle at all. Precisely in this sense did Hobbes and Rousseau, the founders of this modern theory, put forth their doctrine; each one adding a shade of coloring of his own. Their set purpose, in asserting the sovereignty of the people, was to separate and estrange society from any and every relation to a personal God—to establish the State without God. Though it does not always openly avow it, Liberalism employs this principle in the sense of the *contrat social*, and for a like purpose. This theory of popular sovereignty renders it an immense service; for it is a fruitful source whence are derived the means of furthering its plans, and legalizing State-absolutism. We are not to regard the sovereign power of the people in this atheistico-materialistic sense.

Anarchists and socialists openly declare that the sovereignty of the people is to be so understood, and that they intend to carry out their plans on that principle as soon as they have a majority in the legislative bodies.

The cynical saying of Bebel, *Ja gäbe es einen Gott, dann wären wir geleimt*—" If there were a God, we would be trapped "—leaves no room for conjecture on that head.

In Rousseau's system the source of all right is

---

[1] Ephesians iii. 15.

the people, i.e., the majority of those who call themselves the people's representatives, or the State, the government of which is determined by the people. In its political enactments, this sovereign people recognizes no divine or natural law—no inborn or acquired right. Whatever is legal is, according to this theory, allowable and good. Every change of government, every revolution, is *ipso facto* justifiable when it is accomplished by the people, or in their name. *Quod populo placuit legis habet vigorem* —The will of the people has the force of law— under all circumstances.

Shall we, can we, as Christians and as citizens, defend our position on any political question with this notion of popular sovereignty? No; never. That would mean, in other words: To be a good American citizen, one must tread under foot, at least theoretically, the rights of God and man; or, the American citizen as such is a revolutionist against any and every authority above his own! In the name of all that we hold sacred in our religion, in the name of our patriotism, we decline to defend our position on the Roman question, or on any other political or politico-religious question, against the representatives of that principle, whether they call themselves socialists or not. We can come to no understanding with materialism, or make any concessions to it. We are a Christian people. We despise a Robespierre who, in the name of the people, wished to do away with the existence of God by an enactment of the State; we have just as little in common with modern political deists, who are striving to place Almighty God on the retired list with a pension.

On political events, then, such as the overthrow of an existing government, we pass judgment accord- to the divine and natural law; according to the eternal principles of justice which worldly power may thrust aside and despise, but which it can never subvert or destroy. Our only question, therefore, can be the following:

Is it not a principle of natural law that God, the fountain-head of all authority, has placed political authority in the hands of the people, and that all government, whether monarchical or democratic, derives its authority directly from them?

Any one has a perfect right to hold this doctrine, and we do not oppose it ourselves. Most Christian philosophers and theologians have been and still are of the opinion that the popular consent is the proximate basis of civil society, and that the civil power as held by particular persons comes only mediately from God but immediately from the people. But it cannot be laid down as an unquestionable philosophical principle of the natural law. It is at most but an opinion, even though it be a very probable one. There are many acknowledged authorities who do not even recognize the sovereignty of the people to be a principle in that sense, but defend the opinion that the will of the people only designates the bearer of public authority, while God Himself confers on him immediately the power to rule. It would be preposterous to deny this fact, and not at all courteous to assert that the defenders of the last opinion have no good reason for it, and that the opposite must be perfectly obvious at first glance to all.¹ Moreover, it is well to remark that those who hold to the more democratic opinion do not concede to the people the right on the plea of popular sovereignty to violently rid themselves of a lawfully constituted government which has lost favor in its eyes. This would be to sanction revolution indiscriminately, as Rousseau has done. They likewise admit that there may be other legitimate titles to the exercise of supreme civil authority, as there have been at all times and are to this day.

As Catholics, we are entirely free to embrace either one of these two opinions. The Church has defined nothing in this matter. She has been content, at all times, to confront revolutionary machinations with the apostolic doctrine (on that account none the less evident to reason) that God, the author of nature, created man a social being and therefore willed that authority without which a well-ordered society of free agents cannot be conceived. Therefore, all civil authority is mediately from God. In very truth, then, do the bearers of it reign by the grace of God.

When a people determines to adopt a constitution it can, most assuredly, without detriment to the

---

¹ The authorities for both opinions are cited in the works of Costa-Rossetti, S.J., who strenuously defends the first: *Philosophia Moralis*, p. 593, seqq.; *Philosophisches Jahrbuch*, 1888-90; *Die Staatslehre der Christlichen Philosophie*. St. Thomas treats this question, q. 2, 9, 10, a. 10; q. 12, a. 2; q. 105, a. 1; q. 90, a. 3; q. 92, a. 3. One of the most ardent and profound advocates of the rights of the people is Suarez, *Defensio Fidei*, l. 3, c. 2; *De Legibus*, l. 3, c. 4. See also Brownson's *Origin and Ground of Government*.

natural law, choose a democratic as properly as a monarchical form of government. It can positively declare through its representatives that in the government about to be established the supreme authority, divinely ordained, actually proceeds from the people; and that their representatives are only to exercise it as their delegates. In such a State or society the theory of popular sovereignty has the effect of a fundamental law, by which every loyal citizen must abide; which he is to look to for the preservation of his civil and political rights, and which accordingly must guide him in the performance of his duties. Thereupon the representatives of the people may declare: We accept the democratic theory as the principle of the government under which we are going to live. A parliament with a thousand members could not do more than this. It is beyond its competency to change a question of natural and public law into a general principle which shall be universally binding. And if in our day the theory of popular sovereignty has been recognized in most States and has passed into current public law, it is significant of nothing but that modern governments have accepted it as the groundwork of their constitution. This is precisely the case in our glorious Republic. With us the sovereignty of the people is at the bottom of all civic obligation. Indeed, nowhere do we see it exercised so liberally. But the framers of our Constitution, who were by no means hostile to the interests of religion, did not dream of approving the theory of popular sovereignty in the atheistical sense of a Rousseau. Just as little did they wish to decide the abstract question about the origin of civil authority. Considering the peculiar condition in which our people lived, they simply looked upon a constitution founded on the sovereign will of the people as the best for our country.

From what has been said we draw a twofold conclusion. In the first place, we, as citizens of the United States, have an indisputable right to hold popular sovereignty in the highest esteem; to proclaim aloud that it is the best system of government for the American people, because it accords best with our character and the traditions of our country. But, on the other hand, it would be most ridiculous for us to maintain that we had thereby established a principle which is binding for all time and must be accepted by all nations. With precisely the same right might another system be adopted elsewhere, which might meet equally well the desires and be practically as well adapted to the necessities of that country as our system is to us. Did we attempt to impose our political views on other peoples, whose character and wants may be totally unlike ours, we would be untrue to our American sense of liberty. No. A true American is proof against the madness of Chauvinism. God forbid that this foreigner should ever be naturalized here!

The whole matter may be summed up as follows:

There is no popular self-government in the Catholic Church.

No Christian can defend the right of the people to self-government in the sense of Rousseau's theory.

Any Catholic may defend as true the opinion that civil authority comes immediately from the people and mediately from God.

Every Catholic of the United States can, like any other citizen, acknowledge the right of self-government guaranteed by the Constitution, and his religious principles need not suffer in the least. He may also consider this system as the best one for this country. He may also advocate that it be introduced into all countries for which it is suitable. Finally, he, like every other citizen, has the obligation to render obedience to the government established according to the principles of the Constitution.

Now, it may be asked, does all this remain true, if we judge the Roman Question as the pope does? if we not only desire the restoration of the temporal power, but also defend it?

Yes, even in this case, it all remains true. Nor do we contradict in any way our political views, or act contrary to our civil duties. If we Catholics acted otherwise we would be illogical and disloyal to our religious convictions.

15. Let us consider in the first place the *national standpoint*. As citizens of the United States we must unreservedly acknowledge the Constitution, in the above sense, and fulfil our duties accord-

ingly. The obligation of a good citizen extends no further; it cannot extend further unless the liberty guaranteed by this very Constitution be such only in name. Or is it perhaps American to say: Every nation of the earth *must* be governed according to the same principles? This would be a ridiculous assumption. Is it necessary to pronounce death-sentence on all monarchies in order to be a true republican? This would be a contradiction of the very principle of self-government, which allows a people to transfer the supreme authority to any form of government which it may prefer, monarchical or democratic. Indeed, one can be a good citizen of any State without maintaining its form of government to be absolutely or even relatively the best. If this were not so what would become of liberty of thought? of liberty of science and research? It would be downright tyranny if a government or a people strove thus to fetter free thought.

Must a citizen of the United States approve of every revolution by which governments are overthrown? Such theories would declare revolutions the order of the day! Even the American people, notwithstanding its sovereignty, has no right violently to overthrow the Constitution; it has not even a right to forcibly oust the President or a majority in Congress before their term of office has expired. Thus, though every form of government be an immediately human institution, still from the very nature of the case it is a *permanent mode* of exercising authority, and the people must pay deference to it as such.¹

16. Now what must our judgment be on the spoliation of the Papal States by Victor Emmanuel, considering it simply as a *political* event?

Let us first merely glance at the overthrow of the pope's temporal power. The Italian or Roman people as such did not perpetrate that robbery. It was Freemasonry and the Piedmontese thirst for spoils which committed the outrage. The Roman plebiscite of October 2, 1870, was a mere comedy and can in no way be said to have been the manifestation of the "sovereign will of the people," even if we allowed that the subjects of the pope were sovereign. At present, however, we only wish to lay stress on the ground of principle. We therefore say: the pope is as legitimately and rightfully the sovereign of the Papal States as any monarch or executive ruler the whole world over. The legitimate form of government in his kingdom was always a purely monarchical one. Therefore the temporal power could not be set aside upon the plea of popular sovereignty—not by the Romans and much less by

---

¹ We utterly deny the right of revolution, or the right to resist for any purpose whatever, legitimate government in the legal discharge of its functions. We repeat, then, that the right of rebellion and revolution on the part of the people is no right at all. The people can never have the right to act, save through the forms prescribed by the supreme authority. (Brownson's *Works*, xv. p. 398.) The people of the United States and of the several States can amend the Constitution, but only constitutionally, through the government. The notion which has latterly gained some vogue, that there persists always a sovereign people back of the government or constitution or organic people, competent to alter, change, modify, or overturn the existing government at will, is purely revolutionary, fatal to all state government, to all political authority, to the peace and order of society, and to all security for liberty either public or private. (*Id.*, vol. xviii. p. 451.)

other Italians—except by the violation of justice and fidelity.

But it will be asked: Has not the spoliation of Rome been at least approved as a *fait accompli* by the other powers? History answers *No !*

From the point of view of the law of nations, the occupation by force of arms of the pontifical territory by Italy is a conquest which is devoid of international sanction, and which is justified neither by the necessity of legitimate defence nor by the exigency of repression.

The papacy has never committed upon its neighbor any act of aggression which could authorize a defensive war involving as its fatal result the confiscation of the territory of the assailant. Besides, this taking possession has not been regularized by any treaty stipulating the renunciation of ownership in favor of the possessor, or by the general consent of the political community of nations. Yet in 1815 the treaty of Vienna sanctioned anew the temporal sovereignty of the popes, after the spoliation of Napoleon I., and thus the fate of the papacy, closely bound up with the fate of the European equilibrium, finds itself equally under the ægis of the general treaties which form the international code.

The recognition of the title of King of Italy, no more than the transfer of the foreign ministers to the new capital, implied the sanction of the dispossession of the papacy. For no one is ignorant that this double act was accompanied by express declarations and formal reservations which left no doubt of the intention of the powers not to prejudge the situation.'

It is certainly very regrettable, as the Marquis de la Vega de Armijo has said, that the passive attitude of the nations, and particularly of the Catholic nations, has permitted Italy to realize the occupation of Rome. The great war between Prussia and France which arose at the moment will explain to a certain point this apparent indifference, but it can never excuse it entirely. Fouqué might have repeated, in the presence of this sad spectacle: "It is more than a crime, it is a blunder." But it is equally necessary to recognize the importance of the following facts, which must never be left out of sight.

The Italian Government, almost to the very eve of the occupation of Rome, had caused the declaration to be made to the powers by the minister of foreign affairs (August 29, 1870) that it would regulate with the Catholic world the conditions of the transformation of the pontifical power. The representatives of the powers, on being officially acquainted with this declaration, signified to the Italian Government that their governments would not consider the occupation of Rome as a final solution of the Roman question, and reminded it of its duty to "effectually guarantee" the perfect spiritual independence of the head of the Catholic religion and the entire personal liberty of the

---

[1] See "*Lettre de Léon XIII. au Cardinal Rampolla*," by T. D. F. T., Bruxelles, Vennekens, pp. 41, 43.

pope.[1] Thereupon the minister Visconti Venosta declared to the Chamber: "Italy assumes with confidence, in the face of Europe and of Christendom, the responsibility of protecting the Holy See;" and still more: "The sovereignty of the pope bears the seal of the ages, and is recognized by the powers, either by solemn treaties or by diplomatic relations which they maintain with it;"[2] and again: "The Roman question concerns all the nations; it is 'more than international.'"[3] The Senator Cadorna, president of the council of state, recognized in 1871 that the final rearrangement of the Roman question was for Italy an "international obligation," and that "the absolute necessity of an effective liberty for the pope created a right for all Catholics and for all their respective governments."[4]

On the other hand, the powers have never recognized the "Law of Guarantees" as a sufficient assurance of the independence of the Holy Father; eight years after the invasion of Rome, the Italian government took the risk of soliciting before the tribunal of Europe, at the Congress of Berlin, 1878, a diplomatic ratification of the *fait accompli*. The powers responded by a categorical refusal.

The attitude of the same powers has been

---

[1] See the declaration made by Bismarck, October 8, 1870; by M. Jules Favre, in the name of the French Government, September 6, 1870; and the reports in which the ministers to Italy of the various governments express the sentiments of the latter: notably the reports of Mr. Minghetti, minister at Vienna (December 10, 1870), of Mr. Barral, minister at Brussels (September 12, 1870), of Mr. Melegari, minister at Berne (September 6, 1870), and of Mr. Cadorna, minister at London.
[2] April 21, 1871.   [3] April 22, 1871.
[4] See Vaughan, chap. iv.; Vennekens, chap. ii.

entirely different towards other Italian sovereigns despoiled of their territories, such as the dukes of Modena, Parma, and Florence, and the king of Naples, with whom all diplomatic relations were broken off immediately after the annexation of their states to the new kingdom.

We have not here to examine the question whether the annexation of other Italian territories was legitimate, or if it was at least legitimatized by the consent and the well-being of the people. But in treating the Roman question solely from the political point of view, and particularly from the point of view of the law of nations, we observe that the powers have not wished to tie their hands in presence of the "accomplished facts" at Rome, and that in their eyes and in the eyes of the Italian Government itself the Roman question has an altogether special and unique character, a character truly international. All recognize accordingly the perfect exactitude of the words of Leo XIII.:

> This principality has a sacred character, which is peculiar to it, and shared with no other state, because upon it depends the security and stability of the liberty of the Apostolic See in the exercise of its sublime and important functions.[1]

The interior reason of this fact is the intimate connection which the temporal power of the popes has with their spiritual power, as we shall see more clearly still as we now go on to

---

[1] In quo quidem principatu... inest similitudo et forma quædam sacra, sibi propria, nec cum ulla republica communis, propterea quod securam et stabilem continet Apostolicæ Sedis in exercendo augusto et maximo suo munere libertatem. (Allocution, May 24, 1884.)

give expression to our Catholic convictions on this question by considering its *religious aspect*.

17. The dearest of all the liberties which our Constitution permits us to enjoy is liberty of conscience, the freedom to openly profess our religious faith and practise it by fulfilling the duties which it enjoins upon us.

As Catholics we believe that the successor of St. Peter is divinely appointed by God to rule the entire Church, independently of any earthly power; and that all Catholics owe him unqualified obedience. Furthermore, we believe that the bishop of Rome and he alone is the successor of St. Peter. Our faith then teaches us that the bishop of Rome ought by divine right to rule the Church with freedom and independence, and that we owe him childlike submission. It is therefore the will of God that the freedom of the pope be secure in Rome, in order that he may be truly independent in leading the whole flock of Christ.

This conclusion no Catholic can deny without serious detriment to the dogma of the primacy of the bishop of Rome. The following conclusion is just as certain: Against the will of God there is no sovereignty upon earth, whether it be that of a Cæsar, of a people, or of all people taken together.

The Holy Father indicates clearly this difference in the encyclical which he has just addressed to the bishops of France (February 16, 1892):

> Whatever be the form of government of a nation, it cannot be considered as so definitive that it should remain immutable. The Church of Jesus Christ alone has been able to preserve and

will surely preserve unto the end of time its form of government. And, far from needing to change its essential constitution, *it has not even the power to renounce the conditions of true liberty and of sovereign independence* with which Providence in the general interest of souls has endowed it.

But in regard to purely human societies, it is a fact engraven a hundred times in history that time, that great transformer of everything here below, operates profound changes in their political constitutions.

Hence, no Catholic can ever approve of any act or condition of things by which the pope is bereft of perfect liberty.

Illa autem, quæ sursum est Jerusalem, libera est, quæ est mater nostra! "Free she must be, that Jerusalem which is our Mother!"[1] *Itaque fratres, non sumus ancillæ filii, sed liberæ, qua libertate Christus nos liberavit!* "We are not the children of a slave, but of a mother who is freeborn." We claim for her that freedom which Christ our Lord purchased for her.[2] These grand words come to the mind of a Catholic when he raises his eyes and looks aloft to the Roman Church, the mother and teacher of all the churches of the globe. The Lamentations of Jeremias are inadequate to give expression to his sorrow, when this Jerusalem, "the Ruler of nations," "the Queen of the Provinces," is robbed of her freedom.

The Roman Church then must be free in the person of her bishop, the head of the Church. But if the pope has received from God the right to exercise his sublime office most fully and without

---

[1] Galatians iv. 26.   [2] Gal. ii.

molestation, he is thereby entitled also to the means necessary for the perfecting of that liberty, and has a right to determine and demand them.

Accepting, then, the doctrine of the primacy, (*a*) common-sense must tell every one that the pope is truly free in Rome when he is in no way subject there to another, or dependent upon another; and that this independence has its surest guarantee, and is most effectually secure against every extraneous influence, when the pope himself is likewise the temporal ruler of Rome.

If we consult (*b*) history, we find that the popes ever since the division of the Roman Empire have possessed a certain political power in Rome, which for the past eleven centuries has been of a truly regal character.

Now (*c*) the Christian concept of the Church and of divine Providence tells us that God, "Who loves nothing dearer than the freedom of His Church,"[1] thus shaped events that the freedom of the head of the Church should be made secure by his temporal power—"singulari scilicet prorsus divinæ Providentiæ consilio factum est, ut Romano Imperio in plura regna variasque ditiones diviso, Romanus Pontifex . . . civilem principatum haberet."[2]

Furthermore (*d*) the events of the last twenty years sadly but unmistakably prove that the pope is no longer free to exercise his office in Rome in a manner becoming its importance and dignity since

---

[1] St. Bernard.
[2] Pius IX., Allocution "Quibus quantisque," April 20, 1849; Leo XIII., letter to Card. Rampolla.

Victor Emmanuel forcibly entered by the Porta Pia and took possession of Rome as king of Italy; for the pope, in spite of all guarantees, is completely dependent upon government measures and the whims of ministers, the chambers of Parliament, and the rabble.

Lastly, (e) we know from the clear and positive utterances of the popes themselves "that the temporal power of the pope is necessary at present in order that he may, freely and independently of any power or secular prince, rule and guide the entire Church."[1]

The last reason alone would be more than sufficient. The pope is the competent judge in this question; every Catholic must accept humbly his declaration. But we add, and Pius IX. emphasized it in the allocution quoted above, that the episcopacy of the whole world more than once has repeated these same declarations of the head of the Church.

It is not incumbent upon Catholics, therefore, to defend the temporal power because the pope was the legitimate prince of Rome, who was unjustifiably and violently despoiled of his temporal possessions. No, the real and true reason is a deeper one. They defend the liberty of the pope because he is pope, i.e., because he has been lawfully constituted the head of the Church by Jesus Christ. It is a question, therefore, of defending that liberty and independence to which the divine

---

[1] Pius IX., Allocution, "Maxima quidem," June 9, 1862; Leo XIII., l. c.

Founder of the Church has given His representative an inalienable right. In defending his own rights he is defending our rights as Catholics. The means to preserve intact this freedom is the temporal dominion. Therefore we conclude that just as no power on earth has the slightest right to destroy the freedom of the Sovereign Pontiff, which God wills, so also no emperor or king or people has any right whatever to deprive the pope of the temporal power which he needs and must have in order to govern the Church with the freedom willed by Christ. The sovereign freedom of the successor of St. Peter is to-day necessarily conditioned by his temporal sovereignty ; therefore the latter, through the former, is rendered sacred and inviolable, and *to attack it is to assail Christ Himself in the person of His representative.*

Victor Emmanuel had accordingly no more right to deprive the pope of the Papal States than had Napoleon I. The occupation of Rome will always be a sacrilege no matter by what people it is effected. We say a *sacrilege,* for such in very truth it is, being "a sin against the immunity of a sacred place;" and as prescription has no force in sacred things and against ecclesiastical rights, the spoliation of Rome cannot be legalized by any title whatever. Hence the Constitution " Apostolicæ Sedis " places the ban of excommunication (*speciali modo Romano Pontifici reservata*) upon " all who either themselves or through others invade, destroy or retain the cities, lands, places or rights belonging to the Roman Church, or who usurp, disturb or retain the supreme jurisdiction therein; also on all who give help, counsel or favor to any of the acts aforesaid."[1] Is not this excommunication of itself sufficiently expressive for every Catholic, who knows that it is the severest ecclesiastical punishment, and always presupposes grave sin? Can there be any law or principle to justify that sin? Knowing this, must not every Catholic openly condemn the invasion and retention? Unless he does so he is in direct opposition to the pope and to himself, and solicitude for the maintenance of a so-called political or national principle would lead to the denial of an undeniable Catholic principle.

A remark of St. Thomas on a similar subject may appropriately illustrate these deductions. The Angelical Doctor, along with the majority of mediæval theologians, defends, as is well known, the opinion that civil authority proceeds immediately from the people. In treating of the laws and customs of the Old Testament he makes the objection: "With the Jews the election of rulers was not sufficiently provided for, since no direction had been given to the people in this regard." He replies as follows: "That people was governed under the special care of God; whence it is said (Deut. vii. 6.): 'The Lord thy God has chosen thee to be His peculiar people;' therefore the Lord did not commit the election of the supreme ruler, the choice of the king, to the people, but reserved it to Himself, as

---

[1] *Invadentes, destruentes, detinentes* vel per se vel per alios civitates, terras, loca, aut iura ad Ecclesiam Romanam pertinentes, vel usurpantes, perturbantes, retinentes supremam iurisdictionem in eis nec non ad singula prædicta, auxilium, consilium, favorem præbentes. (I. 12.)

is clear from Deut. xvii. 15: 'Thou shalt set him king whom the Lord thy God shall choose.'"¹

Hence according to Aquinas there could be no question about the election of a ruler—the exercise of the sovereignty of the people in the proper sense of the term—because there can be no right of the people against the ordinances of God. Now, reasoning from analogy, we say God provides in a special manner for His "peculiar people," the Holy Catholic Church, and in her, more especially, for the Roman Church, whose bishop by His express command was to be the successor of St. Peter and the head of the Church. By the special providence of God it came about that the temporal sovereignty also over Rome was given to the successors of St. Peter, in order that they might exercise freely and independently their sublime office. Hence with regard to the Roman people it is true that since they are the objects of God's special providence, He has not committed to them the election of a ruler, but has reserved to Himself, i.e., to His Church, the right to determine by the election of the pope the person who is to be the king of Rome.

It is our duty to speak plainly and forcibly. The religious aspect of the Roman question is for us the most important. Our non-catholic fellow-citizens will not recognize this argument as the

---

¹ Ad primum ergo dicendum, quod populus ille sub speciali cura Dei regebatur: unde dicitur (Deut. vii. 6.): Te elegit dominus Deus tuus ut sis ei populus peculiaris. Et ideo institutionem summi principis . . . electionem regis non commisit Dominus populo, sed sibi reservavit, ut patet Deut. xvii. 15: Eum constitues regem quem Dominus Deus tuus elegerit. (1. 2. q. 105, a. 1.)

only true one, because they reject the religious principles on which it is grounded. They deny moreover the spiritual sovereignty of the pope; hence, *a fortiori*, his right to independence. But they cannot gainsay our right to remain true and loyal to our religious principles. Do we Catholics enjoy only a partial and imperfect liberty of conscience? They cannot but respect consistency; and shameful compromise and cowardly faint-heartedness will surely not gain their esteem. Let us cling therefore, above all, to the great American principle that we are free citizens and esteem religious liberty above all else. Let us proclaim clearly and positively that as Americans we hold firmly to our Constitution, to the right of self-government and to republican principles, and believe that in general civil authority comes only mediately from God and immediately from the people; but we maintain that there may be other legitimate titles to such authority. We have neither the right nor the intention of imposing our views upon others. Just as it is not contradictory to our republican principles that monarchies exist elsewhere, so also we cannot reject *à priori* a constitution that does not recognize the sovereignty of the people. In any case, not even the most sovereign people in the world can have a right to violate the ordinances of God! But we Catholics behold in the papacy an immediate institution of God, and in the temporal power the necessary condition of the divinely-ordained freedom of the pope. Therefore no right in the world, not even the right of self-government, can be appealed to against that freedom; and we may apply to the Roman question: "Quod Deus coniunxit homo non separet"—" What God hath joined let not man put asunder!"

18. We will conclude this part of our argument with the words of Brownson, who was always proud of being an American citizen, and whom all Americans claim as their own : " It is enough to say that the pope never was a subject of any temporal prince, and never can be. He represents Him Who is King of kings and Lord of lords. He is above all earthly monarchs, by the law of Christ; .... the status of prince belongs to him by right of his office as vicar of Christ, for by that office he is declared independent, and clothed with plenary authority to govern all men and nations in all things relating to salvation." [1] "The Roman or ecclesiastical state was a donation to the Holy See or to the Church of Rome. Gifts to the Church are gifts to God, and when made are the property, under Him, of the spirituality, which by no laws, heathen, Jewish, or Christian, can be deprived of their possession or use without sacrilege. They are sacred to religious uses, and can no longer, without the consent of the spirituality, be diverted to temporal uses without adding sacrilege to robbery. Whoso attacks the spirituality attacks God. The temporal power of the pope is therefore not within the category of any earthly human government, but is the property of the spirituality. Victor Emmanuel, in

---

[1] See vol. xii. *Pope and Emperor*, p. 456.

despoiling the pope, has usurped Church property, property given to God and sacred to religious uses. The deed, which our eminent jurists and Protestant divines sympathize with and applaud, strikes a blow at the spirituality, at the sacredness of all Church property, of Protestant churches as well as Catholic churches—at the sacredness of all eleemosynary gifts and asserts the right of power when strong enough to divert them from the purposes of the donors. . . . Are they [the Protestant divines] so intent on crushing the papacy that they are quite willing to cut their own throats?"[1]

VI. Salus Publica Suprema Lex

19. We cheerfully admit this principle. It does not militate against the re-establishment of the temporal power, but is rather a confirmation of its usefulness and necessity. It shows both in a brighter and clearer light. Let us therefore briefly consider its essence and the deductions made from it in the light of Christian jurisprudence and according to the teaching of Christian moralists.

The common good is to be placed above that of the individual; hence duties towards society precede, generally speaking, those towards self. The temporal welfare of the people is the immediate

---

[1] See vol. xviii, *Sardinia and the Holy Father*, p. 451. This article carries the greater weight with it because it was written in 1871, a year after the spoliation of the Holy See, and in order to refute the arguments of Dr. Thompson and other Protestants who pretended to defend the "sovereignty of the Roman people," saying that the sovereignty of the Roman State "is in the category of all earthly sovereignties."

end of civil society. Government exists not for its own sake but for the people. A change of government or a change in the form of government, brought about by any event whatsoever, may be legitimate, even though effected by unlawful means. It suffices that the former state of affairs has become hurtful or impossible, and that, consequently, the welfare of the entire society requires the subsequent situation to be upheld by all. Even he who does not admit the lawfulness of our War of Independence, or of the Belgian revolution of 1830, must concede that the governments thus established are perfectly legitimate. But if the above conditions do not exist, the members of such a society may tolerate the change of government, but cannot directly lend their aid to confirm or maintain it.

20. If the claims of different societies be compared, precedence must be given, other things being equal, to the highest and most important. Since every society is made up of a number of rational beings united for the attainment of some more or less definite end, it is evident that the dignity of a society depends upon the loftiness of its end and on the number of intelligent beings who are striving for that end. This truth must always be kept in mind when considering civil and religious society, the State and the Church.

The State has for its immediate end the temporal welfare of its subjects; the Church, the eternal welfare of all mankind. Just so far as the importance of eternal salvation exceeds that of temporal happiness, by so much the Church, by divine appointment the mediator of eternal happiness, must take precedence in dignity over every civil society. There exists therefore a true subordination of the State to the Church. The Church cannot be made subservient to the State, and no transitory temporal considerations can prevent her from using the means necessary for the attainment of her sublime end.

The ecclesiastical as well as the civil power are both supreme in their respective domains; but, though each has its own sphere, they should act conjointly for the welfare of humanity. But the Church, because of her exalted end, is superior to the State, "as the soul is superior to the body, and as the sky is above the earth."[1] "Or should the spirit give place to the flesh, the celestial to the terrestrial?"[2]

Moreover, the Church surpasses also in excellence the civil organization of any people or nation, because her activities embrace a wider field. Her welfare is the welfare of all her children who are scattered over the entire globe; nay, more: it is that of all men, for whom indeed she was instituted.

This is why, in case of a conflict of jurisdiction between Church and State, e.g., when both claim jurisdiction in the same matter, precedence must be given to the Church. This is no "mediæval theory." It is Catholic teaching, which can be proven by sound reason and which Leo XIII., in union with

---

[1] St. Chrysostom.   [2] St. Gregory Naz.

the fathers and theologians, has clearly and distinctly explained.[1]

Suppose that the temporal advantages of a nation come in conflict with the welfare of the Church, to which that nation belongs, or hinders the Church in the attainment of her end, then evidently that nation must make its temporal interests subservient to the higher interests of the Church—which is identical with the nation's own higher interests, and with those of the faithful at large.[2]

These are the conclusions which faith and reason draw from the principle *Salus publica suprema lex*.

21. *The welfare of the whole Church demands the re-establishment of the temporal power.*

The objection brought against this principle when applied to the Roman question may be stated thus, in clear terms:

"Private interests must give way when there is a question of public welfare or of the common good. Now, the welfare of the Romans and Italians, that is, the public welfare of Italy, demands the maintenance of the present political situation of their country; consequently the pope's temporal power must be permanently abolished. It is therefore his duty to renounce his claims to temporal sovereignty, or at any rate Catholics need not strive to re-establish it."

[1] Particularly in the encyclicals *Immortale Dei. Quod Apostolici Muneris, Humanum Genus, Diuturnum*. There is no need of citing authors in confirmation of the above-mentioned principles; they may be found in any treatise on Christian Jurisprudence. Cf. especially Cardinal Hergenröther, *Staat und Kirche*, viii., "Die Lehre von der Superiorität der Kirche und ihrer Gewalt über das Zeitliche."

[2] On the subject "How the Church, notwithstanding her higher aim, or rather by means of it, promotes the temporal well-being of nations," cf. Leo XIII., encyclical "Humanum Genus."

The first proposition is true, but it proves just the contrary of what our opponents deduce from it.

Facts show the second proposition to be false; but even granted it to be true, it would prove nothing against us. Hence, in any case, the conclusion is false.

As the temporal welfare must be subordinate to the spiritual, so likewise must the incidental claims of a single nation be subordinate to the demands of the Church and the Catholic world at large. Now the Roman question means the security of a spiritual good, the security of ecclesiastical liberty, through the territorial independence of the head of the Church; a claim most intimately associated with the well-being of the Church and the interests of two hundred millions of Catholics.

Hence *Salus rei-publicæ Christianæ* suprema lex!

Rome, therefore, belongs to the Church, to her visible head, and therefore to the whole Catholic world. The Papal States are the incontestable heritage of the common Father of Christendom, "the patrimony of Peter." Romans and Italians would have no right to rob Rome of its essential character, that of the centre of the Church, the capital of the Catholic world, even though their claims were unanimous, and they really did gain a national advantage by despoiling the pope, and subjecting the vicar of Christ to a temporal king.

No, Rome is not a city like any other! It is neither an Italian city nor a modern capital; it is the city of the apostles, and the metropolis of the Christian world. It is the heritage of St. Peter, the property of the Church Universal, the head and the heart of Christendom.

Italy, therefore, owes it to the Church, to the Catholics of the whole world, as well as to the pope himself, to restore to him that liberty and independence indispensable to the government of the Church, viz., his temporal power.

This is the unbending logic of philosophy, the logic of the ecclesiastical standpoint, the logic of Catholic consciousness.

The following proposition stands out clearly in the light of present events. In order to enjoy sovereign liberty, as the head of the Church, the pope must be a temporal sovereign. Only lately three enemies of the papacy have furnished eloquent commentaries upon the outrageous occurrences of last October—commentaries that must come home forcibly to the blindest adherents of nationalism and modernism. They were the speech of Minister Rudini at Milan; the circular of the Jew Lemmi, the Grand-Master of Italian Free-masonry, to the Italian ∴ Brethren; and the agitation of the demagogue Menotti Garibaldi against the so-called Guarantee Law.

It is true, as some timid persons are fond of saying, that the Church will survive, though days of worse captivity and still greater affliction be in store for the venerable sufferer in the chair of St. Peter. She lived through ages of persecution when almost all her popes roddened the chair of St. Peter with their life's blood and she would live through the same ordeal again, by virtue of the divine life dwelling within her. But are these the sentiments of a child realizing the sublime dignity of its mother? Is this the language of one who glories in his faith and is proud of being a Catholic? Every true Catholic understands the *non possumus* of the successor of St. Peter in an entirely different sense; and from deep conviction proclaims with him that "the temporal power of the pope is at the present time not only useful but necessary for the liberty of the Church." Necessary, because the Church has not only a right to live, but also the right to live free and unmolested! Necessary, because she has not merely the right to conceal herself in the catacombs, under the surveillance of a questor, by the grace of the State, but she has the right to show her everlastingly youthful, beautiful, and venerable countenance to all people! Because she has not merely the right to pass by the palaces of the mighty in the ragged garb of a poor servant-maid, a beggar imploring a place of shelter, but she has the right to pass majestically through human society, a royal personage with power to command and a gracious blessing for all, a queen adorned with that royal crown which the eternal King placed on her brow when He purchased her upon the cross at the price of His Precious Blood!

22. *The re-establishment of the temporal power a benefit to Italy itself.*

It only remains for us to show in a brief way that in the Roman question it cannot be said that Rome and Italy must sacrifice their temporal advantage for the common good of Christianity. The opposite is true. We will only mention the following facts :

a. It is not true that the overthrow of the pope's temporal power was the work of the Roman or Italian people, and that the present situation fulfils their desire. We do not mean that the Italians may not be justly reproached for lack of energy in proclaiming their Catholic sentiments. Nevertheless, Leo XIII. gave expression to the truth, when he said, on different occasions, that the great majority of the Italian people faithfully adhered to the Roman See. It was the confirmation of this fact by the grand demonstration of October 1, 1891, in St. Peter's, when, with twenty thousand pilgrims, not less than forty thousand Romans and Italians knelt at the feet of the Sovereign Pontiff, that induced the Grand-Master Lemmi to issue a most violent circular.[1]

Apropos of the absurd deception of the plebiscite, says Mgr. Vaughan,[2] let us hear the Jewish editor of the *Libertà*, Edoardo Arbib. He is assuredly an impartial witness.

"The plebiscites," he says, "were made in the midst of the terror of the Revolution. The government is legal, because it has force to sustain it, but it is certainly not the government desired by the

---

[1] The well-known liberal deputy, Fazzari, presented the following programme to his constituents: "The reconciliation between the Roman See and our government is the highest need, the most urgent necessity and the sincerest wish of our Fatherland." He was elected to Parliament by an immense majority. Distinguished *conservatives* wrote to him: "*All Italians feel the truth of your resolution,* but few have the courage to declare it openly to the official world." Cf. *La Conciliazione tra il Papato e l'Italia.* Florence, 1887.

[2] Chap. vi.

people. The true Italy, the real Italy, is with the pope, remains with the pope, and hopes in the pope —*è col Papa, sta col Papa, e spera nel Papa.*

"Do you see how the churches overflow and how the ballot-boxes are deserted? How few go to vote! And do you know why? Because they do not believe in you; because you appear to them a transitional government, destined to disappear."

It cannot be too often repeated that the invasion of Rome is before all and solely a carrying out of plans woven in the anti-christian and anti-religious sects, whose war-cry is the destruction of Catholicity, and by that means of Christianity, by the annihilation of the spiritual power of the head of the Church. Already in 1856 Cavour declared at the Congress of Paris that he "would bring about the fall of Rome and would shake the edifice to its very foundations." His plan miscarried at the time, but Mamiani already could say "that an eighth power had sat in the Congress of Paris—it was the Revolution." Crispi, who has called himself "the First National Conspirator,"."Son of 1789," has also declared: [1] "Between us and the pope there can be no truce." According to him and according to Mazzini: "It is the vocation of the Italian people to destroy Catholicism." Who is the chosen poet of the Italian Revolution? Carducci, the author of the "Hymn to Satan"! And what was the real reason of the apotheosis of the infamous Giordano Bruno and of the grotesque saturnalia celebrated,

[1] June 17, 1887.

with the concurrence of the government, in the city of the popes, if not his unbelief and his ferocious hatred against the Church and the Holy See? The honors rendered to such a man signify, then, that it is necessary to dechristianize the world and drive men to revolt against the authority of the vicar of Christ.[1]

b. Far from having promoted the welfare of Italy, the proclamation of Italian unity has caused it to suffer greatly and has well-nigh ruined it. Rome and all Italy are suffering from the *mal di Roma*, the Roman plague, that is, financial embarrassment and poverty, the outcome of the mania for political ascendency. The straits in which New Italy finds herself plainly verifies the saying of Thiers: "*Qui mange du pape en meurt*"—"He who eats pope dies of it." The Italians, whose sensitiveness in money matters is proverbial, understand the practical application of the well-known adage: *La farina del diavolo va tutta in crusca* —"The devil's meal all turns into bran." Even those who out of inborn cowardice join in the cry *Evviva l'Italia unita* will tell a stranger in a significant and plaintive way: *Si stava meglio quando si stava peggio*—"We fared much better when we were worse off"!

A living proof of what sort of blessings the new kingdom is showering on the population of Italy is the great mass of poverty-stricken Italian emigrants who daily land on our shores.[2]

[1] See Vaughan, chap., iv.; Vennekens, chap. i.
[2] Cf. *La question Romaine au point d' une financier ;* Office of the *Osservatore Cattolico*, Milan. E. de Laveleye, in the *Contemporary Review*.

c. National honor and glory! That Providence selected Italy for the seat of the papacy is her fairest fame, her greatest glory. It was the popes who added the most celebrated pages to Italy's history. The glorious traditions of the land, its splendid achievements in the domain of science and the arts, are all to this day most intimately connected with the names of the popes.[1]

"Those who appreciate aright the lessons of history and Italian traditions, and do not separate the love of the Church from love of country, will see with us that in union with the papacy lies precisely Italy's most fruitful source of prosperity and greatness."[2]

In regard to the cry *Roma, capitale d'Italia!* Massimo d'Azeglio, one of the most skilful politicians of the Garibaldian party, has already said: "All the lofty minds of Italy are convinced that it is impossible to make of Rome the capital of Italy. It is, moreover, no mystery to any one that the Italian government, beginning with the king, do not feel themselves at home there. They do not receive there the visits of sovereigns, and those that they do receive are surrounded with formalities which proclaim loudly that Rome is 'the natural See of the Roman pontiffs, the centre of the life of the Church, and the capital of the Catholic world;' and that consequently the true sovereign of the city of the apostles can be no other

---

[1] Leo XIII. to the Italian bishops, February 15, 1882, and letter to Cardinal Rampolla.
[2] Leo XIII. to Cardinal Rampolla.

than the august prisoner of the Vatican. On the other hand, according to the unanimous opinion of Italian and foreign statesmen, no city is better situated and better constructed to be the capital of the country than Florence—*Fiorenza la bella.*" [1]

d. Even from an international standpoint, Italy's great misfortune is and will be the Roman question. Even without Crispi's notorious declarations, his angry speeches, and his frivolous article in the *North American Review*, it is as clear as daylight to the unbiassed mind that Italy keeps an immense standing army, which consumes millions upon millions, for no other purpose than to guard her spoils against the protestations of the Catholic world. For that very reason the Roman question will always be a question of the day, despite the tricks of diplomacy, until the sacred right of St. Peter's successor is restored to him. Never will the two hundred million children of the pope cease to accuse Italy of the crime committed against their common father, and demand back his freedom. They will be louder in their claims, the longer the head of the Church is kept in prison. The world's legions of soldiery are not able to smother the voice of the pontiffs and deaden the ring of its echo in the hearts of the faithful or prevent its re-echo from their lips.

e. National unity. Is there a unity more precious and more strong than religious unity? And would not Italy in living at peace with the pope

---

[1] See especially Leroy-Beaulieu and de Laveleye.

see that unity powerfully cemented which is the foundation of every other and the source of immense advantages, even in the social order?

And now can there be any question about the lawlessness of a state of affairs which leaves to so many subjects of the usurper no other alternative than to transgress a religious duty and refuse obedience to the Church and the vicar of Christ, or to look upon the Italian kingdom in its present form as the enemy of the Holy See and of the Church? We say Italy in *its present form :* for the union of all under the sway of the king of Piedmont is not at all a necessary condition for the oneness of the nation. Were the popes ever opposed to a federative union of Italy? Did not the united cities of the land in earlier times find precisely in the papacy their most active representative, protector, and defender?

Finally, would not united Italy be powerful enough without having Rome as its capital? Would it not, above all, be a more blissful union? Italian unity is not considered to be destroyed by the independence of the principality of Monaco and the republic of San Marino; it would no more perish by the cession of a territory in which the Sovereign Pontiff would find the guarantee of his spiritual independence.

Furthermore, Leo XIII. has never, as far as we know, raised his voice against such an Italian kingdom as would be compatible with the independence of the Holy See. "He knows very well," says Bishop Vaughan, "he has clearly indicated it, and we all can see, that Italy would be the most happy and the most really united of countries if she would only be willing to concede a little civil principality to the head of the Church, who lives on its borders, to guarantee his independence.

"This union in peace of the consciences of a Catholic people would be for her not only an immense glory, but a formidable rampart."[1]

23. Would it not be a benefit, in the best sense of the word, to all civilized nations, if the popes should again be universally acknowledged and appealed to as the arbitrators in international differences?

But in order that all nations may resort in every instance to such an arbiter and peace-maker with full confidence, he must be entirely independent, a prince himself in his own free right. Who is there who does not pray for such an arbitrator? All, including the enemies of the Church, must admit that there can be no person better qualified for that sacred trust than the pope. Therefore the *salus publica*, the public good of humanity, on this account also, demands his perfect liberty.

We add: The papacy, from a purely human point of view, is the most beneficent of all social institutions. As Leo XIII. remarked in his letter to Cardinal Rampolla, the temporal power has rendered "to Italy and to Europe, even in the political and civil order, most signal services."

The popes have been the soul and the genius of

[1] Chap. ii.

the most noble and useful enterprises which are the honor of the human race. Watchful sentinels, they have uttered the cry of alarm at the approach of every social danger, and have always been and are pre-eminently in our day the most solid barrier against the rising tide of socialism and of anarchy.

Moreover, the pope is the most august representative of what forms the basis of civilized society— moral force. He is the incorruptible guardian and the indefatigable and generous defender of the principles whose maintenance is essential to the very existence of society—the principle of authority, paternal and civic, and the principle of justice, private, political, and international. He is, finally, the foremost initiator of all the moral good which operates in the world; he is the vivifying and luminous centre whence go forth continually, like so many rays, encouragement for feebleness and timidity, exhortations for cowardice and apathy, consolation for those who struggle or who suffer, and inspiration for those who ask only a field for action.

It is, then, out of gratitude as well as from an instinct of self-preservation and self-interest that the peoples should guarantee to the popes the possession of a power of which they have made such noble use in the service of universal humanity.

24. *The Papal States and the District of Columbia.* —The relation of the District of Columbia to the United States strikingly resembles the relation of Rome to the Catholic Church. We shall indicate

the line of thought. The Constitution explicitly states that "Congress shall exercise exclusive legislative power in all cases whatever over a district" set apart for the government of the nation.' Now, the inhabitants of the District of Columbia are more numerous than those of certain States; nevertheless they have no representatives in Congress, no right to vote on national issues in the district, not even the right to elect municipal officers. The proximate reason of such a wise measure is the independence of the legislative and ruling power of the United States; the ultimate reason, the welfare of all the States, of the whole country. Did the decree of 1801 ask the consent of the Washingtonians? By no means. Are the people of Washington "sovereign"? Can they change this article of the Constitution, even if its population of two hundred thousand unanimously demanded it? Not at all. What would be the answer of Congress, of all Americans, to such claims? Simply this: It is an honor and a privilege for Washington to be the capital of the United States; but its citizens must sacrifice some political rights exercised by other citizens, because *Salus publica suprema lex!*—the welfare of the whole country demands it!

We say *à pari* and *à fortiori:* According to the divine constitution of the Church, Rome is the centre and capital of the Catholic world, the seat of the government of the Church. Hence the Roman pontiff must have "exclusive legislative power"

---

[1] Constitution of the United States, art. i, § 8, ¶ 17.

over Rome. Therefore Italy is honored with the highest privilege of divine Providence, but it has at the same time the sacred duty towards all Catholic nations, towards Catholics of the whole world, to sacrifice certain political or national rights, if such there be, in order to insure the complete independence of the pope and thereby the well-being of the whole Catholic Church.'

VII. WHAT SHOULD BE THE SOLUTION OF THE ROMAN QUESTION

25. We see that the Roman question exists; that it has not been settled, but always left open. It is not only an Italian question, it is not only a European question, it is an international question, in the fullest sense of the term. Its solution is not

---

' Rev. H. A. Brann, D.D , in his learned pamphlet, *The Schism of the West*, draws the following weighty argument from the necessity of the freedom of papal elections:

"We learn from this schism how dangerous it is to the peace of the Church to permit any secular power to have influence in the Conclave. The election of the pope should be absolutely free so as to forestall excuses for schism. Hence the place of the Conclave should be subject to no prince. The popes should be temporal sovereigns; their territory, be it great or small, absolutely inviolable; and in that territory the Conclave ought to be held. The Schism of the West furnishes arguments for the restoration of the temporal power of the pope. There are some, I know, who dream of a possible spiritual independence of the Papacy, without temporal power. But we ask when or where the popes were absolutely free, *de iure* and *de facto*, except when they were temporal sovereigns. They should be perfectly free *de iure* as well as *de facto*, and this is only possible with the temporal power restored. All the facts of history are against the platonic dream of a spiritual independence of the papacy when it is subject to king, kaiser, or mob. The restoration of the temporal power is therefore a necessary guarantee to the freedom of the Conclave. The attempt of Crispi, the late prime-minister of the king of Sardinia, to get a pledge from the *Dreibund* to coerce the future Conclave to elect a pope who would sanction Sardinian usurpation, shows what is to be expected of any civil government which can claim the pope as a subject."—*The Schism of the West and the Freedom of Papal Elections.* New York, Benziger Brothers, 1892, pp. 30, 31.

only useful and possible, it is necessary. It is then an error, from a political as well as from a religious point of view, to think that time can ever render acceptable to the Holy See the situation in which it is now placed by the invaders of Rome. Such an affirmation would be altogether inexcusable in the mouth of a Catholic.

26. We do not ask when God will hear the supplications of the Catholic world for its captive father; or how, under the present circumstances, Providence will give to the Bishop of Rome the temporal sovereignty over the Eternal City. History tells us that the pope was robbed of his sovereignty one hundred and seventy times, and that each time it was restored to him; our own century has been the witness, both in 1815 and 1849, of how wonderfully God directs His Church in troublous times, and prepares new triumphs for her in the person of her persecuted head. But to appeal to divine Providence is not to demand of it a miracle, or to expect such a thing and in the mean time cross one's arms. This providence exists, and faith tells us that it extends in a special manner to the beloved spouse of Christ, His Church, and in the Church in a most special manner to the Vicar of Christ. But we know also that Providence does not dispense us from doing what in us lies to further its designs; that it requires the co-operation of men, and that it permits the most cruel trials to the Church precisely in order to stimulate and fortify our zeal in the works of faith.

27. *To whom belongs the duty of co-operating with*

the designs of divine Providence with regard to the Holy See? This duty is incumbent, first, upon those who by their crime have acted directly against the designs of Providence, upon those who have destroyed its work,—the Italian Government.

It is incumbent also upon those who have not prevented the crime, although they could and should have done so, or who have at least encouraged the invaders of Rome by their silence; upon the Christian governments, especially the Catholic governments.

Finally, it is incumbent upon all the Catholics of the world, who ought to do all in their power to lead the authors of the crime to make reparation for it.

28. *In what should this reparation consist?* It consists in rendering to the chief of the Church "the civil sovereignty which in the designs of Providence is ordained as a means for the regular exercise of the apostolic power, as being the efficacious safeguard of its liberty and independence."

29. *To whom belongs the right of determining the conditions under which the re-establishment of the civil power should be made?*

This right does not belong to the Italian Government, nor does it belong to the other powers, either to each of them separately or to all united; it belongs solely and exclusively to the pope. The exercise of his divine rights is in question; he alone is their depository, he alone is their guardian, and consequently he alone has the right of determining the conditions under which they should be exercised.

30. *Can this solution be pacific, and how?*

Yes, it can be pacific; moreover, it is desirable from every point of view that it should be so; it is such a solution which Catholics above all demand, after the example of the Holy Father himself.

The Holy Father has clearly indicated his ardent desire that the re-establishment of the civil sovereignty should be "a work of pacification," that it should be brought about by "reconciliation," that it should "bring to an end the unfortunate disagreement between Italy, such as it is at present officially constituted, and the Roman pontificate." [1]

And the more to indicate their sincere desire to arrive at such a pacification, neither Pius IX. nor Leo XIII. has ever required that the Pontifical States should be returned to them in their original extent. Taking into account the circumstances of the case and the present condition of Italy, Leo XIII. has "taken care to put at the basis of this pacification the justice and the dignity of the Apostolic See, and to claim a state of things in which the Roman pontiff should be subject to none, and enjoy a full and not an illusory liberty." [1] This state of things which the Holy Father demands is more explicitly determined by the declaration "that the indispensable condition for a pacification of Italy is the restitution of real sovereignty to the Roman pontiff." In the same document the Holy

[1] Leo XIII. to Cardinal Rampolla.

Father indicates clearly that this sovereignty should extend in the first place over "the city of Rome, the natural see of the Sovereign Pontiffs, the centre of the life of the Church, and the capital of the Catholic world."

At Rome, continues the Holy Father, "the pope ought to be placed in such a condition of freedom, that not only shall his liberty not be contravened, in fact, by any one whoever he may be, but that this shall also be absolutely evident to every one; and this not owing to conditions subject to change and at the mercy of events, but from their nature stable and lasting." He warns the statesmen "who imagine other projects and plans" that "these are vain and useless attempts;" and that he will never accept an adjustment "which, under specious pretences, leaves the pontiff in fact in a state of true and real dependence." Finally he sums up the restitution that he requires, and consequently the programme of pacification, in the following words: "Without the restoration of a true and effective sovereignty, we do not see any open way to an understanding and peace."

31. Some non-catholic journals have spoken lately of the "desires, more or less avowed, of the court of King Humbert" for a reconciliation with the Holy See. These desires are, they say, based on the conviction that the interest of the dynasty counsels an agreement with the Vatican, in order to resist the rising flood of radicalism and socialism.

We readily believe that they are beginning to

see at the Quirinal the truth of the words of Victor Emmanuel, *Roma è fatale*—that the revolutionary logic goes on from the overthrow of altars to the overthrow of thrones. They will undoubtedly recognize that the future of a dynasty cannot be founded on the *débris* of the most august and the most legitimate of thrones.

But will the court have the courage and the strength necessary to extricate itself from the machinery of the revolution? We would be glad to hope so, but unfortunately history teaches us that such returns are not possible except to vigorous and heroically-tempered souls.

32. A liberal journal, speaking of these "desires of the court," adds with a world of reason that the Roman question is the heel of Achilles to the Triple Alliance, especially in view of the Catholic sentiments of the Austrian court and of the great majority of the people of that empire. It thinks likewise that an agreement with the Holy See "concluded under the auspices of a foreign power would hardly please the Italians." [1]

It may certainly be admitted, as a great defender of the Holy See has said,[2] that a too marked interference of another power in the regulation of the Roman question might wound the sensibilities of Italian patriotism. But there is for the most interested party in the case a very simple means of warding off this inconvenience, which is to dispense with all intermediaries, and take to itself the initia-

---

[1] *L'Indépendance* (Belgian), February 3, 1892.
[2] **Verspeyen**, in his excellent *Bien Public*, Feb. 4, 1892.

tive in the steps which are commended to it both by justice and by its own interests. Is this not the way that Leo XIII. himself has often suggested in his memorable allocutions, in proclaiming that the independence of the Holy See had nothing incompatible with the greatness and the prosperity of Italy?

One might perhaps do well to look over the Gospel with King Humbert, and read again the parable of the prodigal son: "I will arise and go to my father's house"!

From the Quirinal to the Vatican it is not so far!

Let he who can and ought cause the conflict to cease, by restoring to the pope his proper position, and forthwith all these difficulties will disappear. Moreover, Italy would benefit greatly in all that constitutes its true glory and the happiness of a people, or deserves the name of civilization; for as Italy has been designed by Providence to be the nation nearest to the Papacy, so it is destined to receive more abundantly from the latter such salutary influence, if only it does not fight against or oppose them. [1]

VIII. THE DUTY OF CATHOLICS IN REGARD TO THE ROMAN QUESTION

33. "From all this it may be easily understood how incumbent it is on the Roman pontiffs and how sacred is their duty to defend and uphold the civil sovereignty and its lawfulness; a duty which is rendered still more sacred by the obligation of an oath [which every pope has to take after his election]. It would be folly to pretend that they would themselves sacrifice along with the temporal

[1] Leo XIII. to Cardinal Rampolla.

power that which they hold most precious and dear : we mean that liberty in the government of the Church for which their predecessors have always so gloriously struggled. We certainly, by the grace of God, will not fail in our duty."[1]

There are certain Catholics, fortunately not at all numerous, who do not love to hear such language from the mouth of the Vicar of Christ. According to them the best policy would be for the pope to be silent regarding the Roman question. The words cited from Leo XIII. contain an energetic and clear response to such advice, which is equally devoid of authority and of Catholic sense. Others would wish at least to be themselves dispensed from treating the Roman question in the press and in public assemblies. We have given them above the response dictated by the Catholic conscience.

The popes know better the fidelity of the true children of the Church and their attachment to the Holy See. Far from supposing silence on their part, they see, on the contrary, in the action of the Catholic peoples the firmest support of their hopes and of their claims.

Hence it is that Leo XIII., after having spoken of his own duty, adds the following words, which show well the confidence of the father in his children :

> The whole Catholic world, very jealous of the independence of its head, will never rest until justice has been done to his most righteous demands.

[1] Ibid.

34. Pius IX. has indicated clearly in what manner Catholics should co-operate with the views of Providence and second the efforts of their common father. These are his words:

> The Church of God in Italy is suffering violence and persecution, and the Vicar of Christ has neither liberty nor the free and full use of his power. We therefore think it opportune, and we greatly desire, that the bishops, who in many ways have constantly shown their union in the defence of the rights of the Church and their devotedness to this apostolic see, should call upon the faithful under their jurisdiction to make every effort, as far as the laws of each country may permit, to induce their governments not only to examine carefully the serious condition of the head of the Catholic Church, but also to take such measures as may insure the removal of the obstacles which restrict his true and perfect independence.[1]

35. It is by the people that great things are done in our day. It is they who, so to speak, trace for their governments the road which they are to follow. Now the governments represent the rights of the minorities as well as those of the majorities of their citizens, and they will not be able in this matter to ignore their numerous Catholic subjects.

Says Bismarck to the Prussian Chamber of Deputies:[2]

> As the representative of the government, I must place myself at an independent point of view, and I must recognize that the Papacy is not an Italian institution, but a universal one. And because it is universal, it is also for German Catholics a German institution.

We would add, that because it is universal it is also for American Catholics an American institution, that is to say, it concerns intimately the

---

[1] Allocution "Luctuosis," March 12, 1877.
[2] April 22, 1887.

rights and the religious interests of the Catholics of America.

Usurping Italy does not fear anything so much as this manifestation of Catholic sentiment. It is on that account that she has interfered at home with the petitions which were being drawn up in favor of the pope. It is on that account that she has stifled the voice of bishops and priests by a new and tyrannical penal code, according to which the mere expression of an opinion in favor of the temporal power is liable to punishment. It is on that account, finally, that by her diplomatic agents she has made desperate efforts to crush out the public and solemn protestations of the Catholic nations.

It is only several weeks ago that the Austrian minister, the Count Kalnoky, indicated in the open Chamber that the condition of Rome was always an open question. Hence interpellations and explanations without end in the Italian Chamber!

Italy will not be able to long resist such a pressure from the public conscience, and must finally decide herself to make up her mind to pay her "international debt." The unanimous explosion of a sentiment so just, so noble, and so legitimate will be considered everywhere as the voice of Eternal Justice, whose echo resounds in the hearts of the believers of the Old World and of the New.

Being, then, conscious of our strength, let us bring it to bear in our associations, in our assemblies, and above all in our Catholic Congresses. Just claims do not nowadays secure a hearing in any other way. So only does a numerical minority gain public recognition. Those who stand aside and content themselves with calling upon Heaven to witness their protest will never prevent the usurping power from demanding the order of the day.

Our efforts should be persevering and unanimous. In order to have these two qualities, they should before all be frank and decided. Let us not content ourselves with declaring vaguely that independence is necessary to the Holy See, since there is question precisely of guaranteeing this independence by a designated method. Common action supposes an unequivocal platform. Such a platform is furnished us by the popes, and by the situation itself; it can be no other than this: The independence of the Holy See by the re-establishment of the temporal power of the pope.

36. Certain journals have shown a great zeal in proving to Italian Catholics that it is upon them above all that the duty is incumbent of acting in behalf of the Holy See. Articles have even been written to urge them to take part in the political elections of their country, and to instal their deputies at Montecitorio in order to defend there the rights of the pope.

Certainly the Italian Catholics should be in the front ranks of the soldiers of the Holy See. They have already made great efforts, and will make still more. Their first need, unhappily too long neglected, is a powerful *organization*. But in regard to their participation in the political elections, it must be said that in abstaining thus far they

have only followed hitherto the watchword of
the Holy Father; the formula *ne eletti ne elettori*
is simply the putting in practice of the response
of the Holy Father, *Non expedit*. We have not here
to indicate the manifold reasons for this attitude of
the Holy See: they are more numerous and more
serious than any one would think at the first
glance. M. Leroy-Beaulieu, as a profound politician, recognized it, and declared that " the situation of a political party in Italy would be more
difficult than in any other country." But in any
case, the Holy Father is here also the only judge
of the situation, and it is not becoming in a Catholic to criticise his attitude. Moreover, these
criticisms hide too easily a specious excuse for
those who would desire to throw upon the Italian
Catholics alone the accomplishment of a duty which
is incumbent upon us as well as upon them: for
the duty of Catholics is as international as the
Roman question itself.

37. The more active and vigorous international
action is in this case, the greater will be its weight,
the more powerful its efficacy, and the more speedy
its success. Again, the more outspoken Catholics
are in a country where they enjoy greater liberty
the greater will be their influence on public opinion.
It is this conviction that the German-American
Catholics at the congress of Buffalo (September,
1891), have well expressed in their resolutions, so
clear and so energetic, on the subject of the temporal power.

Their open and decided language has also been

justly appreciated and loudly approved by the Catholic organs of the highest standing in the Old World.

In the inspiring language of Father Hecker: "We have the right, as well as the duty, as one of the members of the Catholic Church, to voice what we know to be the unanimous conviction of our fellow-Catholics on this continent, who are no idle spectators of passing events at Rome, who do not listen with deaf ears to one whom they delight to call by the endearing name of father; and when the government of the king of Italy makes, or allows others to make, his position in the Eternal City 'intolerable,' then we have the common right and the common duty to raise our voice, and in the unmistakable tones of sincerity to warn him—*beware!*" [1]

The Catholic people of the United States, whatever be their mother-tongue, are profoundly attached to the Holy See: let us go to them, let us give them an opportunity of manifesting their attachment, let us speak to them clearly and warmly of the unworthy situation in which the chief of the Church is placed, and they will be happy to give us resplendent proofs of their filial sentiments towards the common Father of the Faithful. This is abundantly evidenced by the grand mass-meeting of workingmen which was held a few days ago under the auspices of the Most Rev. Archbishop Corrigan in the city of New York. We have just read with real pleasure and admiration the masterly

[1] *Catholic World*, April, 1882.

discourse of one of our most distinguished Catholic laymen, Judge Dunne, and the excellent resolutions enthusiastically adopted in that memorable assembly.

Let us aid, in the mean time, the captive Peter alike with our charity and with our prayers, and take heed that we may in no way incur the reproach of the Holy Spirit: "Of what an evil fame is he that forsaketh his father." Let us follow the example which he gives us. "We place our trust in God," said Leo XIII. in an address, "and are determined to contend with all our might for the freedom of the Church and its head. . . . We are, moreover, not alone in this conflict."

No, Holy Father, you are not alone in this conflict! Your devoted bishops and priests, all your faithful children, pray and protest with you! Our trust, like yours, is in the Lord, who above all else loves the freedom of His Church! The day will come, the longed-for day of deliverance! The successor of the prince of the apostles will again ascend the venerable throne which centuries have erected for the papacy, to shed new lustre upon the Church, to spread over all the world the beneficent influence of the apostolic word, to be free again to bestow his blessing, without let or hindrance, upon the Eternal City and the entire world—*Urbi et Orbi!*

APPENDIX

APPENDIX

TWENTY THESES ON THE ROMAN QUESTION

I.

The head of the Catholic Church, as the successor of St. Peter, has a right, which by reason of his sublime office and the explicit will of Jesus Christ is divine and inalienable, to direct and govern the whole Church, freely and independently of every earthly power.

II.

Only the bishop of Rome is or has ever been the successor of St. Peter in the primacy. It is theologically certain that this prerogative of the Roman Church is immutable, and can never be transferred to any other episcopal see.

III.

To insure the permanent liberty and independence of the head of the Church, divine Providence has so shaped events that after the age of persecution the popes became by the most legitimate means, without offence or opposition, the masters of Rome even in a political sense, and have remained such until our own day.

IV.

The violent measures of which the Holy See became the victim in the year 1870, could not change these designs of divine Providence. On the contrary, the events of the last twenty years have only served to prove more clearly that the temporal power is an indispensable condition for the normal government of the Church, and a necessary guarantee of the complete freedom and independence of the pope.

V.

The political independence of the popes has always been assailed by the enemies of the Church and the destruction of the temporal power in our, day was instigated by the anti-christian and anti-religious sects, and effected by their instrumentality with the open and avowed purpose of shattering and destroying the spiritual power of the pope and of the Church.

VI.

The Roman question is therefore a religious and not a merely political question.

VII.

The spoliation of the Holy See by the Italian Government in 1870 was consequently not only a flagrant violation of the principles of natural and public right, a breech of the most solemn treaties, and an infraction of the very primary provisions of international law, but also a crime done against the Church of God herself, her property and her freedom, and hence a true sacrilege.

VIII.

Although the Christian powers permitted the spoliation of the papal states without the solemn protest which they should have made, they reminded Victor Emmanuel's government immediately after the event of its duty to make the independence of the head of the Church secure, and the Italian Government has thus far tried in vain to obtain from them an explicit recognition or approval of the occupation of Rome.

IX.

The circumstances under which the law of guarantees was framed, and the manner in which it is understood and executed by the Italian Government, prove clearly and unmistakably that it was a deceit practised upon the Catholic people concerning the real intention of the revolution, and while apparently acknowledging the pope's dignity, it was really a means of degrading it. It is, in fact, a defiance of divine Providence and an insult to the Catholics of the whole world.

X.

This law and the general attitude of the Italian Government towards the Holy See, is a breach of the pledge which it gave to the Christian powers both before and after the taking of Rome, to guarantee full freedom to the pope and to settle the Roman question " with the Catholic world."

XI.

By these and similar declarations the Italian Government itself has acknowledged the international character of the Roman question, and thus has given the lie to Crispi's words that " the question is a purely Italian one."

XII.

The Roman question is in reality an international question, because (a) it is concerned with the most vital interests of Catholics of all nations and of all tongues, and (b) the pope is the highest representative of that moral power which is the basis of a civilized society, and which alone can effectively guard it against the anarchical designs of socialism in its many forms.

XIII.

The Christian powers cannot leave the Roman question to be solved by the Italian Government as it sees fit; for they have to protect the religious interests of their Catholic subjects, which are intimately connected with the liberty and independence of the Papacy.

XIV.

A peaceful solution of this question is most desirable. It can be attained either by the voluntary action of the Italian Government or by the diplomatic influence of the other powers.

XV.

Far from being detrimental to the true interests of Italy, such settlement would make the political independence of the country secure, promote its credit and influence abroad, bestow upon its people the blessing of true unity at home, elevate its religious and moral power, increase the material and financial prosperity of the land, and correspond to the urgent desire of an overwhelming majority of the Italian people.

XVI.

The principle that even violent changes in the political conditions of a people can be legitimated by circumstances cannot be applied to the Roman problem, as it is not a question of dynastic claims or the temporal interests of a particular nation, but rather of the inalienable rights of the head of the Church, the spiritual interests of Catholics throughout the world, and indeed the most important social interests of all nations.

XVII.

As the pope has again and again solemnly declared his love for peace and expressed his desire for a settlement which would not compromise his dignity, and the Italian government, far from taking any steps to meet this wish, has more than once forcibly suppressed the endeavors of its Catholic subjects to that end, the latter alone is answerable not only for bringing about the strained condition of affairs, but also for its continuance.

XVIII.

The only final solution of the Roman question must assure to the Holy See a true territorial sovereignty as a guarantee of its real and manifest independence; and the acceptance of this principle alone can furnish the basis of future negotiations.

XIX.

It belongs to the pope alone to determine the details of the adjustment which, in view of the existing situation in Italy and the present condition of society at large, is necessary for the attainment of that sovereignty.

XX.

The Catholics of the whole world are in honor bound to use every endeavor for the re-establishment of the temporal sovereignty of the head of the Church. Systematic silence is not only disobedience, but cowardice.

EDUCATION:

TO WHOM DOES IT BELONG?

SECOND EDITION,

WITH

A Rejoinder to Critics.

By the Rev. THOMAS BOUQUILLON, D. D.,

Professor of Moral Theology at the Catholic University of America, Washington, D. C.

BALTIMORE:
JOHN MURPHY & CO.
1892.

COPYRIGHT, 1892, BY JOHN MURPHY & CO.

PREFACE.

In these pages theoretical principles only are dealt with. These are exposed from a Catholic standpoint. The practical application of the principles does not come within the purpose of the writer, it is not his office to give directions. He has written this pamphlet at the request of ecclesiastical superiors. They deemed that a clear exposition of the principles underlying the school question would be both useful and opportune at this hour, when the practical difficulties in which it is involved have become national concerns; were it only to show that in the matter of education as in all other social concerns the true doctrine of the church is opposed neither to liberty well understood nor to the just prerogatives of the state.

The writer makes no pretense to originality. He professes to walk in the footsteps of the great theologians, especially of Saint Thomas. He has been guided by the light of the Encyclicals of Leo XIII on civil power, the constitution of states, liberty and the condition of the laboring classes. He could not omit, without sacrificing completeness, certain delicate points of detail on which Catholics are not in agreement. On these he has frankly expressed his opinion and has given for them what he thinks good reasons. He begs the reader to give them serious consideration.

EDUCATION: TO WHOM DOES IT BELONG?

We reduce the subject matter of our paper to the following four questions: right to educate, mission to educate, authority over education, liberty of education. Though these four aspects of the educational question touch at many points, we prefer to treat them separately. This plan may force on us some repetitions, but in compensation, it will enable us to avoid the ambiguities and confusion that too often involve in darkness this important subject.

We will examine these four questions from the point of view of the individual, the family, the state, the church. For man is not an isolated being, he is a social being; in society he finds the helps he needs for the development of intellect, the formation of character and the means of subsistence. Now there are three essential societies instituted by God to work harmoniously in conducting man to his perfection and his end; the domestic, the civil, the religious. Therefore, we must determine what are the reciprocal rights, duties, and powers of these three societies in the intellectual formation of man. To do this safely we shall not take for our only guide *a priori* arguments, but we shall also seek to find a basis in the canonical and civil law of Christendom, moreover we shall look for light in the lessons of history. Principles, laws, facts, in these we shall search for the solution of the questions under consideration.

As to principles, we acknowledge that they are to be found best exposed in the more recent publicists, rather than in the older writers who lived before the modern era of the separation of Church and State. We quote in preference Taparelli, *Saggio teoretico di Diritto naturale*, diss. 7, and *Esame critico degli ordini representativi*, tom. I, p. 314; Card. Zigliara, *Phil. mor.*, p. II, lib. II, c. 1, a. 5; Costa-Rosetti, *Inst. Eth. et jur. nat.* thes. 175, 176; Hammerstein, *De Eccl. et Statu*, p. 146, 158, 181; Sauvé, *Questions religieuses et sociales*, c. 10;

Cavagnis, *Inst. Jur. publ. et Eccl.*, lib. IV, c. 1. Mention must also be made of Coppola, *Sull Diritto della Chiesa in ordine al publico Insegnamento*; Riess, *Der moderne Staat und die Christliche Schule*; Jansen, *De Facultate Docendi*; Conway, *The respective rights and duties of family, state and church in regard to education*; Robiano, *De Jure Ecclesiae in Universitates Studiorum*; and finally the anonymous work of two French priests, *L'École neutre en face de la Théologie.*

As to laws, besides the Decretals, lib. v, tit. 5, *De Magistris*, we have consulted the collection of Councils by Hardouin, and its worthy continuation the collection of Maria Laach, the Capitularies of Charlemagne, the ordinances of past governments, the two collections of Mgr. Roskovany, *De Ecclesiae independentia* and *Romanus Pontifex*, and notably the acts of Pius IX and Leo XIII, the decrees of the papal congregations, and finally the *Schema de Ecclesia*, prepared by the pontifical theologians of the Council of the Vatican, though not discussed by the Council.

As to facts, we shall have recourse to Thomassin, *Anc. et nouv. disc. de l'Eglise*, p. II, lib. I, c. 92; Claude Joly, *Traité hist. des Écoles épiscopales et monastiques*; Léon Maitre, *Des Écoles épiscopales et monastiques de l'Occident*; Stallaert and Vanderhaeghe, *De l'instruction publique au moyen age*; Lebon, *Histoire de l'enseignement populaire*; Du Boulay, *Hist. Univ. Paris*; Jourdain, *Histoire de l'Université de Paris au dix-septiéme et dix-huitiéme siècle*; Bourbon, *La licence d'enseigner et le role de l'écolâtre au moyen age*; Karl, *Ueber die alten und neuen schulen*; Denifle, *Die Universitäten des mittel alters.*

The history of education and of schools is to-day the occupation of a great many erudite scholars in many lands. The *Polybiblion* gives in vols. 10, 11, 12, years 1873 and '74, a bibliography of the subject which is worthy of regard; still later we find another bibliography in the report of the bibliographical and international congress held in Paris from the 3rd to the 7th of April, 1888.

I.

THE RIGHT TO EDUCATE.

Right, considered as distinct from law, justice, authority, is a faculty moral and inviolable of doing, exacting, possessing, disposing of something.—We will not stop to explain the various kinds of Right: natural and positive, innate and acquired, absolute and hypothetical, primary and secondary, independent and subordinate, alienable and inalienable, direct and indirect, right the exercise of which is necessary and right the exercise of which is free. One remark: when we say that Right is an *inviolable* faculty, we mean that Right, as long as it is in existence, must be respected, and may be defended even by force; but we do not mean that a Right may not be regulated, modified, restricted, even suspended. Evidently an acquired right may be taken away, and many natural rights may be, if not entirely suppressed, at least regulated, modified, or restricted in various ways. —Only a rational being is capable of possessing a right; such a being, as possessing a right, is properly called a Person; if the one who possesses the right is an individual, the person is physical; if the one who possesses the right is a corporation, a college, the person is moral. Let us now consider the right of teaching, or of education, in the individual, the family, the state, the church.

(*a*). *The Right of Educating in the Individual.*

By individuals we mean not only men isolated, but also private associations other than the family, the state, and the church.—A theory termed "liberal," at present in vogue in different countries, especially in Germany, rests on the assumption that the right of education in individuals can be only a positive right, delegated by the sovereign authority, because education is a public, a social function.[1]—Against this theory, which is as dangerous as it is false, we affirm that every individual, every legitimate association has by nature the right of educating.

---

[1] Victor Cousin, the philosopher, wrote in the *Journal des Débats*, May 4, 1844: "The state has the right to confer the power of educating, *for to educate is not a natural right, but a public and social right.*"

And 1° we say that the right of educating belongs naturally to every physical person. What is education? In a large sense it is to communicate what we know to one who does not know. In a restricted sense it is to communicate after a methodical and continuous fashion knowledge relative to religion, morals, letters, sciences, the arts; or, it is to instruct and train childhood and youth. But every man has the right to communicate the truth, and to communicate it after the fashion that is most efficacious and best adapted to those who wish to receive it. For this he needs no mandate from government.[1] To allow to every citizen the right of expressing opinions by speech or by the press, and at the same time to deny him, as is done in some countries, the right of teaching is a monstrous contradiction.

We say 2° that the right of educating belongs naturally to every moral person, or corporation. The reason is plain. If every individual has the right of teaching what he is capable of teaching to whomsoever will accept his teaching, a collection or legitimate association of men endowed with a like capability must have the like right. Whatever the lesser may do, that same with stronger reason the greater may do. If the isolated man possesses such a right, men collectively possess it also. Therefore the right of educating is not a right exclusively individual, but a right that may belong to many persons associated and may be exercised by them *in solido*. That an association may have the natural right to teach whatever is the allowable object of teaching, it is only necessary that it be lawful and composed of men fitted to educate.[2]

The right to educate, therefore, which we attribute to individuals is not absolute and unlimited, it is essentially limited to the true, the good, the expedient. No one has by nature the right to teach error, vice, or even truths that are injurious and inopportune.—Neither is it an independent right: the right of individuals in education is essentially subordinate to the action of legitimate authority, civil and religious. Doubtless no authority may arbitrarily suppress this right, but authority may for sufficient reasons regulate it, for instance, by determining what are the due conditions of worth and capability

---

[1] Suarez, *De fide*, disp. 18, s. s.: "Jus docendi ignorantes es*i* quasi connaturale cuicumque homini."

[2] The natural right of association is openly asserted by Leo XIII in the last enc. *Rerum novarum*: "Privatas societates inire concessum est homini jure naturæ."

in the teacher, of which more shall be said later on.[1]—Finally it is not an exclusive right, but coexists with the rights of the family, the state and the church.

This natural right to educate which we attribute to individuals and associations has always been acknowledged by the Church. The Lateran Council, in the pontificate of Alexander III, prescribed that no one shall forbid the right of teaching to him who is capable thereof. The same Pope rigorously ordained that all who are capable and learned and wish to open schools, might do so without undergoing any hindrances or exactions whatsoever.[2] Facts are not wanting to strengthen our position. The history of Abelard shows that he set up his school where he pleased. Dr. Denifle tells us that many of the great mediæval universities were formed spontaneously without the intervention of church or state: the universities of Padua and Verceil were brought into existence by an exodus of students from Bologna. The reader who desires further information on this point may consult Taparelli, *Saggio teoretico di Diritto naturale*, diss. 7, c. 3, not. 140; Sauvé, *Questions Religieuses et Sociales*, c. x, a. 1, § 4; Cavagnis, *Inst. Jur. publ.*, lib. IV, n. 107. We shall often cite these three writers. Taparelli is recognized by all as a high scientific authority. Mgr. Sauvé, who had the honor of being one of the theologians commissioned by Pius IX, to prepare the *schemata* of the Council of the Vatican, and afterwards became the first rector of the Catholic university of Angers, devotes his declining years to the composing of works of the highest order, such as the one we have named. Mgr. Cavagnis is at present professor of Canon Law in the Roman seminary.

(b). *The Right of the Family to Educate.*

We speak not of a general right such as every individual possesses, but of a right special and proper to parents. No one can call into doubt that parents have by nature the right of giving education to their offspring. The end of conjugal society, one of the reasons for

[1] Were we asked how the natural right to educate may be regulated, restricted, modified, we should refer the questioner to the luminous distinctions of Suarez, De Legib., lib. II, c. 18, and we should ask him in turn, how does it happen that the natural right of contract is modified in many ways by civil and ecclesiastical laws.

[2] See lib. V, of the decretals of Gregory IX, tit. 5, de Magistris, c. *Quoniam* and c. *Quanto gallicana.*

its stability, is the education no less than the procreation of children. Parents are called by God not only to generate children to bodily life, but also to form their minds; therefore they are entitled to be the first instructors of their children, themselves, or through teachers of their own choosing. The child belongs to the parents, as S. Thomas very clearly explains in the second part of the Summa. "The child, he says, is naturally somewhat of the father, who generated him. At first he is not separate from the parent as to the body, as long as he is contained within the mother's womb. Later when he has come forth from the womb, he remains, before coming to the use of free will, under the direction of his parents, in a kind of spiritual womb, so to speak. . . . Thus it is a natural right, that the child before coming to the age of reason, be entirely governed by the parents. It would be against natural justice that the child, before coming to the age of reason, be torn from the guardianship of the parents, or disposed of against their will."[1]—Parents may exercise this right either separately or collectively, that is to say, in association. If one father can give education to his children, twenty fathers may associate to give education to their collected children. For number, as Taparelli observes, does not change the nature of things.[2] This right of parents is sacred, no one may suppress or diminish it; for it springs from a paramount duty. Leo XIII insists on this in his Encyclical to the Bishops of Bavaria: "Hisce in officiis simul cum procreatione liberorum susceptis, noverint patres-familias totidem jura inesse secundum naturam et æquitatem, atque esse ejusmodi de quibus nihil liceat sibi remittere, nihil cuivis hominum potestati detrahere, quum officiis solvi quibus homo teneatur ad Deum sit per hominem nefas." [3]

However, this right is neither unlimited nor absolute; it does not extend to error or vice; the parent has only the right to communicate to the child by himself or by others knowledge that is allowable. —Moreover this right is not independent, but subjected to the control of authority religious and civil within the proper sphere of each. Hence, while parents may and should give moral and religious education to their children, the church has the right and duty to scrutinize and guide such education where faith and morals are concerned. On the other hand the State, within the sphere of its powers, has a right of inspection over the education imparted by the family, the right to

---

[1] S. Thomas, 2ᵃ. 2ᵃ. q. x, art. 12.   [2] Esame Critico, 1. c.
[3] Leo XIII. Ency. "Officio Sanctissimo," 22 Dec., 1887.

prevent it from becoming a source of moral poisoning. Thus the judge may take a child from corrupt and corrupting parents who train it up in crime. The supernatural good and the social good may necessitate and demand a suspension of the exercise of parental authority by the ecclesiastical or civil authorities. It is well, however, to remark that Church and State may infringe more easily on the right of educating inherent in the individual than on that belonging to the family.—Let us add with Taparelli,[1] that the parental right has a natural tendency to diminution and undergoes changes in subject matter at least, as the needs of the child change. From this point of view we must admit a certain difference between the primary education of the child and the superior or special education of the grown boy and the young man. We will return to this point presently.

(c). *The Right of the State to Educate.*

By the word "State" we understand not the people but the social authority. This authority, according to the various constitutions of nations, is vested either in one person or in an assembly; but essentially it is one and the same, and always and everywhere has the same rights and attributes.[2]—Moreover, by the word "State" we understand in this matter of education authority in all its degrees, not only in the highest degree or the sovereign authority, but also in the lower degrees, such as the authority in provinces, counties, towns, districts.—Furthermore we suppose the distinction between the two societies, the religious and the civil, between the two powers, the political and the ecclesiastical, between the two spheres in which those powers have their movement, the sphere of temporal interests and the sphere of spiritual interests. Hence we do not inquire whether the State has the right of teaching religion, but we do ask if the State has the special and proper right of teaching human knowledge. We say *special and proper* right: for there can be no question of a vague and general right: it were unreasonable to refuse to the State that which is granted to every legitimate association.—Let us add that teaching, as far as the State is concerned therein, means establishing schools, appointing teachers, prescribing methods

---

[1] Saggio teoretico, n. 1569.

[2] In the last enc. Leo XIII while treating more particularly of the social problem exposes with great clearness the general rights and duties of the State.

and programmes of study: the State teaches in the same way as it governs and judges, viz., through delegates fitted for such functions.— Finally, we are inquiring what is the right of the State considered in itself, omitting the consideration of the conditions and circumstances under which it may prudently and legitimately use the right.

These considerations being premised to obviate all equivocation, we affirm unhesitatingly, and in accord, as we think, with the principles of sound theology and philosophy, and with the testimony of the tradition of the Church, that it must be admitted, as the larger number of theologians do admit, that the State has the right to educate. The following reason, drawn from the very nature of things and, in our judgment, thoroughly apodictical will suffice. Civil authority has the right to use all legitimate temporal means it judges necessary for the attainment of the temporal common welfare, which is the end of civil society. Now among the most necessary means for the attainment of the temporal welfare of the commonwealth is the diffusion of human knowledge. Therefore, civil authority has the right to use the means necessary for the diffusion of such knowledge, that is to say, to teach it, or rather to have it taught by capable agents. We believe the major proposition of this argument cannot be denied, especially if it be kept in mind that we are speaking of *temporal* means that enter into the sphere of action of the State, and of *legitimate* means that trench on and wound no other right. With this double reservation the right to an end evidently implies the right to the means. Neither can the minor proposition of the argument be reasonably denied. You have but to look around you, you have but to consult history to be convinced that from the moral, social, political as well as material point of view, science, possessed in different degrees according to different conditions, is one of the primordial elements of prosperity in any country. A nation needs citizens able to take interest in the commonwealth, workmen that are intelligent, surveyors that are skilful, physicians that are experienced, jurists that are learned. An ignorant people is a people inferior in agriculture, industry, arts, war. If you would have a people instructed, you must look to its instruction, and, if need be, establish and direct it. We look upon this conclusion as impregnable. We will merely add this further view, viz: that the civil power does necessarily teach in one way or another, as for instance, when it exercises legislative and judiciary powers; for a law is an enlightenment, a teaching for the mind as well as a direction for the will; the sentence of a tribunal is likewise an educational agency; and therefore the state as legislator and judge has in virtue of this double capacity the right of imparting education. We will produce facts and documents to show that all Christian nations have always held this opinion. How astonished Charlemagne would have been had he been told that he had no right to found schools; how astonished the bishops of his time had such a doctrine been put before them! Those very bishops were the men who, in the Council of Toul, exhorted princes as well as the ordinaries of dioceses to appoint everywhere teachers of divine and human learning; "Deprecandi sunt pii principes nostri, et omnes fratres et coepiscopi nostri instantissime commonendi, ut, ubicumque Omnipotens Deus idoneos ad docendum donare dignetur, constituantur undique scholæ publicæ, ut utriusque eruditionis divinæ videlicet et humanæ in ecclesia Dei fructus valeat accrescere."[1] It is well known that many universities arose in the Middle Ages in every catholic land. Their eminent historian, Fr. Denifle, divides them into four categories: those that were formed spontaneously, such as Paris, Bologna, Salerno, Oxford; those that were formed by the Church; those that owed their erection to the State; those in the foundation of which both Church and State combined. It stands recorded that previous to the year 1400 there had been founded by the civil authority alone not less than four universities in Italy, viz: Arezzo, Siena, Naples, Treviso; not less than five in Spain, viz: Valencia, Salamanca, Seville, Leṛida, Huesca.[2] Similar instances are not wanting in more modern times. But we desire to call attention to another order of facts. In the XVII century there were in the archdiocese of Spalatro free schools and communal, or as we should say, district schools; in these latter instruction was given by salaried teachers, cleric or lay. The Bishop made no objection as to the legitimacy of these schools, but he desired to know from the Congregation of the Council if he could force the teachers of such schools to instruct the children and ruder pupils (pueros rudesque scholares) in the catechism. The Congregation in its answer, Aug. 17, 1688, does not protest against this system of schools, but declares that the Bishop should exhort the masters to teach religion and even that he may compel them to do it.[3]

[1] Conc. Tullens. an. 859, c. 10.
[2] Denifle, op. cit., and Civilta Cattol. Serie XIV, tom 3.
[3] This answer is to be found in Giraldi, in Bened. XIV, Inst. IX, in Cavagnis, op. cit., n. 27.

In our own century Leo XII by the bull *Quod Divina Sapientia*, Aug. 29, 1824, reorganized the public education of the pontifieal states. Now the dispositions and the authentic interpretations of that bull suppose that the State has the right to educate. No doubt the care and guardianship of all that concerns faith and morals, belong to the Bishop or his delegate, but the school teachers are chosen by competitive examination which the communal magistrate publishes, the examination of the candidates is made in the presence of the magistrate. After the examination the municipal Council hears the report of the examiners and decides the choice of the teachers by a majority of votes given in secret balloting. The admission of children into the communal or public school belongs to the magistrates, to them also belong the duty and power of seeing to the execution of the regulations of discipline.[1] Now the power of choosing teachers, of admitting children into the school is nothing else than the power of teaching by delegation. Finally we have yet to learn that any pope has ever declared that the State went beyond its right in founding schools, *provided the instruction be organized in the spirit of Christianity.*

After studying the documents we have cited—and many more of a like tenor might be added—no one need wonder that the best and most serious publicists of our day explicitly acknowledge the right of the State to educate. Cardinal Zigliara affirms that nobody denies to the State the right to provide the best means for the intellectual and moral education of its subjects.[2] Father Costa-Rosetti, a Jesuit, lays down the thesis that the State has the right to found and direct schools.[3] Father de Hammerstein, another Jesuit, does not hesitate to assert that public schools may be established by the civil authority.[4] To Mgr. Sauvé the opinion denying to the State the right to educate does not seem probable.[5] We will close this list of authorities by giving the opinion of the theologians commissioned by Pius IX to prepare the subject matter of the discussions of the Council of the Vatican. They intended to proclaim the right of the Church to watch over the education, religious and moral, of catholic children, but at the same time they most explicitly recognized the right of the State to educate.

---

[1] See Caterini, "Collectio legum et ordinationum de recta studiorum ordinatione," p. 229, and "Analecta Jur. pontif.," ser. II, col. 1730.
[2] Phil. mor., l. c., n. 7.   [3] Inst. Eth. et Jur. nat., l. c.   [4] De Eccl. et Statu, p. 146.
[5] Questions Religieuses et Sociales, p. 271.

Here are the words of the proposed *schema* on this point: "Non negatur jus potestatis laicæ providendi institutioni in litteris ac scientiis ad suum legitimum finem et ad bonum sociale, ac proinde etiam non negatur eidem potestati laicæ jus ad directionem scholarum, quantum legitimus ille finis postulat."[1]

At times we have heard serious men deny to the State the right to educate under the pretext that the State might abuse that right. This is bad reasoning. The abuse that authority may make of a right cannot destroy the right. You would not deny to the State the right of making laws, of declaring war, because it may make bad laws, or lead the nation into unjust wars. Not only is such reasoning bad, it is very imprudent. It is true that to-day more than ever we must be careful not to attribute to the State rights to which it is not entitled; but neither should we fall into the contrary error and contest the rights to which it is entitled. That would be to deprive the State of powers it may indeed abuse at times, but also might rightly use; it would be to condemn what governments faithful to their mission have done in the past and are doing to-day. The opinion we are criticizing will never prevent civilized nations from having public or governmental schools; but it will furnish the evil-minded a pretext for affirming that the Church is hostile to the prerogatives of the State; it will prevent Catholics, when in power, from using a means that would be in their hands a powerful agent for good.

It has been said that the State cannot teach, because it has no teaching to give. An absolutely false assertion. The State has its own doctrines, and must have them. How otherwise could it make laws? We must, however, admit that the State is not qualified to define and impose religious doctrines. It is from the Church the State must receive such teaching. But the State knows the natural law, at least in its fundamental principles, and is bound to secure the execution thereof; and the State certainly knows the rational sciences on which depend agriculture, industry and the arts.

It is plain that the right of the State in education is not an unlimited right. The State, just as individuals or the family, cannot teach error and vice, *cannot set up schools that are atheistic or agnostic.* Neither is this right an exclusive one, it cannot destroy the rights of individuals and of parents, it supplements these; all these rights co-

---

[1] Schema Constitutionis dogmaticæ De Ecclesiae Christi, patrum examini propositum, c. xv, not. 47.

exist and should be exercised harmoniously. Our conclusion then is this, the State has been endowed by God with the right of founding the schools that contribute to its welfare.

(d). The Right of the Church to Educate.

That the Church has the right to teach results from the words of Our Lord to the Apostles, "*docete omnes gentes.*" The Church is essentially a teaching power. The Church alone has the right to teach Christian doctrines, that is to say, the revealed truths, the guardianship, interpretation and defence of which it has pleased Christ to entrust to her. The words, *docete omnes gentes*, "teach all nations," were not addressed to the heads of nations, but to the Apostles and through them to the Pope and the Bishops in union with the Pope. No earthly power shares this right with the Church, no prince of this world can claim it as being his proper right.—The Church, having thus received *directly* from God the right to teach revealed religion, is thereby *indirectly* endowed with the right to teach the sciences and letters, in so far as they are necessary or useful to the knowledge and practice of revelation. The right to teach religion comprehends the right to communicate whatever may serve religious education. We do not say that the teaching of profane sciences and letters belongs to the church by the same title that the teaching of religion does; much less do we say that such teaching belongs to her exclusively; what we do say is, that the right to spread the revelation entails the right to whatever is profitable to revelation. Now human sciences and letters are destined by God to be handmaidens of faith and of the chief among sciences, theology.—This right is a special right, proper to the Church, direct as to revelation, indirect as to other knowledge.—Moreover, if we consider the Church merely as a human association, we cannot refuse to her the natural right to teach the truths she is adapted and fitted to impart to men. Such right belongs, as we have seen, to associations.

II.

THE MISSION TO EDUCATE.

By the word "mission" we mean not any obligation in general, but a special charge, an office. The right to teach may exist without the duty to teach and especially without the mission to teach; but the duty and *a fortiori* the mission cannot exist without the right. The duty of instructing the ignorant, within a certain measure at least, results from the charity we should have for our neighbor. This duty may be more or less binding. It is ranked among 'the spiritual works of mercy, and for this reason the Church has always and everywhere sought to realize a work so pleasing to God. It is not our purpose to insist on this point, but to inquire what is the mission in regard to education imposed by Divine Providence on parents, the state, and the church.

(a). The Mission to Educate incumbent on Parents.

We need not delay on this point after what we have said on the right of parents; for this right springs mainly from their mission. The end of conjugal society is the procreation and education of children; the mission of parents is to form men for the Church and the State; evidently this formation implies the development of the physical, intellectual and moral faculties. " Let us consider the child," says Taparelli,[1] "at the moment when his reason puts forth its first complete and formal act. Evidently at that moment the child does not know all truth; it scarcely has any clear ideas; for a long while it will need masters to impart to it by their authority the simplest and most necessary notions. As soon as these primal ideas are proposed to it, it sees their fitness, at least, vaguely and confusedly; and if they were not proposed to it, it would remain in ignorance of them for a long time. The intention of nature is that they be proposed to it, for nature has formed intellect for the knowledge of the truth, and society to facilitate and develop such knowledge. And so the parent has the obligation of instructing and the child the obligation of attending to the instruction, until the day when the reason of the youth is matured and he can discover for himself the principles of conduct, the laws of his moral activity. Then only, when the reason of the child is nearly as well developed as that of the father, the child being equally capable of knowing the truth by himself, is he bound to give to his own reason that obedience which formerly he yielded to the reason of the parent." We have cited this passage in its entirety, because, while giving the reason for the parents' mission to educate, it clearly marks the extent and duration of that mission.

[1] Saggio teoretico, n. 1565, 1566.

(b). The Mission to Educate incumbent on the State.

The end of civil society is to secure the material, intellectual and moral perfection of the citizen, that is to say civilization, for true civilization comprises these three things. The purpose of civil authority is: 1°, to maintain peace between citizens, protect their mutual rights, their legitimate activity; 2°, to supply the insufficiency of individuals. Such is the traditional and Christian notion of the State.[1] Such, also, is the notion expressed in the preamble to the Constitution of the United States. "We, the people of the United States, in order to form a more perfect union, establish justice, insure domestic tranquillity, provide for the common defense, promote the general welfare, and secure the blessings of liberty to ourselves and our posterity, do ordain and establish this Constitution."

To this double purpose of civil authority correspond functions of a different order; some essential, exclusively proper to the authority and to be exercised by it constantly; some accidental, belonging to individuals as well, and liable to be exercised or not by the authority according to circumstances. The essential functions correspond to the primary end of the State, the maintenance of peace. Such are, for instance, legislation, courts of justice, infliction of penalties, declarations of war. The accidental functions correspond to the secondary end of the State, supplying the insufficiency of individuals. Such are, for instance, the laying out and repairing of roads, the foundation of hospitals, and the like. Mgr. Cavagnis has made a very clear exposition of this matter in his *Instructiones Juris Publici Ecclesiastici*.[2] He is in perfect accord with Professor Wilson in his estimable work, *The State*, and with Messrs. Westel W. Willoughby and William P. Willoughby in their recent contribution, *Government and Administration of the United States*. We take this extract from them: "Among the many functions of government there are many so obviously necessary to the existence of a nation, however organized, that there is no discussion concerning the expediency of their exercise by the State. We may therefore group governmental duties under two heads: the necessary and the optional, or as Prof. Wilson has named them, the constituant and the ministrant. Under the first head are embraced all those functions which must exist under

---

[1] S. Thomas, *De Reg. Princ.*, I., 15. [2] Cavagnis, op. cit.

every form of government; and under the second title those undertaken, not by way of governing, but by way of advancing the general interests of society."[1]

This being well understood, we affirm without hesitancy that the State has the mission, that is a special duty, of providing education in the letters, sciences and arts. This duty is comprised in the general duty of providing the common good. We have seen above how the diffusion of knowledge promotes the common welfare of society. It will be enough to state here the teaching of Taparelli. This great philosopher thus writes in the work we have quoted more than once: "No one can contest that it is the duty of society to protect the intellect of its members against injustice, fraud, error and ignorance, against all the elements that attack the first principles of human activity. If the individual man is bound to procure for his neighbor the good of truth, in as far as this good of truth is for his neighbor a means to his end, evidently this obligation is more binding on society, destined as it is by the Creator to protect the individual in the attainment of temporal happiness. The existence of this duty is beyond question, the manner, however, of fulfiling it depends on the degree of perfection to which society has risen."[2]

The duty of teaching is not for the State an essential duty, it is accidental. Individuals, families, associations may have provided all the education that is necessary. In that case the State is freed from its obligation. But we must add that in primary education this hypothesis is rarely realized. For, as Cavagnis remarks, it is almost impossible that the zeal of parents and private charity should suffice for the instruction of the poor.[3] We may therefore assert that, generally speaking, the State is bound to take measures for the diffusion of human knowledge. It can accomplish this glorious mission by encouraging private efforts, helping parents, establishing schools, appointing capable teachers. If this duty falls on the State at large, it binds more particularly, as to primary education at least, the local authority of municipal communities, as they represent more immediately the families. Certainly among the local interests for which the

---

[1] Johns Hopkins University Studies in Political and Historical Sciences, Ninth Series, I–II.

[2] *Saggio teoretico*, Diss. 4, c. 4, § 2, n. 903 et seqq.

[3] Op. cit. liv. 4, n. 107, "Ex parte (scholæ privatorum) semper deficient, cum pro pauperibus vix possibile sit adsint universim charitate privatorum constitutæ."

municipality should provide, the education of children holds the first rank.—Finally, to avoid all danger of misconception, we wish to state that for civil society, as for individuals, right goes beyond duty in this matter. Therefore, while saying that the State should provide instruction, where private individuals fail to do so, we do not mean to say that the State may teach only when and where individuals fail to do their duty. The exercise of the duty of the State is allowable whenever the State judges the exercise of this duty to be useful, without being absolutely necessary.

(c). *The Mission to Educate incumbent on the Church.*

The Church has received from her Divine Founder the mission to teach the supernatural truths. Her duty is to make known to man his relations to God, his end, the rules he must follow and the means he must use to attain that end. But the Church has not received the mission to make known the human sciences, she has not been established for the progress of nations in the arts and sciences, no more than to render them powerful and wealthy. Doubtless, in virtue of the general harmony that reigns between all things, the Church, while communicating the science of things heavenly, contributes powerfully to the development of human sciences; just as she contributes to the temporal happiness and strength of nations by inculcating the practice of the supernatural virtues. But this is a *result* not the *object proper* of the mission of the Church. Her duty of teaching human sciences is only indirect, a work of charity or of necessity : of charity, when they are not sufficiently taught by others who have that duty ; of necessity, when they are badly taught, that is, taught in a sense opposed to supernatural truth and morality. This is why the missionary, setting foot in a savage land, though he begins with the preaching of the Gospel, very soon establishes schools. In this case his action is a necessity. For to make Christians you must first have men using their powers of mind. When the Roman Empire was falling into ruin, bishops took in hand the administration and defence of cities.[1] That was a work of necessity, for in order to serve God, men must be able to lead a tranquil life. In these days of religious indifference, in the presence of an

---

[1] Paul Violet, *Histoire des institutions politiques et administratives de la France*, tom. I, p. 380.

education that is indifferent or hostile to religion, bishops found schools, colleges, academies, universities. Clearly this is a case of necessity, regrettable necessity, implying the regret that the State is indifferent to Christianity in the premises.

There are men who seem to assert that the Church has received the mission to teach human as well as divine science. They give to the words of Christ, "*Euntes, docete,*" an indefinite interpretation. But such an interpretation is evidently false. The context indicates the restriction we have placed. What the Apostles are to teach is the doctrine and the morality of Jesus Christ, "*Quæcumque mandavi,*" "whatsoever I have commanded," and this teaching is an object of faith, "*qui crediderit salvus erit,*" "who believeth shall be saved." The interpretation we criticize, is highly imprudent. To assert that the Church has received the direct mission and duty of imparting the human sciences, is to make the Church responsible for the condition of the sciences, letters and arts among Christian nations. Let us not be understood as saying that Catholic nations are inferior to the non-Catholic in true civilization. We assert no such thing. But we do think that Christian apologetics should not be handicapped by useless and dangerous assumptions. In this respect, and also as being replete with profound considerations bearing on the subject matter, we recommend to our readers Cardinal Newman's masterly work, "The Idea of a University," especially discourses I, II, III, IV, VIII, IX and the discourse entitled, "Christianity and Letters."

III.

Authority over Education.

Authority over education, or the control of education, must not to be confounded with the right to teach. The right to educate, being, as we have defined it, a moral faculty to impart to others those things which one is fit to impart licitly and usefully to the end of forming the mind and heart, belongs to whomsoever has the fitness required. Authority over education is the right of watching over, controlling, and directing education. This authority belongs to him or to those who are vested by natural or positive law with the powers required and sufficient in the premises. Now there are three societies intended by God to conduct man to his end: the family, the state, and the church. Each of these societies has its proper authority, the character and extent of which authority are indicated by the nature of the society itself. We are not called upon to explain the character and extent of parental, civil, and religious authority. The matter in hand only demands that we examine their respective powers in the sphere of education.

(a). Parental Authority in Education.

Parents have authority to regulate, direct, and control the education of their children. They may teach their children themselves or get them taught by others; they may choose the masters to whom they confide them, determine the sciences they wish to be imparted to them, the means of correcting them. Other individuals, associations, municipalities, and the State should take account of the wishes of the parents in the organization of schools; for the father can never lose control of the education of his child. Need we add that parental authority is subordinate to another authority which certainly may not annihilate, but may direct it. " There is," says Perin, " between public power and domestic power, a certain equilibrium of authority and liberty, a certain harmony of properties which cannot be disturbed without injury to both. The family cannot claim complete immunity in the presence of the political power. In the interest of social law as well as in the interest of the family, those who live in the bonds of domestic life must respect that law. The father, supreme in the home, is not infallible. Those who are under obedience to him have always the right, as a safeguard to their liberty and the inviolability of their person, to claim from the State that protection which parental authority might fail to give. At times they may need defence against the abuses of that very parental authority which should protect them. It is the right and the duty of the political power to see that the essential order of the family be not disturbed. The more extensive the rights of the political authority the greater may be the danger, arising from the ever increasing complications of social relations, that disorder might find way into the various parts of society, and produce disturbances, and overturn the order that should reign between the different groups of the social whole. Hence, there is a limitation of the parental jurisdiction corresponding to the extension of the political jurisdiction. Certain acts of high jurisdiction, allowed to the father in primitive societies, cannot be allowed him in more advanced societies." [1]

(b). The Authority of the State over Education.

The question here is not of the authority of the State over the teaching of religion and over theological schools. It is clear that the State has no jurisdiction in that sphere.[2] Nor is there question of the authority of the State over schools founded by the State; from our statements concerning the right of the State to educate, it is evident that the State can govern the schools it founds. The question then is about schools of human science founded by individuals, families, associations. Furthermore, we are speaking of the State's authority *in se*. We have no intention of defining when and under what conditions the State may or should put its authority into operation. That is a question of prudence and justice.

Having thus cleared the ground, we affirm that the State has authority over education. This authority is included in that general authority with which the State is invested for promoting the common good, for guaranteeing to each man his rights, for preventing abuses. Education, well-directed or ill-directed, is one of the great means of good or of evil to the social body. It is on the education he receives that the future of the child depends; and the child needs protection all the more that he is weak and at the mercy of others. There is no need that we should insist on this motive, it seems to us self-evident. As a fact, the assertion is not contested to any great extent, at least by serious minds. We have already seen that the pontifical theologians of the Council of the Vatican protest they do not mean to refuse to the State the power of regulating education as regards the temporal welfare. Cardinal Zigliara admits the State's right of overseeing that the intellectual and moral education of its future citizens be maintained within the limits of honesty and truth.[3] A Roman Canonist, in a book written for the use of bishops specially, deplores the fact that the authority of the Church over schools is too often disregarded; but he adds immediately that he does not mean to deny to the State the direction and patronage of the natural sciences nor to diminish the

---

[1] Perin, *Les lois de la Société Chrétienne*, lib. III. c. 2.
[2] Encycl. of Leo XIII. to the Bishops of Prussia.   [3] L. c.

civil jurisdiction in regard to them.[1] We refrain from quoting other authorities, such as Sauvé, Cavagnis, etc. We pass on to the examination of some practical applications of the principle enunciated. The State has the right to prevent the unworthy and the incapable from assuming the role of educators. But has it the power to exact from those who wish to enter into the work of education that they give evidence of worth and capability? We think that the State can not be refused the power of exacting ordinary and reasonable conditions of qualification. Such was in the XVI century, the opinion of the famous Jesuit Mariana. In his well-known work, "*De Rege et Regis Institutione,*" he reminds the reader of the care taken by the Persians, as related in Xenophon, to entrust the education of their children not to slaves, like other nations, but to old men specially chosen and renowned for probity. He then adds: "Quam industriam vellem ex parte principes nostri civitatesque imitarentur, viris eximiis ei curæ ex utroque ordine sacrato et populari præfectis cum potestate de præceptorum moribus, docendique dexteritate (in quo gravissime peccatur multis modis) judicandi publice. Quid enim? Calceos vestesve non conficiat nisi qui artis peritiam ante probarit, filios, sine delectu cuicumque se obtrudenti erudiendos tradamus?" Such also is the opinion to-day of many and notably of the Roman professor we have often cited. And to his reasoning which we quote we really do not see what can be objected. "Illud (sc. normas quasdam præventivas quibus idoneitas docentium verificetur constituere) posse probamus ex jure Status normas quasdam generales præventivas constituendi in iis quæ sunt majoris momenti, cum id valde expediat bono publico, et aliunde non multum gravet privatos, si res intra limites a nobis constitutos retineatur, id est simpliciter idoneitatem verificari, non autem extraordinariam et sæpe inutilem peritiam. Hinc videmus et in aliis pluribus has normas præventivas constitutas esse, ut circa emptiones et venditiones et alia negotia privata, v. g. de justis mensuris et ponderibus."[2] What is the meaning of *Licentia* as known to Canon Law? In the middle ages there was in every diocese an official, named *Scholasticus,* whose special office was to exercise control in the name of the Church over all educational institutions, especially as to the choice of teachers. To these he granted or refused a license to teach. This license became necessary as far back as the XII cen-

---

[1] Lucidi, *De Visitatione Sacrorum Liminum*, Tom. II., c. 7, § 2, a. 4, n. 207.
[2] Cavagnis, op. cit.

tury, and thus was given to education a direction corresponding to the spirit and views of the Church.[1] Now, what the Church may do within the spiritual sphere and in view of the spiritual welfare, that the State may do within the temporal sphere and in view of the temporal good. In fact the older Canonists acknowledge that the right to confer degrees in the human sciences, law, medicine, philosophy, belongs to the sovereign authority of the State.[2] Now what are grades? Not only titles scientific and literary, not only honors, but declarations that the bearer is fit for certain professions and especially for the profession of teaching.

The State has authority to see to it that parents fulfil their duty of educating their children, to compel them, if need be, and to substitute itself to them in the fulfilment of this duty in certain cases. In the use of this authority the State does but lend a hand to the execution of the natural law. It forces the parents to fulfil a duty that binds them most strictly, it protects the child and safeguards his future, it removes from society most serious perils. Here again we quote Mariana: "Sed et eisdem præfectis jus sit, me quidem auctore, inquirendi in civium mores, censorum instar, ac coercendi malo privatim parentes in filiorum institutione negligentes, includendi etiam si opus est rebelles, ingenio præfracto, præsertim qui defunctis parentibus aut domo profugi sine lare familiari incertis sedibus vacantur pueri puellæque, unde scelerum licentia existit, animi depravantur, multorum corpora libidinum tabe contaminantur." As to modern writers on education they seem to us to be almost unanimous on this point. Taparelli teaches that the State has a strict duty to remedy the shameful and unnatural negligence of so many parents, who forgetting the first of their obligations, the education of their children, accustom them to idleness, misery, and crime; that the State has the duty to see to it that every child receives that education to which it is entitled, as soon as bud in him the first germs of reason; that it has the duty, as holding the place of the Sovereign Father from Whom comes paternity, to rouse parents from lethargy, to compel the unnatural father to behave as a true father.[3] Perin is not less positive. "If the father forget, as too often happens in our days, that he owes himself

[1] Bourbon, *La Licence d'enseigner*, in the "Revue des Quest. Hist." Tom. XIX, 1876, p. 518.
[2] Schmalzgrueber, Dec., Lib. V., Tit. 5, n. 19.
[3] *Saggio teoretico*, l. c., n. 919.

to his offspring to the very abnegation of self, if within the family he seeks only a life of selfish ease without any concern as to the obligation imposed on him by God to make of his children true men for the Church and the State: who, in the presence of so grave an evil, will dare deny to the State the power to provide by compulsory education for the future of the rising generation, and for the conservation of the social body?"[1] We will not multiply quotations of a like import. The reader may consult, if he wishes, Sauvé,[2] Cavagnis.[3] We have deeply at heart to remark most emphatically right here, that the above named writers have a reputation for orthodoxy so well established that no vague and wild accusation of liberalism will avail against them.

If the State may coerce parents who neglect the education of their children, so also may it determine a minimum of instruction and make it obligatory. Who admits the former must admit the latter. The consequence seems to us logically necessary and we are surprised that all do not see it. Consider, when are parents called negligent? Evidently, when they do not give their children a minimum of education. If then you grant to the State power over cases of neglect, you at once give it power to define what is the minimum of education, and to exact that minimum by way of prevention and of general precept. A law prescribing a minimum of instruction is nothing else, it seems to us, than the application of a principle of natural law to the given circumstances of this or that country. We are aware that distinguished writers, such as the editors of the Civiltà Cattolica[4] and Costa Rosetti,[5] do not admit this conclusion. We have carefully examined their arguments, they are far from convincing us, they seem to us very faulty. On the one hand they restrict the power of the State to what is strictly necessary for the protection of the State, on the other hand they deny that a certain level of instruction for the people is necessary. We do not undertake at present to refute in detail the considerations advanced by these authors for their views; we beg the reader to examine them for himself, we trust to his judgment without fear. Just one remark. If the State can hinder parents from sending their children to labor above the strength of their

---

[1] *Les Lois de la Société Chrétienne*, tom. I, p. 457.
[2] Op. cit., p. 303. [3] Op. cit., tom. 3, n. 49.
[4] Ser. VI, vol. 2, p. 708; ser. VII, vol. 1, p. 458; ser. VIII, vol. 8, p. 5.
[5] Op. cit., thes. 176.

age, say in the mines, a proposition that no Catholic contests, we do not see why the state cannot force parents to give these same children a minimum of instruction.

At any rate, we are not left without respectable authorities in favor of our opinion. St. Thomas[1] teaches that the legislator may take measures concerning "bonam disciplinam per quam cives informantur ut commune bonum justitiæ et pacis conservent." Jerome de Medicis, one of the best commentators of St. Thomas, in the XVI century, adds to the above sentence, "sicut si princeps condat legem ut adolescentes debeant litteris studere, ut hoc studio cives informentur, ut commune bonum justitiæ et pacis conservent." To our forefathers compulsory education was not a bugbear. In our days, Mgr. Sauvé declares that he dares not refuse to the State the authority to make obligatory so much of elementary education as is strictly necessary or useful.[2] Nor does Cardinal Zigliara dare deny that power to the State.[3] Cardinal Manning acknowledges that the State has the power to punish the father who neglects to send his child to school, and this power is incontestably within the competence of the State.[4] At times we have seen missionaries make obligatory on the faithful not only the elementary religious, but the elementary secular instruction in reading and writing;[5] and yet over such instruction the missionaries have only an indirect authority and control.

We think we have said enough to justify our position. In granting to the State the power of making obligatory a minimum of instruction, we do not grant the power of prescribing a standard arbitrarily set up. This minimum is naturally determined by public opinion, it will comprehend everywhere reading, writing, and the elements of arithmetic, the three Rs. In certain countries and under certain conditions the standard may be higher. "For," as Taparelli[6] very well says, "the words, 'elementary studies, higher sciences,' are terms relative to the condition of each society, to the progress of the sciences that are taught in it, to the century in which it lives. A science which to-day is classed among the 'elementary,' might have

---

[1] 1, 2, ques. 95, a. 3.   [2] Op. c., p. 306.   [3] L. c., 3a. obj.
[4] Pastor. Letter for the Lent of 1872, quoted by P. Pradié, "Traité des Rapports de la Religion and de la Politique," p. 247.
[5] See what is done in the Philippine Islands, "Les Missions Catholiques," Nov. 1880.
[6] Op. cit., n. 917.

been simply marvellous in the middle ages."—While granting to the State the power to force the father to give to the child a minimum of education, we do not grant to the state the power to force the father to send the child to a certain determined school, if the father chooses to give the prescribed minimum at home, or in any school of his choice. Compulsory State schools are not logically included in compulsion of education. In a word, to recognize in the State a power is not to recognize in the State the moral right to abuse the power, however much the possibility of the abuse may be admitted.

If the State may exact on the part of teachers evidences of capability, on the part of the children a minimum of instruction, if it may punish negligent parents, it follows that it may also prescribe the teaching of this or that branch, the knowledge of which, considering the circumstances, is deemed necessary to the majority of the citizens. No more difficulty in the one case than in the other.—Moreover, it is not needed that we should remark that the State has over all schools the authority of inspection as to hygiene and public morality.

The powers we believe necessary to admit in the State, have for their object the protection of the weak and the prevention of abuses. The exercise of such powers is the more necessary the less advanced in civilization the country is, and the less capable are the citizens of knowing their true interests and of securing them unaided. It may well be that a country might arrive to such a social perfection, that abstention in this matter by the civil authority will be preferable to its intervention. Even in that lower social condition that may require the intervention of the State, the intervention may be more useful if it come under the guise of persuasion rather than of coaction. And this remark applies especially to compulsory education. However, these are questions of governmental prudence, not of right, strict, pure and proper.

(d.) *Authority of the Church in Education.*

It is not question here of the authority of the Church over schools founded by her, but the question is of the authority of the Church over teaching given by individuals, the family, associations, and the State.—The Church has a direct authority over the teaching of the Faith and Christian law, or over the religious and moral education of Catholic youths. Hers it is to regulate, direct, and control the religious education. This authority is evidently comprehended in her general mission.—As to the teaching of letters, sciences, arts, the Church has only an indirect authority over that, she can busy herself with it only in its relations to religion and morality.—Schools, colleges, and other like institutions, are subject to the ecclesiastical authority, not only in religious teaching, but also in secular teaching, with this notable difference, however; that religious teaching comes directly and exclusively under her control, whereas secular teaching, which directly is under the control of the civil or domestic authority, depends on the Church only indirectly in the name of faith and morals. This comes to saying that the Church has the right to see to it that any teaching whatsoever do not injure faith, morals, the salvation of men, things of which she has the guardianship. This is the doctrine as laid down the proposed Vatican *Schema* already quoted. "Non asseritur potestati ecclesiasticæ, velut ex divina constitutione consequens auctoritas ad positivam directionem scholarum quatenus in iis litteræ et scientiæ naturales traduntur; sed vindicatur ecclesiæ auctoritas ad directionem scholarum, quantum ipse finis Ecclesiæ postulat; adeoque asseritur jus et officium prospiciendi fidei et christianis moribus juventutis *catholicæ*, hocque ipso cavendi ne pretiosa haec bona per ipsam institutionem in scholis corrumpantur. Hoc jus Ecclesiæ in se spectatum non minus ad superiores quam ad inferiores scholas extenditur. . . . Cæterum per se clarum est exercitium hujus juris in applicatione ad diversos terminos necessario debere esse diversum." It is the denial of this authority of the Church which is condemned in the 45th and 47th propositions of the Syllabus.

In the course of ages the Church has exercised this authority more or less extensively according to circumstances. She has exacted from teachers certain guarantees of religion and piety; in this sense she has demanded a profession of faith from whomever would teach.[1] She has also demanded guarantees of fitness in exacting the licentia docendi already spoken of. She has reminded parents of their strict duty of giving to their children sufficient instruction. She has at times taken severe measures in regard to unworthy parents. In a word she has employed in view of the spiritual end means analogous to those used by the State in view of the secular end of mankind.

[1] "Neque magistro cuiquam docendi potestas fieri quin prius fidei professionem in manus ordinarii sui emittat, quæ quotannis erit renovanda, ut sacri canones præscribunt." Letter of Clement XIV, to the King of Poland, 18th Dec., 1773.

IV.

Liberty of Education.

The word "liberty" has many meanings, and is open to misunderstandings. It means either the absence of internal determining necessity, free will, or the absence of obligation, moral liberty, or the absence of coaction, civil liberty, or the absence in general of hindrances to the regular evolution of man's powers. Evidently, by liberty of education is meant moral liberty, civil liberty, and that more general liberty that often goes under the name of Christian liberty.[1] After all that has been said on the right, mission, and authority of education, we may be brief in this question of liberty. Though the concept of liberty is not the same as the concept of right, the former meaning a permission to act or the absence of obligation, the latter an inviolable faculty to act; nevertheless, right and liberty almost always merge into one another. It must not be forgotten that the exercise of authority necessarily limits liberty when it is bad and secures it when it is good. From the principles we have laid down it is easy to deduce what is and should be reasonable liberty in education.

It is at once clear that the moral liberty of teaching is restricted. Teaching, like any human act, is subject to divine law. No one is at liberty to teach evil, error, or inopportune truth, for inopportune truth is truth accidentally injurious.—It is clear that civil liberty in education is also more or less restricted. The state has for mission to hinder, as far as it can prudently, any evil coming from physical liberty, and to secure liberty in that which is good. The State, therefore, cannot allow an education that is corrupting.—But the State cannot prevent and hinder all evil, cannot secure all good, its action is limited. Hence the State may, and at times should, tolerate a teaching that is bad, reproved by divine law; it may permit such a teaching positively from a legal stand-point. Indeed by such permission the State does not grant the right to teach evil, but it does grant legal impunity, which impunity, as Suarez remarks, contains a moral

---

[1] It is of this liberty that Leo XIII speaks in the Encyclical "Libertas." Igitur in hominum societate libertas veri nominis non est in eo posita ut agas quodlibet, ex quo vel maxima existeret turba et confusio in oppressionem civitatis evasura, sed in hoc ut per leges civiles expeditius possis secundum legis æternæ præscripta vivere.

right of some importance, the moral right to be hindered by no one, individuals or agents of the State. If we are asked how civil law can give a moral right to impunity when it cannot give a moral right to a bad act, we answer thus. The right to evil can never be a moral right, no one can ever get the right to commit a crime, no law can ever recognize such a right. But when the civil authority finds itself in the necessity of permitting legally vicious acts, it may grant to its subjects the right to be legally undisturbed, if they do in fact commit such vicious acts. This is a real right founded in reason itself, which advises and commands a legislator to allow his subjects to perform certain acts with impunity, in order that greater evils may be avoided or greater good procured. In a word, you have only to apply to education those general principles by which are solved the questions of liberty of worship, liberty of associations, and that larger question, tolerance of social evil. We conclude that the civil liberty of teaching may reach greater extension than moral liberty would allow.

And now were we to define in what consists true liberty of education, that liberty which is the honor of a people, worthy and capable of self-government, we should say that it consists in the absence of all useless obstacles to the communication of truth on the part of individuals, families, associations, of all those in a word, who are fit to teach. This liberty, thanks be to God, exists in the United States, nowhere so wide and sacred.

Education : to whom does it belong, is the question with which we started out. We now make answer. It belongs to the individual physical or moral, to the family, to the state, to the church ; to none of these solely and exclusively, but to all four combined in harmonious working for the reason that man is not an isolated but a social being. Precisely in the harmonious combination of these four factors in education is the difficuity of practical application. Practical application is the work of the men whom God has placed at the head of the Church and the State, not ours.

APPENDIX.

A REJOINDER.

My pamphlet on Education has provoked adverse criticism. Critics, notably Rev. R. I. Holaind, S. J.,[1] have seen in it what I did not say, and have not seen in it what I did say. I feel called on to offer some explanations that, I trust, will put the truth in clearer light, end misunderstandings and dissipate prejudices.

I.

OBJECT AND PURPOSE OF THE PAMPHLET.

I. The special object I had in view is indicated in the title, explained more fully on the first page, summarily and emphatically asserted in the concluding sentences of the last page. I wished to show that education belongs to men taken individually and collectively in legitimate association, to the family, to the State, to the Church, to all four together, and not to any one of these four factors separately. In other words, education is one of those mixed matters in which many powers concur, and which is to be regulated amicably by the parties interested. Leo XIII speaks of this amicable concordance in mixed matters when he says in the encycl. *Immortale Dei:* "Nature's law first of all, then God's law prescribes that in mixed matters there should be between the powers interested not divorce, much less contention, but full accord.[2]"

---

[1] *The Parent First: An Answer to Dr. Bouquillon's Query, Education: To Whom Does it Belong?* By R. I. Holaind, S. J. Benziger Bros.

[2] "In negotiis mixti juris maxime esse secundum naturam itemque secundum Dei consilia non secessionem unius partis ab altera, multo minus contentionem, sed plane concordiam." Again in the Encycl. *Nobilissima Gallorum gens:* "Verum quoties quidquam constitui de eo genere oportet, de quo utramque potestatem, diversis quidem causis diversoque modo, sed tamen utramque constituere rectum sit, necessaria est et utilitati publicæ consentanea utriusque concordia; qua sublata omnino consecutura est anceps quædam mutabilisque conditio, quacum nec Ecclesiæ nec civitatis potest tranquillitas consistere."

The object of the pamphlet was not the *religious organization* of the school. That question has been so clearly determined by the Holy See, so fully explained by our national and provincial councils, so learnedly and eloquently expounded by many of our bishops, that I thought it useless to go over a settled point and prove once more that the system of so-called neutral schools may not be accepted by Catholics. How came I to be misunderstood on this point, since I have been sufficiently categorical, it seems to me, and have frequently stated throughout the pamphlet, (p. 15) italicising the statement, that the State may not found schools prejudicial to religion?

Neither was it my purpose to speak *ex professo* and at length of the obligation of parents to entrust their children to worthy masters and support good schools. Such obligation is of the domain of practical morals, and has been so often defined by competent authority that I might be dispensed from passing my opinion on it. And notwithstanding, have I not expressed my conviction on this very point most unmistakably, since more than once I have asserted in the pamphlet (pp. 10, 20) that parents have not the right to give to their children an education detrimental to faith and morals, that in the presence of a system of education indifferent to religion the Church has the duty of establishing Christian schools?[1] By the way, I would remark that the obligation of parents and the duty of the Church in this regard depend not on the solution given to the question of *Right*, viz : May the State, and in what measure, busy itself with the teaching of profane sciences, but rather on the solution given to the question of *Fact*, viz : Are the schools of the State good or bad. Suppose that the State had no right whatever to teach and yet opened its school ; parents could certainly avail themselves of the school, provided it were of the right sort. Grant the State, on the contrary, an unconditional right to teach ; then, evidently, its schools, if they are of the wrong kind, can be of no use to parents. Hence, it is clear that the questions with which we have dealt are important when viewed from the standpoint of political action ; but viewed in their bearing on the duty of the Christian parent in educating his children, they have not that same importance.

---

[1] It must have been in a fit of distraction that a certain Catholic journal quoted against me a passage of the Encyclical *Sapientia*, where the Holy Father insists on the obligation of parents in regard to the Christian education of their children.

II. Such was the special object of the pamphlet, and now my reasons for taking that special view of the matter are the following. I wished to throw light on a point that I and others better informed than myself thought to be involved in confusion and darkness in many minds. The lack of a full perception and grasp of the principles that underlie education is the cause that in journalistic polemics imputations of liberalism and even heresy are too easily cast on adversaries, even Catholic adversaries.[1] Hence, political action may get based on ground that is not solid, and be forced to a platform from which there is little chance of gaining our cause before the public opinion of the country. Is there not some utility in showing our non-Catholic fellow citizens that the doctrine of the Church is not opposed either to a reasonable liberty or to the just prerogatives of the State in the matter of education, just as in all other questions where the two powers come in contact?

A thorough understanding of principles is the basis of a sound policy, is the one means to prevent those politico-religious conflicts so dreaded by the Holy See, because so difficult to allay. Let it be kept in mind that in order to oppose a State law, to prevent its promulgation or to obtain its repeal, there is no need of claiming that every enactment in such matters goes beyond the limit of State authority; it suffices—and this course is often the fairest and wisest—to insist on the fact that the State, in passing and upholding such a law, has abused its right. The whole world has given praise to the political sagacity of the German Centre. On the school question that party found itself in the presence of most tyrannical measures adopted by the government. It had to vindicate the essential rights of the Church; the exclusive right of educating the young clergy; the right of inspecting and guarding the religious instruction of all her children. The Centre did not fail to do its duty and gained more or less success. But while resisting the unjust claims of the State, the Catholic party was careful not to compromise its cause by denying

---

[1] The *American Ecclesiastical Review*, Jan., 1892, p. 74, asserts that nobody "among those who have studied the subject" would object to my conclusion. I thought so too, still I am glad to have it said by others. But the *Review* will admit that among the Catholic leaders of public opinion there are at least some who have not studied the subject. The objections made, prove it beyond any doubt. It is for such that I wrote my pamphlet.

the real and true rights of the State, and notably it has recognized that the State can have its own schools and can make education obligatory for all children. Quite lately, on the last Sunday of October, 1891, an electoral meeting was held in Treves, at which were present many members of the Centre, and among them one well known in America, Herr Lieber. At that meeting, the deputy Koehler explained the platform of the Catholic party on the school-question. He laid down that there were four factors in education: the State, the Church, the municipality, the family. He proclaimed that the Church cannot give up her indefeasible right of teaching herself her own doctrines, but at the same time he proclaimed *that no one dreams of denying to the State its rights of inspection;* he admitted that the State may make education compulsory; what he does not admit is that the State may so far usurp the rights of the father as to compel him to send his child to a school determined by the State.[1]

Such has been my purpose. Now, shall I protest against certain intentions imputed to me? If Father Holaind had known me better, or if he had taken pains to inform himself, as he might very easily have done, as to the origin of the pamphlet, he would have been convinced, I am sure, that I never had the ridiculous pretension of influencing an assembly of Archbishops; and I fear that the breathless haste with which he rushed into print himself to save them from some fatal mistake will not be fully appreciated by them. But I do pretend and declare that my work was not done hastily. The doctrine exposed in the pamphlet has been taught by me more than once, and is substantially contained in the treatise *De Legibus* of my *Theologia Fundamentalis*, printed as early as 1887.[2] I may add that the English version of the pamphlet had been made almost a year ago.

[1] *Courrier de Bruxelles*, 16 November, 1891: Une assemblée des Catholiques de la Prusse Rhénane.

[2] *Theologia Moralis Fundamentalis*. Ratisbonæ, Neo-Eboraci et Cincinnati. Fred. Pustet, 1890. The theological reviews of Germany, England, Ireland, Belgium, France, Italy have given this work a reception so favorable that I cannot bring myself to repeat their appreciations. I may, however, be permitted to refer to the *Civiltà Cattolica* of August 5, 1891, those who should be tempted to suspect my orthodoxy.

II.

Authorities and Quotations.

I. A question, such as the one treated in the pamphlet, demands for proper treatment that we should have constantly before our eyes the true notions of family and nation, of paternal power and political power, of Church and State. On these grave and fundamental matters I hold to the doctrine of S. Thomas, Suarez and Leo XIII. Cardinal Newman has taught us that in an *Apologia* for one's teaching as for one's life egoism is truest humility. Accordingly I make bold to say that I am by no means ignorant of the instructions of the present Pope; for not only have I read attentively and used in my teaching the acts of Leo XIII as they successively appeared, but I have edited them with accompanying analytical notes and made a complete index of all the questions they touch on.[1]

II. In the exposition of the subject I have made use of various contemporary publicists of different schools and countries. Thinking that serious readers would like to know the sources from which I drew, the works which I consulted, I gave a brief *literature* of the question, not indeed to make a show of erudition, but to make easy to students the verification of my assertions and the deeper study of points which I merely hinted at. To be sure, I did not name only the authors favorable to my views; such a proceeding would be unworthy the sincerity of a true scientist. I have indicated impartially the writers who, in my opinion, have treated the question with talent and science, be they with me or against me. Strange that Father Holaind did not see this, and tried to throw discredit on my quotations by insinuating (p. 4) that some of the publicists named in the bibliography prefixed to my thesis were against me on this or the other point of detail. Evidently the authors invoked in my favor are those indicated in the text itself or in the foot notes. I have gone over all such citations once more, and I challenge Father Holaind and those who have made like insinuations to prove, text in hand, that the authors cited by me as favorable to me do not say what I make them say.

---

[1] *Sanctissimi Domini Nostri Leonis Papæ XIII, Allocutiones, Epistolæ, Constitutiones aliaque Acta præcipua.* Vol. I, 1878–1882; vol. II, 1883–1887. Typis Societatis Sancti Augustini. Desclée, De Brouwer et Soc., Brugis et Insulis, 1887.

III. Frequent use has been made of Mgr. Cavagnis, not only because of the intrinsic worth of his writings, but also because of his special position. He is a member of the Sacred Congregation of extraordinary ecclesiastical affairs and Professor in the Pontifical Seminary of the Apollinare. May we not repeat in America what is taught in the seminary of the Pope himself and is published in Rome?

IV. I have placed great reliance on the *Schema de Ecclesia*. Doubtless, and I have remarked it in the pamphlet, it is not an official document; but no one will deny that its authority is superior to that of any individual writer; it is the work of a commission of theologians named to prepare matters for the Council. That commission was made up of men learned, known for their orthodoxy, devoted to the Church and the Holy See, chosen from all the Catholic nations. I will name Archbishop Cardoni; Mgr. Monaco Lavaletta, since Cardinal; Professor Pecci, since Cardinal; Franz Hettinger; the Jesuits, Perrone, Franzelin, since Cardinal, Schrader; the Dominicans, Ferrari and Spada; Dr. Corcoran, Mgr. Schwetz, Mgr. Gay. The *schema*, the fruit of the knowledge and labors of such men, was approved by a directing congregation and judged worthy of being laid before the Council as the basis of the Conciliar discussions on the subject.[1] I beg my opponents to remember all this, and then to read attentively chapter XV and note 47, in which the chapter is commented. They will find in it, I trust, nothing heterodox or imprudent. After that, let them read my pamphlet and show in what my doctrine differs from that of the *schema*.

III.

GENERAL OBSERVATIONS.

I. In the wake of many publicists, I distinguished four points in regard to education and laid them down in this order: Right, Duty, Authority, Liberty. Father Holaind (p. 6, l. 18) thinks I should have begun with Duty, seeing, says he, that Right springs from Duty. The stricture is not well founded. Doubtless the imposition of a duty implies the right to fulfil such duty; but it is not true that every right comes from an obligation. For instance, I may have the right to embrace a religious life, to work, to give alms, and yet not be obli-

---

[1] Cecconi, *Storia del Con. Vat.*, lib. II, c. 2, p. 305 and docum. 61.

gated to do those acts. If Father Holaind is correct, what becomes of my right to follow the evangelical counsels? I hold, then, that in education, as in other acts morally honest, Right goes beyond Duty, and that the order I laid down is logical—the only one logical. Father Holaind (p. 6, l. 20; p. 13, l. 26) finds fault with the phrase, "Mission to teach." Let me say, that if I have given to the word "Mission" a meaning not usual in ordinary English, I took good care to define the term, and to state precisely what meaning I gave the word (p. 16). No calm reader could have mistaken me.

A critic of the *American Ecclesiastical Review* attaches a peculiar meaning to my classification of the factors in education, intimating that I set the State over the Church. "He unconsciously selects them (principles) and disposes them in a way which gives us a comparatively clear sight of how he would have us apply them. There is a noticeable tendency to say 'the State and the Church,' rather than 'the Church and the State,' even in places where the logic of the subject would demand the latter position."[1] Against this accusation I appeal to the sense of fairness of my Rev. Critic. If in my former writings I had given proof of any preference in favor of the State, then might he find a meaning in the disposition of the words "State and Church." But it is not the first time that I treat of those subjects before the public. I did it in 1877, in my work, *De virtutibus theologicis* (chapter *de fidei defensione*), again, in 1880, in the first volume of my work, *De virtute religionis* (chapter *de juramento*); and recently in my *Theologia Moralis Fundamentalis*. I had reason to think that the critic of the *American Ecclesiastical Review* would be better acquainted with the principles exposed in this last work.[2] I beg to refer him to the chapters on Church, State and Family, on law, ecclesiastical and civil; on parental authority, and he will see if he can justly accuse me of tendency to stateworship! And even had I made use of a less correct expression, he should have remembered the words of S. Ambrose, *Epist.*, 40: "Verbum si offenderit, virtutem professionis interrogato. . . . Etiam sermonem dubium mens non dubia obumbrat et defendit a lapsu." I do not say this by way of apology, far from it! Had my critic read the pamphlet without prejudice, he would have noticed that in my enumeration and in all the arrangement of my essay, I meant to

---

[1] *American Ecclesiastical Review*, Jan., 1892.
[2] See *American Ecclesiastical Review*, vol. III, p. 48.

proceed by way of gradation, from the lower to the higher, putting first the individual, and then the Family, the State, and the Church: it is in this order that the three societies, necessary and established by God for the complete good of man, are superposed one over the other; and that is all that I wanted to insinuate.[1] Moreover, such an ontological order was imposed upon me by the laws of Logic, for what I had to say of individuals and of associations, became applicable when I had to treat of the Family, of the State and of the Church. I, therefore, affirm that it is not "unconsciously," but on the contrary very consciously that, when enumerating the parties concerned, I put the State before the Church, and that, in the disposition of the parts of my essay, I spoke of the right, mission and authority of the State before speaking of the right, mission and authority of the Church. Would my critic cast a suspicion on Suarez for having treated of civil laws before treating of ecclesiastical laws? Outside of this no one can find in my pamphlet anything like a determination as to the order of the words State and Church. For instance (p. 8, l. 31–32), I write "civil and religious authority," but p. 10, l. 32, I put "authority, religious and civil." Let me add that the so-called *procès de tendance* are everywhere odious, and contentions merely about words, ridiculous. In olden times such things flourished in Byzantium; I did not expect to find them to-day in the free and fair land of America!

II. The general notion of Right determined, its various kinds indicated, I went on to state (p. 7), that a natural right may be regulated, modified, even suspended, by competent authority. This pleases Father Holaind little (p. 8). "'Tis a subtle problem," quoth he, "abstract theory." I beg to differ. The question is elementary; any one may see the point from a few illustrations. Every man has the natural right to be a proprietor; but the Church has made (*jure communi*) a religious incapable of possessing by virtue of his solemn vow of poverty. Every man has the right to dispose of what is his own; but the State restrains, nay, suspends this right in the case of

---

[1] *Cf.* T. Meyer, S. J., *Inst. Jour. Nat*, tom. I, n. 392: "Tres numerantur societates intrinsecè completæ, societas domestica, civilis, religiosa (see here the State before the Church!), quippe quæ singulæ bonum sociale simpliciter humanum seu cunctis hominibus quâ talibus commune aliquomodo ut finem prosequuntur; eædem tamen simul ratione finis specie inter se differunt, et similiter diversis socialibus mediis utuntur."

minors and married women. Every man has the natural right to work; but this right is regulated and restrained in women, children, and even adult men as far as the hours of work are concerned. Furthermore, the question is not mere theory.[1] Whence comes it that so many writers hold that the State could not, without injustice, limit the hours of labor, man having the natural right, argue they, to use his forces as he pleases to his own advantage? They do not understand this principle which Father Holaind calls "abstract theory," and which may be termed: modification of natural rights by competent authority. Hence, the one who wants to "grapple with the difficulties which beset the live issues of the hour," and especially the question of education, must keep that principle before his mind.

III. A capital objection against me is, that in my treatment of education I make no distinction between the State Christian and the State non-Christian (Father Holaind, p. 5). Most assuredly I make none, and no more do I make any between the family Christian and the family non-Christian, the individual Christian and the individual non-Christian. I repeat, I make no such distinction, and this is why:

(a) Civil society and its inherent authority are in the natural order; the Church and its inherent authority are in the supernatural order.

(b) Civil society and authority retain in a Christian people the character they derive from the natural order, they remain substantially what they were under the gentile dispensation, what they might have been in *statu naturæ puræ*. Such is the commonly received doctrine of theologians, proved by Suarez in his treatise, *De Legibus*, lib. III, c. 10, and especially c. 11, where he answers the question: "Utrum finis potestatis et legis civilis, prout nunc est in Ecclesia, sit alius a fine ejusdem potestatis et legis, ut in natura pura, vel in gentibus spectari potest."

(c) Civil authority is co-extensive with the end of civil society as ecclesiastical authority is co-extensive with the end of religious society. Whatever is *sacred* by any title whatsoever falls under the religious authority, whatever is *profane*[2] falls under the political society. This

---

[1] See in the acts of the Catholic social Congress of Liege, 1890, the paper of Comte de Kuefstein: *Réglementation de la durée du travail;* also *Civilta Cattolica*, 14ª. Ser., vol. 2, p. 37, and G. Howell, *Conflicts of Capital and Labour*.

[2] The word "profane" is here used in the strict not the common sense, in the sense marked 1 at the word "profane" in Webster, 1884.

is the doctrine of Leo XIII in the encycl. *Immortale Dei:* "Quidquid est in rebus humanis quoquo modo sacrum, id est omne in potestate arbitrioque Ecclesiæ; cætera vero, quæ civile et politicum genus complectitur, rectum est civili auctoritati esse subjecta." Therefore the domain of the State comprehends all that of its nature is not sacred, all that is profane in the intellectual and moral as well as in the material region. Thus S. Thomas, 1-2, q. 96, a. 3, and Suarez, *De Leg.*, lib. 3, c. 12, admit that the civil legislator may prescribe acts not only of justice but of all the other moral virtues.

(*d*) Hence the sovereign political power, the State, is everywhere the same; save the restrictions that written constitutions agreed to by men may impose, everywhere substantially the same, in infidel and protestant as in catholic nations. See here the very words of Suarez, *l. c.*, n. 9: " Potestas hæc ut nunc est in principibus christianis, in se non est major nec alterius naturæ quam fuerit in principibus ethnicis." It extends to and is limited by what is *profane;* it is competent in the domain of the *sacred,* only by concession or delegation. This principle is at the bottom of those agreements between States and the Church, known as Concordats.

(*e*) Therefore the difference between the State non-Christian, the State Christian non-Catholic, and the State Catholic, consists not in the rights and attributes inherent in the State, but in the manner of exercise of those rights and attributes. The State non-Christian in the execution of its rights follows the natural law, has no eye to the Gospel; the State Christian non-Catholic follows the natural law and the Gospel, has no eye to the discipline of the Church; the State Catholic follows the natural, the divine, the canonical laws.[1] All this is fully explained by Leo XIII in the Encyclical *Libertas.*[1] In a word the Christian and Catholic State lives in union with the Church, the non-Christian and non-Catholic State in separation from the Church. However, to prevent exaggerations in this matter, I will add the observation of Suarez, *De leg.*, lib. III, c. 12, n. 11, that the acceptation by the State of the divine law, the union of State and Church, has two aspects, negative and positive. The negative is the obligation on the part of the State to make no enactments contrary to spiritual interests. The positive, which is often of counsel only, is the active concurrence of the State with the Church in procuring

---

[1] The reader will find a commentary on this encyclical in my *Theologia Fundamentalis*, pp. 455-465.

and furthering spiritual interests.[1] The theologians of the Vatican Council have made this doctrine their own. It comes simply to saying that in public as in private life, temporal interests should not be furthered at the expense and sacrifice of spiritual interests.[2]

(*f*) Moreover I call attention to this consideration, that between a non-Christian and a thoroughly Christian State there is an indefinite series of degrees and shades; that a State may be regarded as Christian in one point and non-Christian in another. For proof of this, witness the condition of various European States to-day. As to this country, it may be said truly that it is Christian *in a certain sense*, that less than any country on earth does it hinder by enactments spiritual interests, that Christianity is an essential part of its laws. Many eminent judges have so affirmed in the verdicts of their courts. After Kent, the great Webster has held this view with energetic eloquence in one of his most famous speeches. This is not the place to give complete treatment to the question; I must refer the reader for further study to writers who have treated it *ex professo*, pointing out to him especially the remarkable and impartial work of a French publicist, *La République Américaine*, par Aug. Carlier, vol. III, p. 470.

(*g*) Let it be remembered, moreover, that it may be very difficult to legislate on certain mixed matters pertaining at once to Church and State, and notably on education in a nation where many religious beliefs prevail. Of this no one doubts. Now such a condition of things, I mean multiplicity of beliefs and its consequences, may incline the State to waive the use of its rights in education, but it can never put those rights out of existence.

---

[1] "Est observandum hanc relationem (potestatis et legislationis civilis ad bonum spirituale) posse dupliciter fieri: primo per positivam ordinationem, et sic regulariter erit in consilio, nisi ubi speciale præceptum vel necessitas ad illam obligaverint. . . . Secundo intelligi potest per negationem tantum, seu per circumspectionem nihil statuendi per hanc potestatem, quod sit contrarium fini supernaturali, vel ejus consecutionem impedire possit, quæ prudens cautio ex fide procedit, estque non tantum in consilio sed etiam in præcepto maxime proprio Christiani et Catholici principis."

[2] "Sicut in negotiis privatis ita transeundum est per bona temporalia ut non amittantur æterna; pari modo etiam in rebus et negotiis publicis felicitatem temporalem, quam societas civilis societatisque administratio per se et directe tanquam finem propositum habet, non ita quærere fas est, ut finis hominis ultimus ab oculis dimittatur." *Schema de Ecclesia*, not. 45.

In conclusion I ask, why in the matter of education certain writers clamor so loudly for a distinction between the Christian and the non-Christian State, whereas they have no word to say about the same distinction equally to the point, I should judge, between the Christian and the non-Christian family and parent. I said equally to the point; I should say, much more to the point, for the relations of the natural and supernatural are closer in the family than in the State, for the simple reason that marriage is a Sacrament.

I do not make nor admit the distinction between State and State my critics demand of me, because (1) it is unfounded, (2) it implies that the government of the United States is not Christian, an assumption I regard as untrue in its full extent. Are my critics conscious of the unenviable position to which they are driven by denying that the State has the right to educate?

IV. I am blamed for confusing *Teaching* with *Education*, and urging in favor of the right to educate arguments that avail only for the right to teach. The answer is easy and very clear.

The words Teaching, Education, may be used in a strict or in a loose sense. In the strict sense, education is the formation of the heart, the will, the interior dispositions of the soul; it is the imparting of virtuous habits. Teaching in the strict sense is the formation of the mind, the communication of truth. In a loose sense education and teaching equally mean the complete formation of man in general, or of man in any special avocation, of the Christian, the priest, the soldier, and the like. But it is ordinarily in regard to the special work done in schools that the terms *teaching* and *education* are used; and in reference to this they are commonly employed almost indiscriminately. The reason of this is not hard to find. For it is well to remark that there are three sorts of schools. First come boarding-schools, colleges and academies: in these the teacher is almost a *substitute* for the parents, in regard to the physical well-being of the pupils, their moral and religious training and their instruction. In another class of schools, more special in character, and devoted to such particular branches, as geography, history, music, drawing, etc., the teacher merely coöperates with the parent in a certain limited sphere, while the responsibility of the child's education rests wholly with the parent. Finally, there is the ordinary sort of school, where the child spends five or six hours each day. In this case, especially as regards children of the lower class, the teacher takes the parents' place as instructor and coöperates with them as educator. And though in these schools more time is allotted to instruction as such than to education as such, yet the work of education is of greater importance, because morality takes precedence of knowledge. This explains the indiscriminate use of the words *instruction* and *education* when people get to talking about schools; it shows too how reasons that apply directly to instruction and only indirectly to education, or *vice versa*, are brought forward without the least regard for this distinction. This I have not hesitated to do, where my context was so clear that misunderstanding of my meaning seemed impossible. Having carefully shown that the religious side of education is not within the province of the State, I proved that the State has a right to found schools, " to provide education in the letters, sciences, and arts," to inculcate the moral principles of the natural law,—in a word, to provide and to exercise authority over all that part of education which concerns the temporal welfare of human society. My meaning being thus perfectly clear from the entire context, the reader may judge, first, whether it is correct to say that the right of the State extends only to instruction and has nothing to do with education; and, secondly, whether it is just to force upon my words a meaning foreign to their obvious sense and then boast of having refuted what I evidently never meant to say. All this will be made clearer as we go on.

IV.

THE RIGHT OF INDIVIDUALS AND ASSOCIATIONS.

I. With Suarez I have asserted (pp. 7, 8) that every individual has from nature the right to teach, being careful at the same time to add that this right is not unlimited but limited to the true and the good, not absolute but subject to competent authority, not unconditional but conditioned by capacity and worth on the part of the would-be teacher.

As proof of this assertion, I adduced the very purpose of teaching which is to develop the intellect by the communication of truth, and I argued that, since every man has the right to communicate truth and to speak, so has he the right to teach. It is Taparelli's argument (*Saggio teoretico*, diss. VII, not. 140).

I am met with the plea that the argument may be admitted for teaching, but not for educating in the strict sense of the term (F. Holaind, p. 6).—I answer: there is no essential difference between the formation of the mind and that of the heart, if the point under consideration be the right to effect that formation. But let us exchange words and see what kind of argument we get. What is education? The formation of character, the inculcation of virtue, the correction of faults and defects. But every man has the right to inculcate virtue on his neighbor, to correct his neighbor's faults. Among the works of spiritual mercy, we find not only the teaching of the ignorant, but also the correction of sinners, and if you should want to know what that implies, I refer you to Valentia, 2–2, disp. 3, quaest. 10. Correction is "qualiscunque sermo quo quis vel monendo, vel reprehendendo, vel hortando, vel rogando, vel quippiam indicando, vel alia hujusmodi ratione nitatur proximum a peccato revocare et ad officium virtutemque traducere?" Is education anything else? Therefore every individual has the right to educate.

But we have not yet done with this objection and the fallacy that lurks in it. The individual man, say my critics, has not the right to teach, much less to educate, because teaching, and especially education, suppose a certain jurisdiction (F. Holaind, p. 7).—This argument reveals a sad confusion about *right* and the *exercise of a right*. I have the right to practice medicine, but I may not and can not be a physician except to those who will put themselves under my care. Just so I have the right to teach and to educate, but I can exercise the right only on those who have the goodness to take me as master. If the client I solicit is *sui juris*, his consent suffices to give effect to my right: thus the founder of a religious community gets his right made practical, the right, namely, to give a religious education to those who associate with him, by their consent. If my would-be client is a child, I must needs get the consent of his parents. Is my position plain? Must I say in so many words, that when I assert for every individual the right to teach, I do not assert the right to take pupils by the collar and teach them willy nilly? My right to teach does not imply a right to force myself on others, but does imply an obligation on the part of others not to hinder my giving education to those who are willing to accept my services as a teacher. So elementary is the distinction I have just drawn out that I had thought it enough when writing the pamphlet to hint it, trusting the keenness of my readers to see the point at a glance. I did hint it when I wrote on page 8: "Every individual has the right of teaching what he is capable of teaching *to whomsoever will accept his teaching,*" and when (p. 22) I added, treating of parents in education, *that parents have the right to choose the masters of their children.*

II. On the authority of Leo XIII I affirmed (p. 8), that the right of association is a right which men hold from nature. In whatsoever things they act individually, in those same they may act collectively. If Peter, Paul, and John can do business individually, why can they not combine their resources and energies for a more extensive and successful method of doing business? If Peter, Paul, and John can pursue and cultivate knowledge individually, can they not unite their efforts and studies for a more extensive and useful cultivation of the sciences? It seems to me a truism, an elementary axiom of the first evidence. Applying this to education, I have argued that if twenty isolated individuals have the right to teach, they have the same right when united collectively. Now many individuals, putting their talents and efforts into a common fund for the pursuit of a common end, make up what is called a *society*, an *association*, a *corporation*. The logical consequence is that such an association has the right to teach just as well as individuals and under the same conditions.—There is nothing new in this process of reasoning; on the contrary it has been made use of by all the defenders of religious congregations to prove their right to existence, to their special mission, whatever it may be, to the possession of the means, financial and otherwise, necessary to these objects.[1] I wonder that Father Holaind does not see this truth. Yet the denial of this elementary principle is in his pamphlet. Finding my list of factors concurring in education too long, he scratches "associations" from it (pp. 7, 21).

III. I need not tarry to refute certain flashy, flimsy objections made by journalists, guided more by passion than by reason. However, there is one to which I must advert, because it gives me the opportunity to point out a principle as dangerous as it is false.

We are told that it is illogical to attribute to associations or moral persons the rights attributed to individuals or physical persons, since an association is only a fictitious being and can be called a moral person only by a legal fiction, by a courtesy of the law. *Association a fictitious being, association a person created by the law and depending on the law,* is with many an axiom laid down as gospel. Now let us

---

[1] For instance see the paper of R. Father Sengler, S. J., in the *Revue catholique des institutions et du droit*, Janv. 1882.

see what underlies that. A collection of individuals, who combine their means and talents in view of a common end, is certainly something real, something concrete, and not at all a fiction; it is a *body* (the meaning of *corporation*) made up of parts and members united by a common bond. Those members are free and intelligent beings; that body acts, it has rights, it has duties; hence it may be called a *person*. The bond that unites them is moral, and so the association is called a *moral* person. Since the right of association is anterior to positive legislation and is not a concession made by law to men, no more than is the right to speak, to labor, it follows that an association or a moral person with its inherent rights and duties is not necessarily a creature of law. I grant that the law recognizes the association, and that it may endow it with privileges; then it becomes a *legal* moral person, but that does not make it a mere figment. Remark well that I do not deny that there are in law fictitious beings of pure legal creation. For instance, if we consider society as something distinct from individuals who compose it, we have an *abstract* being, an *ens rationis*, or less exactly a *fictitious* being. And if the State or the Church recognizes this *ens rationis*, we have a moral person which will be a creation of the law.[1] I do not deny it. What I assert is that the *associations* to which I attribute the right to teach, have their right to exist and to teach, by natural law, not merely by courtesy of the civil law. This suffices to make good my position.

The axiom against which I am arguing is full of peril. It gives a basis to all those European legists who are foes to religious associations. From it they draw conclusions like the following: donations and legacies to associations, which the law does not clothe with moral personality, are null and void, because of the absolute incapacity to receive and inherit in donees and legatees who have no existence before the law; the State may divest associations of the civil personality formerly granted and then may seize their property which now belongs to nobody. These iniquitous consequences have been discussed and refuted by a learned professor of the University of Louvain, Mr. Van den Heuvel, in a work which has made a great sensation in the legal world, *De la situation légale des Associations*. Let us beware how we put false coin in circulation, even for the temporary needs of war;—we might perhaps be

---

[1] See Cavagnis, *Inst. jur. eccl.*, III, n. 342.

the very first to suffer from our action. Enough on this point. I do not stop to examine the strange proposition that an association cannot have greater right or more rights than the individuals that compose it. Has not civil society, the State, more rights than the citizens? How about the right of legal punishment and of capital punishment?

V.

The Right, the Mission, the Authority of Parents.

At the start let me say that I am glad to find myself absolutely in agreement with Father Holaind as to the title of his pamphlet. He headed it "The Parent First," and I wrote "The parents are entitled (by the Creator) to be the first instructors of their children, themselves, or through teachers of their own choosing" (p. 10).

I. I asserted the rights of parents, and I indicated the qualities of that right. I admitted that the right is very extensive, without, however, being unlimited, since the teaching must be bounded by the true and the good. I have emphasized with Leo XIII that the right is sacred and must be respected; but I had to acknowledge that the right is not independent; so does Leo XIII in his Letter of June 26th, 1878, to the Cardinal Vicar. In that letter he teaches that the father has not the right to deprive his child of religious instruction, even should the civil law favor such a wish of the father, and that the case occurring, the school authorities should look to the spiritual welfare of the child.[1]

I have pointed out the foundation on which the parental right rests, bringing forward a passage of S. Thomas, at once the briefest and clearest formula of doctrine on the question, in my judgment. Likely enough Leo XIII is of the same opinion, for he makes the same quotation in the late Encyclical *Rerum Novarum*.[2] And yet

[1] "Se vi fossero genitori che o per malvagità di animo o molto piu per ignoranza e negligenza, non pensassero a chiedere per i loro figli il benefizio dell' istruzione religiosa.... non sarebbe un dovere da chi presiede alla scuola remediare all'altrui malizia o trascuranza?"

[2] "Patria potestas est ejusmodi ut nec extingui, neque absorberi a republica possit, quia idem et commune habet cum ipsa humana vita principium. *Filii sunt aliquid patris*, et velut paternæ amplificatio quædam personæ; proprieque loqui si volumus, non ipsi per se, sed per communitatem domesticam, in qua generati sunt, civilem ineunt ac participant societatem. Atque hac ipsa de causa quod filii sunt naturaliter aliquid patris, antequam usum liberi arbitrii habeant continentur sub parentum cura. Quod igitur *Socialistæ*, posthabita providentia parentum, introducunt providentiam reipublicæ, faciunt contra justitiam naturalem."

Father Holaind (pp. 8–12) thinks that I have not done enough. He puts the argument under four different forms, appeals to Grotius, Puffendorf, Blackstone, Kent, even to Justinian, Ulpian, Lycurgus. I have not a word to say anent all that, except *quod abundat non vitiat*.

II. I have asserted and proved (pp. 10, 16) that it is the duty of parents to give their children education, not education of an indifferent, vague kind, but a civic and Catholic education, that will make the children into good citizens and good Christians; that this parental duty is strict and paramount, though by no means a duty of commutative justice, as Father Holaind would hold (p. 10, line 35). Why, then, does he quote against me (p. 16), the decree of the Holy See and the American Hierarchy on neutral schools? Where is the word of mine contrary to those decrees? This mode of dealing deeply pains me, I confess, because those who have read only the pamphlet of Father Holaind are deceived by that mode of dealing as to my position. Has not a Catholic journal, as I remarked above, opposed to me the Encyclical *Sapientia?* May not others think that I grant all power in education to the State only? There are rules of justice from which the most praiseworthy zeal dispenses no one.

III. As to the authority of the parents, I have asserted and proved that parents never can lose it; that, if the State establishes public schools, it is bound to take account of the reasonable wishes of parents, and allow them a legitimate share in the carrying on of such schools (p. 22). For this very reason I have said that primary public schools ought to be, not governmental as in some countries, but municipal as in this country, because the municipality more nearly and completely represents the families, and is the immediate emanation of them (p. 19). True, this point has not been attacked, but I have at heart to repeat it as it gives a very good understanding of the relations of the State and the family in the matter of education.

VI.

THE RIGHT, THE DUTY, THE AUTHORITY OF THE CHURCH.

When I came to treat this part, I found that I had either to spread over many pages, if I wished to be complete, or confine myself to the mere statement of general principles and indication of principal proofs. This latter alternative was imposed on me by the very nature of my work.

I. I asserted then that the Church is a teaching power—*magisterium*. Father Holaind (p. 12) insists to add that the Church is also an *educating* power. I have no objection to that. Even Guizot has written that the Church is "*la plus grande école de respect.*" Now, frankly, is not all that Father Holaind says on this point so emphatically that he gives the impression that I have not said it, sufficiently indicated in my pamphlet? Again, *quod abundat non vitiat*.

II. Father Holaind (p. 13) thinks me too hard on those who hold that the Church has received the direct mission to teach human sciences, and reminds me that those who so hold, find in the text, John, XVI., 13, a corroboration to their interpretation of the text of St. Matthew, "Going, therefore," etc. Thanks for the information; though to tell the truth, I was acquainted with this trifling plea, but did not think it worth noticing. However, since Father Holaind challenges, I will say, (1) that in the text of St. John supernatural truth is in question: "I have yet many things to say to you, but you cannot bear them now;" (2) the text deals with the teaching given by the Holy Ghost to the Apostles, and not with the teaching given by the Apostles to the world; it deals, in a word, with the completion of Revelation: "But when he, the Spirit of Truth, is come, he will teach you all truth; for he shall not speak of himself: but what things soever he shall hear he shall speak: and the things that are to come he shall show you." If this text is to be of any service to Father Holaind, he should make it prove that the Holy Ghost was sent to communicate to the Apostles human sciences. Can Father Holaind do it? I pray you avoid that kind of Exegesis that would cover us with ridicule in the eyes of the world.

III. Father Holaind regrets (p. 13) that I have omitted to speak of the philosophical verities of the moral order, and that I have not given the Church the mission to teach them. This is not serious polemics. Turn to page 20 of my pamphlet. There I wrote, "her (the Church's) duty is to make known to man his relations to God, his end; the rules which he must follow and the means which he must use to attain that end." Is not that the supernatural moral order, and does not the supernatural moral order comprehend the natural moral order? It surely does. So at least I was taught by my regretted Master, Cardinal Franzelin, in his treatise, *De divina traditione et scriptura*, p. 110 (1ᵃ. edit.). I ask the impartial reader, was I bound to explain everything at length, especially when my purpose was only to sketch the main outlines of a very complex question in a limited pamphlet? I was addressing an enlightened audience, and I was counting and I still count on the intelligence and fairness of my readers.

But, as Father Holaind calls my attention to this point, and as some persons seem not to understand truths of the most elementary kind, I shall here express myself very plainly.

(*a*). The natural moral law is the foundation of the civil order (economical and political) as it is also the basis of the religious order itself.

(*b*). The precepts of the natural law may be known naturally by the very light of reason, as S. Paul teaches in his epistle to the Romans. But they are known more fully and perfectly by the light of revelation ; for revelation is necessary in order that these precepts should be known by all, easily, certainly, and without any mixture of error : *ut ab omnibus expedite, firma certitudine et nullo admixto errore cognosci possint.*[1]

(*c*). The principles of the natural law are the patrimony of all mankind, which preserves and explains them ; and hence it is that on the fundamental questions both theologians and philosophers avail themselves of the wisdom of nations. Still these truths are in a more special manner the patrimony of the Church to whose guardianship they were intrusted and who interpret them authentically.

(*d*). It is the duty of the State to sanction the precepts of natural law and to determine its application as to the temporal good ; it is the duty of the Church to sanction and apply the same principles as to the spiritual good. Theft and adultery, for instance, may be punished at the same time by civil law, inasmuch as they are opposed to the temporal good of society, and by ecclesiastical law as opposed to the spiritual good.

(*e*). The State, which is bound to sanction the principles of moral law, is consequently bound to inculcate them on the members of society ; the Church has a similar duty, but of a higher order, in regard to the faithful ; for these two authorities have both the mission to procure the moral education of men, though each one at a different point of view.

[1] Conc. Vat. const. *Dei Filius.*

(f). To admit a system of moral principles grounded on nature, known by reason, the observation of which is necessary to the temporal good of society, and which the State, whatever it may be, must sanction, is not the same as to admit the so-called "morale civique, indépendente." The "morale civique" or "indépendente" is the one that some pretend to establish outside the first foundations of all justice and righteousness, without consideration for God as Creator and of his Providence, the eternal law, the last end of man, as it has been so well exposed by Leo XIII in the Encyclical *Humanum genus*.[1] I repudiate such a system of morality as inefficacious, inadequate and dangerous : it is impossible to separate either politics from morality, or morality from religion. I beg my opponents to read what I have written on the subject in my "*Theologia fundamentalis.*"

Let me be permitted to make here a final remark. Much is said of the knowledge of natural moral truths when it is question of education; also, when the doctrine of the Church is explained against fideists and traditionalists; and when it is question of the means of salvation among the heathen. Do those who make this discussion bear in mind the logical consequences which follow from their premises ?

IV. I have asserted and proved (pp. 28 and 29) that the Church, by her divine constitution, has direct authority over religious instruction, indirect authority over secular instruction. I added that the Church has varied in the enforcement of this authority according to time and place. I wish to remark here very explicitly that the Church has enforced in her sphere the system of compulsory education and imposed a minimum before the State had begun to do so. Here I transcribe, as one instance, a decree of the first provincial Council of Mechlin : " Since the poorer classes are often careless in the instruction of their children, they should be forced by the withdrawal of the alms usually allowed them for subsistence to send their

---

[1] "De officiis loquimur quæ ab *humana honestate* ducuntur. Mundi enim opifex idemque providus gubernator Deus: lex æterna naturalem ordinem conservari jubens, perturbari vetans: ultimus hominum finis multo excelsior rebus humanis extra hæc mundana hospitia constitutus: hi fontes, hæc principia sunt totius justitiæ et honestatis. Ea si tollantur, quod Naturalistæ idemque Massones solent, continuo justi et injusti scientia ubi consistat, et quo se tueatur omnino non habebit. Et sane disciplina morum, quæ Massonum familiæ probatur unice, et qua informari adolescentem ætatem contendunt oportere, ea est quam *civicam* nominant et *solutam* ac *liberam;* scilicet in qua opinio nulla sit religionis inclusa."

children to school. . . . In order that schools may not seem to be established in vain, but be frequented with good results, it is the duty of the magistrates of each district to devise means whereby the attendance of children may be enforced, so long at least as they shall be ignorant of the Christian religion. The magistrates may exact this attendance by fines from those parents, who, after due monition, continue to neglect sending their children."[1] Is it not with some reason that a Catholic writer states that the principle of compulsory education, rightly understood, is a Christian principle?[2]

VII.

The Right, the Duty, the Authority of the State.

I.—Right.

I. Unhesitatingly have I affirmed (p. 12) that the State has the right to teach, adding, however, very carefully, (1) that the right is not absolute; the State any more than individuals may not teach error; (2)—that the right is not exclusive; the State's right does not mean the right to hinder others, and notably the family from teaching; (3)—that the exercise of this right is subject to the moral law, which governs both States and individuals; the State's right does not mean the right to squander the people's money in the building of useless schools, nor of schools indifferent and harmful. All this I have insisted on with a clearness, an emphasis such that my thought cannot be possibly mistaken, and I cannot permit any one to impute any other doctrine to me, be the imputation open or hidden.

II. I proved the State's right by the following syllogism (p. 12): "Civil authority has the right to use all legitimate temporal means it judges necessary for the attainment of the temporal common welfare. Now, among the most necessary means for the attainment of the temporal welfare of the commonwealth, is the diffusion of human knowledge. Therefore civil authority has the right to use the means necessary for the diffusion of such knowledge, that is to say, to teach it, or rather to have it taught by capable agents."

Father Holaind (p. 15) criticizes the major, the minor, and finds that the conclusion does not follow from the premises. Let us see.

---

[1] Tit. XVIII, c. 5 et 6; ap. De Ram, *Syn. Belg.*, tom. I, p. 122.
[2] Pierre Pradié, *Rapports de la Religion et de la Politique*, 12ᵉ note à mes Collègues.

As to the *major*, namely, the State has the right to use all legitimate temporal means it judges necessary for the attainment of temporal common good, Father Holaind seems not to deny the principle. But in view of the application I make of that principle he asks what are the *legitimate* means and makes his objection hinge on that word. Pray look at page 12, line 23. Legitimate means are those " that trench on and wound no other right." Yes, there I have defined the term " legitimate." And yet Father Holaind goes on to ask me, do I consider as legitimate, measures opposed to the anterior and inalienable rights of parents ! I have answered *No* more than ten times. Father Holaind continues, " The doctor *would* answer that no right is infringed, because the parents are free to send their children to the government schools or to keep them at home. *If* so we are satisfied ; but let this qualification go on record." This time Father Holaind goes too far. Has he read my pamphlet ? If he has, why did he not see what is there printed in *Italics* (p. 28, l. 4), so that the most distracted and prejudiced reader might not fail to see ? "*Would answer !* " Good heavens, I *have answered.* And yet Father Holaind uses a dubitative and conditional form of speech of a nature to make his readers suppose that I sacrifice the family to the State, that I set no limit to the right of the State, but that Father Holaind is considerate and gracious enough to presume that in my heart's heart I do admit some limit. If I did not know how much must be allowed and pardoned to the partisanship of criticism, I should qualify most severely the proceeding of Father Holaind. I am content to point it out to the reader who realizes the necessity of fairness in important discussions, and to Father Holaind himself, who knows now that, by his trifling, a portion of the public has been impregnated with an absolutely false conception of my doctrine.

The *minor* of the argument is not less displeasing to the Rev. Father. He would have much to say to it, but time failed him, he was in such a hurry to be on hand at St. Louis to counteract the baneful influence of my pamphlet on the archbishops. I am very sorry, indeed. It would have been so interesting to know the opinion of the Rev. Father as to the importance of the instruction of the masses. True, further on (p. 20, l. 27) he ventures to state that it is not absolutely correct to say that the welfare of the laboring classes depends on their knowledge of the three R's. That is a vague assertion, and I should want for it proofs, and proofs more convincing than those given by

Costa-Rosetti. Meanwhile, I maintain what I have said on this point, and I repeat it, making my own words of Prof. Moulart, of the University of Louvain.[1] "Civil instruction, after religious instruction, is the first means of civilizing a people. The first duty of the public power is to favor and propagate knowledge. The State is bound to promote scientific, literary, technical or industrial training, to safeguard its subjects against fraud and injustice by providing means whereby they can know *persons* and *things*, and know the laws that regulate *relations* between persons, the *enjoyment* and *use* of things and the *exercise* of rights." I maintain my proposition, that the social condition of the individual depends on the education which he has received, and which alone can fit him for most occupations, even the lowest in society; that the agricultural, industrial and political condition of a people depends in great part on the intellectual culture of the citizens.

And now for the *conclusion:* Poor logician that I am, it does not follow from the premises! At best I might conclude that the State can help those who teach, but not that the State itself can teach. Let us look at this more closely. My argument proves that the State may use all honest, legitimate means which the State judges necessary for the diffusion of knowledge among the people. Therefore, if giving aid to voluntary teachers is considered by the State a necessary means to the diffusion of knowledge, the State can give such help. If the State judges that to be not enough, and thinks necessary the establishment of schools by itself, the State can establish such schools. But, insists the Rev. Father, this proves at most that the State can give teaching, but not education. Excuse me, it proves both. Morality is not less necessary than knowledge. Does not S. Thomas teach that there is no virtue the acts of which the State may not prescribe, and Suarez, that "the end of civil law is the temporal happiness of the Commonwealth, which cannot be obtained without the observance of all the moral virtues; hence, the civil law may prescribe in the domain of all the moral virtues."[2]

But, enough. Until stronger objections are brought against me, I hold my argument to be apodictical. To this argument I added a

---

[1] *L'Eglise et l'Etat*, p. 467.

[2] 1-2, q. 96, a. 3. "Nulla est virtus de cujus actibus lex præcipere non possit." *De Leg.*, lib. III., c. 12, n. 8. "Finis juris civilis est felicitas vera naturalis politicae civitatis; haec autem obtineri non potest sine observantia omnium virtutum moralium; ergo in omnibus potest præcipere jus civile."

cursory remark of minor importance, that the State necessarily teaches, if not in schools, at least in its laws and juridical verdicts. The Rev. Father answers that legislating and judging are not quite the same thing as holding school. I knew that. In order that no one might impute to me so childish a *naiveté*, I wrote, p. 12, "That the civil power does necessarily teach *in one way or another*" when it legislates and judges. The Rev. Father might very well have passed so secondary an observation, but he is wrong in calling it *metaphorical*. It is not in a metaphorical, but in a very proper sense, that divine law in Scripture is called *Lux, Lucerna, Lumen,* and that S. Basil says, *Lex doctrix et magistra*.

III. In confirmation of my opinion I adduced (p. 13) the fact, that among all Christian nations of all times the civil power has engaged in teaching without any opposition on the part of the Church.

In so doing I have shown, thinks the Rev. Father, the extent of my erudition (pp. 15, 16), not the sharpness of my judgment; for (1) I am wrong in supposing that Christian princes have not essential rights more extensive than non-Christian princes, (2) I do not see that the princes of the Middle Ages may have received from the Church the power of founding schools, (3) I do not attend to the fact that the princes of past times gave to schools a Christian organization and accepted the authority of the Church.[1]

I answer to No. 1: I have demonstrated that Christian princes have not larger powers than non-Christian princes. The Holy Oil that shone on Charlemagne's brow has nothing to do with the question, whatever may have thought some old French writers.[2]

[1] See Father Holaind's Pamphlet, p. 5, l. 20; p. 16, l. 3; p. 18, l. 25.
[2] "The brow of Charlemagne is glossy with the sacred unction," says Father Holaind, p. 5. The consecration was a religious ceremony instituted to call down God's blessings on the King and his family. It was a public acknowledgment that authority comes from God, and must be exercised for his glory; it was also a lesson both to the prince and to the people: to the prince that he should govern according to the laws of justice; to the people, that they should be faithful and loyal. But it did not confer any prerogative. This latter signification is made evident by the history of Charlemagne himself. Pepin had been already consecrated by S. Boniface, but he felt the necessity of consolidating his dynasty, and therefore, as Pope Stephen II had come to implore the aid of the Franks, he was requested to give again to Pepin the sacred unction. On July 28th of the year 754, the Pope consecrated not only Pepin, but *his wife*, and his *two children*—Charles, then 12 years of age, and Carloman, aged 3 years. He blessed the nobles (*Francorum proceres*), and prohibited them under the pain of excommunication to ever elect a King sprung from the loins of any one else but Pepin. See Pertz, *Scriptores*, tom. xv, *De unctione Pippini regis*.

The Rev. Father tries, p. 18, to prove the contrary, but I do not see clearly his reasoning and I must turn him over to the tender mercy of better logicians, say of his brother Jesuit, Father E. A. Higgins. Here is his reasoning: "The end of the Church is the union with Christ and life everlasting. The end of the family is the procreation and education of children. *Hence* (!) the civil power can claim ampler rights when it is in union with ecclesiastical authority and acts under its direction."

To No. 2 I answer: when we study the Middle Ages, the intimate relations of the two societies forces us at times to inquire, if the Church in certain of her actions acted by her proper inherent authority or by an authority borrowed from the State, and again to inquire if the State in certain of its actions acted by its own authority or by an authority borrowed from the Church. To resolve this double question, the essence of the two powers must be held in mind and it will be well also to ask from each, what notion and what consciousness each had of its respective attributes. Just what I have done. First I have proved that the right to teach profane sciences is essentially within the natural domain of the State's rights; then looking at facts, I have found that princes did exercise this right; nowhere have I found that they believed that such right came to them from the Church. Doubtless they almost always petitioned for canonical institution, not as a condition of existence but as a condition of privilege, a condition availing for degrees in the eyes of the Church : for it is a mixed matter.[1]

And now for No. 3. It was not because they gave to their schools a Christian organization that the princes had the right to establish schools; but because they were Christian they made a Christian use of the right and submitted their schools to the legitimate inspection and guardianship of the Church.

Moreover, I did not restrict myself to the Middle Ages and, had brevity not prevented, I would have adduced many modern facts. In the beginning of his Pontificate Leo XIII found in Rome so-called *neutral* schools established by the revolutionary municipality of that city. He wrote a letter to the Cardinal Vicar about the matter. Does he protest against the fact of the establishment of those schools? Does

---

[1] See C. M. de Robiano, *De jure Ecclesiæ in universitates studiorum*.

he pretend that in the establishment of them the municipality has gone beyond its native attributes and powers? There is not in the letter a word to justify such a supposition. What he does strongly protest against is the organization of those schools in which religion had not its proper part and place. In so doing Leo XIII did but apply to Rome the traditional policy of the Popes towards all lands. In our days almost all European governments have withdrawn more or less completely from the dominion of the Church, and all have set up some system or other of public schools. Now, where do you find the Holy See condemning the fact of the erection of such schools? Nowhere. The Holy See has been content with condemning the defective mode of organization of those schools, where they were organized without religion; in a word, the Holy See has denied to the State not the right to teach, but the right to teach wrong. In the Encyclical *Immortale Dei*, Leo XIII makes a strong appeal to Catholics to take an active part in the politics of their country, even where the constitution is rationalistic, and does not recognize the Church. He advises them especially not to neglect municipal politics. Now, why? Please attend: because schools are of the jurisdiction of municipalities, and Catholics should not neglect this most powerful means of assuring to their offspring a good education.[1] On August 18th, 1886, the Holy Father made a concordat with the Prince of Montenegro, who is a schismatic. Naturally the question of schools was taken into account. The Sovereign Pontiff accepts that the Schismatic State shall establish schools for its Catholic subjects as well as for the others; he insists that the religious teaching of the Catholic children shall be subject to the bishop; and, moreover, that wherever the Catholics are in the majority the school teachers shall be approved by the ecclesiastical authority.

IV. Finally, I brought (p. 14) to the support of my thesis the authority of some serious publicists of the day. I selected from Austria and Germany two Jesuits, Costa-Rosetti and Hammerstein; from France, Mgr. Sauvé, who, for his knowledge of the positive science, and for the accuracy of his judgment, is recognized as a man

---

[1] "Illud etiam publicae salutis interest, ad rerum urbanarum administrationem conferre sapienter operam, in eaque studere maxime et efficere, ut adolescentibus ad religionem, ad probos mores informandis ea ratione, qua aequum est Christianis, publice consultum sit."

of the first order; from Italy, I chose Cardinal Zigliara, a Dominican. I might have added others; I regret, especially, the omission of the illustrious Bishop of Mayence, Mgr. Ketteler. But these were surely sufficient.

Father Holaind slyly insinuates (p. 4) that these references deserve a relative confidence. Father E. A. Higgins, S. J.,[1] is bolder; he plainly tells the readers of the *Catholic News* that he has carefully looked up my references, and that of all the writers quoted by me not one gives to the State the right of education as I have formulated it, that is, the right to establish schools, pay teachers, prescribe programmes; not a single one even holds my opinion to be probable. Evidently some one does not know how to read, or is lying to the public. That some one is either Father E. A. Higgins, S. J., or Dr. Bouquillon. As no one is judge in his own cause, I produce the documents and appeal to the public. Let its verdict be Father Higgins' punishment or mine.

I have quoted Costa-Rosetti, Hammerstein, Sauvé, Zigliara. Here are the texts. Costa-Rosetti, *Inst. Eth. et juris nat.*, th. 175, p. 691, 1st ed.: "Auctoritas civilis quidem *scholas* fundare et a se fundatas dirigere potest; sed per se prohibere nequit ne cives ipsi scholas etiam publicas erigant, ab ipsis erectas ordinent et dirigant, quin tamen absolutam docendi libertatem concedere possit."—Hammerstein, *De Ecclesia et Statu*, 1st ed., II, 2, p. 98: "Concedimus ipsius (status) esse *scholas* fundare, si opus sit, ut parentes meliorem nanciscantur opportunitatem ad liberos instruendos;" item, III, 3, p. 146: "*Scholæ* publicæ tum ab Ecclesia tum a potestate civili institui possunt;" again, III, p. 182: "Negari non potest, statui jura quædam circa liberorum educationem et scholas competere. Ipsius enim est, supplere familiam. Hinc primo parentibus media offerre potest, ut melius et efficacius educationi provideant. Quod facit *scholas* fundando et dotando secundum parentum necessitates et vota."— Sauvé, *Questions Sociales*, c. 10, p. 269–271: L'État a de lui-même le droit d'enseigner . . . ce qu'il est licite de communiquer à d'autres. Oui, l'état a le droit d'ouvrir des *écoles*, qui, sans préjudicier aux droits de l'Eglise, à ceux des familles et des individus, peuvent être nécessaires ou utiles au bien social, dont l'état est juge. . . . Entendu de la sorte, le droit d'enseigner peut-il être raisonnablement dénié à l'état? Ne serait-ce pas lui refuser le droit de communiquer à d'autres ce qui est bon et utile, et même d'accomplir ce qui peut être pour lui un

[1] *Catholic News*, Dec. 16, 1891.

devoir? . . . Ma thèse est donc celle-ci: Le pouvoir civil a été investi par Dieu du droit de procurer le bien commun temporel, et par là même de favoriser et d'ouvrir au besoin des écoles qui contribuent à ce bien. . . . La thèse opposée à la nôtre qui refuserait à l'état tout droit d'enseigner ne nous paraît pas probable."—Zigliara, *Phil. Mor.*, lib. II, c. 1, a. 5, n. 7 : "Statui jus simul et officium inesse procurandi media aptiora ad *educationem* tum *intellectualem* tum *moralem*, negat profecto nemo. Cum enim in societatem civilem formandam familiæ conveniant, ut auxilia a communitate habeant, quæ solæ aut nullo modo aut nonnisi imperfecte in promptu habere possunt, necesse est ut de jure et officio socialis auctoritatis sit illa media aptiora suppeditare."—Cavagnis, *Instit. jur. publ. eccl.*, III, n. 89, p. 59 : "Facultatem statui civili scholas instituendi nemo unquam denegavit."

Is comment needed? Let not Father E. A. Higgins say that those writers mean *teaching*, not *education:* they speak of *schools* and, therefore, of education, as well as teaching, and at any rate they use expressly the word *education*. Let not Father Higgins say that those writers allow no probability to my thesis; it is to his they give no value whatsoever! Hammerstein and Costa-Rosetti did not even deign to discuss his opinion; Sauvé expressly says it is not probable; Cavagnis and Zigliara assert that nobody ever taught it. Let not Father Higgins hereafter say what he has said. But let me say that Father E. A. Higgins has given to the world an instance of audacious negation in the face of truth such as I have never met with. To break down my thesis he would make me a forger. I resent it.

V. It is not only theologians I have quoted in favor of my thesis, but also the Dogmatic Commission of the Vatican Council.

It is sought to weaken the force of this authority by the statement that in chapter XV of the schema and in note 47, which is the explanation of the chapter, there is no question whatever of education but only of instruction, no question of the right to teach, that is to build schools, employ masters, prescribe programmes, but only of the right to *provide* (*providere*) for the instruction of youth, that is to aid, stimulate and supply in cases the defect of parents.

The force of the *schema* cannot be evaded by such artifices. In the text of the *schema* it is question of *schools*, and therefore of education as well as instruction. Moreover, education is expressly named in the *schema*. Besides, to provide for the instruction of youth means not only to aid and encourage others in the giving of such instruction, but to give instruction directly, just as to provide food means not only to aid those who furnish it but to give it directly and at first hand. The context of the *schema* is absolutely opposed to the fanciful and Byzantine interpretation that is fastened on it by my opponents. The authors of the *schema* warn us that the actual condition of things makes necessary an exposition of the principles that concern the instruction and education of the youth in schools.[1] Then they take note of that error that gives to *the State alone* all right and discretion over schools.[2] To this error they oppose the doctrine to be held by Catholics, viz.: that the Church has the right to see to it that Catholic children are trained in the principles of faith and Christian morality.[3] But to refuse to the State the *exclusive* right of teaching is not to refuse it the right to teach, and to grant the Church the right to superintend the religious and moral education of Catholic children is not to grant the Church the right to superintend, much less to monopolize, the civic teaching and education of these same children, and this is precisely what the theologians hasten to state in the most explicit terms.[4]

VI. Before entering upon the study of the right of the State to teach, page 11 of my pamphlet, I threw out a previous consideration in these words: " We ask if the State has the special and proper right of teaching human knowledge. We say *special and proper* right, for there can be no question of a vague and general right; it were unreasonable to refuse to the State that which is granted to every legitimate association." Thereupon the Rev. Father E. A. Higgins, S. J., actually says that this previous remark is all the argument I

---

[1] " Declarationem distinctam quoad institutionem et educationem in scholis." Not. 47.

[2] " Contendunt scholas omnes directioni ac arbitrio *solius* potestatis laicae subjiciendas esse, ita ut auctoritas Ecclesiae ad providendum religiosae institutioni et educationi juventutis christianae omnino impediatur." Cap. XV.

[3] " Ab omnibus agnoscendum esse jus et officium quo Ecclesiae pervigilat ut juventus catholica, imprimis vera fide et sanctis moribus rite instituatur." Cap. XV.

[4] " Tum in expositione errorum, tum in affirmatione veritatis, non negatur jus potestatis laicae providendi institutioni in literis ac scientiis ad suum legitimum finem, ac proinde etiam non negatur eidem potestati laicae jus ad directionem scholarum, quantum legitimus ille finis postulat. Non asseritur potestati ecclesiasticae velut ex divina constitutione consequens auctoritas ad positivam directionem scholarum, quatenus in iis litterae et scientiae naturales traduntur." Not. 47.

have for the State's right, he puts this pretended argument in form, declares it a caricature and bids me go to school to learn logic.

He has set up a man of straw and knocks him down. Again I appeal to the fair minded reader and beg him to give verdict. I have gone to school many years ago, to the school of Franzelin, Patrizzi, and Ballerini, S. J.; to that same school I go as often as I can. But Father Higgins' school! No, I hie me not thither, it is a school of deceit. And now shall I tarry to justify—not my argument, I have done that just now in answering Father Holaind's objections to my syllogism—but a simple preliminary observation made by the way in one line? I will merely say that I am not the first who has made this observation, and that it has been advanced in favor of the Church, especially in lands where the Church is not recognized as a perfect society. If Father E. A. Higgins, S. J., has read, as he affirms, the writers I have quoted, he may have read in *Questions Sociales*, p. 275, of Mgr. Sauvé, formerly pontifical theologian in the Council of the Vatican, and first Rector of the University of Angers, the following words: "I shall prove in a moment that the right to teach belongs naturally to every individual and legitimate association endowed with the requisite ability for the exercise of the right. Now, what an individual and an association may do in this regard, why should not the State do? Why and on what pretense will you refuse to the State a natural right that belongs to the simple individual and to an association inferior to the State? The State, the sovereign, be he one or multiple, may be as able, oftentimes abler to give teaching than simple individuals. What reason is there then why you should object to the State's teaching those who are willing to take it for a teacher, if it offers all reasonable guarantees and does not teach against the order established by God." Father E. A. Higgins, S. J., whose name is attached to no great scientific work that I know, may apply to Mgr. Sauvé, author of first class works, the epithets with which he has honored me, may bid him go back to school! Here I drop the Rev. Father. May the reader excuse me for wasting on him so much of his and my time. I should not have stopped to answer his unfair criticism had it not been signed with a name, the religious affixes of which attached to the criticism credit in the eyes of Catholics.

VII. I come back to my original opponent. Father Holaind (p. 16, l. 15) asks what sort of school can a State that ignores revelation set up, and he answers, the best it can establish are neutral schools, and neutral schools are condemned. This answer is incomplete and too easy.

In turn I answer, first by asking Father Holaind what kind of education can an immoral and free-thinking parent give his child; and does Father Holaind deny all right to educate to such a parent?

Secondly, I answer that the Father's argument proves, perhaps, that the non-Christian State is not qualified to exercise over Christians its rights in the matter of education, but does not prove that the non-Christian State has not the right to teach.

But this is not enough, and I answer, thirdly, that the non-Christian State may exercise its right of teaching towards its Christian subjects by establishing denominational schools; the non-Christian State may do for Catholics what Christian States have done for Mahometans. Do not bishops, priests, and laymen in the United States earnestly ask for denominational schools? Moreover, if the State non-Christian will not grant denominational schools, he may enter into some compromise whereby on the one hand its neutral position towards all religions may be maintained, and yet on the other hand the demands of the various denominations as to religious instruction may be safeguarded.

I answer, fourthly, that if the neutral school is condemned on principle, it does not follow, after learned theologians and canonists, that in a peculiar condition of political affairs the State is absolutely prohibited from establishing schools not religious, schools negatively indifferent. Such is, for instance, the doctrine of Mgr. Cavagnis, Professor in the Pope's Seminary and Consultor of the S. C. of extraordinary Ecclesiastical Affairs, the very Congregation charged with the questions of the relations of Church and State; p. 78, n. 128, vol. III of the work already referred to, he says: "Etsi nunquam liceat nisi per accidens ex erronea conscientia malum facere, ut esset constituere scholam acatholico spiritu imbutam, tamen licet aliquando a bono alias obligatorio abstinere, cum nempe id sive physice sive moraliter impossibile est, seu præstari nequit absque gravioribus malis. Schola autem negative se habens quoad religionem est tantum omissio boni et non mali positio."[1] Let it be understood that I am here speaking of the establishment of schools by the State, not of the use of such schools by the parents. Be the State reprehensible or not in establishing schools negatively indifferent, more or less dangerous, the duties of Catholic parents remain those indicated in the Third Council of Baltimore, n. 198, and in the *Instruction* given by the Holy See, 24 Nov., 1875 : "Sacra Congregatio non ignorat talia interdum rerum esse adjuncta, ut parentes catholici prolem suam scholis publicis committere in conscientia possint. Hoc autem non poterunt, nisi ad sic agendum sufficientem causam habeant; ac talis causa sufficiens in casu aliquo particulari utrum adsit, nec ne, id conscientiæ ac judicio Ordinariorum relinquendum erit ; et tunc ea plerumque aderit, quando vel nulla præsto est schola catholica, vel quæ suppetit parum est idonea erudiendis conditionis suæ . . . . adolescentibus. Tunc autem ut scholæ publicæ in conscientia adiri possint, periculum perversionis cum propria ipsarum ratione plus minusve nunquam non conjunctum, opportunis remediis cautionibusque fieri debet ex proximo remotum." [1]

II.—*Mission.*

Let the reader be patient. I have only a few words to add on the mission of the State in education.

I. Before explaining my views, I thought it well to lay down in the pamphlet the traditional theory of the duties of the State (p. 18). I had to warn my readers against two opposite errors,

---

[1] Mgr. Sauvé is not so explicit and furnishes a very good example how prudent we should be in deducing conclusions from general principles. On page 259 of his work already referred to, I find these words : "Un gouvernement ou un souverain qui présiderait aux destinées d'un peuple divisé de croyances, ne pourrait-il pas licitement, non par indifférence doctrinale ou impiété, mais sous l'empire de nécessités urgentes et pour éviter de plus grands maux, ouvrir, par exemple, telles écoles où seraient reçus des élèves professant des cultes divers et dont les maîtres devraient, dans l'intérêt de la paix et de l'ordre, s'abstenir de parler pour ou contre la religion ? Je suppose, pour bien me faire comprendre, une société ravagée à tel point par l'erreur et l'impiété que le gouvernement, si chrétien qu'il soit, ne puisse établir, vu l'état pervers des esprits, des écoles où la vraie religion soit enseignée sous ses auspices, ni même des écoles confessionelles ; et je suppose d'un autre côté que les écoles dues à l'initiative privée ne soient pas suffisantes ; l'état en une telle situation pourrait-il, *faute de mieux, crainte de pire,* fonder des écoles dans lesquelles les maîtres, par raison de prudence, devraient s'abstenir de parler de religion ? Telle est ma question. Je la pose et je ne la résous pas." One need not be a prophet, however, to conjecture how he would answer, if he were put to it. Here I wish to recall a sentence of my pamphlet, page 31 : "You have only to apply to education those general principles by which are solved the questions of liberty, of worship and tolerance of social evils."

the error of those for whom the State is only a policeman, the error of those for whom the State is a parent. Those two errors, pregnant with conclusions affecting the whole social life of man, find even among Catholics many upholders. Father Holaind knows this as well as myself; or, if he did not, he might have learned it from an article of Father Caudron, S. J., in the *Revue Catholique des Institutions et du droit* of January, 1891. To those two errors I opposed the doctrine of S. Thomas, lib. I, c. 15, *de Reg. princ.* I should have given the text, so luminous is the doctrine of the great teacher. But it is within easy reach of my clerical readers. Had I not written my pamphlet before the publication of the Encyclical *Rerum Novarum*, I should have quoted from it that passage which refers to the duty of the State; it holds as good for education as for labor. I now quote the text: "Per quos civitas regitur, primum conferre operam generatim atque universe debent, tota ratione legum atque institutorum; scilicet efficiendo ut ex ipsa conformatione atque administratione reipublicae, ultro prosperitas tam communitatis quam privatorum efflorescat. Id est enim civilis prudentiæ munus, propriumque eorum, qui præsunt, officium. Nunc vero illa maxime efficiunt prosperas civitates, morum probitas, recte atque ordine constitutæ familiæ, custodia religionis ac justitiæ, onerum publicorum tum moderata irrogatio, tum aequa partitio, incrementa artium et mercaturæ, florens agrorum cultura et si quæ sunt alia generis ejusdem, quæ, quo majore studio provehuntur, eo melius sunt victuri cives et beatius." Finally, wishing to show that on this fundamental point (the mission of the State) Catholic teaching was in harmony with the American idea, I quoted from the preamble to the Constitution of the United States (p. 14). All this is pure waste in the eyes of Father Holaind.

II. As to the functions of the State, I accepted the division into functions essential and functions accidental. And to show that theological and political science were in harmony on this point, I quoted on the one side Mgr. Cavagnis, on the other side an American writer, Mr. Wilson, and two employés of the government. Three, that is all. Waste of erudition, thinks Father Holaind. Mind you, I quote three on a controverted point to show that Catholic theologians and political writers are at one. On a point that no one among Catholics controverts, Father Holaind (pp. 8–10) allows himself the luxury of Grotius, Puffendorf, Blackstone and Kent, of Justinian, Ulpian, Lycurgus! Yet it is I that play the charlatan, beat the drum, display erudition, and waste my powder in harmless fireworks!

III. I have affirmed and proved (p. 19) that the State is invested with a mission to teach human knowledge. Father Holaind exclaims, (p. 13) with some excitement: "Where, when, from whom has the State received such a mission?" Why, dear Father, the State has received the mission from God, when God created man a social being, just as the parents receive their mission to be the educators of their children, when God grants them children; or rather, they received it once for all, when God created man, male and female; and commanded them to increase and multiply.

IV. While admitting in the State a mission to teach, I declared (p. 19) that the mission was an accidental function, *supplying the insufficiency of individuals;* that the State is not bound to exercise it in all circumstances; that the State can and should exercise it only when *necessity* or *utility* demands the State's intervention. By that distinction, utility or necessity, I applied to teaching what is applied by all to the other accidental functions of government, post-offices, telegraphs, roads, &c, and I wished to be aloof from those who admit the intervention of the State in such matters only in cases of absolute necessity. Father Holaind thinks, perhaps, that to admit the intervention of the State for cases where the intervention is useful is to admit it for cases where it is not useful. So he interprets my thought; for he says, p. 14, l. 28 : "that is, the State may establish schools, even when the public could do without them," and he quotes a text of Jansen to the effect that the State should observe distributive justice and not favor one class of citizens at the expense of another!

III.—Authority.

I. I have asserted the right of the State to educate; but at the same time, I have carefully determined the object, the limits of this authority, and the conditions within which the State must exercise it. Again and again have I said that this authority is not absolute, nor arbitrary, nor exclusive of the Church and the family, but that in the divine plan these three authorities should combine their efforts for the common good of humanity. I beg the reader to read again this important passage of the pamphlet, pages 22–28, and to judge if I have made all necessary reservations and if they are to be excused who attribute to me the doctrine of the omnipotence of the State and quote against me passages from the encyclicals where Leo XIII proclaims against the *Socialists* that the State may not invade the family and thrust aside the parent to take his place.

II. As to the argument by which I have proved the authority of the State, it is reducible to this : this authority is included in that general authority with which the State is invested for promoting the common good, guaranteeing to each man his rights and preventing abuses. Father Holaind finds (p. 19) that this argument proves too much, and, therefore, proves nothing; for it would prove, he says, that the State has the right to invade our kitchens and prescribe our eating and drinking; and so the good father sends me to Utopia, Salento, Icaria.

The argument *ab absurdo* is a weapon of little effect at times, of very careful handling, of some danger to the fencer. If Father Holaind has read the Encyclical *Rerum Novarum* since he wrote that hasty pamphlet of his, he must be sorry that he tried to fence with that treacherous weapon. Let us examine the reasoning of Leo XIII in the question of labor. *Major:* " Eis qui imperant videndum ut communitatem ejusque partes tueantur." *Minor:* " Atqui interest salutis cum publicae tum privatae. . . . validos adolescere cives, juvandæ tutandaeque, si res postulat, civitati idoneos." *Conclusion:* " Quamobrem . . . . si valetudini noceatur opere immodico, nec ad sexum ætatemve accomodato, plane adhibenda *certos intra fines* vis et auctoritas legum." I have reasoned in the question of education exactly on the same line as the Pope in the question of labor. If the culinary objection of Father Holaind has any force, it hits the Holy Father more directly than it hits me; for good victuals are surely of the highest importance to the health of the growing citizen. But I hasten to assure Father Holaind that he is guilty of no irreverence, because his objection is of no account, and Leo XIII has quietly brushed it aside with three little words, *certos intra fines*, which I took the liberty of italicising in the quotation. He explains the three little words thus : " quos fines eadem, quæ legum poscit opem, causa determinat, videlicet, non plura suscipienda legibus, nec ultra progrediendum quam incommodorum sanatio, vel periculi depulsio requirat." I had made precisely the same observation : we may grant to the State what is reasonable and possible without granting to it what is unreasonable and impossible. At any rate does not the State busy itself within reasonable limits with the material welfare of the citizens? Does it not inspect food, meats, drinks, the sanitary conditions of homes, the justness of weights and measures and a thousand other matters? Why then give out exclamations of holy horror when you are told that this same authority, that does all those things without a protest from you, can protect the intellectual and moral life of the children of the people by imposing a minimum of instruction!

Oh! says Father Holaind (p. 20), the State can interfere only when a public wrong has been committed and the judge takes cognizance of it. "The fact is that all those matters are relative . . . requiring State intervention only when there is a public wrong committed and the existence of that public wrong must be determined by the judge on the individual merits of the case." Will Father Holaind please understand the distinction between the legislative and the judiciary? The existence of a social necessity, viz., the fact that some parents neglect the education of their children, may induce the legislator to remedy the defect by a general law. After the promulgation of the law the judge sees to its execution by taking cognizance of individual breaches of the law, and inflicts punishment as the gravity of the case requires. But the judge does not make the law, he applies it. If it is difficult for the legislator to foresee all eventualities and predetermine every detail, it is perhaps still more perilous to leave all to the discretion of individuals, even of executive magistrates.

III. Finally Father Holaind expresses the wish that I had discussed the reasons adduced by Costa-Rosetti against compulsory education. I have not done so, because I had provided against them in my pamphlet, and I will not do so because some of them, even with the approbation of so excellent an author as Costa-Rosetti, seem to me unworthy of discussion before the people of the United States. For instance, the instruction of the masses in their rights and duties in order that the observance and administration of justice be made more easy is one of the arguments in favor of compulsory education: Costa-Rosetti objects that this argument is suggested by sloth on the part of the magistrates, and that it must not be forgotten that magistrates are for the people and not the people for the magistrates. Here are his own words: "hoc argumentum potius ex molestia magistratuum quam ex prosperitate publica repetitur, ita ut inde illi solum merito commoveri possint, qui tenent cives esse propter magistratus, non magistratus propter cives: propter quos si magistratus existant, hi incommoda subire debent, quæ sine comparatione minora sunt quam onera gravissima civium, per quæ magistratus se ab molestiis liberare possunt." What are those *onera gravissima*? Remember that the State by making education compulsory and demanding a minimum of instruction does not impose any burden on good citizens, for we suppose the State to be reasonable in such legislation; it imposes, therefore, a burden only on the bad citizens. I do not see that anything more can be objected to the law of compulsory education than to any other law that sanctions our natural obligations.

Conclusion.

In my pamphlet I purposed to prove, and, I take it, have proved that education belongs to individuals isolated and collected, to the family, to the State, to the church; to these four together, to none of them exclusively. Such is the theoretical doctrine. The practical application of it demands the combination, more or less harmonious, of these four interested parties in the work of the schools.

Objections have been made to my thesis—not one, however, that has not been foreseen and guarded against in my first pamphlet. Notwithstanding this, I have thought it advisable to scatter the clouds and mists that have been cast about me, and to put the truth in a new and clearer light. I have proved in particular that the objections drawn from the distinction between instruction and education, the Christian and the non-Christian State, have been urged against me without justice. I have shown the solidity of all the arguments which I deduced from principle, law and fact. I owed this defence to myself, to the institution of which I have the honor of being a member, to the distinguished persons who have advised me, to the Catholic people of this country who cannot afford to be led astray.

In the fulfilment of this duty I have been moved by two sentiments. On the one hand a sentiment of satisfaction and confidence that I am in the truth, that there is little strength in the reasoning of my adversaries. On the other hand a sentiment of pain caused by the controversial methods of my adversaries, methods to which I have been unaccustomed, which I had not expected. I spoke of the right to educate: I am met with the question of the organization of the schools. I upheld the right of the State: this is taken to mean that I deny the right of the family. I spoke of a determinate right of the State and carefully fixed its limits: it is inferred from this that I preach State omnipotence—in a word, neither my explanations nor my reservations, emphasized by the use of italics, have received the slightest notice. I took care to back each statement with the authority of Catholic writers of acknowledged standing: to this comes the printed reply that not one of those writers looked on my opinion as even probable! And yet, I had taken my stand in the serene region of pure science. No allusion, no imputation, no qualification that could wound is to be found in my pamphlet.[1] With St. Jerome I could say, "Asked by my brothers what I thought, I gave my answer, taking from no one the right to think for himself: "Interrogati a fratribus quid nobis videretur, respondimus, nulli præjudicantes sequi quod velit."[2] Whence all this impassioned opposition

[1] And yet the *American Ecclesiastical Review* writes (p. 76) that my essay "bears, in the light of existing facts, an aggressive character;" that I threw down the glove, and that "I have given sign of being an adversary, in deed if not in words." An adversary to whom? Aggressive in what? Those "existing facts"—are they mine? I have made merely an abstract and impersonal exposition of principles. And even had I made a challenge, the one who took up the glove should have fought with lawful weapons. I dedicate to such critics the following words which R. F. De Smedt, S. J., Superior of the Bollandists, pronounced December 6th, 1885, in the Catholic Congress of Rouen: "I do not hesitate to put fairness in the first line of the duties of Catholic writers in discussion with co-religionists. . . . What name would you give to the practice of a writer who, to refute more easily an opinion that displeases, presents it under an appearance that disfigures and falsifies it out and out; who strains wording so as to make the author say the thing which he did not say, nay the contrary of what he did say; who attributes to him hidden thoughts, intentions, which are far from his mind; who masks explanations and restrictions essential to the real bearing of his propositions? What would you say of the tactical craft that strives to take the discussion from the main field of the contest and bring it to a corner of very subordinate importance, where an easier victory is hoped for and the onlooker is deceived into the belief that the enemy has been routed. All this, I grant, may be done unconsciously; none the less does it shock the calm and disinterested witness of the strategy, and above all him who is the victim."

[2] *Apol. adv. Ruf.*, lib. 1.

these insinuations, these suspicions, this *procès de tendance*, even these calumnies? Was the light so dazzling that it hurt the eyes of some? However that may be, I forgive those who have so forgotten themselves as to use against me unfair weapons. I offer to their meditation the following words of Leo XIII: "Illud in controversiis agitandis cavendum est, ne modus transiliatur quem æquitatis caritatisque leges præscribunt, neve temere insimulentur vel in suspicionem adducantur, viri cæteroquin Ecclesiæ doctrinis addicti." [1]

---

[1] Epist. *Licet multa*, 3 Aout, 1891.

Public Schools

OR

Denominational Schools?

PASTORAL LETTER

ON

"The Separation of the School from the Church"

ISSUED IN 1873 BY

RIGHT REVEREND W. E. VON KETTELER,

BISHOP OF MENTZ.

FROM THE GERMAN

BY A CATHOLIC PRIEST.

NEW YORK, CINCINNATI, CHICAGO:
BENZIGER BROTHERS,
Printers to the Holy Apostolic See.
1892.

COPYRIGHT, 1892,
BY
BENZIGER BROTHERS.

BIOGRAPHICAL SKETCH

OF

WILLIAM EMANUEL von KETTELER.

By The Translator.

W. E. von Ketteler was born December 25, 1811, at Munster, Germany, and ordained priest in the same city June 1, 1844. The funeral oration which he delivered at the grave of those who had fallen victims of the revolution at Frankfort in September, 1848, and his address on "The Liberty of the Church and the Social Crisis," held in Mentz at the first Catholic Congress, 1849, established his fame all over Germany. Only six years after his ordination he was raised by Pius IX. to the episcopal see of Mentz and consecrated bishop July 25, 1850.

For more than a quarter of a century Bishop Ketteler was an ornament of the Catholic hierarchy, and the foremost champion of the rights and liberties of Catholics in Germany. Indefatigable in the discharge of the special duties towards his diocese, he was ever ready as orator or publicist to defend the true interests of the Church and of society at large. He issued 50 pastoral letters and 7 larger memorials addressed to his diocese; he published, moreover, 30 books or pamphlets such as "Liberty, Authority, and Church" (1862); "The Social Question and Christianity" (1864); "The True Basis of Religious Peace" (1868); "The General Council and its Significance for our Time" (1869); "The Infallible Teaching Authority of the Pope" (1871); "Liberalism, Socialism, and Christianity" (1871); "The Breach of Religious Peace and the only Way of Restoring it" (1875). Several of these works reached four, five, six, that at the head of the list even eleven, editions, and were translated into various languages.

The social question and the school question formed Ketteler's favorite subjects which he studied continually and treated of in many of his writings and sermons or addresses. In regard to the social question Leo XIII. once declared Ketteler his "great predecessor," and Cardinal Manning said, "In the social movement Ketteler made room for the cross." His last publication contained four sermons "On the Duties of

Parents and the Home under the Modern Conditions of School Education." (1877). In 1876 he had written on "The Dangers of the New School Legislation for the Religious and Moral Education of Children in the Common Schools." All the writings of Bishop Ketteler show his great and clear mind, his deep religious convictions, his sincere love for mankind, particularly the laborers and the young.

Bishop Ketteler was most firmly attached to the apostolic chair of Peter, and was a great friend and admirer of Pope Pius IX. As member of the Vatican Council (1869) he belonged to the so-called minority, deeming the solemn declaration of the infallibility of the Pope "inopportune," though he always adhered unwaveringly to the doctrine itself. In 1877 he went for the fifth time to the Eternal City on the occasion of the episcopal jubilee of Pius IX. On his way home, however, he fell dangerously ill in a Capuchin monastery in Bavaria, and died there July 13, 1877. His remains rest in the cathedral of Mentz.

CONTENTS.

	PAGE
I. What are Denominational Schools?	8
II. What are Secular Public Schools?	9
III. What did our Forefathers think of the Separation of the School from the Church?	12
IV. What do Religion, Reason, and Man's Nature, what the Interests of the Family and Experience, tell us concerning the Separation of the School from the Church?	13
V. What must we, therefore, judge of the Suppression of the Denominational School and the Establishment of the Secular Public School?	23
VI. Who Demands, after all, the Separation of the School from the Church? Who alone can Demand it?	27
VII. Duty of Christian Parents concerning the School Question	29

PUBLIC SCHOOLS

OR

DENOMINATIONAL SCHOOLS?

WILLIAM EMANUEL,

by the mercy of God and favor of the Holy Apostolic See, Bishop of Mentz, Domestic Prelate and Throne-Assistant to his Holiness the Pope, to all the priests and faithful of our diocese health and benediction in the Lord!

THE school question is undoubtedly one of the most important questions of our times. It affects deeply and lastingly every home, every family. For it relates not to the temporal property which the family have inherited, or acquired by the sweat of their brow; it touches that which is nearest and dearest to parents, their children. The question at issue is whether the children should be conscientiously instructed and thoroughly educated according to the spirit of Christianity, as they hitherto have been, or misinstructed and perverted according to the party spirit of the age, and thus be ruined for time and eternity.

For this reason it is a sacred duty incumbent on all parents to direct their whole attention more than ever to the management of the schools to which the existing laws force them to entrust their children. The schools are intended for your children; you must support them at the cost of great sacrifices. You can, therefore, demand such an arrangement of the schools as is best suited to the education of your children.

Here, then, arises, first of all, the question: which of the two school systems is the better one for your children—the denominational school which is intimately connected with the Church, or the public school which is separated from the Church? You must make yourselves thoroughly acquainted with the advantages and disadvantages of these two systems. All parents must arrive at a clear judgment on this question: which is the better for the salvation of my child—the denominational school or the secular public school? This may soon become a practical case, as this subject may be submitted to the decision of the community. Who among you would be so indifferent as not to examine this vital question carefully? Who would not uphold with all lawful means that school which he reasonably deems the best? Any one who leaves the decision in so important a matter to others is most assuredly a father, a mother, devoid of all conscience, unconcerned about that on which the future happiness of their offspring most essentially depends.

I shall, therefore, answer a number of questions concerning school education in order to induce you, dear parents, to consider and weigh them seriously and conscientiously. Allow me to ask:

I. WHAT ARE DENOMINATIONAL SCHOOLS?

Denominational schools, first, are such schools into which, as a rule, only children of one and the same religious denomination are admitted; secondly, in which only such teachers are appointed as profess the religion of the children; and thirdly, in which religion forms the basis of the whole education and instruction. In the denominational schools, accordingly, the pastor of the congregation has the necessary authority to watch over the religious education of the children.

According to the existing laws, the school as just described was, up to the present date, the school of our country. The edict of June 6th, 1832, which regulates the primary schools, ordains expressly that the teacher must ordinarily belong to the Christian denomination of his pupils; that, besides the other conditions required for his appointment, he must faithfully comply with his Christian duties, and that religion shall be the basis of all common schools. The teacher, moreover, shall, as the edict very beautifully says, share with the family "to which the child belongs" the duty of educating it; he shall "form it into a pious and solid man;" he shall endeavor to accomplish this purpose "by instruction, example, and charity, by an amicable intercourse with the parents," and, as far as necessary, "supply what is wanting in the home education." To the same end he shall also attend the divine service with the children, and watch over them while at church. True, the supreme direction of all the schools is entrusted to the state alone, to the exclusion of the Church. But this principle, which we cannot admit as just, is essentially modified by the fact that an important share in the direction of schools is conceded to religion on all the official school boards.

Such has been till now the condition of our schools, allowing religion still to exercise on them the most necessary influence. On the basis of such laws our schools have hitherto enjoyed a satisfactory development. As to their results, our schools are no doubt on a level with the best of other countries, and have, as far as it depended on them, solved to a great extent the task of forming "pious and solid men." On that account you had also confidence in our schools. You could commit your children to them with the consoling assurance that piety, virtue, and all the good you had instilled into their hearts in your families, would not be destroyed, but rather be fostered and promoted under the hand of a pious teacher. If parents, therefore, hitherto were not so actively interested in matters of school education as it was properly their duty and as they formerly always had been, the reason for it lay chiefly in the confidence they could place in the school authorities and teachers.

II. WHAT ARE SECULAR PUBLIC SCHOOLS?

I wish to remark at this stage that I do not speak here of the common schools as they exceptionally still exist even after our edict. Since the primary schools, as a rule, are denominational; since, moreover, the spirit of the edict is based on denominational schools, and religion is everywhere represented in the directing authorities; since, finally, the teachers themselves are trained in denominational seminaries, a pure system of secular public schools could not as yet develop itself in our country. Thus, the appointment of Jewish teachers would scarcely have been possible. I speak, therefore, of the secular public schools as they should be introduced according to the intention of the party which now demands everywhere the complete separation of Church and school.

Such public schools, then, are schools which receive children and engage teachers irrespective of any religious denomination. All children of a community or town, Catholic, Protestant, Jewish, and such children as have been brought up in complete infidelity, are instructed together in the same school, and distributed in the various classes exclusively according to the grade of their knowledge. Side by side with a Christian teacher a Jewish teacher, or one without any religion, is with the same right appointed to instruct Christian children.

A natural consequence of this arrangement is that the position of religion in such a public school is just the opposite of that which it has in a denominational school. In the latter religion, and not only its doctrine but also its practice, is the basis of the whole instruction and education. In the secular school, on the contrary, the religious instruction and life of the child can at best be considered as a matter which is cared for outside the school, and which is incumbent exclusively on the parents and pastors. The school itself has nothing to do with it; it is not connected with any denomination, and, since without any denomination religion itself cannot be conceived, it is truly irreligious, or godless.

In a secular public school Catholic children dare not even bless themselves, because non-Catholic children would be shocked, and their teacher may be a Jew or an infidel, as well as a Christian. For the same reason no prayer whatever may be pronounced as is customary in the church and in the family. One may not speak of the Church, of the holy sacraments, of the ecclesiastical year, and the difference of the holy seasons. The holy season of Christmas with all its impressions and blissful joys for the hearts of the children, the holy season of Lent, the holy season of Easter with its thousandfold Alleluia, the holy season of Pentecost and Corpus Christi,—all this passes for the secular public school without meaning, and can never be mentioned there. The walls of such a school are empty and bare, showing no crucifix, no sacred image or picture; likewise the whole year passes monotonous and joyless for Christian children.

The pastor of the child, he who is most apt to work upon its soul, has no longer any power in the school. Neither do parents exercise any influence there, since the pastor represents, at the same time, the interests of the parents. All that religion has imparted to the children through the medium of pious parents, brothers, and sisters, all those happiest and most ennobling sentiments and pleasures, are entirely banished from the children during all the hours of the many years which they must spend at the public school. As often as the school-room opens the child finds itself in a sphere totally different from that in which it lives at home. What in the eyes of virtuous and good parents is the principal thing it sees and hears treated at school as if it were the most insignificant and worthless matter in the world, since the teacher does not so much as even mention it.

In this point, dear parents, you must not give yourselves up to the delusion that the fatal consequences of the public schools can in reality be avoided through the influence of a pious and good teacher. For, all I have just said cannot be averted or prevented even by the best teacher, painful as this may be to his heart. He can neither in general nor on special occasions give vent to his personal pious sentiments, because by so doing he would give the children of other denominations a cause for complaint. Even the most pious teacher is, therefore, compelled to banish religion as far as possible from the school and all subjects of instruction, and to treat the children as if in fact religion, Christ, and the Church did not exist at all.

True, some maintain that this is not exactly the case, and that the secular public school, though it is not denominational, is not an irreligious school. They speak, therefore, of a universal religious instruction which is not denominational, and of a universal school morality which is sufficient to form the child into a good and moral man. But all these are great illusions.

Imagine, for example, a school in which children of Catholics, Protestants, and Jews are gathered. What kind of religion could a teacher treat of there? He dare not speak of all the doctrines in which Catholics differ from Protestants; the Protestant children and parents would not suffer it. Moreover, he dare not speak of the teachings concerning Jesus Christ and the Redemption; the Jewish children would not tolerate it. Consequently, there would remain only a general teaching about God which he could explain. But since men go so far in their folly, according to Holy Scripture, as to deny even God, or, at least, distort and corrupt the teaching on God to such an extent that in the minds of many nothing is left but gods and idols which they have made for themselves, it might finally come to such a pass that a teacher could not even speak of God, lest he should wound the ears of those children who are the offspring of infidel parents. Such is the universal religion of the secular public school.

The same may be said as to the universal school morality. The entire history of heathendom preceding the advent of Jesus Christ demonstrates in the most fearful manner what value the so-called universal religion and morality has for the formation of men. Undoubtedly in man's nature, even without revelation, there lies the capacity of knowing God and the principal duties towards Him. But because men no longer wished to read the divine handwriting in their souls God wrote His commandments on the solid stone of the tables of the law, and when even this writing on stone was not sufficient, He gave us, finally, through His only-begotten Son a celestial, supernatural light and power to enable us to escape the corruption of heathendom. As the universal religion and morality in heathendom could not save mankind from the lowest degradation and the most hideous depravation, so it can now save neither us nor our children.

The other pleas for secular schools are of the same kind: that the cultivation of the understanding makes the child moral; that faith is incompatible with knowledge, and that the school, therefore, should occupy itself only with science and the Church with faith; finally, that dogma should be learned only after one has left the school.

Heathendom has been showing for 4000 years what our natural reason without faith can accomplish towards morality, and daily experience shows the same by the great number of those who, notwithstanding all their culture, have fallen a prey to the deepest immorality. That knowledge and faith are incompatible is a doctrine which has been condemned as an error by the Church, and which can only be asserted by such as have, through their infidelity, lost all idea of the true faith. The same holds good with the third assertion, that man should learn the teachings of faith only in his after-life. This, too, can only be maintained by people who have in reality lost the belief in a divine revelation. Whosoever believes that God has, through His divine Son, revealed Himself to us, must be convinced that these divine teachings cannot be imparted to the child too early.

To the secular schools, therefore, we may apply what the Redeemer said of those builders who build on sand. With their universal religion, with their universal school-morality, with their exclusive cultivation of the understanding, etc., they are institutions in which the whole future of the children is being built on sand; and when the young have scarcely been dismissed from school, and withdrawn from the guardianship of their parents, then the first blast will suffice to overthrow the whole moral structure, and to deliver them, lacking all moral strength, to the many seductions and passions of youth.

Such is the secular public school—in the full sense of the word, an irreligious, godless school.

III. WHAT DID OUR FOREFATHERS THINK OF THE SEPARATION OF THE SCHOOL FROM THE CHURCH?

In former ages secular public schools were not known. Even among the heathens it was never doubted that education and instruction must be religious. With the Jews this was likewise an established truth. During all the Christian centuries, moreover, the conviction was incontestable that religion and school must be intimately connected. Our Christian forefathers without exception would have considered the separation of school and Church as irrational, impious, and pernicious. With all Christian nations the school is in the best and fullest sense a daughter of the Church. All schools, the higher, middle, and lower, sprang originally from the Church. When the Church founded her new colonies in the midst of uncivilized, savage races, when barbarity was reigning up to the very walls of the cloister, she established everywhere within these same walls nurseries of science and schools for the training of youth.

The reformation of the sixteenth century did not change this intimate union of religion and school. In the treaty of Westphalia both Catholics and Protestants unanimously expressed the old Christian view as to the proper position of the school; they declared that the school was an "annexum exercitii religionis," a necessary appendage for the free practice of religion, and, consequently, inseparably connected with religion. According to this Christian and absolutely correct conception, therefore, the free exercise of religion is curtailed and impeded wherever the school is withdrawn from the Church. Also, later on, when the state began to take charge of the schools, the principle, nevertheless, was firmly adhered to, that the influence of religion should not be impaired, and that religion should remain the basis of the school. The abovementioned regulation of the school edict of 1832 shows that only a few years ago the opinion was still universally held in our country that denominational schools, not secular public schools, correspond to the true interests of our people.

Hence you see, beloved parents, that up to the present day secular public schools were never and nowhere wanted. Let this be a warning for you not to abandon this sacred tradition without the most serious examination, and to be on your guard in such an important question which is most closely bound up with the welfare of your children. Do not accede thoughtlessly to the opinions of the day. We must, therefore, put to ourselves another question:

IV. WHAT DO RELIGION, REASON, AND MAN'S NATURE, WHAT THE INTERESTS OF THE FAMILY AND EXPERIENCE TELL US CONCERNING THE SEPARATION OF THE SCHOOL FROM THE CHURCH?

They tell us unanimously that the secular public school destroys Christian education; that it is in contradiction with all principles of religion and reason, with the nature of the child, with the interests of the family; and that, finally, wherever it has been introduced it has been attended with the most pernicious consequences.

1. The secular public school is in contradiction with all principles of religion.

As Christians we must judge all important questions chiefly according to the principles of religion, and not according to the changing opinions of the day. Religion contains God's revelation and the teaching of Jesus Christ. Religion alone, therefore, can with full certainty answer the great questions which present themselves to us; it alone can show, in particular, the ways that lead to the true welfare of our children.

But religion teaches us that man is placed on earth to know, to love, and to serve God, and thereby to become happy here and hereafter. With this destiny all other conditions of man must agree, as the road we are to take depends on the goal we want to reach. The school, therefore, which has such an important influence on the course of the child's whole after-life, must likewise lead it to the knowledge, love, and service of God, and thus assist it towards its true temporal and eternal welfare. From this conviction sprang the old Christian principle that religion must form the basis of all human concerns, and, in particular, of the school. The secular public school, however, denies this truth, because it knows nothing of the true destiny of man, and aims at nothing higher for the child beyond this life. It is, accordingly, essentially based on infidelity.

Religion teaches us, moreover, that mankind has fallen deep through sin; that our mind has been obscured and our will weakened; that we need, therefore, a Redeemer; that Christ alone points out the true way which leads to our happiness; that He alone by His grace frees our understanding from innumerable errors, and renders our will again strong and powerful. All these truths pervade the whole treatment of the child in the denominational school; but they are all completely ignored by the secular public school, and in this respect also the public school is based on infidelity.

2. The secular public school, in consequence, destroys also all Christian education.

In the school, instruction and education are most intimately and indissolubly connected. Every instruction is, at the same time, education. This lies in the nature of the child who is fast developing all its faculties and powers of both body and soul. Whatever it sees and hears affects its education. At school it learns not only to read, to write, and to figure, but also to live a good or a bad life; it imprints in its mind the principles according to which it will arrange its after-life; it contracts good and bad habits which soon become a second nature. What a destructive influence must, therefore, the secular public school exercise on the whole education of the child !

The Christian education, furthermore, derives its educational means, first and above all, from Christ Himself, from the Christian faith and Christian duties, from the graces and sacraments of Christ. These living fountains for the education and formation of the child are totally obstructed in the public school. What God complained of in the old covenant, that His people have "forsaken the fountain of living water and have digged to themselves cisterns,"* holds pre-eminently good with the secular public schools. All the fountains of divine assistance which Christ offers us to make our children pious, good, and happy have in them run dry. There you find only cisterns, i.e., means of instruction which men have invented.

What, however, will the public school system substitute for the great and wonderful educational means of Christianity? It has nothing but its miserable, sickly school-morality of which we spoke above, and which without the aid of Christianity is absolutely unable to make men truly good.

Besides, the secular public school destroys Christian education also directly, because all subjects of instruction must be treated without that immediate reference to God, to Christ, to religion, which is an essential feature of the denominational school. All things have been created by God and for God, are continually preserved, governed, and directed

* Jerem. ii., 18.

by God, and are, therefore, most intimately connected with God. In the same manner, a good instruction must in all the various subjects constantly direct the attention of the pupils to this connection of the world with God. A pious teacher, accordingly, brings everything into connection with God, and thereby accustoms the child to refer all things to God, to find, and love, and serve God in all things. Oh, how beautiful and beneficial is such an instruction ! How it forms the mind and character of the child, and rewards the teacher with the happiest results ! How all these little germs of truth and virtue grow strong and vigorous, which God has planted in the hearts of the young to be fostered and developed by pious parents, teachers, and priests! A child's soul in which all these divine germs are daily cherished by education and instruction is indeed a heavenly flower-garden, and the gardeners who, full of love, walk about tending the flowers, are good parents, good teachers, good priests.

All this, however, is entirely neglected by the secular public school; nay, more: the contrary effect is produced by it. Whereas the denominational school uses everything to lift up the soul of the child to God, to direct its eye and heart heavenwards, the public school treats all subjects of instruction as if there were no God, no Christ, and it accustoms, therefore, the child to view all earthly things in such a manner as if there were no God and no Christ. But thus the public school is by its very nature, even against the will of the teacher, a veritable school and institute of godlessness; for, as the essence of religion consists in the union of man with God and, accordingly, the essence of a religious education in the training to this union, so the essence of an irreligious, godless education consists in the child's being accustomed to look upon itself and the world without reference to God. But if the child for the many years of school attendance has been accustomed to hear so many things spoken of without their connection with God, it must finally come to look at nature in a similar way as the brute animal does, which knows "by the things that are made" * neither the existence nor the attributes of its Creator.

Now, if the secular school is, by its very nature, destructive of Christian education, this will be much more the case if the teacher himself is not a Christian, or is even hostile to all religion. The public school does not care about the faith of the teacher: it cares only about his knowledge, his examination. A necessary consequence of this system is, besides, the irreligious seminary for teachers. Who could, therefore, for any great length of time keep away from such schools teachers who are imbued with those materialistic opinions concerning God and

* Rom. li., 20.

nature which are so wide-spread nowadays; teachers who, perhaps, in your children hardly recognize an immortal soul or anything more than a lump of earth shaped in this way or that way; teachers who are ignorant of all those heavenly doctrines of Christianity which make us revere and love in the soul of every child an image, a temple, a child of God, and an heir of heaven?

When you think of these public schools you must be careful not to represent to yourselves such a teacher as you had when you were young, —a pious Christian, a father during your childhood, who in union with your parents and pastors introduced you into a truly Christian life. The public school system would deprive us of these pious teachers, and in their stead we should often receive teachers who, having themselves fallen a prey to modern infidelity, would with cold hearts and darkened minds be strangers and enemies to the pious faith and love of religion which your children would bring along from their homes. Now consider, beloved parents, what an immense influence a teacher who for eight long years spends so many hours daily with your children in their most tender and susceptible age exercises on their whole development; and then reflect what consequences the influence of a man as I have described him must have on the whole Christian education of your offspring. The children will soon instinctively feel that all which they were, at home and at church, taught to consider and to love as the highest and holiest is to their teacher an object of complete indifference and, perhaps, even of mockery and scorn. How great, then, is the danger that the children will follow the sentiments of the teacher rather than those of their parents!

Another very important circumstance is to be considered. Teachers who have no longer before their eyes the educational principles of Christianity, and are no longer guided by them, must necessarily form for themselves other principles according to which they treat and educate the children at school. Now, there is scarcely another field where in the last hundred years so diverging and contradictory views have been advanced as in the field of education. Great and renowned schoolmen have applied principles which, if I proposed them to you, would make you shudder. True, afterwards they were found out to be erroneous, and were abandoned. But we shall learn on the day of judgment what incalculable harm the poor children suffered on whom these experiments of modern educators were practised. The very same thing would happen in our primary schools. Young teachers would apply now such principles, now others, now this method of education, now that, and your poor children would be the subjects to be experimented upon.

Till now, beloved parents, you knew with perfect clearness and certainty according to what principles your children were treated and educated at school. They were the principles of your faith according to which you yourselves treat your children at home; the principles according to which you yourselves were once educated by pious parents, priests, and teachers; principles the value of which you yourselves have tested and experienced in your lives. All this ceases in the secular public school. If you were, however, to call the teacher to account for his perverse educational opinions, he would answer you that you understand nothing about the matter, and that he has the right to educate your children according to his own views.

Accordingly, a Christian education is out of the question in the public school system. If you, therefore, decide in favor of this system, you burden your soul with a fearful responsibility by depriving your children and all your descendants of all the blessings of a Christian education.

3. The secular public school, in the third place, is in contradiction with reason itself and with the nature of the child.

Viewing the matter merely in the light of reason, we cannot conceive anything more unreasonable and unnatural than the endeavor to exclude from the cultivation of the mind and heart of the child Almighty God, from whom all things proceed, in whom we live and move, from whom we continually have our being. The children are far more dependent upon God than even upon you, beloved parents. Now, a school which would try to separate the children from their parents under the pretext of culture would undoubtedly be a pernicious and unnatural institution. How much more is the public school, which loses sight of the relation of the child to God, a pernicious and unnatural institution!

But considered from the Christian stand-point in particular, a school which ignores all that the Son of God Himself offers us in the Church for the education of man is irrational and unnatural in the highest degree. How can any one who is sincerely convinced of the divine origin of the Christian religion reasonably exclude from the school Christ, the divine Master and educator of mankind? This would be an inconceivable climax of folly and absurdity. We can, therefore, but maintain that the public school system disclaims Christianity as the divine institution for the salvation of men, and that only such can support this kind of schools as have already lost the Christian faith. The public school, therefore, is essentially a part of the great apostasy from Christianity. Its true significance lies in this, that it is intended by the advocates of infidelity to be a school against Christianity, a means to stunt and, if possible, to crush the very first germs of the Christian faith in the hearts of the children. Parents, on the contrary, who still believe in the Redeemer of the world must necessarily, if they wish to act according to reason, demand that the whole school education of their offspring be pervaded and guided by the spirit of Christ.

Still in another respect we see how irrational and unnatural the secular public school is. Many console themselves with the thought that religious instruction need not be entirely excluded from the public school, since for it as for other subjects of instruction special lessons may be arranged. Religion is only forbidden to exercise its influence in the school itself, but the Church is not prevented from instructing the children thoroughly in the Christian doctrine during those appointed hours. Apart, however, from all I have already said above concerning this point, those who deem such an arrangement sufficient to impart a Christian formation to the children entirely misconceive the nature of the child. The soul of the child has, indeed, divers faculties, but all these faculties are not separated from one another : they form together the one, indivisible, spiritual nature of the child. We cannot, therefore, disconnect, as it were, its faculties, and separately hand them over for their education, one to the parents, another to the teacher, another to the priest, and afterwards again gather and join them into one man. We cannot educate one portion of the child to be pious and God-fearing, and bring up the other, in complete separation from God, for the world and all the wants of this earthly life, and finally form a true and solid Christian. These are mechanical ideas; in this way we deal with machines which we can take asunder and construct at will ; but this will not do with a living human being. Such notions are absolutely contrary to reason and nature. Children at school who spend the greatest part of their youth without any regard to their faith cannot in some few hours of religious instruction be trained to a lively faith and a truly Christian life. In such a school, where all relations to God are cut off, their mind gradually becomes insensible to whatsoever partakes of the supernatural, their will turns more and more away from God, and clings exclusively to earthly things, since they hear of nothing else at school. How can, then, the short religious instruction raise to God and to Christ those minds and hearts entirely bent on this earth ? But on such an irrational and unnatural supposition is the public school system based.

4. The secular public school, furthermore, injures likewise the interests of the Christian family. It is not only, as the German bishops said in their last memorial issued at the tomb of St. Boniface, an anti-church, it is also an anti-family, system.

There are, in fact, but two institutions founded by God for the spiritual and moral formation of man. These two institutions are the family and the Church. Both have their mission immediately and directly from God. The child belongs, in the first place, to its parents. Besides, it belongs through baptism to the Church. The school is equally attached to both of these institutions; it is an aid of the parents and of the Church. The teacher has, to repeat once more the significant words of our edict, "the important calling to share with the parents the duty of education, to make of the children pious and solid men." Now, if this formation and education of the child shall be successful, all depends on this, that the family, the Church, and the school are intimately united, and in the instruction and education supplement one another by always working on the same principles. The teachings which the child receives from the priest, the parents, and the teacher, about the great fundamental principles that are to be deeply imprinted in its mind and heart for the guidance of its whole life; the teachings it receives about the principles of what is right, true, and good, about its end here on earth, about the duties it has to fulfil to become good and truly happy,—these teachings must evidently always be substantially the same, though they may differ as to the manner. It is only by such an internal unity that those three institutions really aid one another: at the same time, the child's respect for its parents, teachers, and priests increases, and their influence on it becomes more efficacious.

Now, religion alone is the sacred bond which unites the home, the school, and the Church. Only by a common faith is it possible that all those who share the calling of educating the child start from one truly uniform plan and are guided by the self-same principles. Where this unity of faith is wanting there the greatest confusion prevails among those who work at the development of one and the same child. If the child hears one teaching at school, another in the church, another again at home, there arises necessarily in its soul, not unity of formation, but complete confusion. Such a child is in the position of a man who, being ignorant of the right road, receives on his inquiry three different answers from three different persons. Thus the guides of youth become their seducers, and the school becomes but too often an enemy of the family, by destroying in the soul of the child what pious parents are daily building up.

5. Experience, finally, confirms what has hitherto been said of the secular public school.

Wherever this system was introduced, or is still in vogue, the religious life of the children, families, and congregations, and the authority of the teachers were greatly damaged, the discipline and morals of youth were sapped, and even their accomplishments in the ordinary branches of instruction were superficial and defective.

Our own city of Mentz, during the period of its occupation by the French, furnishes us with an obvious illustration of the results of secular school education. The parochial schools were not expressly abolished, but in reality they were separated from the Church. By the decree of Commissary Rudler of the year 1798 the catechism and other manuals of religious instruction had to be removed from the schools, and in their stead "the fundamental rules of civic and republican morality" had to be taught. This "civic and republican morality" of the French revolution coincides pretty much with what is now called "the universal school-morality." When the zealous Bishop Colmar came to this city the work of dechristianizing the schools of Mentz was, in spite of his opposition, promoted with might and main by the prefect of that time, a man exceedingly hostile to the Catholic religion. The consequences of this separation of "the civic and republican morality" from faith and religion became manifest but too soon. Scarcely had some years elapsed, when the schools of Mentz, which had flourished under the electors, were decayed to the utmost degree. The voices which were then raised from all parties can hardly find words to describe the hopeless condition and total ruin of the schools of Mentz during the French period. But the source, too, of this decay was recognized and found to be the separation of the schools from the Church. The French Minister Portalis, therefore, began at length to negotiate with Bishop Colmar to put a stop to the corruption, and requested him repeatedly to direct his priests to devote themselves again with all energy and love to the schools.*

Similar were the results in Holland. In the year 1848 the new constitution ordered public instruction to be arranged in such a manner "that no one's religious sentiments and ideas should be offended. For the rest, the imparting of instruction is given free, save the inspection by the authority and a state examination of the teacher." This law, however, based as it was on freedom and tolerance, was not suffered by modern liberalism to last long. By the new school law of August 13th, 1857, the secular public school, or, as it is there termed, the neutral school—viz., neutral with regard to religious denominations—was introduced.

But there, also, voices are since being heard from all sides giving information of the deplorable consequences of the new arrangement. A certain preacher, Schwarz by name, a Lutheran missionary and the editor of the "Heraut," has written an instructive little book on those consequences in the Protestant districts of Holland. Among other things he says: "The final results are distressing enough; more and more people, of both sexes, remain unconfirmed, often only baptized; more and more marriages without religious blessing; ever increasing ignorance in religious matters, which makes many a fervent believer an easy prey of fanatics, whilst it leads the light-minded and indifferent without resistance into the arms of the basest rationalism; ever increasing morbid dismemberment of the [Protestant] Church in various sects." The author goes

---

* See "Die kath. Pfarrschulen in der Stadt Mainz" [The Catholic Schools in the City of Mentz], by Christopher Monfang, 1868. Pages 4 ss.

on assuring us that, while he was engaged for six years in the direction of a Dutch mission society, he had many occasions to hold examinations, and that he found the saddest ignorance in a very large number of young people. On the moral effects of the neutral schools he remarks: "The condition of public morals, according to the unanimous testimony of experienced observers and official statistics, has not become better since the introduction of the school law, as many expected it would. True, the great cities have their proportionate share in the moral depravation which seems to be inseparable from the gigantically increasing development of international communication; this is a product of different factors easily accounted for. However, the continually growing immorality among the country population forms such a glaring contrast with the simplicity and severe manners of former days as to justify us perfectly in inferring therefrom the moral insufficiency of the irreligious schools." *

Catholics in Holland express themselves in the same way. The writer of a series of instructive articles on this subject which were published in Munich says: "In fact, the number of illegitimate births is continually increasing; divorces are increasing; suicides are increasing; cases of insanity become more and more numerous, the victims of drunkenness more and more frequent." †

A very noteworthy phenomenon in Holland—which, however, must occur in all countries where the public school system is adopted—is the variety of views among the schoolmen concerning the position which the neutral school should maintain towards the teaching of the Church. One says the neutral school, in opposition to the Church, must patronize freedom of inquiry; another, the school must lead to liberalism in religion without adhering to any denomination whatever; another, the mere utterance of the teacher's own conviction made in the simplicity of his heart and with delicacy, without either touching upon the error of others or teaching his own opinion as a positive truth, cannot morally be considered as a transgression of the law; another again, in order to teach Bible history without offence the doctrines of the Bible and the supernatural stories must be thrown overboard; another, finally, the fear of clashing with the teachings of faith need not hinder any one from pointing to the supreme truth which manifests itself in the eternal laws of nature both in the material and moral order.‡ From all this we see clearly that a really neutral or non-denominational school is, in fact, a chimera, and that it always, by its very nature, develops into a school

---

* "Die religionslose Schule der Niederlande und ihre Fruechte " [The Irreligious School System of the Netherlands and its Fruits], pages 24 and 57.
† Historisch-polit. Blaetter, 1871, vol. 68, p. 367.
‡ Ibid. pp. 179–181.

which directly combats and destroys the teachings of revelation in the hearts of the children. The secular public school must of necessity become an irreligious school.

In no country, however, has the system which separates the school from the Church in such a measure become prevalent as in North America. There all the public schools are entirely separated from the Church. But in no country either have all the evil consequences of these schools shown themselves to such an extent as in North America. It may suffice to adduce here one testimony on this matter. Professor Agassiz, of Harvard University, a friend of the public school system and a well-known free-thinker, made for some time past "the social evil, its cause and propagation" the subject of special inquiries; the result of his studies filled him with horror, and considerably shook his faith in the much-prized civilization of the nineteeth century. Thus he alleges as a sure fact that in the city of Boston very many women who habitually lead an exceedingly immoral life openly avowed that the original cause of their fall and disgrace had its source in the influence which the public schools had exercised over them.

In what this influence consists, a daily paper of the city of Boston explains in words that are not fit to be repeated here. Suffice it to mention that in the schools such filthy and shameless pictures are handed round among the female pupils that it would be a miracle if the children were not totally corrupted. This is a fearful thought for the parents and the country. There occurred cases of systematic general immorality, and they were kept secret lest the public schools be exposed. And thus, rather than have these bad schools fall into discredit, the children are allowed to go to moral destruction.*

Agassiz's crushing verdict is fully confirmed by an eminent physician who published an anonymous work with the title "Satan in Society." He discloses without mercy the vices and crimes particularly prevalent in the higher Puritan world, and asserts that these modern pagans have sunk much lower than even the ancient Romans. The author finds the root of all these vices in the free public schools and boarding-schools, in the description of which he inexorably tears the hypocritical mask from the American public school system.†

No less severe is the weighty judgment of the American bishops of the Council of Baltimore, 1866. It runs as follows: "The experience of

---

* Baltimorer kath. Volkszeitung, Dec. 2, 1871.

† Ibid., Dec. 28. [From the third edition of "Satan in Society" (1890) we learn that the author of this remarkable work is the late Nicholas Francis Cooke, M.D., LL.D., who joined the Catholic Church in 1866. The first edition of his work appeared in 1869.—*Note of Translator.*]

long years has more than sufficiently shown what serious evils and great dangers are entailed upon Catholic youth by their frequenting the public schools in this country. Such is the nature of the system of teaching therein employed that it is not possible to prevent young Catholics from incurring, through its influence, great danger to their faith and morals; nor can we ascribe to any other cause that destructive spirit of indifferentism which has made, and is now making, such rapid strides in this country, and that corruption of morals which we have to deplore in those of tender years. Familiar intercourse with those of false religions, or of no religion; the daily use of authors who assail with calumny and sarcasm our holy religion, its practices, and even its saints—these gradually impair in the minds of Catholic children the vigor and influence of the true religion. Besides, the morals and examples of their fellow-scholars are generally so corrupt, and so great their license in word and deed, that through continual contact with them the modesty and piety of our children, even of those who have been best trained at home, disappear like wax before the fire." *

V. WHAT MUST WE, THEREFORE, JUDGE OF THE SUPPRESSION OF THE DENOMINATIONAL SCHOOL AND THE ESTABLISHMENT OF THE SECULAR PUBLIC SCHOOL?

This question can now be answered with perfect clearness.

1. The separation of the school from the Church is a great injustice against God.

The child belongs, above all, to God, not to the world exclusively or to the state or to a party, not even to the parents exclusively. When God blessed the common mother of the human family with her first child, she acknowledged in the name of all parents that it was a gift from God. The child belongs to the parents only in so far as God entrusted it to them to be reared and educated. God has created it, He is its supreme and ultimate end; the possession of God is its everlasting happiness. Again, when man was lost for God through sin, Christ redeemed him with His blood. God has, therefore, the supreme right to the child, consequently also the right of demanding that it be educated according to His will, and that the school be arranged according to the destiny He has given the child. To separate the school from God is, therefore, manifestly a great wrong against God; but this is done, if the school is separated from the Church.

* Concilii Plenarii Baltimorensis II. Decreta. Baltim. 1868. Tit. IX, cap. 1, n. 426.

2. The separation of the school from the Church is a great injustice against the Church.

Through baptism the child belongs also to the Church which Christ has founded to lead men to God, and in which He has deposited for this purpose all graces and resources. Hence the Church is, according to the apostle St. Paul, the mother of the faithful, consequently also that of the children; in her they receive supernatural life, in her this life is nursed and fostered. To banish our religion from the school means, therefore, to make the task imposed upon the Church by her divine Founder impossible to her; it means to tear her children from her own motherly heart; it means, in the proper and true sense, to destroy religion. After the Church has christianized the nations through the blood of her martyrs, after she has transformed the world through the power of the gospel, all shall be destroyed through the separation of the school from the Church. This is a detestable scheme and a great injustice against the Church of Christ.

3. It is a great injustice against Christian parents.

To the parents, in the first place, the children have been given by God. They have, after God, the first right to the children. There is no right more natural and more sacred than this. But God did not give it to them to dispose of their children at pleasure; He connected with it the most sacred and most stringent duties. The first and noblest one among them is to rear their children for their supreme destiny, for the Father in heaven, Whose name the head of every family here below has the privilege to bear. This duty lies in nature itself. But it is increased by the fact that the children have through baptism been made truly children of God and heirs to heaven. The school does not change anything in this sacred relation. Being, in the first place, supplementary to the family, it should not hinder the parents in the fulfilment of their duty, but should, on the contrary, be a powerful help thereunto. All the religious sentiments, knowledge and love of God, which the parents have implanted in the hearts of their children, must be carefully nourished and fostered by the school.

But from this it appears clearly what a great wrong, nay, what a great cruelty it is to separate the school from the Church. This wrong and this cruelty are the greater, if parents are forced by compulsory school laws to send their children to these schools. To compel parents to entrust the children they have received from God to schools which prevent them from fulfilling their most sacred duties towards them is the greatest abuse of power, and the hardest slavery to which man can be subjected. A mere sense of justice would demand that where school attendance is compulsory the schools be arranged in such a manner that

Christian parents can entrust their children to them without violating their consciences and their duties towards God.

4. The separation of the school from the Church is a great injustice against the children.

How great this injustice is can scarcely be expressed in words. If we estimate it according to the damage which is done to the child, and the advantages of which it is deprived, it cannot suffer a greater harm nor lose greater advantages than by being compelled to spend its youth in a school that is separated from God and religion. Both its temporal and its eternal welfare are thereby endangered. This is self-evident when everlasting happiness is considered. But the temporal welfare is most closely connected with the eternal. The more a man cares for his eternal welfare, the more he cares, also, for the temporal. All that religion teaches and commands the child serves to make it already here on earth as happy as possible. God engraved on all temporal things the law that even earthly enjoyment is true enjoyment only as far as man has the moral power to avoid all excess in the use of creatures. Self-denial alone, as taught by Christianity, makes earthly joy pure and true. But man finds only in religion sufficient strength for this self-denial which must accompany us throughout our life. Religion, moreover, helps him to carry the numerous crosses connected with every man's earthly career. Religion, finally, preserves him from many sufferings and trials which the Almighty has attached as a natural punishment to the gratification of every sin and every passion. Of all these divine remedies which are at man's disposal from his childhood to make him happy for time and eternity, the child is deprived in the school which is separated from the Church. Hereby the public school becomes in all reality an institution for the temporal and eternal ruin of our youth.

5. The separation of the school from the Church is a great injustice against the teacher.

As religion bestows through the sacraments a sacred character and dignity on man that far exceeds all earthly things, so it gives a similar dignity to all conditions and affairs connected with it. This is also true with regard to the teacher's calling. The Christian teacher in a denominational school, who is at the same time teacher of religion and representative of God, occupies a very different position from that of a teacher in a school which is separated from religion. What a Catholic teacher is in a Catholic school is very beautifully expressed by the pious Overberg in the following words containing the gist of a longer treatise: "I am a teacher;—this means, therefore, I have an office which is one of the most venerable and important offices on earth. For, what office could be more important and more venerable than that of being a teacher of truth and virtue for so many ignorant, a representative of so many parents, a spiritual father of so many children, a fosterer of the nursery of the community, a visible guardian angel of the children of God, a custodian of the price of the blood of Jesus, a guard of the temple of the Holy Ghost, a companion and guide of so many young pilgrims to God, their Father? As teacher I must be all this!"*

The same author exhorts the teacher often to make the following reflections:

"Often consider your pupils, when they are sitting or standing around you, with the eyes of faith, and ask yourself: Are these not children of God, favorites of God, heirs of God? Are they not the innocent minor brothers of my Saviour, the price of His blood, the temples of His holy Spirit? Are they not the charges of the angels, the joy of their parents, the flower of humanity, the hope of a better posterity?

"Sometimes reflect: If these little ones who have been entrusted to me knew how much they could profit by my piety, what would they do? Would not many, perhaps, fall on their knees before me, stretch out their little hands towards me, and address me with tears in their eyes: O dear teacher, please do your best to be good and pious, that you may the better teach us to be so too! Live so as to go surely to heaven, in order that you may help us the better to go there too!

"Another time you may consider: If my Saviour would appear to me in order to recommend to me these little ones whom He loves so much, could and would He not tell me: Behold the marks of My wounds in My hands and feet and side. The souls which I have confided to your care have been bought by the blood that streamed from these wounds. Sanctify thyself for them as I have sanctified Myself for all of you.† I shall require their souls also at thy hands.‡

"It is very useful to ask one's self frequently: What will these pupils of mine think of me on their death-bed and before the judgment-seat of God? Will they have cause to pronounce upon me a blessing or a curse? What shall I myself on my death-bed think of my conduct during my teaching generally and, in particular, during the religious instruction? Will the thought of it cause me anguish or consolation?"§

So sublime is the teacher's calling in the light of faith. In this manner the Christian teacher regards himself and his vocation. In this manner he is looked upon and respected by the priest who works with

---

* "Anweisung zum zweckmaessigen Schulunterricht" [Directions for a Proper Instruction in School], by Overberg, page 21.

† John xvii. 19.

‡ Ezechiel xxxiv. 10.

§ "Christkatholisches Religionshandbuch" [Hand-book of the Catholic Religion], by Overberg. p. 6.

him in the school, by the parents of his pupils, and by the children themselves. What consolation, what strength, what holy joy do not these Christian ideas afford the teacher in his difficult calling! The school, however, which is separated from the Church divests him of this higher dignity, of this sacred character, of these consoling and elevating sentiments. The teacher who is no longer a teacher of religion, who does no longer regard himself and the children in the light of faith, and is no longer considered by them in this light, suffers, therefore, an unspeakably great loss. He loses the higher mission he has received from God; he loses that higher authority in virtue of which he took towards the child the place of God, the place of the Christian father, the place of the Christian mother; he loses, at the same time, all the graces which through the Church flow to him as a co-laborer in the vineyard of the Lord. Thus he sinks down to the level of a mere instructor, of an ordinary business-man, of one who does a very troublesome and often ungrateful business, solely for the sake of an earthly compensation and for a temporal end.

6. The separation of the school from the Church is, finally, the greatest injustice against civil society itself.

Society is again made unchristian by the secular public school. As Christianity is also the nursery of true civil virtues, these civil virtues are diminished wherever the influence of Christianity is diminished. The fruits of dechristianizing the higher, middle, and lower schools make their appearance everywhere in proportion as the dechristianizing of the schools is proceeding.

VI. WHO DEMANDS, AFTER ALL, THE SEPARATION OF THE SCHOOL FROM THE CHURCH? WHO ALONE CAN DEMAND IT?

1. The Catholic people do not demand it. If they had to give their votes, only few would rise in favor of the public schools. Universal experience proves that wherever Catholic parents have the free choice of schools, they always prefer those schools which are intimately connected with religion. Their love for their children shows them what is truly useful or injurious to them. They are, therefore, less influenced by the agitations of parties and the opinions of the day in the things that directly affect the welfare of their offspring. From the daily experience of their own family life they have come to know the blessings of religion and its influence on the child, as well as the corruption that takes hold of it when it is estranged from religion. Hence it is that parents consider themselves happy if they can confide their child to a school that is intimately connected with the Church. Even in small Catholic congregations of the Palatinate, for example, many parents cheerfully make

the greatest sacrifices to secure this blessing for their children. The Catholic people, therefore, do not want the separation of the school from the Church.

2. That the Church herself does not demand, but rather detests and rejects, the secular public school as the greatest curse, needs no proof. Wherever the Church has raised her voice, wherever popes, bishops, and priests have pointed out the duties of parents, they have admonished them to send their children only to such schools in which instruction and education rest on the eternal foundations of revelation.

3. Believing Protestants and believing Jews reject, in the same manner, secular public schools. This follows necessarily from the belief in divine revelation. Where the living faith exists that God Himself has manifested to men the fundamental principles of truth and of a truly human life, the imperative conclusion naturally follows that at the age when the young receive their training, when they are to be shown the right path for their after-lives, they must by no means be excluded from these divine teachings and precepts.

4. The government itself held, until of late, that the secular schools are pernicious: a conviction which was shared by a large number of the most eminent schoolmen of all denominations. If the government has shown itself, of late, more favorably inclined to secular schools, we may well maintain that this is not owing to a conviction that these schools are really good and advantageous, but rather from a lamentable obsequiousness to the intrigues of influential parties.

5. There are only two classes of people who do, and who can, demand secular public schools.

It is, first, those impious men who have lost the light of divine revelation. All believing Christians insist on having their schools united with the Church, because they believe in the divinity of the Christian religion. He who believes in this must necessarily demand that Christ with His doctrine and His graces shall also reign in the schools. To refuse this demand is, properly speaking, the same as to deny us the right of believing in the divinity of Jesus Christ and in the divinity of His Church. On the other hand, he who has lost the belief in Christ cannot, of course, admit the value of the union between school and Church. The demand, therefore, of separating the school from the Church springs from infidelity, from apostasy from Christ. This is the proper and true reason of that policy. Those pitiable men in our midst who have lost the light of Christian faith, and have fallen back into the darkness of paganism, evidently cannot appreciate the value of that light for the school and the child. They want the school separated from the Church, in order to rob even the children of that light which they themselves no longer know, and to draw them back again into the darkness of paganism.

The second class of those who demand secular public schools is made up of people without self-dependence and without judgment of their own. They have not, it is true, lost their faith completely. Nevertheless, owing to vanity, lack of principles, or disgraceful egotism (because they fear loss of position, of patronage or gain), they do not decide questions of public life according to their faith or conviction. They are rather guided in their decisions by empty phrases about enlightenment and progress, or by shallow pretexts that reading and figuring are nothing denominational, or, finally, by the direct order of those on whom they depend. Unfortunately, there are in every community such dependent people. Their master is not God and Christ, but the favor of the world, the patronage they enjoy, their self-interest which they always have in view. They live on the waste thrown to them by the world, and for the betrayal of their faith and conscience they find a compensation in this, that in certain circles of which they are but the blind instruments they are commended as educated, enlightened, and progressive men. These conceited, dependent, and selfish people are the disgrace and the ruin of our communities, and the hired emissaries of infidelity.

VII. DUTY OF CHRISTIAN PARENTS CONCERNING THE SCHOOL QUESTION.

We have seen, beloved parents, what the school is when connected with the Church, and what it is when separated from the Church; we have seen what our forefathers thought, and what we have to think, of secular school education; we have seen how manifold the injustice is which is contained in the secular public school system; finally, we have seen that only those can ask for secular public schools who have abandoned the belief in Christ.

From this follows, dearly beloved parents, the duty to reject with united efforts every attempt of introducing among us the secular public schools. To act thus you have the most sacred right, because the children belong to you, because you furnish the resources by which the schools are supported, because even the state has till now sanctioned this right by its laws. But to act thus you are also bound in conscience, because on it the temporal and eternal welfare of your children depends, because God will on the day of judgment demand the souls of your children from you.

If some one were to devastate your fields, or to poison the bread you eat and give your children to eat, would you not oppose him with all possible means? But far more pernicious is the attempt of separating from the divine sources of all truth and virtue your schools where spiritual nourishment is daily offered to your children. Parents who look with indifference upon a matter of so great importance either have no conscience or are apostates from their faith.

The united opposition of all parents to the threatening measure is the more necessary, the more violent efforts the party of unbelievers make to take hold of the schools in order to use them in their combat against Christianity. That they cannot recognize the true worth of the denominational schools is, as we have seen, a necessary consequence of their unbelief. If they, therefore, for themselves and for their children prefer schools which are separated from religion, we cannot be surprised, though we lament their baneful error for their own sake. But they are not content with this. They want, at the same time, to make their unbelief and its consequences a law for the entire Christian people. Herein lies the unheard-of injustice which this party strives to commit against the nation. Because they deny Christ, the schools of the Christian people too shall be arranged in such a manner as if the whole nation had apostatized from Christianity. In their scheme there is no question of progress and enlightenment, as they pretend, but only of realizing their hostile intentions against religion.

In order, moreover, to make their success surer, they recur, besides, to that other pagan principle that the children belong not to the parents in the first place, but to the state, and that, accordingly, not the will of the parents, but the will of the state, i.e., of the party which endeavors at the present moment to rule the state, has to decide on the whole formation and education of the children. All these pernicious plans and efforts, however, have their proper root in those secret societies, chiefly that of freemasonry, which extend their influence everywhere, without betraying anything of their machinations to the people, and which have, without your being aware of it, almost in every community their dependent creatures who serve them as instruments for the accomplishment of their plans.

Therefore, beloved parents, take care of your schools, and follow with the greatest attention everything that takes place on the field of educacation. But above all, strain every nerve to keep your schools, as hitherto, intimately united with the Church. It is only through this intimate union with the Church that the schools will be enabled to promote the true temporal and eternal welfare of your dear children.

That your efforts may be successful, beloved parents, I give you and all your dear children the episcopal blessing in the name of the Father, and of the Son, and of the Holy Ghost. Amen.

AN ANSWER

TO DR. BOUQUILLON'S QUERY,

"EDUCATION: TO WHOM DOES IT BELONG?"

BY

REV. R. I. HOLAIND, S.J.

SECOND EDITION.

NEW YORK, CINCINNATI, CHICAGO:
BENZIGER BROTHERS,
Printers to the Holy Apostolic See.

PREFACE.

LAST night (Nov. 19, 1891) we had the good fortune to receive a pamphlet written by the eminent Dr. Bouquillon, professor of moral theology at the Catholic University of America. To those who have the honor of knowing the distinguished writer it is needless to say that his little book is teeming with erudition; it is, moreover, highly interesting, for it deals with the burning question of the rights of the civil power with regard to the education of children. The Doctor says very truly that a clear exposition of the principles underlying the school question must prove both useful and opportune at this hour, " when the practical difficulties in which it is involved have become national concerns." He tells us that in the pages of his pamphlet *theoretical principles only are dealt with*, but he knows that these theoretical principles bear directly on practice; he is fully aware that both in Wisconsin and Illinois they have given rise to a sturdy political conflict; that the fate of elections may depend on the issues taken by the candidates with regard to parochial schools; and that a lawsuit involving the freedom of Catholic teaching is at this very moment before the Supreme Court of Ohio. Moreover, in a few days, important meetings will be held in St. Louis; great interests are at stake, and his modesty cannot blind him to the fact that his authority will have great weight, both with the hierarchy and with the laity. The importance of the question should, perhaps, have prompted him to give us sooner the benefit of his extensive learning; nobody knows better than Dr. Bouquillon that the scientific treatment of moral questions involves very serious difficulties; that a slight inaccuracy leads to dangerous consequences; and that a statement, perfectly clear to its author, is often misapprehended both by his friends and by his opponents.

We wish more time had been given us to study and discuss the pamphlet. But as the matter stands, we have no choice; we must act on the spur of the moment; the pamphlet reached us on the 19th of November, at a late hour, and the important meetings in which it must have great weight will begin on the 28th of November. In so short a time we cannot do justice to the subject, compare all the quotations with the texts from which they are drawn, nor show how far they go in making good the peculiar conclusions at which the author has arrived. But if want of time and dearth of books prevent us from accomplishing all we fain would do, nothing forbids us to set forth our difficulties and objections. We shall do so freely; happy shall we be if the Doctor's explanations enable us more firmly to grasp the true principles on which Catholic education is to be established and maintained. After asking for explanations which, for us at least, are much needed, we shall make up for our deficiencies by quoting at length two of the standard writers whose names appear on pages 5 and 6 of the pamphlet. The reader will be able to judge for himself whether their principles and their conclusions always agree with those of the author of the pamphlet.

THE PARENT FIRST.

§ 1. IS THE STATE CHRISTIAN OR UNCHRISTIAN?

After perusing the pamphlet one cannot help asking : "What is that State which is represented as one of the four owners of educational rights and which stands forth as the general manager of the joint property? Is it a Christian State united with the Church, obedient to her in things spiritual, and (although itself supreme in the temporal order) acknowledging her indirect authority when she calls on rulers to come to her assistance? If so, we may acknowledge in the civil power not only the rights which essentially belong to it, but also those which may have been delegated to it by the Church. The brow of Charlemagne is glossy with the sacred unction.

If the State be such as it is defined (p. 11), " not the people, but the social authority,"—that is to say, a body of men who govern the people and who may be individually very good Christians and may even teach a Sunday-school, but who in their official capacity ignore the authority of the Church and have no special use for Canon Law, then in order that arguments drawn from the Decretals or from Catholic theologians may be used to determine their powers, it is necessary to prove, first, that the powers attributed to the rulers are neither accidental nor derived from the Church, but are essential to the State precisely because it is a social, autonomous, corporate body. We may live on excellent terms with our master, but we must not take him for Charlemagne.[1]

It might be alleged that the mistake would be without importance, because the authority " is one and the same, and always and everywhere has the same rights and attributes" (p. 11). This must not be taken to the letter, for it is evident that a physical or moral person that has delegated powers besides its own has more authority than

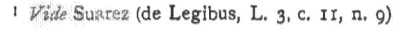
[1] *Vide* Suarez (de Legibus, L. 3, c. 11, n. 9).

one which must be content with the grants of nature. Moreover, the author himself (p. 18) has distinguished the essential from the accidental powers of the State, and has told us (p. 19) that "the duty of teaching is not for the State an essential duty." It is true that he adds that right goes beyond duty in this matter; but if right does not spring from an essential duty, it is necessarily conditioned by the essential duties of other physical or moral persons, namely, the parents and the Church.

For these reasons we must beg of the reader to bear in mind the distinction which we have made: it is commonly found in theologians, and it is explained by Costa-Rosetti in the first corollary to his 171st thesis, p. 731.

The author has reduced the subject-matter of his pamphlet to four questions: right to educate, mission to educate, authority over education, liberty of education; in our observations we shall follow a somewhat different order. As rights originate in duties, at least as far as man is concerned, we shall consider first the duty, then the rights, of the four claimants to educational privileges. Moreover, as the Church alone may be said in a strict sense to have received *a mission* to teach, we shall assume that with regard to other educators mission and duty mean the same thing.

§ 2. HAS EVERYBODY A RIGHT TO EDUCATE?

The first contention of our author is that every individual, every legitimate association, has by nature the right of educating. We would let this proposition pass unchallenged were it not for an equivocation which might perplex readers less versed than Doctor Bouquillon in matters of morals. If education consisted only in communicating to others the useful knowledge that each one may have acquired, then we also would say that each man may educate all those who of their own accord come to him for information. To communicate our knowledge to others, as far as may be useful, is a duty of charity, for we must do by them as we would wish them to do by ourselves; as a rule, it is a precept of charity, not a strict command of justice. Let us grant, then, that every individual man, and every lawfully constituted society, is entitled to give useful information, *to teach*, as long as persons are found willing to be taught by that individual or that society, without, however, overstepping the limits assigned by natural law or by *just* civil laws. But *education* is a very different thing: it comprises, according to Costa-Rosetti and others, "all those functions which promote not only the preservation and development of the body, but also the perfection of the mind and the evolution both of the intellectual and of the *moral* powers." To educate is to exercise jurisdiction; it supposes *authority* in the educator and submission in the scholar. We deny that any one has the right to educate the children of anybody else *unless the parents give him that power*. The reason is briefly this: jurisdiction (unless derived or delegated) cannot be found where the peculiar relation on which it is founded is wanting; but the peculiar relation on which the jurisdiction of parents is based is found in the parents *only;* therefore that jurisdiction can be found in nobody else except by derivation or delegation. The same thesis will be found in Jansen at the end of this volume; moreover, we shall have occasion to dwell again on this topic. Of course this argument does not exclude a jurisdiction founded on a relation other than paternity, and, *a fortiori*, on a title superior to it, such as a direct divine command; but it excludes all individuals, moral or physical, who would claim education against the will of the parents without showing a title superior to paternity. Moreover, it enables us to get rid of one of the claimants mentioned at the end of the pamphlet; those claimants are: the individual, physical and moral; the family, the State, the Church. We always thought that there were too many. We may leave as a consolation to the individual the right of teaching those who want to listen to him, just as the physician has the right to treat all the patients that apply to him, and the lawyer has the right to plead all the honest suits that he can get.

Should we intentionally lead the reader to believe that the Doctor has done nothing more than prove a truism, we would be guilty of great injustice. There is really a school of so-called liberals who ignore natural law, and try to find in legality the fount of every right; against that school his arguments are decisive. The right of teaching comes primarily from natural law, the limitations come chiefly from positive law. But we want to emphasize the difference between mere *teaching* and *education*, because a confusion in this case is a fruitful source of sophisms. It is also necessary to insist on this point: the right of teaching *does not* involve necessarily the obligation of hearing the teacher. Surely the right of healing the sick is based on nature itself, yet Esculapius cannot compel the sufferers to take his pellets.

The quotations and references which adorn page 9 of the pamphlet are not levelled at the upholders of parental power, but at those who assert that the right of teaching is always delegated and derived from the ecclesiastical authority. We do not feel called upon to enter into that controversy. The reference to the treatise of Suarez (*de Legibus*) brings before us all the subtle problems attending the modifications of natural law—not in its essence, which is immutable, but in its varied applications. This question alone would require a volume.

This is not the time to discuss *abstract* theories: we must grapple at once with the difficulties which beset the live issues of the hour.

§ 3. THE DUTY AND RIGHT OF THE PARENT.

To whom does education, and especially elementary education, belong? We said: To the parent first. This is exactly what the Cardinal Archbishop of Rennes asserts in his catechism. We quote two of the questions:

Q. With whom rests the right to educate children?

A. The right to educate children rests with their parents.

Q. What is the duty of Christian parents with respect to the education of their children?

A. The first duty of Christian parents with respect to the education of their children is to see that they know and practise their religion.

"The power of the parents over their children," says Blackstone, "is derived from their duty."

Dr. Bouquillon does not dissent: "This right of parents" (the right of education) "is sacred, *no one may suppress or diminish it*" (the italics are ours); "for it springs from a paramount duty" (page 10, l. 20).

Leo XIII., quoted by Dr. Bouquillon, adds another feature. This right is inalienable: "In those duties which are assumed in the very act of imparting life, let the fathers know that many rights are contained, according both to nature and to justice. And those rights are of such a nature that man cannot in any particular either free himself from their exercise or take away anything from the power of any other man; for to relax duties by which man is bound to God would be criminal on the part of man."

These solemn words are the authoritative declaration of the conclusions of ethics and of human law. According to Blackstone the duties of parents are maintenance, protection, and education.

Four evident reasons show that this threefold duty follows directly from natural law:

First, every moral agent is accountable for the consequences of his own acts, so far as he can foresee them; on him it is incumbent to provide that those consequences be not hurtful, but beneficial. But the birth of the children is the result of an act of the free will of their parents. Therefore it is the bounden duty of the parents to see that the life which they have given be not a curse, but a blessing. It could not be a blessing were the duties mentioned, especially that of education, neglected; therefore it is the duty of the parents to provide for the maintenance, protection, and *education* of their children;

and that duty would exist of necessity even if positive law should fail to sanction it; for even in that case the natural relation of parent to children would immutably subsist. Grotius, Puffendorf, and Blackstone use the same argument with some differences which are not material. We will quote only Grotius: " It is a maxim of Aristotle that he who gives the form (i.e., the specific principle of activity) must give what the form requires. Therefore, he who has caused a man to exist must, as far as it is possible and necessary, secure to him the things which are necessary for a human and social life—this being the kind of life to which man is born" (*De jure belli et pacis*, l. ii. c. vii. sec. 3). Immediately after, Grotius quotes several authorities, and, among others, Justinian, who says: " A natural impulse and instinct moves the parents to educate their children."

Secondly. The chief end of nature in the marriage relation is to secure the continuance and perfection of the human race; but this purpose would evidently be defeated if the three obligations above mentioned were neglected by the parents; therefore these obligations are laid upon them by nature itself. Blackstone says: " The last duty of parents to their children is that of giving them an education suitable to their station in life; a duty pointed out by reason and of far the greatest importance of any. For, as Puffendorf very well observes, it is not easy to imagine or allow that a parent has conferred any considerable benefit upon his child by bringing him into the world, if he afterwards entirely neglects his culture and education, and suffers him to grow up like a mere beast, to lead a life useless to others and shameful to himself" (Bk. I., c. 16). We must add that by this neglect the parent not only sins against the child and against society, but also thwarts the beneficent purpose of the Creator in instituting matrimony.

Thirdly. A universal impulse which is not only rational and human, but which is reproduced in the instinct of animals, is, according to Roman jurisconsults and to reason itself, the unmistakable token of natural law. But such is the impulse of parents to accomplish the three duties mentioned and it finds its counterpart even in the instinct of animals. Therefore those duties are imposed by natural law. We quote in full the celebrated text of Ulpian: " Natural law is that which nature has taught all living beings, for it is not the exclusive property of man, but it reaches all the animals which live in the air, on the earth, or in the depths of the sea. Hence flow the union of man and woman which we call matrimony; hence the procreation of children; *hence their education.*"

Fourthly. Where there is a special and natural fitness, there also is laid a special and natural duty; but parents have a special and natural fitness to educate their own children; hence it is their special and natural duty. The minor premise is evidenced by observation both of private and of social life. Nothing can supply the love of a mother or the mild firmness of a father. Young orphans are at a disadvantage from the start, as keen observers of human nature well know. In political life, history tells the same tale. One of the Grecian States, Sparta, shifted the responsibility from the parents to the State. It interfered with nature's law, and the consequence was that Sparta did not produce a single poet, a single orator, a single statesman of superior ability—unless it be Lycurgus, who invented the system, but was not reared according to it. For a time it had warriors, but even those at last were wanting, and Sparta was conquered by the other commonwealths, on which in the beginning she was wont to impose her will. Rome committed another fault—that of giving by law to the father an authority which had no warrant in nature; but although she paid the forfeit in the end, yet she could boast of a succession of great men down to the last period of decline. "The duties of parents to their children as being their natural guardians," says Chancellor Kent, "consist in maintaining and educating them during the season of infancy and youth, and making reasonable provision for their future usefulness and happiness in life, by a situation suited to their habits, and a competent provision for the exigencies of that situation.

"The education of children in a manner suitable to their station and calling is another branch of parental duty, of imperfect obligation generally in the eye of municipal law, but of very great importance to the welfare of the State."

For the better understanding of this passage I must observe that *imperfect duty*, in ethics and in law, means a duty which the holder of the corresponding right cannot enforce, or a duty based on fitness, but not on commutative justice. In our opinion the duties enumerated by Blackstone and Kent are imperatively demanded by strict justice, and therefore are *perfect duties;* but, according to Kent, municipal law takes the view that the State is not bound to enforce them as long as their violation is not evident enough to become a public inconvenience. From the stand-point of municipal law this view is correct. "Several of the States of antiquity," continues the eminent jurist, "were too solicitous to form their youth for the various duties of civil life to entrust their education solely to the parents; but this was upon the principle, totally inadmissible to the modern civilized world, of the absorption of the individual in the body-politic, and of his entire subjection to the despotism of the State" (Comment., lect. xxv.).

"The father," says Blackstone, "may delegate part of his parental authority, during his life, to the tutor or school-master of his child, who is then *in loco parentis*, and has such a portion of the power of the parent committed to his charge, namely, that of restraint and correction, as may be necessary to answer the purpose for which he is employed."

"The power of the parents over their children is derived from their duty."

The learned Doctor would probably accept this doctrine, for he himself says (p. 9):

"The end of conjugal society, one of the reasons for its stability, is the education no less than the procreation of children. Parents are called by God not only to generate children to bodily life, but also to form their minds ; therefore they are entitled to be the first instructors of their children, themselves, or through teachers of their own choosing." But at the end of the same page he makes an assertion which we must beg leave to call misleading. "On the other hand," says the Doctor, "the State, within the sphere of its powers, has a right of inspection over the education imparted by the family—the right to prevent it from becoming a source of moral poisoning." No doubt the State has a right to prevent education from becoming a source of moral poisoning, but does this involve the right of invading the privacy of the household ? Leo XIII. does not think so, for the Holy Father says: "The idea that the civil government should, at its own discretion, penetrate and pervade the family and the household is a great and pernicious mistake" (Encycl. *Rerum Novarum*).

The sphere of civil authority is determined by its end, and it is described by the Doctor himself in the following lines: "The purpose of civil authority is: 1. To maintain peace between citizens, protect their mutual rights, their legitimate activity; 2. To supply the insufficiency of individuals." Moreover, we must bear in mind that the direct object of social activity is not the individual but the social good, and that a wrong must be exterior, and must visibly, though perhaps indirectly, attack society before the civil authority can take cognizance of it and follow it within the precincts of the household. "If the citizens of a State,—that is to say, the families,—on entering into association and fellowship, experienced at the hand of the State hindrance instead of help, and found their rights attacked instead of being protected, such association were rather to be repudiated than sought after" (Encyl. *Rerum Novarum*).

In concluding these remarks on the right of parents to educate, we must observe: 1st. That the family is a true society, anterior to every kind of state or nation, with rights and duties of its own totally independent of the commonwealth (Encycl. already quoted). 2d. That since the household is anterior, both in idea and fact, to the gathering of men into a commonwealth, the former must have rights and duties which are prior to those of the latter, and which rest more immediately on nature (ibid.). 3d. That the right of education is one of those rights, that it is inalienable, and that no man can either abridge or destroy it (Encycl. *Officii sanctissum*, Dec. 22, 1887). 4th. That the State cannot, at its own discretion, penetrate and pervade the family (Encycl. *Rerum Novarum*). 5th. But if a family finds itself in great difficulty, utterly friendless and without help, it is right that extreme necessity be met by public aid. 6th. That if within the walls of the family there occur great disturbance of mutual rights, the public power must interfere to force each party to give the other what is due (ibid.). 7th. But the rulers must go no further; nature bids them stop here (ibid.).

Unless we retain a strong hold on these principles, all ethical and social theories referring to the family and to the State will be doomed to inextricable confusion.

§ 4. MISSION OF THE CHURCH.

"That the Church has the right to teach results from the words of Our Lord to the apostles: 'Docete omnes gentes.' The Church is essentially a teaching power" (p. 16). Yes, but she is an *educating* power as well: for she imparts spiritual life to her children, feeds them with the word of God and the living bread, watches over their spiritual growth, and brings them (as far as they let her) into the measure of the fulness of Christ; she is a true and perfect mother; she is also the best of educators. The passage from which we have taken the first words of this paragraph is admirable, and we do not think that Dr. Bouquillon would object to the few words we have added.

The statement of the mission of the Church (p. 20) does not seem to strengthen the advocacy of her rights contained in the sixteenth page, yet it supplies us with the following significant passage: "In the presence of an education that is indifferent or hostile to religion, bishops found schools, colleges, academies, universities. *Clearly this is a case of necessity*,[1] regrettable necessity, implying the regret that the State is indifferent to Christianity in the premises."

In the following lines the Doctor might have been more tender for those who assert that the Church has received the mission to teach human as well as divine science. It is but fair to state that they try to make good their interpretation of the celebrated text, "Go ye, therefore, and teach all nations," by bringing in the 13th verse of the

[1] The italics are ours.

sixteenth chapter of St. John, "But when the Spirit of truth is come,. He will teach you all truth ;" but as the Doctor emphatically declares that the Church is *indirectly* endowed with the right to teach the sciences and letters, in so far as they are necessary or useful to the knowledge or practice of revelation, the question is more speculative than practical.

But there is an omission that we regret. The Doctor does not speak of the mission of the Church with regard to those *moral* truths which belong to the natural order, but which the pagan philosophers have never fully known, and which modern pagans forget or distort. Shall we have a sort of *morale civique?* What shall be the foundation? State Law, Utilitarianism, Altruism, Evolution? It would have been good to state explicitly that the Church had the mission to teach those truths ; for, although they do not *singly* transcend natural reason, yet it is *morally impossible* for men to acquire the knowledge of *all*, and even to retain the knowledge once acquired, without the help of an infallible exponent.

§ 5. THE SO-CALLED MISSION OF THE STATE.

At the top of page 18 of the pamphlet we read the following caption : *The Mission to Educate incumbent on the State.* When, where, by whom was this mission given? We know that Our Lord said to His apostles : "Go ye, therefore, and teach all nations." Here is a clear, distinct, unequivocal command to teach, and from the context and the nature of the teaching it is evident that it is not *bare teaching* which is commanded, but the duty of *educating* is imposed. The Church has unquestionably a mission to *educate*. When was such a precept imposed on *civil* society? Well, by *mission* the Doctor means *duty*. We need not quarrel about words ; and yet metaphorical expressions often confuse ideas instead of making them clearer. What is meant is that the State is bound to teach, not that it has some control over education, not that it has the right to establish schools, but that it must be an educator. Let us see how this is proved. The author tells us that the purpose of civil authority is: 1st, to maintain peace between citizens, protect their mutual rights, their legitimate activity ; 2d, to supply the insufficiency of individuals. To this double purpose correspond functions of a different order, some essential, and others accidental. We are told moreover that the duty of teaching is not for the State an essential duty, it is accidental ; if individuals, families, associations have provided all the education that is necessary, the State is free to doff the teacher's gown. Moreover, its way of educating is to erect schools and appoint competent masters. And so this very scientific presentment of the thesis may be reduced to the simple statement: that, when schools and teachers are wanting, government must try to supply both. There can be no objection to this proposition; moreover, it is easily proved. It is the secondary function of the government to supply the insufficiency of individuals—when schools and teachers are wanting, individuals are deficient. Therefore the State must supply both as far as the exchequer will allow. Candidly it was not necessary to bring St. Thomas, Mgr. Cavagnis, Professor Wilson, Messrs. Westel W. Willoughby and William P. Willoughby to tell us that. In a man less wealthy than the learned Professor, I would call this a waste of science. But the conclusion contains something more: "While saying that the State should provide instruction where individuals fail to do so, we do not mean to say that the State may teach only when and where individuals fail to do their duty. The exercise of the duty of the State is allowable whenever the State judges the exercise of this duty to be useful, without being absolutely necessary." That is, the State may establish schools, even when the public could do without them. We would here beg leave to insert a remark of Jansen: "Private citizens, erecting schools at their own expense, are perfectly independent; but the government, using the money of the treasury which is obtained by taxation, must, as a faithful administrator, observe distributive justice and make sure that the studies promoted are useful for the common good, and do not benefit one class only of citizens" (Thesis XLIX. Schol. $1^{um.}$). Some late developments make this remark very timely.

The *mission* of the State consists in erecting schools and supplying teachers when private enterprise is inadequate. But as the right "goes beyond the duty in this matter," let us consider the right of the State with regard to teaching.

And first we must ask again whether the State is Christian or un-Christian—at least in its *corporate* capacity. Certainly Dr. Bouquillon does not consider the United States of America as coming under the rule laid down by Cavagnis, his favorite author, who says: "States are parts of the Church, and as such are bound to procure the good of the whole" ("Nozioni di Diretto," etc., p. 231). In that duty we might find a good foundation for a right. But let us take up the arguments. The following is considered by the author as *apodictical*, and he says of the consequence: "We consider this conclusion as impregnable" (p. 12). The argument is substantially as follows: "Civil authority has the right to use all legitimate temporal means it judges necessary for the attainment of the temporal welfare of the Commonwealth. Now, among the most necessary means for the attainment of the temporal welfare of the Commonwealth is the dif-

So-called Mission of the State. 15

fusion of human knowledge. Therefore civil authority has the right to use the means necessary for the diffusion of such knowledge, that is to say, to teach it or to have it taught by capable agents." With regard to the major, we must ask what are the legitimate means ? Are measures which infringe pre-existing and inalienable rights, such as those of parents, to be called legitimate ? The Doctor would answer that no right is infringed, because the parents are free to send their children to the government schools or to keep them at home. If so, we are satisfied: but let this qualification go on record. We let pass the minor, although explanations might be useful. (But the printer sends us notice that no work can be done on Thanksgiving.) The consequent of the argument is, unfortunately, double, for it is one thing to use the means necessary for the diffusion,—that is to say, *to help, to encourage* those who diffuse—and place the means at their disposal; it is another thing *to teach directly*, or through the medium of agents. Moreover, to teach directly or indirectly those who are willing to be taught, is *to instruct;* the thing to be proved is that the State has the right *to educate*. Now, *to educate*, one must form the minds and hearts of pupils and teach them *morals*. Now, does it not strike the Doctor that one who sets aside revelation makes himself unfit to teach *Christian* morals ? Nothing is left but to teach *la morale civique*—a doubtful sort of education.

The Doctor tells us that the State cannot help teaching, because it exercises the judicial power. Now to pass a judicial sentence is not generally understood to be the same as to teach a school, and so we must beg leave to consider this argument as metaphorical.

The Doctor proceeds to prove from history that Christian sovereigns have often established schools, and even universities, without waiting for the consent of the Church, and without eliciting from the Church any protestation. The argument evinces great learning and we would be the last man to question the learning of our gifted friend (we hope the Doctor will not refuse us the title of friend, which is for us an object of legitimate pride). But we are compelled to say that his enumeration proves nothing, because those princes took the teaching of the Church as the moral basis of their institutions, acknowledged the right of inspection on the part of the bishops, and considered the Pontifical direction as supreme. The Doctor concludes his arguments as follows: " Finally, we have yet to learn that any pope has ever declared that the State went beyond its right in founding schools, *provided the instruction be organized in the spirit of Christianity.*" Such a declaration would have been strange indeed; but the popes have often condemned godless schools and godless education. But you will answer that you have expressly said that the State may not establish Agnostic schools. Certainly. But what sort of schools can be established by a government which, in its *corporate* capacity, ignores revelation? At best they can be but neutral. Well, the Holy Father, Leo XIII., says explicitly:[1] "The Church has always condemned *mixed* or *neutral* schools."—But the government will limit itself strictly to the teaching of secular matters. This is the very case embodied in the 48th proposition *condemned* in the Syllabus: "Catholics may approve a system of education according to which the training of the young is severed from the Catholic faith and from the power of the Church; and which, having for its *only object* the knowledge of natural sciences, aims only or chiefly at the ends of earthly social life."

No one, Rev. Doctor, knows better than you do the import of the instruction sent by the Congregation of the Inquisition to all the bishops of the United States, November 24, 1875 (Conc. Balt. III., p. 279). That declaration, and the decrees of the council which it accompanies, belong, as you know, to the *jus canonicum novissimum*. In that instruction, after having quoted a pontifical utterance in which those are condemned who send their children to schools unfriendly to the Catholic Church, the Congregation adds the following significant words: "As these teachings are founded both on natural and on divine law, they enunciate a universal principle and have a universal binding force wherever the same system is prevailing."

As a commentary on the 48th proposition of the Syllabus, let me quote an authority who is equally revered by us both. In his latest work Cardinal Gibbons speaks as follows:

"The religious and secular education of our children cannot be *divorced* from each other without inflicting a fatal wound upon the soul. The usual consequence of such a separation is to paralyze the moral faculties and to foment a spirit of indifference in matters of faith. Education is to the soul what food is to the body. The milk with which the infant is nourished at its mother's breast feeds not only its head, but permeates at the same time its heart and the other organs of the body. In like manner the intellectual and moral growth of our children should go hand in hand; otherwise their education is shallow and fragmentary, and often proves a curse instead of a blessing" ("Christ. Her.," p. 493).

Do I then condemn the State for erecting *mixed* or *neutral schools?* No. Our rulers have on hand a bad bargain, and they often do what they can to meet its conditions without hurting any one: yet the bargain remains a bad one. But I am free to find fault with those Catholics who in the face of the repeated warnings of the highest authority

---
[1] Letter to the French Bishops, 1884.

in this world continue to send their children to *mixed* or *neutral* schools without necessity, without using the required prophylactics, without securing the authorization of the Ordinary.

You may say that you speak of an ideal State and of ideal schools, and consequently take it for granted that the instruction is organized in the spirit of Christianity ; this is where I am compelled to be at variance with you. We professors have a tendency which at times is mischievous. We are apt to soar to the t᠎᠎᠎᠎ ; of metaphysical peaks, and ignore the real issues that are debated at the foot of the mountain. You discoursed on an ideal State and ideal schools, but we have to deal with a *concrete* State, and schools which do a great deal of concrete damage by rapidly disintegrating all the creeds, and undermining the foundations of *Christian* morality.

§ 6. STATE-CONTROL.

We have but one question of some importance to treat : it is the control of the State over private schools, or at least over the teaching of secular branches in those private schools. The author tells us that he has "no intention of defining when and under what conditions the State may or should put its authority into operation," for "that is a question of prudence and justice." We must observe that it becomes at times a question of validity, for authority exercised without justice is no authority at all. No authority is valid except within its own sphere. No authority can be put into operation except to attain the end for which it has been given ; no authority can absorb a power which had a prior existence, and which rests more immediately on nature. Hence Leo XIII. tells us that the "parental authority can neither be absorbed by the State nor abolished by it, for it has the same origin as human life itself." Again the same pontiff says: "The Socialists, in setting aside the parent and introducing the providence of the State, act against natural justice, and threaten the very existence of family life." It must therefore be clearly understood that whatever power the State may wield, it must leave intact the rights of the parents. What rights, then, remain to the State ? The right of suppressing immoral or treasonable teaching; the right of promoting education by supplying *the means* that private enterprise could not secure, and offering incentives to the learned ; the right of standing *in loco parentis* when the parents are dead or notoriously vicious or cruel, and when there is no one bound to the child by closer or holier ties ready to claim its guardianship. This description of State-control with regard to the child sums up substantially what can be deduced from the nature of State functions, without making them run against and interfere with the rights of that society which, as the Holy Father has it, " is anterior to every kind of State, and totally independent of the commonwealth" (Encycl. *Rerum Novarum*).

This control, of course, is *indirect*, and nothing will satisfy some philosophers but a direct control. As we have neither time nor space, we have left them to the tender mercies of Von Hammerstein, whose criticisms will be found in Appendix No. 2.

Of a higher and more complete kind is the control of the Church; her mission is of the supernatural order: the duty of the family springs from natural law and from parental relations. The end of the Church is the union with Christ, and life everlasting. The end of the family is the procreation and education of children. Hence the civil power can claim ampler rights when it is in union with the ecclesiastical authority and acts under its direction.

This is an observation which Dr. Bouquillon might have made: it would have rendered his pamphlet far more useful. The authorities which he draws from canonical sources are all weakened by that fatal flaw. For instance, he quotes Lucidi (de Visitatione, tom. 11, c. 7, § 2, n. 207); the passage begins as follows: "It is to be regretted and vehemently to be deplored that supreme rulers have taken this department from the bishops. No wonder if the foundations of empires are quaking and if the princes fall from their thrones. . . . We do not mean to wrest from the civil power all control and right of patronage with regard to science, chiefly with regard to physical sciences, especially when (as sometimes happens) they have no connection with religion, and to give the whole authority to the Church," etc. He gives us the constitution of Leo XII., in which it is ordered that schools should be opened in every city by the magistrates; but those schools must be under the authority of the bishops, the students must make an annual retreat, etc., etc. Give us schools of this kind by all means; they shall never be condemned by the Church, and magistrates under episcopal jurisdiction are welcome to quiz the students.

Dr. Bouquillon would seem to claim *direct* control for the State: he pleads that it is of great importance for the commonwealth that men should be well instructed; therefore the *control* of instruction should belong to the State. He proves too much.—It is of great importance to the State that the citizens should be well off; therefore the State should have control of property. It is important that citizens should be healthy: this depends in a great measure on cooking; therefore the State should have the control of the kitchen, etc., etc. The general answer is this: The department of the State is to promote the welfare of the commonwealth by social means, not by controlling directly individual activity, much less by invading family rights; individual activity and family rights are simply outside of its sphere of action, and it would be a fatal error either to hamper the one or to violate the other; by so doing the State would sap the foundation of its own prosperity.

Costa-Rosetti (theses 175–176) holds this doctrine, and refers to thesis 174, where he proves that individual and personal goods do not formally and directly belong to the sphere of civil authority, although civil authority may indirectly reach them: instruction is *per se* an individual good, hence the control over it on the part of the State is only *indirect*. Since Dr. Bouquillon has quoted Prof. Wilson, Messrs. Westel W. Willoughby and William P. Willoughby, we may be allowed to bring in a quotation from John Stuart Mill, which seems to express the common-sense view of the question.

"One thing must be strenuously insisted on—that the government must claim no monopoly for its education either in its higher or lower branches, must exert neither authority nor influence to induce the people to resort to its teachers in preference to others, and must confer no peculiar advantages on those who have been instructed by them.... It is not endurable that a government should, either in law or in fact, have a complete control over the education of the people. To possess such a control and actually exert it is to be despotic. A government which can mould the opinion and sentiments of the people from their youth upwards can do with them whatever it pleases."

Many other questions we should like to treat, but time and space forbid. One word more, however, about the power which the learned Doctor grants to the State to exact a minimum of instruction. He says that if you grant to the State power over cases of neglect, you must grant it also the power to define a minimum. This does not follow. The State may punish parents who starve their children, or leave them in a state of destitution with regard to clothing; yet will you allow the State to determine by law how many ounces of food must be given to the children, and what sort of clothing they shall wear? We may as well repair at once to Icaria, to Salentum, or to Utopia. The fact is that all those matters are relative, undefinable *a priori*, and requiring State intervention only when there is a public wrong committed; and the existence of that public wrong must be determined by the judge on the individual merits of the case. The learned Doctor admits that the Civiltà and Costa-Rosetti are against him, but he rules them out of court on the ground that their reasonings seem to him very faulty. It would have been fairer to let us know what those reasonings are. First let us state the thesis; it reads as follows in Rosetti: "Considering natural law only, parents cannot be compelled by the civil authority to send their children to an elementary school. But they may be obliged in particular cases." This is not exactly the contradictory of the Doctor's position.

Let us state briefly the reasons of Rosetti: First, parents alone are judges of the material and intellectual wants of their children; the control is due to them in strict justice: an obligation of that kind is an abridgment of their control, and therefore a violation of justice. Secondly, the only reason why the State could interfere would be the violation of the right of the child; but all the child is strictly entitled to is to receive the education necessary to live in comfort in the condition of his parents. On the other hand, it is not universally true that the three R's are necessary to live in comfort; hence it cannot be proved by natural law alone that the parents can be compelled to give their children a knowledge of the three R's. The author adds, that ignorance, though itself an evil, often saves men from great dangers which result from the reading of bad books, etc., etc.

In point of fact, neither Rosetti nor any other Catholic writer objects to knowledge: they object to State *programmes* and to *compulsion*. They object to State interference in domestic affairs, and whenever the government leaves its imperial duties to cross the family threshold, Catholic writers resent the intrusion and bid the rulers halt. Moreover, they fully know that he who can make and unmake programmes of studies can crush competition and rule the social forces for his own private ends.

Dr. Bouquillon tells us at the end of his pamphlet that there are four claimants to the right of educating children: the individual, the parent, the State, the Church. He leaves to the hierarchy the duty to harmonize their contending claims. He might have been bolder, and the hierarchy would have thanked him for it: it is in such learned men as the distinguished professor that they seek the comfort afforded by distinct and unfaltering assertions of truth. May we not reject one of the claimants, the individual, moral or physical? We remain with three: the parent, the Church, and the State. The parent has the *priority* both in concept and in fact. The Church has the supreme direction, because she has the noblest end and the most sacred mission. By her side stands the State, aiming at the public good without interfering with private or domestic rights, but ready to answer the call of the humblest member of society, ever watching over that order on which depend the peace and happiness of nations.

THREE THESES OF JANSEN
ON THE
SCHOOL QUESTION.

(*De Facultate Docendi Institutiones Juridicae.*)

THESIS XXI.

PARENTS ALONE HAVE THE RIGHT OF EDUCATION.

I.

From duty. For if, by the natural law, God has imposed upon them, before any other person or persons, the duty of *education*, surely it stands to reason that it is not lawful for others to put obstacles in their way, or to rob them to any extent of this privilege. They enjoy also the same liberty in specifying the *method* of education, since he who has a right in the substance of a thing has also the corresponding right in the mode which accompanies the substance.

II.

From the nature of the family. Again, the right itself being entirely dependent on relations peculiar to the constitution of the family, the parents *alone* can be judges in the matter.

III.

From absurd conclusions. Finally, the liberty of the family would be infringed, nay, wholly abolished, by the interference of another power. The unity of education, and consequently education itself, would be at an end, since that education which would be acceptable to the parents would often miss its aim, owing to the interference of a contrary system. And this by the very force of nature itself, from which the two contending powers would have sprung,—a supposition entirely out of keeping with the order of nature. Therefore, parents have the sole right in education, and consequently they alone can derive from the order of nature that authority which is indispensable for the performance of their duty. Hence Grotius has justly said, "Parents are by nature educators" (l. ii. c. 20).[1]

But since instruction is nothing but *a part* of education, these same parents have alone the natural right of instructing their children; and it is their right also to determine the limits and method of that instruction.

Instruction.

Scholion.—Therefore, although the duty of education is not imposed upon parents by a law of strict justice, yet those who place obstacles to the exercise of the paternal power infringe upon justice, since they take away from the parents something that is exclusively their own. Lugo's teaching is to the point:

Personal authority.

"The power of directing belongs to the parents; hence, he who takes from the father this power takes from him something that belongs to him and commits an injustice, since he deprives the father of something *useful*. For it cannot be denied that to possess such a power is useful to the father, because, though the father's command ought to be directed to the good of the child, yet the right to command for his own good redounds to the benefit of the father. It is an advantage to him to exercise his power in the interest of his son."—*De jure et just. Disp. L.S.I., n.* 13.

IV.

It is with perfect right that parents call their children *their own*, and hold them as such. For, inasmuch as the children owe obedience to their parents alone and have not yet the full use of their faculties, they are not yet fully independent or *sui juris*.

The children belong to the parents.

There is, besides, the fact that parents are, both in physical and moral order, the source of the children's life. For these reasons, we should not be surprised at the extent of the authority that is vested in the parents, nor wonder why they exercise a liberty almost unlimited in the government of their children; for the Author of nature, who has entrusted to them this liberty, has protected it against abuse both by a certain division of power between father and mother, and by a strong natural tendency, owing to which the parents, of their own accord, in spite of every difficulty, seek the good of their children, and really consider the good of the little ones as their own. To this

---

[1] The word used by Grotius is *magistratus*, from "magister."

care, instinctive in the natural order, God has appointed a further safeguard in the supernatural order, which perfects nature and gives it a supernatural aim. In this matter we can easily see, from its mode of acting, what prudence the Church has always observed in securing at the same time the safety of the child and the liberty of the family. It uses at first, for a long time, moral means only; and it is only in an extreme case that it has recourse to compulsory measures against unnatural parents.

THESIS XXII.

"IT IS NOT LAWFUL FOR ANY ONE TO INSTRUCT CHILDREN UNLESS HE HAS OBTAINED FROM THE PARENTS THE AUTHORITY OR THE RIGHT OF TEACHING."

Instruction. There is no doubt that it is indispensable for a teacher to have authority over his young pupil; for instruction, and especially elementary instruction, is a part of education, and without this authority it cannot be carried out. "Who," says Lactantius, "can educate children unless he has the power of a master over them?" (*Divin. Inst.*, l. iv. c. 3. Migne vi. 455.) But if there is question of the order of nature, there is no one except the parents that is by natural right endowed with this power. Since it is vain to expect this authority from the voluntary submission of the child itself, inasmuch as it is not yet in the full exercise of its own rights, it only remains to ask from the parents the needed **Ministers of the Church.** power. If there is question of the supernatural order, the proposition must be restricted; for the ministers of the Church, whose office it is to give moral and especially religious instruction to the children, with or without the consent of the parents, do so on their own authority, which God has conferred upon them with a view to the salvation of men. But if we consider the question of literary instruction apart from religion, then the ministers of the Church cannot impart this kind of instruction, except in the name of the parents. If the parents, therefore, considered it necessary, or even useful, to send their children, together with those of the same locality, to a school, and place them under the care of one teacher, they should diligently inquire whether this school is of such a character as to justify them in entrusting to it their children; moreover, they should take every precaution to ward off whatever could endanger the child's salvation. Wherefore they should hold in abhorrence that school, where such a danger would arise, either from the character or religion of the teacher, from the defect of the method, or from the companionship of school-fellows. Should there be any ground for suspicion, they should prefer to see their children remain ignorant rather than grow wicked. It is evident that it is not lawful for them to send their children to *neutral* schools, for they are prohibited from doing so by the natural law as well as by the precept of the Church. Ecclesiastical authority has the right to *tolerate* exceptions in those cases where the danger of perversion *is removed* or *counteracted*, and when a sufficient reason is given for attending such schools. This is in accordance with the instruction sent to the bishops of America, June 30th, 1875, by the Congregation of the Inquisition.

THESIS XXXIII.

IN THE PERFORMANCE OF THEIR DUTY WITH REGARD TO EDUCATION, PARENTS ARE NOT AT ALL SUBJECT TO STATE-CONTROL.

I.

The title of the State to claim that control should be derived from *the duty* to maintain the rights of its subjects, from *the obligation* to promote the public welfare, or lastly, from *the right* to maintain its own existence: none of those sources can be assigned to State-control. For if we consider the first, children can claim in strict justice nothing but what is necessary to human life—we have shown this in other parts of this work; hence, children have *no strict right* to higher instruction or to the expenses that this higher instruction entails on the parents. Hence the civil power cannot penetrate and pervade the family and the household under the plea that it must protect the rights of its subjects. Nay, more; this very duty forbids interference, for such is the constitution of the family that the head of the household enjoys full administrative freedom on his own responsibility. Far from impeding this freedom, the mighty arm of the State must protect it. Nor can the right of control be based on the second plea; for it requires that those things be accomplished by the State which exceed the power of the citizens in their individual capacity, and which for this reason must be left to the State, which controls greater resources. But the business of education is such that, according to the divine will, it must be carried on by the parents themselves; or, if entrusted to others, it must remain under the unceasing control and responsibility of the parents. For let the kind reader bear in mind that the duty of education is laid upon the parents in so divine a manner that they can never entirely free themselves from it. Without their consent, any other person, even the ruler of the Commonwealth, is without authority. If the reason alleged proves anything, it goes to show that the government must, when circumstances require, place at the disposal of the parents the means to fulfil their duty with greater facility. Lastly, the argument which the ruler might draw from the duty of self-preservation is nugatory. For nobody will deny that it is the interest of the Commonwealth that the parents should educate their children in the best manner possible; for the Commonwealth needs valiant soldiers and citizens imbued with respect for authority, a deep sense of justice, and a love for social harmony. Although those blessings flow chiefly from education, we cannot conclude that education must be subject to State-control. For that cannot be a State right which conflicts, by its very nature, with social order. That order is so designed by its divine author that its very elements are drawn from the order of the household; for the family, considered in its *nature*, is prior in existence, and the same thing may be said of parental authority. But this priority is an evident token of the will of God that parental authority should not depend on the State, but that it is left to the family itself, under the guidance of a natural impulse, so to perfect its members that they may become valuable social elements. Moreover, the principle advanced by our opponents would, if it were true, utterly destroy civil society, because it would transfer to the government not only parental but also conjugal authority; for there is almost nothing within the domestic circle concerning the rearing and education of children which, according to this rule, could not be claimed by the government as subject to its control.

II.

The duty of education is of such a nature that it requires the tenderest charity; for without the living principle of love the educator is utterly unfit to accomplish his mission. But the civil control, proceeding by compulsory laws, strips this duty of its loving character. Now, it is the nature of man to do reluctantly what he does under compulsion. Moreover, in that case, man will often do less than he is really bound to do, and thus the Government will defeat the purpose of its laws by its own interference.

III.

Order within the household requires that children should be perfectly obedient to their parents and grateful for the education which they receive. But if parents gave it under compulsion, the children could not help thinking that the benefit conferred is nothing but the payment of a debt. We can find an illustration in the laws which restrict the liberty of parents in the making of wills. The legal restriction leads the children to think that they can, even during their parents' life, claim as their own a part of the father's property. A sad experience has shown how much such legislation relaxes the family ties. But as even greater perils would attend the enactment of laws which would make the giving of education compulsory on the part of the parents, government interference must be condemned.

IV.

Lastly, this compulsory legislation, to have any value, ought to meet the wants and the conditions peculiar to different families; for the nature and the measure of education must be adapted to the various circumstances in which families are placed. What is enough for a child belonging to one family may be totally inadequate for a child belonging to another. Nay, the law, to be practically enforced, should be so well defined that it could reach all the individual cases; but the deepest lawgiver would not attempt to frame such a law with regard to education. We conclude that the constitution of the household, the nature of political authority and the special features of the duty of education, make it imperative to leave full liberty to the family.

RIGHTS AND DUTIES OF PARENTS WITH REGARD TO THE EDUCATION OF CHILDREN.

(*Hammerstein, De Ecclesia et Statu*, p. 181.)

I.

We have seen the relations between the Church and the State in regard to the first element of human society, that is, matrimony. Let us now examine these relations with regard to the second element of human society, that, namely, which flows from matrimony—the family, I mean: and thus we come to consider the relations existing between parents and children.

In the first place, it must be noted that, as in matrimony religion holds the most prominent place, so in the family, which is the result of matrimony, religion is above all else. Whence it follows that the relations that subsist between parents and children are under ecclesiastical rather than State jurisdiction, though not so exclusively as in the case of the relation between husband and wife. The reason of the exclusive dependence of the latter on the Church is that matrimony constitutes a sacrament, while the relation between parents and children does not. Yet the chief obligation and right of parents, namely, education, for another reason, is chiefly under the authority of the Church, because Christ appointed the Church to teach and direct all men.

As little need be said on other points that concern the family, we shall consider carefully a few points in regard to education, and particularly in regard to the subject of instruction, and of schools, which impart both education and instruction. Three agents concur—the parents, the State, the Church. Let us see what are the functions of each.

II.

The parents have the obligation of education and all the rights of education before the Church and the State, and in this sense, that even before the existence of any State or Church the parents could and ought to educate and instruct their children, and, if need be, to send them to school. Let us suppose that neither is yet existing. Should the children then born live without education until the State should arise or until the Church should be founded? Or could any one else be designated that should educate and instruct the children? As a consequence, parents have the right to compel their children to learn what is necessary and useful; they have the right to compel them to go to such a school as they may appoint; they have the right to punish if the children refuse to obey. Without these rights there can be no sound education.

The parents therefore have the right of excluding the interference of all others who might wish to educate their children or in some way to hinder them in the performance of their duty by forcing on them methods which to the parents seem inconsistent with the proper kind of education: without this privilege, their right would be a mockery.

However, one condition is to be observed: parents have the right to exclude others, unless such others can prove that they also have some right over the education of the children.

III.

In our times the State is that agency which attempts to interfere in the education of the children by *controlling* the schools. Let us examine with what right it does this. We cannot deny that the State or Commonwealth has some rights in regard to the schools and the education of children. It is the State's duty to supply what is wanting on the part of the family. Hence, in the first place, it can offer *means* to parents whereby they may better and more easily provide for their children's education. This the State does by founding and endowing schools according to the needs and wishes of the parents. But with regard to endowments, or any other form of assistance, the State has no right to give them unless they contribute to the public good, to which they certainly do not contribute if sufficient provision has already been made for the schools in other ways, as, for instance, through the medium of religious orders.

In the second place, the State may *supplement* the family in educating the children, if need be, compelling negligent parents to fulfil their obligations in this regard.

In the third place, the State may so far supplement the family as to take upon itself the education, in the case of orphans, for instance; or if, for any reasons, the parents themselves cannot educate their children. This, however, supposes that those also are unable to supply the education who, next to the parents, and in preference to the State, have the right and duty to fill the place of parents, namely, relatives, a municipal organization, or the Church (where the Church does exist).

In the fourth place, the question suggests itself whether, beyond the duty of supplementing the family, the State has a direct right, jointly with the family, of educating the children, in so far as to have the right to compel parents to send their children to certain appointed schools—those, for instance, under State control ; or in so far as to have the exclusive right to establish schools; or, in a word, to educate and to teach ; or finally, in so far as to have the right to insist upon a certain method of education, a certain kind of school, or a certain amount of matter, which all are bound to learn,—matter, I mean, in excess of what is absolutely necessary; for to omit this would, of course, be sheer negligence.

IV.

Danton implicitly held this doctrine, declaring that children belong to the State before they belong to parents ; but we must absolutely deny this *direct* right of the State in conjunction with the parents. It is altogether outside of the domain of the State; and, as a consequence, whatever would flow from such an assumption would be outside of State right. The reason for this is that the assumed right rests on *mere assertion*, without any solid reason to support the claim.

Let us, however, view the reasons that are brought forward. Cousin, in the French Senate in 1833, said:

"The law which makes elementary instruction obligatory, it seems to me, does not exceed the rights of the legislative power any more than the law of military service and that other law just passed, the law, namely, of forced expropriation for purposes of public utility. If the demands of public utility entitle the legislator to invade the rights of ownership, why should not utility, in a much higher order, entitle him to do that which is less—namely, to require that children receive the instruction that every one needs to prevent him from becoming a source of injury to human society."

We might give our assent, to a certain extent, to these last words, taking them in their ordinary sense, namely, that the State has a right to insist that the children receive, in some way, such education as is absolutely necessary. But more than this seems to be contained in these words, not perhaps in the mind of the distinguished orator, or at least in the minds of those who are in the habit of using similar arguments; for they say that the State can require every one to receive such instruction as is generally called elementary; this, as a matter of fact, in our day, means many things altogether *superfluous* and even *hurtful*. I know for a fact a State in which the sons and daughters of country-people are compelled, in their elementary instruction, to learn the mythology of Greece. The defenders of these principles would also maintain the right of the State to exact the reception of this elementary instruction in no other schools than those established by the State; but they *cannot prove* this right of the State by any such reasons as the above.

For, in the first place, the violation of parental rights in the forced attendance of the children at certain appointed schools, against the will of parents, is far greater than the violation of the rights of property which is inflicted by the appropriation of an estate which the State needs, for instance, to build a railway. In the second place, the conscription of men for military service is to be admitted as a serious invasion of the rights of human liberty—as serious, perhaps, as the drafting of children into the public schools; and for this reason it is not practised either in England or in America. But such conscription can be defended on the ground of the absolute necessities of the case, because that State which would neglect to levy soldiers could not defend itself against a neighboring State provided with a superior army.

V.

But let us meet our Prussian opponents on the same ground, for it is probably in Prussia more than anywhere else that the rights of parents have been invaded.

Trendelenburg claims for the State the right to see "that the same moral principles sway the minds of all. . . . Thus the State, by its very nature, is educator."

This assertion we completely deny. It is indeed the will of God that there should be a certain conformity of principles, not only between the members of the same Commonwealth, but even between all the members of the human race. But this conformity is sufficiently secured by the very fact that all the parents bring up their children in their *respective national principles*. For instance, English parents will impart to their children English ideas; but should a

French or German family dwell in England, doubtless the English government would have no right to send the children of that family to English schools to imbibe English ideas, should the parents prefer French or German schools.

Stahl of Berlin says: "Education and instruction emanate both from parental authority and from State power: from the parents as far as the culture is individual, from the State as far as it is national."

Let us test the soundness of this proposition by applying it to a similar subject-matter. Let us say: The administration of property flows both from the right of dominion and from the power of the State. From the former, in so much as it is for the benefit of the individual owner, from the latter in so much as it is the interest of the State that the citizens be wealthy. Would such a proposition be admitted? Doubtless it is the interest of the State that the citizens should be rich; but this does not justify the State in wresting from the citizens the administration of their property, or compelling them to administer it according to this or that method. *A pari*, it benefits the State that the citizens be well-behaved or even learned; but this does not give it the right to take the education from the father or to determine by law the methods, the schools, or the teachers.

I shall add an argument (?) of charming simplicity, brought forward by Juergen Bona Meyer, the Bonn professor. According to him

"The people themselves transfer to the State the right and assign to the State the duty to promote the instruction of the people, and all other improvements whatever, by all the means it can control. Naturally, therefore, to the State power, jointly with the popular power, belongs an absolute right to determine the extent and duration of that compulsory training."

By the way, according to Meyer, boys, to the age of seventeen inclusively, and girls, to the age of sixteen inclusively, should be compelled to attend school.

Magnificent! But we will ask the learned professor one question: Can he show us the *document*, executed before a notary public and in presence of witnesses, by which the parents have transferred to the State the right of educating their children? Until he can show us this document, we must be allowed to have some doubt with regard to its existence.

Those repeated and strange attempts to prove that the State owns, jointly with the parents, or even above the parents, the right to educate, and to compel the attendance of children, show clearly that the right cannot be made good, and therefore has no existence. The conclusion is that the parents hold the right of training and instructing their children as they judge fit and through masters of their own selection, provided that they do not overstep the boundaries of reason: should they disregard the behests of reason, then, indeed, the State, as the civil superior, may provide for the education of the children.

The freedom of the family, sad to say, is now, in accordance with socialistic theories, too often infringed even by those who otherwise abhor socialism. For it is a socialistic system to transfer to the State the rights of individuals and the rights of families. And it is in accordance with that system to assail the rights which ought to be most sacred to the State: we speak of the rights of parents over their children.

VI.

Having thus determined the relative functions of the family and of the State, we must come to the Church, which *has* received its mission from Christ, when Our Lord said: " Go ye, therefore, and teach all nations, . . . teaching them to observe all things whatsoever I have commanded you." This mission comprises two mandates: the first, to teach faith and confer Baptism; the second, to teach men to observe all things whatsoever Christ has commanded—that is, to direct the moral practice. Therefore, to the Church has been committed by Christ the care of instructing and training all men in faith and morals—that is, in religious matters.

Hence arises a relation which we have often mentioned: the whole education with regard to faith and morals—that is, with regard to religion—falls *directly* under the authority of the Church; but as religious training is by far the most important part of education and instruction, the Church has also an *indirect* power over the rest. To both rights, *direct* and *indirect*, the children themselves must yield submission and obedience; for the Church, in the religious order, is, as it were, the mother of the children which it has brought forth to supernatural life by Baptism. Parents also are subject to both rights, so that in the whole work of education they depend directly or indirectly on Church authority. Civil organizations and the State itself are also subject to the Church in so far as both in common schools and in the institutes, in which the youth are trained for the public service, the Church may interfere *directly* in religious and moral questions, and *indirectly* in other matters, lest dangers threatening the faith or morals of its children should come from evil-minded masters, bad books, or bad associations.

"EDUCATION: TO WHOM DOES IT BELONG?"

A REVIEW

BY

REV. S. BRANDI, S.J.

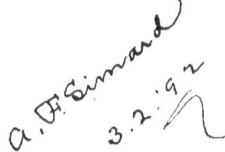

The Civiltà Cattolica, Jan. 2, 1892.

NEW YORK, CINCINNATI, CHICAGO:
BENZIGER BROTHERS,
Printers to the Holy Apostolic See.
1892.

Copyright, 1892, by BENZIGER BROTHERS.

"EDUCATION: TO WHOM DOES IT BELONG?"

A REVIEW.

EDUCATION: TO WHOM DOES IT BELONG? By the Rev. THOMAS BOUQUILLON, D.D., Professor of Moral Theology at the Catholic University, Washington, D. C. Baltimore, John Murphy & Co., 1891.

We have reason to believe that we shall be doing a work of some interest, and perhaps of no little service, to our readers, if we devote a few pages of our present issue to the consideration of a question which has been already discussed in former numbers of our Review. The importance of the matter is such that it will bear repetition; for it is one of those topics which need to be studied and understood by all those who care to guard themselves against being misled by the publications of a certain school, the tendency of whose writings is to exaggerate the rights of the State to the detriment of the rights of the Church and of the family.

The appearance of Dr. Bouquillon's pamphlet is the occasion of the present article. The Doctor undertakes to discuss the question of education in the form of a reply to the question, "To whom does it belong?" His answer is that "it belongs to the individual physical or moral, to the family, to the State, to the Church; to none of these solely and exclusively, but to all four combined in harmonious working; for the reason that man is not an isolated but a social being" (p. 31).

Setting aside the consideration of the three parts of this "harmonious combination" which belong to the Church, the family, and the individual, let us examine briefly what should be, according to the author of the pamphlet, the function of the State; for here we find what we deem the capital error of granting to the State rights which do not belong to it.

"The State," he says, "has authority to see to it that parents fulfil their duty of educating their children, to compel them, if need be, and to substitute itself in place of them in the fulfilling of this duty in certain cases" (p. 25).

More than this. "If the State," says the Doctor, "may coerce parents who neglect the education of their children, so also may it determine a minimum of instruction and make it obligatory" (p. 26). "This *minimum* is naturally determined by public opinion; it will comprehend everywhere reading, writing, and the elements of arithmetic" (p. 27). And further: "If the State may exact . . . on the part of the children a minimum of instruction, if it may punish negligent parents, it follows that it may also prescribe the teaching of this or that branch, the knowledge of which, considering the circumstances, is deemed necessary to the majority of the citizens" (p. 28).

In other words, according to Dr. Bouquillon, the State has *the right to oblige* all parents, be they rich or poor, members of the nobility or of the middle-class, mechanics or peasants, to give or to procure to their offspring an amount of instruction which shall comprehend, at least, reading and writing and the elements of arithmetic, and whatever other branch the State may deem necessary to the majority of its citizens.

The distinguished Professor announces very frankly (p. 26) that on this point he is not at one with the editors of the CIVILTA CAT-

TOLICA. He adds that he has carefully examined their arguments, that they are far from convincing him, and seem to him "very faulty." We regret that the learned Doctor has not thought it worth his while to point out these grave defects in our reasoning. This he has not done, but he seems to have taken it for granted that his word alone was more than sufficient to establish the fact that we have erred; and he contents himself with advising his American readers, the vast majority of whom either do not understand Italian, or, if they do, have no means of consulting the collection of 166 volumes of our Review, to "examine them for themselves"! (p. 26.)

Our articles on Education, and, in particular, those against obligatory primary instruction, from the first issue in April, 1850, to that of September, 1872, (to which the Doctor refers his readers, p. 26,) were written by Fathers Taparelli and Liberatore.[1] And since the author of the pamphlet has not thought it proper to acquaint us with the passages in which our above-mentioned colleagues have gone astray, we shall content ourselves with an examination of the arguments which he puts forward to support his own views, and we shall endeavor to show to our readers what we deem their weak points.

What may be styled his fundamental argument is given by the author on page 12 of his pamphlet. For the sake of clearness, it may be set down in strictly syllogistic form, as follows: "Civil authority has the right to use all legitimate temporal means it judges necessary

---

[1] The high reputation of these two authors, not only as able writers but as sound and accurate philosophers, is now universally recognized in the literary and learned world. Accordingly, we were not a little surprised on reading the words ascribed to a person on other grounds worthy of respectful consideration, to the effect that those who are opposed to the teaching of Dr. Bouquillon on education are "short-sighted people with their false philosophy" (St. Louis *Daily Globe Democrat*, Nov. 29, 1891, p. 9). The philosophy of which these two writers are followers and exponents is, as everybody knows, the philosophy of St. Thomas. Can this philosophy safely be styled "false," especially since the publication of the great encyclical of Leo XIII. ?

for the attainment of the temporal common welfare, which is the end of civil society." But obligatory instruction in reading, writing, etc. is a legitimate temporal means which civil authority judges necessary for the attainment of the temporal common welfare. Therefore civil authority has the right to use obligatory instruction; and, consequently, to impose it by law on parents.

The "very faulty" reasoning in this specious argument, which Liberatore styles a "sophism," was exposed by him in the second volume of our sixth series (p. 709). The major proposition of this argument, which the author (p. 12) believes to be undeniable, can and must be denied. If we needed to be convinced that it is false, it would be enough to recall the principle thus expressed by Aristotle: "Non omnia quæ necessaria sunt civitati, partes sunt civitatis" (7 Politic. 7) —Not everything that is necessary to the welfare of civil society lies within the competency of civil authority. From the fact that a thing is necessary to civil society we can infer only that the well-being of such a thing is of the greatest importance to the State. Whether or not it comes under the dominion of civil authority must be determined on other grounds; that is, from its nature, from its end, and from the extent and limits of the authority in question. Thus, from the fact that religion, the life and basis of the State, is supremely necessary to the well-being of civil society, it does not follow that it is an emanation or an appurtenance of the State.

The learned Professor evidently perceived this defect, and he modified accordingly the principle of his reasoning. He does not intend to speak of any kind of means, but only of "legitimate temporal means." Very well! But is not the propagation of the race a legitimate temporal means which may be judged necessary, by the civil authority, for the end of civil society? And shall it be said that the State has, consequently, the right to make this propagation obligatory, and to impose it by law on all its subjects? If the principle laid down by the author were admitted, even with this modification, to be true, its application would impose upon the people an oppressive and unbearable yoke, since anything and everything that belongs to the sphere of domestic life and of individual right may be styled "a legitimate temporal means" and may be "judged necessary by the civil authority."

But this is not all that is to be said about the author's process of reasoning. For, even admitting his principle, we may fairly ask him by what right he asserts gratuitously, in the minor proposition of the syllogism, the very thing that is to be proved. At least it seems to us that the legitimateness of making primary instruction obligatory is the very thing that is called in question. The Rev. Professor should first prove this legitimateness, and then, from the fact that the State has the right to use all legitimate, temporal, and necessary means, he might *perhaps* prove his thesis. We say "perhaps," first because it might still be denied that the obligatory instruction, which is said to be necessary to the aid of civil society, is, strictly speaking, a temporal means, and second, because the essential point of the argument, namely, that this obligatory primary instruction is a *necessary means* for the attainment of the end of civil society, is not proved, and cannot be proved.

The reason assigned by the Doctor (p. 12) that "a nation needs citizens able to take interest in the commonwealth, workmen that are intelligent, surveyors that are skilful, physicians that are experienced, jurists that are learned," proves only that it is necessary for the welfare of the social body that there should always be in it *some* men who know more than the alphabet; but certainly it does not prove that it is *necessary* for the end of civil society that *all*, even the rudest peasant, should learn, not only to read and write, but also the elements of arithmetic and whatever other branch of instruction the State may prescribe. For the attainment of the end of civil society, it is sufficient that these receive a religious and moral education which may certainly be given, and preserved in its results, by *oral* teaching without any help from the alphabet or arithmetic.

We may recall here what we have drawn out in a previous number of this Review.[1] It cannot be said that anything is *necessary* to society unless the end of society cannot be attained without it. Only the evidence of this kind of necessity can give to any element of social life or progress such importance that every other interest must yield to it. Now can it be asserted that the teaching of the alphabet to every member of the social body constitutes any such necessity as this? Or again, will any one say that civil society has never yet been able to attain its end because a considerable number of its members could not read? But, it may be answered, the times are changed. If they are changed, they are so chiefly in this, that now we need less interference of the State in the relations of social life, and that it should be admitted only in so far as it is absolutely necessary to safeguard the rights of individuals.

The Rev. Professor infers (p. 26) the right of the State to determine a *minimum of instruction* and to make it obligatory, from the right, which all philosophers grant to the State, of coercing parents who neglect the education of their children. "Who admits the former," he says, "must admit the latter. The consequence seems to us logically necessary." We must ask the learned Professor to bear with us if we take leave to deny his inference.

The right which philosophers commonly grant to the State[2] is the right to coerce and even to punish parents, who either neglect entirely the *moral education* of their children or, if they do provide for it, make it a means of moral perversion; for moral education is the only education to which the child has a strict and undeniable right. In the

---

[1] Vol. 8, ser. 8, p. 7.
[2] Vid. TAPARELLI, Saggio Teoretico, vol. 2, § 1571.

antecedent proposition, then, the philosophers mentioned above treat of *moral education* only. The Doctor, on the other hand, in his inference, is dealing with an entirely different matter, that is, with *primary instruction in letters*. Now it is a truth which no well-informed person will deny that *moral education* does not depend necessarily on *primary instruction in letters*, and that there is no indissoluble connection between the two. It follows, then, that just as the one can exist without the other, so also it is by no means "logically necessary" that neglect of the one must imply neglect of the other.

His Eminence, Cardinal Gibbons, in his excellent work, "Our Christian Heritage," clearly confirms our position.[1] "It does not appear," writes his Eminence, "that vice recedes in the United States in proportion as public education advances. Statistics, I fear, would go far to prove the contrary to be the fact." Dr. Bouquillon seems to have an altogether wrong idea of *education;* for he uses the term as if it meant the same thing as *instruction.* Now this confusion of ideas, as Cardinal Gibbons points out, is the source of the many errors which now prevail concerning the question of education.[2]

The Rev. Professor declares (pp. 26, 27) that he does not see how Catholics can admit the right of the State "to hinder parents from sending their children to labor above the strength of their age, say in

---

[1] C. 33, p. 464.

[2] "The second evil that bodes mischief to our country and endangers the stability of our government arises from our mutilated and defective system of public-school education. I am persuaded that the popular errors now existing in reference to education spring from an incorrect notion of that term. To *educate* means to *bring out*, to develop the intellectual, moral, and religious faculties of the soul. An education, therefore, that improves the mind and the memory, to the neglect of moral and religious training, is at best but an imperfect system. According to Webster's definition, to educate is to instil into the mind principles of art, science, *morals, religion,* and behavior. To educate, he says, in the arts is *important;* in religion, *indispensable.*" (Ibid. c. 35, p. 849.)

the mines," and yet deny its right "to force parents to give these same children a minimum of instruction." That the learned Professor "does not see" a distinction so elementary must certainly be a matter of surprise to many. Because the State has power to forbid what is *intrinsically wrong*—as, for example, the violation of the absolute right of the child to the preservation of its own life—it does not at all follow that the State has the right to oblige all citizens to do everything that is good or useful, even in favor of those who have no strict right to such benefit. The Doctor ought not merely to suppose, but he is bound to prove, that children have, as against their parents, an absolute right to primary instruction in reading, writing, arithmetic, etc.; and that, therefore, parents who do not furnish such instruction to their children are guilty of a violation of justice and of a crime against society.

The right teaching on this matter is set forth compendiously by Father S. Schiffini, of the Gregorian University, in his recent work on Moral Philosophy : "Excepta institutione morali et religiosa, quæ cura parentum tradenda est sub directione non politicæ sed ecclesiasticæ potestatis, doctrina in artibus et scientiis, quæ in scholis tradi solet, nequit esse onus necessario subeundum ab omnibus. Istæ enim artes et scientiæ sunt de genere illorum bonorum quæ pertinent quidem ad debitam perfectionem multitudinis collective sumptæ, non vero pertinent aut pertinere possunt ad debitam perfectionem singulorum. . . . Bona autem hujusmodi, ut alibi notavimus cum S. Thoma, nequeunt cuilibet indiscriminatim imponi per modum præcepti, reipsa tamen obtinentur in societate ob diversitatem inclinationum singulorum, accedente impulso divinæ providentiæ quæ omnia moderatur."[1]

In the preface to his treatise, the Doctor "professes to walk in the footsteps of the great theologians, especially of St. Thomas, and to

[1] Disp. Philosophiæ Moralis, vol. 2, § 517. Augustæ Taurinorum, 1891.

be guided by the light of the Encyclicals of Leo XIII." This sounds very well; but we would not have our readers, or the Professor's either, misled by this profession into the belief that the principles laid down by him concerning *obligatory instruction* are those of Leo XIII., of St. Thomas, and of the great theologians. The name of Leo XIII. is not even mentioned by the Doctor, in confirmation of his views, as put forth by him in pp. 26-28 of his work. Indeed it is not easy to understand how it could have been advanced in favor of those views, since the Sovereign Pontiff expressly teaches that "natura parentes habent jus suum instituendi, quos procrearint: hoc adjuncto officio, ut cum fine, cujus gratia sobolem Dei beneficio susceperunt, ipsa educatio conveniat et doctrina puerilis. Igitur parentibus est necessarium eniti et contendere ut omnem in hoc genere propulsent injuriam; *omninoque pervincant ut sua in potestate sit educare liberos*, uti par est more Christiano."[1]

To the Angelic Doctor, who is quoted on p. 27, are ascribed the following words said by the Rev. Professor to be found in the $1^a\ 2^{dae}$ q. 95, art. 3, of the Summa Theologica : "The legislator may take measures concerning 'bonam disciplinam per quam cives informantur ut commune bonum justitiæ et pacis conservent.'" We have searched in vain for these words in the place quoted by the Rev. Doctor, and consequently we have not been able to verify the words of De Medicis, which the author quotes as a commentary on the text of St. Thomas. But even so, and admitting that these words may be found elsewhere in St. Thomas, they certainly do not prove the Doctor's thesis. For how would he prove that, by the words "bonam disciplinam" St. Thomas meant reading, writing, arithmetic, etc.? Could he prove from this text, or from its context, that, according to St. Thomas, primary instruction is necessary to children "ut bonum justitiæ et pacis con-

---

[1] Encyc. SAPIENTIÆ CHRISTIANÆ.

servent"? Finally, how can it be proved that the power granted by St. Thomas to the legislator "to take measures" is a coercive power, and consequently different from that which Taparelli,[1] and Catholic philosophers generally, assign to the legislator—that is, the power of "furnishing means, of opening up to the young safe and wholesome sources from which they may learn what is true and right, of providing parents, for this same end, with a faithful helper in whom their confidence may be assured by public guarantees"?[2]

Let us now turn to the theologians quoted by the Rev. Professor (p. 27) in favor of his opinion. These are Mgr. Sauvé and the two Cardinals, Zigliara and Manning. Now these eminent writers do not defend the opinion of Dr. Bouquillon. Mgr. Sauvé, on page 300 of his work "Questions Religieuses et Sociales," proposes this question: "de savoir si l'État a le droit de rendre obligatoire pour tous ses sujets une certaine dose d'instruction," and he answers, "de ne vouloir se prononcer absolument sur cette question." Sauvé, therefore, is simply neutral, and just as he does not feel justified in denying this right to the State, so neither does he venture to affirm it. The same must be said of Cardinal Zigliara, who, as our author assures us, in answer to a difficulty on this point, does not "dare

---

[1] Saggio Teoretico, vol. 2, § 1570.

[2] In art. 3, quest. 96, we have found what we suppose to be the passage quoted by Dr. Buoquillon. But here St. Thomas is answering the question "Utrum lex humana præcipiat *actus omnium virtutum;*" but among these "actus" the Angelic Doctor does not even dream of placing *primary instruction.* We quote the whole text as found in the place mentioned above: "Non de omnibus *actibus* omnium *virtutum* lex humana præcipit, sed sólum *de illis* qui ordinabiles sunt ad bonum commune ; vel immediate, sicut cum aliqua directe propter bonum commune fiunt; vel mediate, sicut cum aliqua ordinantur a legislatore pertinentia ad bonam disciplinam per quam cives informantur ut commune bonum justitiæ et pacis conservent." We may observe that in the quotation from Sauvé there seems to be some error, perhaps a printer's mistake. On page 306, quoted by the Doctor, Sauvé is dealing with an altogether different subject.

deny that power to the State." In all seriousness, does the learned Professor really mean to say that not venturing to deny a thing is the same as to affirm it? Is he unable to conceive that state of mind in which there is simply a suspension of judgment, a state of mind which logicians call "dubium"; and is he not aware that an authority which is, in this sense, doubtful, is in reality no authority at all? But the authority of Cardinal Zigliara, in this matter, is not doubtful; for in the passage quoted by Dr. Bouquillon the learned Cardinal explicitly *enumerates* and *determines* the rights which he concedes to the State in the matter of education; and among these the Doctor will seek in vain the right of obligatory primary instruction. "The rest," that is, the rights not enumerated here, "which the State arrogates to itself, *vehementer negamus*."[1]

The last theologian quoted by Dr. Bouquillon is Cardinal Manning, who is supposed, on the authority of a certain P. Pradié, to have more or less recognized, in a Pastoral Letter for the Lent of 1872, that the State has the power to punish the father who neglects to send his child to school. As we have not at hand the document thus quoted, we are not able to determine the sense in which those words, if written by the great Cardinal, were understood by him. We have already admitted that the State may punish a parent who neglects altogether to provide for the moral education of his offspring; but we have also pointed out how illogical it is to infer, from this principle, that the State has the right to oblige that parent to give to his children primary instruction in letters or in any other branch of learning.

Much more might be written, in addition to what has been already said, on the matter treated in Dr. Bouquillon's pamphlet. There would be abundant matter for discussion, especially in that part of

[1] Philosophia Moralis, l. 2, c. 1, a. 5.

his work in which the Rev. Professor, dealing with "Liberty of Education," lays down the following proposition: "Civil liberty of teaching may reach greater extension than moral liberty would allow" (p. 31). The learned author makes a mistake when he insinuates or supposes that the principles which he has undertaken to defend against the CIVILTA CATTOLICA, in the matter of *obligatory instruction* and, in general, concerning the right of the State and of every individual in it to *educate*, are "the true teaching of the Church."

To conclude, we cannot help saying that, as we read the pamphlet under discussion, the doubt more than once occurred to our mind: Can this be a *genuine* work of that same moral theologian whose "Theologia Moralis Fundamentalis" we praised in our issue of last August? If so, then we can only exclaim: "Quantum mutatus ab illo!"

33/

Joseph Gagnon,
Sorilda Dion }

George, né le 1er Mars, 1892

The Church and the Age.

THE CHURCH AND THE AGE.

A Sermon preached in the Cathedral of Baltimore, October 18th, 1893, on the occasion of the Twenty-Fifth Anniversary of the Episcopal Consecration of

HIS EMINENCE, JAMES CARDINAL GIBBONS,
Archbishop of Baltimore.

By Most Rev. JOHN IRELAND,
Archbishop of St. Paul.

BALTIMORE:
JOHN MURPHY & CO.
1893.

THE CHURCH AND THE AGE.

Most Eminent Cardinal—Brethren of the Clergy and of the Laity:

Twenty-five years in exalted office, a bishop, a chieftain of bishops, in the Catholic Church, in America, in the latter days of this nineteenth century of the Christian era! Great the opportunities and weighty the responsibilities.

Of those years what record should I, who revere and love the Cardinal Archbishop of Baltimore, fain have to write? Should it be that they went by without harm done or good prevented, without blemish or reproach? This, whatever its value along the dark lines of frail humanity, is, at best, but the story of the talent wrapped up in napkin folds and securely guarded from misuse. Not this record did Christ expect from apostles, and from this pulpit I will not speak it.

Should the record be that of common duties performed in zeal and loyalty, of useful ministry in blessing and ordaining, in building temples and asylums, in exhorting souls unto their salvation? This record would be that of the ten hundred; it merits no special praise; it teaches no special lesson, and it shall not be the theme of this evening.

Let others tell of the many. I wish to tell of the few. I am tired of the common; I am angry with it. If I am myself compelled to plod over its wearying pathways I want, at least, to see others shun them, to see men rise far above their fellows, and by their singular thoughts and singular deeds freshen human life and give to it the power to place itself in those high altitudes wherein is born progress. The common never puts

The Common! We are surfeited with it.

humanity forward, never begets a great movement; nor does it save humanity when grave peril comes upon it. The common! We are surfeited with it; it has made our souls torpid and our limbs rigid. Under the guise of goodness it is a curse. The want in the world, the want in the Church, to-day as at other times, to-day as never before, is of men among men, of men who see farther than others, rise higher than others, act more boldly than others. They need not be numerous. They never were numerous. But, while the few, they take with them the multitude and save humanity. The one man of sufficient grandeur of soul and firmness of hand saves a whole country; the one man saves the whole Church.

This evening it is my coveted privilege to honor a man among men. The record of the Cardinal Archbishop of Baltimore! I speak it with pride and exultation; it is the record I should have traced for my ideal bishop and leader of men in these solemn times through which the Church is passing.

The times are solemn. In no epoch of history, since the beginning of the Christian era, did changes so profound and so far-reaching occur. There is in the physical sphere of human activity a complete revolution. Discoveries and inventions have opened to us a new material world. Social and political conditions have been transformed. Intellectual curiosity is intense and peers with keenest eye into the recesses of sky and earth. Intellectual ambition, maddened by wondrous successes in many fields, puts on daring pinions and challenges all limitations of knowledge. The human heart is emboldened to the strangest dreams and frets itself into desperate efforts in presence of all barriers to the impletion of its desires. Let things be new, is the watchword of present humanity, and to make things new is its strong resolve. To this end are pledged its most fierce activities, which, in whatever part of man's realm they are exer-

A new era has come: the Church needs to adapt herself to it.

cised, have their illustration in the steam and electricity of the new material creation.

In the midst of these times the Catholic Church moves and works, professing, as her charter obliges her, to conquer minds and hearts, individuals and society. Her mission to the world is what it was for long centuries: but the world wears a new aspect. The Church sails upon the waters of the same ocean upon whose bosom she has glided since her first departure from Palestine: but new winds trouble those waters and toss them into unusual billows. No long argument is needed to show that there ought to be new movements of the helm in the ship of state and new unfurlings of canvas from her masts.

Now is the opportunity for great and singular men among the sons of God's Church. To-day old-time routine is fatal; to-day the common is worn-out senility. The crisis demands the new, the extraordinary, and with it the Catholic Church will score the grandest of her victories in the grandest of history's ages.

There is a discord between the age and the Church. I recall the fact with sorrow. The interests of society and of religion suffer, while misunderstanding and separation last. The peace of harmony is the price of well-being and of progress.

There is a discord between Age and Church. Where the fault lies.

The fault lies with the age and with the Church, or rather with spokesmen of the age and spokesmen of the Church. Age and Church, rightly apprehended, are in no manner at war. The age, as it is represented to us, is at fault. Elated with its material and intellectual successes, it is proud and exaggerates its powers. It imagines that the natural, which has served it so well, is all sufficient; it tends to the exclusion of the supernatural; it puts on the cloak of secularism. In its worship of the new, which the march of progress brings to it, whatever is old is suspected. It asks why its church may not be new as well as its chemistry or its science of mechanics. A church bearing on her front the marks of nineteen centuries is in its eyes out of date and out of place. Pride and thoughtlessness are the evil and misleading characteristics of the age.

The Church, as she comes before us in the speech and actions of churchmen, deserves her share of reproach. I speak as a Catholic with sincere love for the Catholic Church. I know the divine elements in the Church which Christ has made the repository of truth and grace, and I have full faith that those elements are at all times guarded under the unerring breathings of the Holy Spirit. But I know, too, the human elements in the Church. Men in the Church retain their human parts, and upon their wisdom and their energy very much of the Church's outward weal is made dependent. The Church has had her epochs, differing one from another in light and glory, as Catholic pastors and Catholic people scanned the world with clearer sight and unsheathed the spiritual sword with greater alacrity. The dependence of the Church upon her human elements is often too easily forgotten, although the Church herself authoritatively teaches that undue reliance upon divine grace is a sin of presumption.

I am not afraid to say that, during the century whose sun is now setting, men in the Church have made the mistake of being too slow to understand the new age and too slow to extend toward it the conciliatory hand of friendship. They were not without their excuses, the strength of which I respect. The Church in her divine elements is unchangeable, supremely conservative. Her dread of change, so righteous in a degree, is likely to be carried beyond the legitimate frontier and made to cover ground where change is proper. The movements of the age, it is also true, were frequently ushered into existence under most inauspicious and repellent forms. The revo-

The mistakes of Churchmen in not seeking to conciliate the Age.

lution of 1789, whose waters, rushing and destructive as those of the maddest mountain torrent, were crested with the crimson of blood, was the loud signal of the birth of the new era. The standard-bearers of the age often bore aloft the insignia of impiety and of social anarchy. Certain men, as Lamennais, who attempted an alliance between the age and the Church, were imprudent in speech, and in their impatience they courted failure for themselves and discouragement for their allies. But with all these excuses churchmen thought and acted too slowly. They failed to grasp the age, to christianize its aspirations and to guide its forward march; it passed beyond them. There were the few Lacordaires, who recognized and proclaimed the duties of the hour : timid companions abandoned them ; reactionaries accused them of dangerous liberalism, of semi-heresy, and they were forced to be silent. The many saw but the vices of the age, which they readily anathematized ; its good and noble tendencies they ignored and denied. The age was for them the dark world against which Christ has warned his followers. The task of winning it to the gospel was considered a forlorn hope. It was a task to be accomplished only through some stupendous miracle from heaven, and until the miracle came the ministers of Christ withdrew, as into winter quarters, into sacristies and sanctuaries, where, surrounded by a small band of chosen ones, they could guard themselves and their friends from the all-pervading contagion. The age, abandoned to itself and to false and mischievous guides, estranged each year more and more from the Church on account of the Church's isolation of her energies, irritated by her unfriendliness, became hardened in its secularism and taught itself to despise and hate religion. This deplorable condition prevailed in some countries more than in others; but from none was it totally absent. The Church had seemingly furled her flag of battle, her flag of victory.

It was a mistake and a misfortune. Go and teach all nations, the Christ had said once for all times, and in obedience to these words the first apostles rushed into the Roman Empire, speaking to the sages of Athens on Mars' Hill, to the patricians and senators of Rome in the very courts of emperors, to the slaves in their huts, and the Roman Empire was christianized. Radically erring and evil-doing as the present age may have been, the methods and zeal of the early apostles would have won it to the Saviour. But, in veriest fact, the present age, pagan in its language and in the excesses of its qualities, is in its depths instinct with Christian emotions; it worships unwittingly at Christian shrines and awaits but the warm contact with the living Christian religion to avow itself Christian.

The opportunity for the great and singular churchman.

I indicate the opportunity for the great and singular churchman. His work is to bridge the deep valley separating the age from the Church, to clear off the clouds which prevent the one from seeing the realities of the other, to bring the Church to the age, and the age to the Church.

We must know that the age and the Church are not hopelessly apart.

The age has, assuredly, its errors and its sins, and these the Church never can condone. With the age conceived as the embodiment of errors and sins the Church cannot be reconciled. But these are the accidents, not the essentials, in the make-up of the age. For my part, I see in the present age one of the mighty upheavals which occur from time to time in humanity, causing and marking the ascending stages in its continuous progress. Humanity strengthened by centuries of reflection and of toil, nourished and permeated by principles of Christian truth, is lifting upward its whole mass to higher regions of light and of liberty, and demanding a fuller and more universal enjoyment of its God-given rights. All this is praiseworthy; all this is beautiful and noble. It is all this

The bad and the good in the age.

that we are asked to accept when we accept the age, and in accepting the age we give ourselves the right to chide it for its defects—we put ourselves in a position to correct them.

The Church, too, has her accidents and her essentials. We must be able to distinguish the former from the latter; we must be prepared, while jealously guarding the essentials, to let go the accidents as circumstances of time and place require.

The Invariable and the Variable; the Permanent and the Transient in the Church. What the Church at any time was, certain people hold she ever must be. They do her much harm, making her rigid and unbending, incapable of adapting herself to new and changing surroundings. The Church, created by Christ for all ages, lives in every age and of every age. We find, consequently, in her outward belongings the variable and the contingent. The Church, at one time imperialistic in her political alliances, was at another feudalistic; but she never committed herself in principle to imperialism or feudalism. She spoke Greek in Athens and Latin in Rome, and her sons wore the chlamys or the toga; but she was never an institution confined to Greece or to Italy. In later days she lisped the nascent languages of Goths and Franks, and showed in her steppings through their lands not a little of their uncultured bearing and of their defective civilization without being a Gothic or a Frank product, limited in life and conditions to the life and conditions of her contemporaries. Her scientific knowledge at different epochs was scant as that of those epochs; her social legislation and customs, as theirs, were rude and tentative. She was simply in her human elements partaking of the life of her epoch, her divine elements always remaining the self-same, however shifting the mundane scenes around her. Two or three centuries ago she was courtly and aristocratic under the temporal sway of the Fifth Charles of Spain or the Fourteenth Louis of France; but this again was a passing phase in her existence, and she may be at other times as democratic in her demeanor as the most earnest democracy would expect. Her canon law, which is the expression of her adaptibility to circumstances, received the impress at one time of the Justinian code, at another that of the capitularies of Charlemagne, at another that of the Hapsburgh or Bourbon edicts: but she was never mummified in Justinian or Bourbon molds, and her canon law may be as American as it was Roman, as much the reflection of the twentieth century as it ever was of the middle ages. Were not all this most true the Church would not be catholic, as her founder was catholic, the teacher and Saviour of all ages and of all nations. Let us be as broad and as catholic in our conceptions of the Church as Christ was, and we shall find no difficulty in recognizing her fitness to all lands and to all ages—the past as well as the present and the present and the future as well as the past.

What! the Church of the living God, the Church of ten thousand victories over pagans and barbarians, over false philosophies and heresies, over defiant kings and unruly peoples—the great, freedom-loving, philanthropic, truth-giving Catholic Church—this Church afraid of the nineteenth century! afraid of any century! not seeing in the nineteenth the fervent ebullitions of noblest sentiments, the germinations of her own Christlike plantings; this Church not eager for the fray, not precipitating herself with force irresistible upon this modern world to claim it, to love it, to foster and admire or to correct and cure, to own it for Christ, and with her impetuous arm to lift it to the very summit of its highest aspirations, to which only by the Church's aid this panting, hoping, despairing world can ever reach! Far, far from Catholics be the chilling, fatal, un-Catholic thought!

The New Crusade—Bringing into close contact Church and Age.

I preach the new, the most glorious crusade. Church and age! Unite them in the name of humanity, in the name of God.

Church and age! Bring them into close contact; they pulsate alike; the God of humanity works in one, the God of supernatural revelation works in the other—in both the self-same God.

Let us note the chief characteristics of the age. The age is ambitious of knowledge. Its searchings take no rest and submit to no limitations of territory. Be it so. The Catholic Church proclaims that all truth, natural as well as supernatural, is from God, and that the mind, whose proper aliment is truth, grows more God-like as it absorbs truth in more generous proportions. Two sources of knowledge there are according to Catholic teaching, both from God,—the individual reason of man and the voice of God in revelation. Between reason and revelation there never can be a contradiction, the so-called war between Church and science being a war between the misrepresentations of science and the misrepresentations of faith, or rather between certain ignorant scientists and certain ignorant theologians. The Church desires the spread of intellectual light among all men and over all regions of truth; the age in its tireless studying of nature does the work of the Church. The discoveries of the age, whether in minute animalcules or in vast fiery orbs, demonstrate God. They show forth through all the laws of the universe an absolute cause, all-wise, all-powerful, eternal, and this cause is God. The fruits of all historical inquisitions, of all social and moral meditations, give us Christ rising from the dead and raising the world from the dead. They give us Christ's Church as the enduring embodiment of Christ's mission. The knowledge of the age! The age has not a sufficiency of it, and the need of the hour, the duty of the Church, is to urge the age to deeper researches, to more extensive surveyings, leaving untouched no particle of matter that may conceal a secret, no incident of history, no act in the life of humanity that may solve a problem. The knowledge of the age! the Church blesses it; the

The Characteristics of the Age—Its ambition of knowledge.

Church aids its onward growth with all her might, with all her light.

It is an age of liberty, civil and political; it is the age of the democracy, when the whole people, tired of the unrestricted sway of sovereigns, become themselves the sovereigns, and exercise with more or less directness the power which was always theirs primarily by divine ordinance. The age of the democracy! The Catholic Church, I am sure, has no fear of the democracy, this flowering of her own most sacred principles of the equality, fraternity and liberty of all men, in Christ and through Christ. These principles are spread upon every page of the gospel. From the moment they were first confided to the Church they have been ceaselessly leavening minds and hearts towards the fullest recognition of rights and dignity among all men, towards the elevation of the multitudes of men, and the enjoyment by them of freedom from unnecessary restrictions, and of social happiness mingled with as few sorrows as earth's planet permits. The whole history of the Catholic Church is the record of the enfranchisement of the slave, the curbing of royal tyranny, the defense of the poor, of the people, of woman, of all the social entities that pride and passion choose to trample upon. The great theologians of the Church, an Aquinas, a Suarez, provide in their teachings complete foundations for the political democracy, which assumes in the present age its plenary form. They assert and prove that all political power comes from God through the people, whose delegates kings and princes are, and that when rulers become tyrants the inalienable right of revolution is reserved to the people. The Church lives under all forms of government. When ratified by the people all forms are legitimate; but the government which more than another is that of the people, by the people and for the people, is the one where the Church of the

It is an Age of Liberty—the Age of the Democracy.

people, the Catholic Church, breathes air most congenial to her principles and her heart.

It is an age of social battlings for justice to all men, for the right of all men to live in the frugal comfort becoming rational creatures, to all of whom birth into the world gives title to a sufficiency of the things of the world. Very well; is not this sudden revolution which has come upon men in the plea for social justice and social comfort the loud outburst of the cry which has ever been going forth from the bosom of the Church since the words were spoken by her founder: "Seek first the kingdom of God and His justice and all things else shall be added unto you?" It is not sufficiently made public that the principles underlying the social movement of the times in all its legitimate demands are principles constantly taught in Catholic theological schools, as, for instance, this chief one proclaimed by Cardinal Manning, to the horror of aristocratic England, that in case of extreme need of food all goods become common property. Catholics have of late been so accustomed to lock up their teachings in temple and seminary that when the same teachings appear in active evolution upon the broad sea of humanity they do not recognize them: they even fear and disown them.

It is an Age of Social Justice; it is an Age of material Progress.

It is an age of material progress, of inventions, of the subjugation of nature's forces to the service of man, of the building up of man over all irrational creation. Does the Church in these things condemn the age? It is her doctrine that the earth was given to man that he dominate over it. Progress of every kind the Church blesses; for progress along the lines of all human activities and human uses is the divine ordering,—stagnation and inactivity calling down from God reprobation, as we learn from the parable of the talents.

I have described the intellectual attitude which it befits us to take toward the age. What should be our practical relations with it? Let them be those which the warmest apostolic zeal and the best human prudence counsel. We desire to gain the age. Let us not, then, stand isolated from it. Our place is in the world as well as in the sanctuary; in the world, wherever we can prove our love for it or render it a service. We cannot influence men at long range; close contact is needed. Let us be with them in the things that are theirs—material interests, social welfare, civil weal—so that they be with us in the things that are ours—the interests of religion. Let us be with them, because their interests are our own, because nature and grace must not be separated. The age, I shall be told, is following wrong roads. I reply we have abandoned it to itself, and allowed it to err. Let us now repair the fault and go with it in order to guide it in the future.

What must be our practical relations with the Age.

The age courts knowledge; let us more than others be the patrons of knowledge. Let Catholics be the most erudite historians, the most experienced scientists, the most acute philosophers; and history, science and philosophy will not be divorced from religion. The age demands liberty with good government; let us be models of patriotism, of civil virtue, of loyalty to the country's institutions; and no suspicion will ever exist that Catholics are the allies of buried regimes, the enemies of liberty, civil or political. In all social plannings and organizations let us be the most active, the most useful; and men will recognize the great truth that religion, having the promises of the life to come, has those, too, of the life that is, and seeing in the Church the friend and the protectress of their terrestrial interests, they will easily accept her in her supernatural offerings. Let us love men as Christ loved them, even when they love us not, and affection for them will beget in them affection for us and for our doctrines. Above all, let us love and work earnestly and energetically. The world succeeds in its enterprises through tireless perseverance and Titanic labors. In like manner shall we succeed in our task. The half-hearted measure in which we evangelize the age deserves and brings failure. Steam and electricity in religion co-operating with divine grace will win; old-fashioned, easy-going methods mean defeat. We have not heretofore won the age; let us not put all the blame upon the age.

I will not pause long to reply to objections which rise in many minds. The age, one may say, is turned away from the Church and will not listen. I believe that if minds and hearts properly attuned reach out to it, the age will listen.

Let us give no heed to opposition. Men are always convertible to God; the age is convertible to Him. I am afraid, says another, of the opposition that will come from men in the Church if I talk of the age as talks the speaker of this evening, if I act toward the world as he advises me to act. Friends, if you are afraid of this opposition, you will not succeed; you are not, " of the seed of those men by whom salvation is brought to Israel." The opposition will surely come. In every historic transition there are the reactionaries, who would fain push back into Erie the waters of Niagara, to whom all change is perilous, all innovation damnable liberalism and even rank heresy. Mind them not; pass onward with Christ and His truth.

The Church and the age! Their union is secured. The nineteenth century has seen in its latter days men "by whom salvation is brought to Israel." I name a few—and in naming

Men through whom victory comes: the chief among them, Leo XIII. them I send to them in their heavenly or earthly abodes my soul's tribute—Von Ketteler, of Cologne; Lavigerie, of Carthage; Manning, of Westminster; Gibbons, of Baltimore; Leo, of Rome. Two we especially revere.

Leo, I hail thee, pontiff of thy age, providential chieftain of the Church in this great crisis of her history! How true it is that God has care for His Church! It seemed to be a supreme moment in her life among men. The abyss between her and the age was widening; governments had set her aside and warred against her; peoples trusted her not; the intellectual and social movements of humanity ignored her. Catholics, clergy, and laity, terrified and disheartened, made of their isolation a rule, a dogma. Humanly speaking, the horizon was dark with fateful forebodings. Then Leo comes to the helm; quickly he discerns the angry elements, the shoals and breakers, and, under his hand, the ship moves in new directions with quickened vigor; she tops the highest billows, fearless of their fury, and soon she reaches calm seas, where triumphantly she plows the waters, the peerless queen.

Leo talks to the age in its own language; he tells it what indeed the Church is and the age wonders and admires. By his decrees opening to the scholarship of the world, non-Catholic or Catholic, the archives of the Vatican, establishing universities in Europe and America, lifting upward the standard of studies in all the schools of the Church, he places the Church in the leadership of the race for knowledge. His immortal encyclical on "The Condition of Labor" consecrates him the pontiff of the workingmen; it becomes the charter of the laborer, teaching him not merely his duties, of which he had heard so much, but his rights, of which clerics heretofore had spoken with bated breath. The masses of the people, the poor and the oppressed, know that the Church is with them, not merely their counsellor, but their defender and their champion. The glorious encyclicals to the French nation bring to the democracy the long-coveted kiss of the Church; the smiles of the Church, which emperors and kings had claimed as their exclusive inheritance, now descend upon the fair face of the highest embodiment of popular rights, the republic. O God be praised that we live to know and to love Leo.

Not merely does Leo teach, but he acts, and he demands that others act. No opportunity to reach out to the world, to benefit it, to teach it in sympathetic words, is neglected. By letters, in private conversation he urges bishops, priests and laymen to be soldiers of the Church, bearing in her name to peoples and governments not the sword of war, but the olive branch of amity and concord. His letters to Decurtins and De Mun instance his enlightened zeal. Nor would he narrow down the lines of combat to pious confraternities. His letter to the Bishop of Grenoble declares that Catholics must work for truth and virtue wherever they are allowed to work, and in the society of men who, while well-meaning and honest, may still be outside the Church. "I try to do everything, everywhere, for the Church," said Leo to myself, "and so would I have bishops do wherever circumstances permit it." His joy over the proceedings of our late American Catholic Congress shows how far he approves unusual manifestations of energy on the part of the clergy and laity.

Leo has the courage of his high mission. Pope as he is, he has his opponents within the Church; men whose sickly nerves suffer from the vibrations of the ship moving under his hand with accelerated velocity; reactionaries, who think that all the wisdom and the providential guidance of the Church are with the past; obstinate advocates of self-interest, who place their own ideas and their own likings above the welfare of the Church of Christ. But Leo works in spite of all opposition, and Leo reigns. The Roman Pontificate to-day before governments and peoples is invested with high prestige and moral power unknown to it for years; the Church is out upon the broad world, felt, esteemed and listened to as she has not been in the century. Whole nations are saved. Leo is doing for France what France is unable to do; he is uniting her people, giving to her a durable government and staying the hand of religious persecution. Say what some may, these are in

France the results of the Papal encyclicals in favor of the French republic.

Leo shows forth in especial splendor the Church's catholicity—her divinely-begotten fitness for all ages and all nations. He severs the Church from political and social entanglements, makes her independent of the transient traditions of the past, and sets her before the world radiant in her native beauty and freedom, prepared to embrace and bless the new humanity of the twentieth century, as she embraced and blessed the humanity of previous centuries amid its manifold phases and transformations, the Church of to-day as of yesterday, the Church of to-morrow as of to-day.

Surely, much is yet to be done before the union of age and Church is complete; but the work has begun and has progressed to a surprising degree. Let us pray that Leo live yet many years, and that when death at last comes Leo's spirit still dominate in the Vatican, and all will be well. Meanwhile, in America, let it be our duty to cluster around him, to inhale his ideas, to work with him, as Americans should work, in energy and earnestness. We are especially favored by him. He lives among us in an especial manner, having sent to us his chosen representative, who makes Leo known to us as no other man could; whose words, whose acts, prove to us daily how truly Leo is the Pontiff of the age,—Monsignor Satolli. The Church and the age! Rome is the Church; America is the age. And Monsignor Satolli's command to Catholics of America is: "Go forward, on the road of progress, bearing in one hand the book of Christian truth—Christ's gospel, and in the other the Constitution of the United States."

Leo's representative in America—Monsignor Satolli.

Gibbons, of Baltimore! I cannot give to my words the warmth of my heart. I shall give to them its sincerity. I have spoken of the providential Pope of Rome. I speak now of the providential Archbishop of Baltimore. How oft, in past years, I have thanked God that in this latter quarter of the nineteenth century Cardinal Gibbons had been granted to us as primate, as leader. Catholic of Catholics, American of Americans, a bishop of his age, and of his country, he is to America what Leo is to all Christendom. Aye, far beyond America does his influence extend. Men are not confined by frontier lines, and Gibbons is European as Manning is American. A particular mission is reserved to the American Cardinal. The Church and the age fight their battles with especial intensity in America. America is watched. The prelate who in America is the representative of the union of Church and age is watched. His leadership guides the combatants the world over. The name of Cardinal Gibbons lights up the page of nearly every European book which treats of modern social and political questions. The ripplings of Cardinal Gibbons' influence cross the threshold of the Vatican. Leo, the mighty inspirer of men, is inspired and encouraged by his faithful lieutenants, from whom he often asks: " Watchman, what of the night?" The historic incident of the Knights of Labor, whose condemnation Cardinal Gibbons averted by personal interviews with Leo, was one of the preparations to the encyclical on the " Condition of Labor." But Cardinal Gibbons is an American; let him be judged from America.

Cardinal Gibbons— the providential Archbishop of Baltimore.

The work of Cardinal Gibbons forms an epoch in the history of the Church in America. He has made known, as no one before him did, the Church to the people of America; he has demonstrated the fitness of the Church for America, the natural alliance existing between the Church and the freedom-giving democratic institutions of America. Through his action the scales have fallen from the eyes of non-Catholics; prejudices have vanished. He, the great churchman, is the great citizen. Church and country are united in him, and the magnetism of the union pervades the whole land, teaching laggard Catholics to love America, teaching well-disposed non-Catholics to trust the Church. How noble the mission which heaven has assigned to him! How well it has been followed out! Church and country in America, the Church and the age, moderns aspirations and ancient truths, the democracy with its republican liberties and the spiritual princedom of the Catholic Church harmonized, cast into bonds of warm amity, laboring together for each other's progress, for the progress of humanity upon earth and in heaven!—O God of time and of eternity, God of Church and of country, we praise Thee, we thank Thee! Unceasing be to us this flow of Thy bounty!

I need not tell the qualities of mind and heart which have brought the reward of success to the labors of Cardinal Gibbons,— the nation knows them. He is large-minded; his vision cannot be narrowed to a one-sided consideration of men or things. He is large-hearted; his sympathies are limited by the frontiers of humanity; careless of self, he gives his best activities to the good of others. He is ready for every noble work, patriotic, intellectual, social, philanthropic, as well as religious, and in the prosecution of it he joins hands with the laborer and the capitalist, with the white man and the black man, with the Catholic, the Protestant and the Jew. He is brave; he has the courage to speak and to act according to his convictions; he rejoices when men work with him; he works when men fall away from him. Bravery is as needful in labors of peace as in those of war.

Cardinal Gibbons, the most outspoken of Catholics, the most loyal co-laborer of the Pope of Rome, is the American of Americans. I desire to accentuate his American patriotism, for it has been a wondrous factor in his victories. We have heard it said that frequent declarations of patriotism are unseeming in loyal citizens, whose silent lives ought to give sufficient evidence of their civic virtue. Let it be said, then, that frequent declarations of religious faith are not in place among devoted Christians, that the "Credo" should be seldom repeated.

I have spoken my tribute to the Cardinal Archbishop of Baltimore. A wide field remains untouched from which other men may gather other tributes.

Reasons for Hope and Gratitude.

My whole observation of the times, and in particular of this memorable Columbian year, convinces me that the Church has at present her season of grace in America, and I often put to myself the anxious question: Will she profit of it? At moments my soul sinks downward to the border land of pessimism. I hate pessimism; I believe it to be one of the worst of crimes against God and humanity; it ends progress. Yet it tempts me, when I read in so many souls indifference and inertia, when I hear of the trifles with which soldiers of truth busy themselves, when I perceive the vast crowd looking backward lest they see the eastern horizon purpled by the rising rays of the new sun, and moving at slowest pace lest perchance they leave the ruts of the past and overtake the world, whose salvation is their God-given mission. This evening far from me pessimism is driven. I feel that religion will surely conquer. My soul throbs with hope. For I remember the God above me; I remember the leaders He has given to the Church—in Rome, Leo XIII; in America, Cardinal Gibbons. What one man can do is wondrous; what could not ten men—a hundred men do? O Church Catholic, fruitful mother of heroes, give us in unstinted measure men, sons of thy own greatness and of thy own power!

The jubilee of Cardinal Gibbons is not a celebration of song and tinsel; it is a lesson to bishops, priests and laymen of God's Church in America.

THE STATE LAST:

A STUDY

— OF —

DOCTOR BOUQUILLON'S PAMPHLET:

Education: To whom does it belong?

With a Supplement

REVIEWING

DR. BOUQUILLON'S REJOINDER TO CRITICS.

— BY —

REV. JAMES CONWAY S. J.,

CANISIUS COLLEGE, BUFFALO, N. Y.

1892.

FR. PUSTET,

Printer to the Holy Apostolic See and the S. Congregation of Rites.

FR. PUSTET & CO.,
NEW YORK AND CINCINNATI.

COPYRIGHT, 1892,
BY ERWIN STEINBACK,
Firm of Fr. Pustet & Co.

PREFACE.

The study of which these pages contain the result was begun immediately after the publication of Dr. Bouquillon's pamphlet. The author, having himself once travelled the same ground, was naturally eager to compare notes with the learned Doctor. He had no intention, however, of rushing into print, especially as he thought he had already said all he had to say on the matter. But believing, as he read, that certain authors with whose teaching he was familiar were misconceived and misconstrued, and judging that some of the leading principles laid down were either false or misleading, and that the whole tenor of the brochure was likely rather to prove detrimental than advantageous to the cause of Catholic education in this country he did finally come to the determination to prepare a review of Dr. Bouquillon's teaching for the press.

His work was well nigh finished when, after the conference of the Archbishops held in St. Louis at the beginning of December last, he was given to understand from a reliable source that discussion—at least in the form of personal controversy—was no longer desirable. So he cheerfully shelved his work and devoted himself to more peaceful and congenial occupations.

Seeing, however, that the controversy was not only continued, but even waxed fiercer than ever, after the St. Louis conference, and that Dr. Bouquillon's doctrine was not only publicly defended, but freely cited in favor of the theory and practice of state education, the author soon came to the conclusion that discussion was not only not undesirable, but plainly invited, and even necessary. He, therefore, readily yielded to the many kindly solicitations brought to bear upon him by his friends, took his notes again from the shelf, and arranged them for the press. It was not for some weeks, however, that his local superiors, who were naturallly opposed to all personal controversy, could prevail upon themselves to give the necessary permission for the publication.

After he had sent his study of Dr. Bouquillon's first pamphlet to the printers, the "*Rejoinder to Critics*" reached him. Though this second publication did not strictly concern him, yet he deemed it due to Dr. Bouquillon, and to the public to review it in a supplement to be appended to this essay.

Though much has been written on the subject since his paper was practically finished, the author did not deem it expedient to make any material changes—not even after reading the Doctor's "rejoinder." He preferred to give his first impressions of Dr. Bouquillon's brochure; which, for the rest have only been confirmed by whatever criticisms have since come under his notice. He endeavored to treat Dr. Bouquillon with that fairness and deference, which he would consider due to himself, and much more to a man of such deserved reputation and true merit as Dr. Bouquillon. Should a single word of this paper seem harsh, or unduly severe, to the readers the author would fain have it unsaid.

Canisius College, Buffalo, N. Y.
January 31, 1892.

CONTENTS.

                                                                PAGE.

   PREFACE   .   .   .   3
I. INTRODUCTION   .   .   .   7
II. DR. BOUQUILLON'S ARGUMENTS   11
III. DR. BOUQUILLON'S AUTHORITIES   18
IV. DR. BOUQUILLON'S METHOD   .   .   . 43
V. DETAILS OF DR. BOUQUILLON'S PROCEDURE   .   46
VI. CONCLUSION.   .   .   71
   SUPPLEMENT—DR. BOUQUILLON'S REJOINDER   .   . 81

THE STATE LAST.

A STUDY OF DR. BOUQUILLON'S PAMPHLET.

Education : to whom does it Belong ?

I. INTRODUCTION.

Dr. Bouquillon's long looked for [1] pamphlet has brought thus much satisfaction to those interested in the juridical aspect of education, that the advocates of state education now know all that can be said in their favor, while the defenders of domestic rights against state encroachment have learned how little can be advanced against them. However, we cannot consider the general effects of this publication as by any means gratifying to either party, beneficial to the Church, or serviceable to any good purpose. The general impression we believe is disappointment. Dr. Bouquillon's opponents, who, we believe, form the bulk of those interested and capable of having an opinion on so difficult a matter, are disappointed, though not disagreeably, that only so light a force could be mustered against them from such a quarter aroused to hostilities. Many of them expected a much more formidable array. Those few, on the other hand, who are known to covet and court state interference were doubtless more painfully disappointed at finding so weak a support upon which to

---

[1] It is now an open secret, made common property by Dr. Bouquillon's own friends, that his pamphlet was written for the *American Catholic Quarterly Review*, but rejected by the editors, for reasons which will probably strike the reader as he peruses these pages. Its publication as a separate pamphlet was awaited early last summer; but for reasons best known to the author, it was withheld from the public until the latter part of November last, about ten days before the meeting of the Archbishops in St. Louis ; at which meeting the school question was to come under consideration. How far this delay was premeditated, or accidental, we do not take upon ourselves to judge.

See *Northwestern Chronicle* December 11, 1891, and January 1, 1892. Cf. *The parent first* by Rev. R. I. Holaind, S. J., Preface.

rest their cause. Besides, this class of social philosophers are used to frothy declamation rather than sober reasoning; and Dr. Bouquillon, instead of spreading the American eagle to their wondering gaze surprised them with a modest, severe, albeit scholarly, dissertation, giving them all the benefit of his profound erudition and varied reading in almost rigid scholastic form. Were Dr. Bouquillon less of a scholar and more of a demagogue he would, we think, have written a more satisfactory, and probably a more successful, plea for state education.

We unhesitatingly call Dr. Bouquillon's pamphlet a *plea for state education*, although he himself does not introduce it as such, and although he does not confine himself exclusively to the discussion and defence of state rights. The proportions of the book itself, to say nothing of the *animus* with which it is written, justifies this view of it. For, apart from the introductory and concluding remarks, we find that fully two-thirds of the space is devoted to the defence of the rights, duties and power of the state, while only one-third is left to the treatment of the rights, the mission, and the authority of the individual, the family and the Church. Whatever share, then, the state may have in the education of the child, it gets, at least, the lion's share of the pamphlet. It might, therefore, be justly entitled: The State *versus* individual, family and Church—not that the author wishes to give undue rights to the state, but that he is so very anxious to give it its dues as against the individual, the family and the Church. This is a sort of distributive justice very commendable in the learned moralist; but he should also remember the old saw: *Summum jus, summa injuria*. The greatest right is often the greatest wrong.

The purport and motive of the learned author, as we read in his preface is "to show that in the matter of education as in all other social concerns the true doctrine of the Church is opposed neither to liberty well understood nor to the just prerogatives of the state." Those "just prerogatives of the state," are, as we subsequently learn, the *right to educate*, strict, special and proper. The Doctor's point, therefore, as we understand it, is this: *That the state has the right to educate, in the ordinary sense of this word ; that this right is a special and proper right (p. 11), such as the state has to govern and to judge, i. e., through its delegates (p. 12); that having such right it has also the mis-*

sion, or obligation to educate (p. 18, sq.), and certain authority or control over education (p. 23, sq.).

Now, in this proposition, taken in its generality, there is much that is unobjectionable. That the state has a certain control over education may be conceded; but the extent of this control must be defined by certain principles and concrete circumstances; else it does little towards the solution of the problem on hand. That the state has an educational mission (or, in the Doctor's meaning, a certain duty in regard to education) is also beyond dispute. But that the state has a right, *special* and *proper* to *educate*, in the accepted meaning of this word, as it has to *govern* and to *judge* by its agents, we cannot grant; and this is the precise point on which we take issue with the learned Doctor, as far as principles are concerned—and he strictly confines himself to the discussion of principles. We deny that the state is an educator *per se*, or has the *special and proper right to educate*, (this right we vindicate in the *natural* order to parents exclusively); though we do grant the state extensive rights, a certain mission, and certain authority in regard to education. We have treated this question at length long before the present controversy arose; and on further reflection, in the light of all that has been written since upon the problem, we do not believe that we have modified our opinion. In 1883 we summed up our views in these words:

"Abstracting from the prerogatives of the Church, we say that, according to the natural law, which is the basis of the moral order and of all positive legislation, education is the business of parents, to the exclusion of all others; that they have, therefore, the sacred and inviolable right to educate their own offspring, or intrust them to the care of those who will educate them, according to their moral and religious convictions; that the state, according to the same divinely-constituted order, should not be the educator of its children, but only the promoter and patron of education; that this is its only function in regard to education, by which alone it can lead the people to true civilization; that any further interference on the part of the state, in the matter of education, is not only violent and unjust, but must needs prove destructive to religion, to morality, to genuine culture, and to the social order of nations." [1]

[1] Respective Rights and Duties, etc., p. 32. (2 ed.). New York, Pustet, 1890. Cf. *American Catholic Quarterly Review*, Jan., 1884.

We cannot afford here to set forth the arguments which led us to the above conclusions; we can only refer the reader to the preceding pages of the work cited. The point in which all arguments in support of our position taken from reason meet is, in our opinion, the following: Parents have the *indispensable duty*, arising from the fact of procreation, by themselves, if possible, or by reliable representatives, if they themselves are unable to discharge this duty, personally, to educate their offspring according to the dictates of conscience. Now, to an indispensable duty corresponds an *inalienable right*. Therefore parents have the inalienable right to educate their offspring according to the dictates of their own conscience. The force of this argument is admitted by Dr. Bouquillon himself (p. 10) where he says: "This right of parents is *sacred;* no one may *suppress* or *diminish it; for it springs from a paramount duty*" (Italics ours). And he cites in confirmation of this assertion the unmistakable words of Leo XIII. to the Bavarian Bishops Dec. 22, 1878: " In these duties, assumed by the fact of the procreation of children, parents should know that just as many rights are inherent (inesse) according to natural right (naturam et æquitatem); and that these rights are such that they may not in aught dispense with them, that no human power can detract aught from them, since one cannot lawfully be absolved by man from the duties by which he is bound to God." [1]

Hence it is manifest that parents can never renounce or forfeit this right, to educate their own children, or to have them educated by teachers, or in schools, of their own choosing—not even by free suffrage in a democratic commonwealth; for an inalienable right can no more be put at the mercy of a popular majority than in the hands of an absolute monarch or of a constitutional government. The only case thinkable in which this right can be forfeited is that of crime or inability (insanity, poverty, &c.). Strange that Dr. Bouquillon, after stating the premises so clearly (p. 9–10) fails to see the conclusion, and rather goes out of his way to seek limitations to parental rights.

[1] "Hisce in officiis simul cum procreatione liberorum susceptis, noverint patresfamilias totidem jura inesse secundum naturam et æquitatem, atque esse ejusmodi de quibus nihil liceat sibi remittere, nihil cuivis hominum potestati detrahere, quum officiis solvi, quibus homo teneatur ad Deum, sit per hominem nefas." Encycl. "Officio Sanctissimo."

This is, briefly stated, our doctrine and the main argument on which it rests as contrasted with Dr. Bouquillon's teaching. It will be seen in the course of our investigation that it is the common teaching of Catholic writers, particularly of those cited by the Doctor in defence of his own opinion. It must be borne in mind, however, that we have to deal with Dr. Bouquillon's teaching, not to establish an argument or a *consensus* of theologians and philosophers. We shall, therefore, introduce positive matter only in as far as it will be deemed expedient, to show the untenableness of the Doctor's position.

In order to treat Dr. Bouquillon's pamphlet with that thoroughness and completeness due to the work of so eminent a man, and required by the importance of the subject, we shall examine:—

1. *His arguments.*
2. *His authorities.*
3. *His method.*
4. *Some details of his procedure.* After this is done we shall have something to say in *conclusion* of its general character and its opportuneness.

II. Dr. Bouquillon's Arguments.

If we have rightly understood the Doctor's process of reasoning he has two chief arguments; the one of a general, the other of a more special nature.

1. The first argument we take to be this: *Every person*, whether physical or moral, i.e., every individual, or corporation, *has a right to educate.* But *the state* is a moral person, or corporation. Therefore the state has a right to educate.

If the *major* of this syllogism is granted the conclusion is inevitable; as the minor is evidently true. Therefore the author is concerned only with the major and devotes to it the greater part of pages 7–9 under the heading: *Right of Educating in the Individual.* This whole section is apparently directed against the *positive right* theory, which claims that the right of education is derived from, or delegated by, sovereign authority, or positive legislation. The conclusion we find referred to (p. 11), where the author says: "It were unreasonable to refuse to the state that which is granted to every legitimate association [i.e., the vague and general right to educate]." But what of the *major?*

We grant as against the *positive right theory* that the right to teach is an individual, personal, or domestic right, antecedent to, and independent of, all positive law or enactment. But is this right vested in *every individual*, whether physical person or corporation? This we deny, unless we are to understand by education the mere communication of thoughts and ideas. But to communicate one's thoughts or ideas is not to teach in the sense of *educating*. And herein lies the Doctor's fallacy. He proceeds from a defective definition of education. We insert the entire passage lest we should seem to misrepresent the Doctor's meaning.

What is education? In a large sense it is to *communicate what we know to one who does not know*. In a restricted sense it is to *communicate after a methodical and continuous fashion* knowledge relative to religion, morals, letters, sciences, the arts; or, it is to instruct and train childhood and youth. But every man has the *right to communicate the truth*, and to communicate it after the fashion that is most efficacious and best adapted to those who wish to receive it. For this he needs no mandate from government. To allow to every citizen the right of expressing opinions by speech or by the press, and at the same time to deny him, as is done in some countries, the right of teaching is a monstrous contradiction. (Italics ours).[1]

This definition of education, on which is based the Doctor's argument is altogether insufficient. The idea of education is not covered by that of teaching or instructing; much less by the idea of incidental communication of ideas. The salient, the essential feature of education is the training of the human faculties, the building up of the perfect man or woman, the development of human power, the direction of youth in the way it should walk to gain its end in this life and the life to come.

Cardinal Gibbons in *Our Christian Heritage* (p. 489) justly emphasizes the necessity of a clear and correct definition, and brings out prominently this feature, of education. "I am persuaded," he says, "that the popular errors now existing in reference to education spring

---

[1] Dr. Bouquillon allowed himself to be mislead to this definition by his admired friend Sauvé, from whom he takes it almost *ad verbum*. "Pris dans sou sens le plus général, l'enseignement signifie *la communication d'une chose que l'on sait à quelqu'un qui l'ignore* (p. 236).... Pris dans un sens plus restreint, l'enseignement signifie la *communication méthodique et continue* de connaissances relatives à la religion, à la morale, aux lettres, aux sciences et aux arts, ou, si l'on vent, l'instruction et l'education de l'enfance et de la jeunesse. Dans ce second sens, comme dans le premier, l'enseignement n'est un droit que s'il s'applique à des connaissances qu'il soit licite de communiquer aux autres." Questions religieuses et sociales, p. 238.

from an incorrect notion of that term. *To educate* means *to bring out*, to develop the intellectual, moral and religious faculties of the soul. An education then which improves the mind and the memory, to the neglect of moral and religious training, is at best but an imperfect system."

Instruction is but a subordinate function, albeit necessary, in the entire process of education. To teach, therefore, in the sense of educating implies much more than merely to communicate knowledge to one who does not possess it.[1] The teacher, that is, the educator, has to deal with the intellectual, moral and religious life, growth and development of the child. This is a sacred function into which no intruder may thrust himself. One has no more right to undertake the instruction or education of another's child without his consent, than one has the right to plow or sow or reap his neighbor's field. The reason is this: the right to teach, in the sense of educating, supposes authority in the teacher and submission in the pupil; unless it is simply a question of contract between a teacher and grown up pupil; in which case the teacher may put conditions, but cannot exact obedience except conditionally. But such a relation between pupil and teacher can hardly be called education in the true sense of the word.

Whence, then, does the schoolmaster derive his right or authority to teach? Like every other right this right must be based on some fact; and here it is the fact by which the schoolmaster receives his pupils; for there is a co-relation between teacher and pupil. Now, by what facts can one become the educator of another? By the very fact of procreation parents (the father in the first instance) become educators, with strict duties and corresponding rights. The facts by which any other may become an educator are, as far as we can see, either *free contract* between teacher and pupil (but in this case, there is hardly question of education in the strict sense), the *choice* of *parents*, or the incorporation in a teaching body (e. g., a college or university), by which fact pupils of such institution become *his*. Whatever authority the schoolmaster has over his pupils, therefore,

[1] " Educatio non in sola corporis nutritione primis infantiæ annis consistit; sed educatio est complexus omnium actionum, quibus non solum conservatio, sed et perfectio corporis atque animi liberorum et physica et intellectualis et moralis in facultatum evolutione usque ad adultam ætatem promovetur, ita ut liberi vitam natura rationali dignam et conditione parentum sociali saltem non inferiorem agere possint." Costa-Rossetti, Phil. Mor., ed. 2. p. 434. Cf. Respective Rights and Duties, etc., pp. 9-11.

(abstracting from ecclesiastical jurisdiction) is delegated by the parents, who either choose him personally or the institution to which he belongs. This, is as far as we could gather, the common opinion of Catholic writers on the authority of schools and schoolmasters.

When, therefore, authors say that individuals have a right to educate they either mean the right of exchanging ideas, or the right of instructing the ignorant, which is a work of mercy that all have a right to perform, or the right of teaching the rudiments of the faith privately (not publicly) to those who are not instructed; or finally they understand a *negative right* (Dr. Bouquillon himself p. 11. calls it a "vague and general" right) i. e., a right not to be unjustly hindered from exercising the profession of teachers or educators, if possessed of the necessary attainments. But no other author, to our knowledge except Dr. Bouquillon simply and unqualifiedly vindicates to every individual the right to educate.[1]

On this assumption Dr. Bouquillon proceeds: "If every individual has the right of teaching what he is capable of teaching to whomsoever will accept his teaching, a collection or legitimate association of men endowed with a like capability must have the like right" (p. 8). The *condition* of this hypothetical argument as we have seen is not verified, but requires to be essentially modified; and, therefore, the *conditional* conclusion calls for the same modification. Nay, more, we cannot refrain from noticing that the individual is in a much more favorable condition in regard to the right to educate, than societies and corporations as such. For every rational individual is at least free to qualify himself for the office of teaching and to acquire the right to teach; but the case is different with societies; they can acquire this right only when teaching, or education, lies within their special scope. A base-ball association, for instance, or an insurance company, or the Farmers' Alliance, could hardly acquire the right of educating. And this, be it borne in mind, is true also of the state, if it can be shown that education as such is not one of its proper functions.

The positive arguments adduced by Dr. Bouquillon (p. 9) have no force whatever. The Lateran Decree[2] referred to only forbids unjust exactions and the refusal of the *license* to teach to those who are

[1] When we wrote the above we had not yet read Sauvé's *Liberté d'enseignement.*
[2] Decretales, lib. v. tit. 5, de Magistris, cc. *Quoniam* and *Quanto Gallicana.*

qualified, but it manifestly supposes that the *license* itself must be obtained; and that from the ecclesiastical authorities. Abelard and the Professors of Padua and Verceil (Vercelli ?) received their authority to teach either by express or implicit contract with their pupils or their pupils' parents, or by the sanction of the communities among whom they taught, or by the tacit consent of the Church, or by all these collectively. We shall have occasion to return to the other learned authorities whom the Doctor here quotes for his opinion.

It is but fair to note, however, that the Doctor does not lay any great stress on this general argument: he may not even look upon it as an argument in the strict sense; but certainly we must consider it as a step, however unimportant, towards establishing his main point, as we see no other reason for giving it such prominence in his treatise, and precisely in this part. [1]

2. The *second* or main argument (p. 11-12) is to be found under the heading: *The Right of the State to Educate.* By the state the Doctor here understands " not the people but the social authority," whether vested " in one person, or in an assembly." This authority, he says, is essentially *" one and the same and always and everywhere has the same rights and attributes"* (Italics ours). Here we would warn the reader that these words are misleading. In the merely *natural order* and in the *abstract* this might be granted; but in the *positive* and *concrete order*, the power of civil authority may be modified in diverse ways by constitutional concessions and restrictions; and, above all, in the *supernatural order* the power of the state may vary indefinitely according to the relation in which it stands to the supernatural authority. In the *concrete*, therefore, the extent of civil power may be very different according as it is vested in a Charlemagne, a Sixtus V., a Garcia Moreno, a Queen Victoria, or a President Harrison. Had Dr. Bouquillon borne this diversity in mind, he would have come to a more satisfactory solution of the tangled school question.

Here the Doctor vindicates for the state, not "a vague and general" right as " granted to every legitimate association," but a *"special and proper* right, of teaching human knowledge " or of *educating* as expressed in the heading and elsewhere. This right of teach-

---

[1] We have been confirmed in this opinion by reading the work of Mons. Sauvé, whom Bouquillon follows as his master. This author gives great prominence to this argument to vindicate the right of educating not only to the state, but chiefly to the Church.

ing on the part of the state is described as that of "establishing schools, appointing teachers, prescribing methods and programme of study.... in the same way as it [the state] *governs* and *judges* (It. ours), viz, through delegates fitted for such functions." Some of rights here ascribed are in a certain sense unquestioned and unquestionable; as, for instance, in *certain cases*, the right of establishing schools, appointing teachers, and, *with certain restrictions*, prescribing methods and programmes of study *for such schools* ; not, however, in the same manner as the right of governing and judging, but as a secondary and accidental function as the Doctor elsewhere concedes. But such rights cannot be categorically asserted as they are by Dr. Bouquillon. We give the Doctor's argument in full (p. 12), italicizing those passages to which we would draw special attention.

These considerations being premised to obviate all equivocation, we affirm unhesitatingly, and in accord, as we think, with the principles of sound theology and philosophy, and with the testimony of the tradition of the Church, that it must be admitted, as the larger number of theologians do admit, *that the State has the right to educate.* The following reason, drawn from the very nature of things and, in our judgment, thoroughly apodictical will suffice. Civil authority has the right to use *all legitimate temporal means it judges necessary* for the attainment of the temporal common welfare, which is the end of civil society Now *among the most necessary means* for the attainment of the temporal welfare of the commonwealth is *the diffusion of human knowledge.* Therefore, civil authority has the right to use the means necessary for the diffusion of such knowledge, that is to say, to teach it, or rather to have it taught by capable agents. We believe the major proposition of this argument cannot be denied, especially if it be kept in mind that we are speaking of *temporal* means that enter into the sphere of action of the state, and of *legitimate* means that trench on and wound no other right. With this double reservation the right to an end evidently implies the right to the means. Neither can the minor proposition of the argument be reasonably denied. You have but to look around you, you have but to consult history to be convinced that from the moral, social, political as well as material point of view, science, possessed in different degrees according to different conditions, is one of the primordial elements of prosperity in any country. A nation needs citizens able to take interest in the commonwealth, workmen that are intelligent, surveyors that are skilful, physicians that are experienced, jurists that are learned. An ignorant people is a people inferior in agriculture, industry, arts, war. If you would have a people instructed, you must look to its instruction, and, if need be, establish and direct it. *We look upon this conclusion as impregnable.*

This argument, the conclusion of which its author looks upon as "impregnable," has very little, if any weight. For, in the first place, it *proves too much* there is hardly a tenet advocated by socialists or modern social reformers generally but could be equally ved from this argument. "Civil authority has a right to use all legitimate temporal means for the attainment of the temporal common welfare." Now "among the most necessary means for the attainment of the temporal welfare of the commonwealth" are the judicious administration of temporal goods, the wise regulation and distribution of all industrial products, the proper control of the means of communication, the cultivation and utilization of the soil to its utmost degree of productiveness, the choice by each citizen of the most suitable calling or profession, the choice of good and congenial wives and husbands. Therefore civil authority has the right to administer all private property, to regulate and distribute all productions, to control all the means of communication, to cultivate the soil and work all the mines of the country, to choose a vocation or employment for each of its citizens, and to assign to each individual a congenial partner for life. With such an argument you may prove anything, therefore it proves nothing. Hence there must be a flaw in it. Where is the fallacy?

The *major* might pass if we are to understand by "legitimate temporal means" *what is really for the common good, within the proper scope of civil authority; and what does not trench on the inalienable rights of the individual, the family and the Church.*

The *minor* omits "legitimate" and substitutes "among the most necessary." Now, *some* "diffusion of knowledge," by *some means*, and *to some extent*, is a "necessary means" for the common good; but not the diffusion of all kinds of knowledge, or any certain kind of knowledge conveyed by certain special means (say, a certain programme, taught according to a certain method, in a public school). This latter kind of knowledge—communicated by the state through its public schools—is not "necessary;" neither is it a "legitimate means" if obtained by the violation of personal or parental rights. Therefore the state may not use it as a means unless in certain cases, when it is for the common good, and when it is within the scope of the state, and does not infringe on higher and more sacred rights. Thus, for instance, the state may establish schools for its special purposes, such as military and naval academies, common schools where such are needed and not otherwise provided for; industrial schools for the children of the criminal an [hel]pless classes, who are not otherwise cared for; or schools generally where necessary or useful, provided it conforms to the just wishes of parents and of the Church [1]—but not a system of public schools to be regarded as the only acknowledged means or standard of education to which all have to submit or conform; such a means of diffusing knowledge would be *illegitimate*. The argument, therefore proves nothing and we are just where we started.

The learned author will, moreover, permit us to draw his attention to the technical looseness of this syllogism. In the major we have as middle term: "*all the means it* [the state] *judges necessary*"; in the minor we have: "*among the most necessary means ;*" in the conclusion the writer jumps to "*the necessary means* [for this means i. e.] for the diffusion of such knowledge." In a man of less gravity than the learned Doctor, this would sound very much like quibbling. The author himself shows the weakness of his "impregnable conclusion" when he descends to the following remark (p. 12–13).

The civil power does necessarily teach in one way or another, as for instance, when it exercises legislative and judiciary powers ; for a law is an enlightenment, a teaching for the mind as well as a direction for the will ; the sentence of a tribunal is likewise an educational agency; and therefore the state as legislator and judge has in virtue of this double capacity the right of imparting education. [2]

This is education in a rather metaphorical sense, the right to which no one will deny the state.

To his "impregnable conclusion" that the state has the right to educate Dr. Bouquillon subsequently appeals to prove the so-called mission of the state to educate, and its authority over education (pp. 19, 23). This is about the only serious attempt at philosophical argumentation in the pamphlet ; and with this argument stands or falls the Doctor's opinion, as far as he would have it based on reason. We may, therefore, take leave of it and proceed to the examination of—

III. DR. BOUQUILLON'S AUTHORITIES.

The author "professes to walk in the footsteps of the great theo-

[1] Cf. Respective Rights and Duties, &c. p. 29, sq.: Rights of our Little Ones, questions 49, 50, 56.

[2] Here the Doctor allowed himself again to be misled by his admiration for Sauvé: "C'est ce que fait l'Etat en exerçant la puissance ou législative ou judiciare, puisque toute loi est une lumière, un enseignement pour l'esprit et en même temps qu' une direction pour la volonté, et que toute sentence est aussi une sorte d'enseignement. Législateur et juge, l'Etat ou le souverain est, en cette double qualité, investi d'un certain droit d'enseigner : *Lex*, dit saint Basile, *et doctrix et magistra*." Opus. cit. p. 254.

logians, especially of St. Thomas. He has, he says, "been guided by the light of the encyclicals of Leo XIII." Now, it is true, he quotes St. Thomas and the encyclicals of Leo XIII. a few times, but not a single time bearing upon the main issue that the state has a *right proper and special to educate* as it has the right to judge and govern by its representatives, but only on secondary issues, which we all admit, or in cases in which they are manifestly against his teaching (as on p. 10, and p. 23), as we shall have occasion to notice hereafter.

Now, who are the great theologians in whose footsteps he professes to walk? He permits us to review them in his introduction (p. 5-6).

As to principles, we acknowledge that they are to be found best exposed in the more recent publicists, rather than in the older writers who lived before the modern era of the separation of Church and State. *We quote in preference* (Italics ours). Taparelli, *Saggio teoretico di Diritto naturale*, diss. 7, and *Esame critico degli ordini representativi*, tom. I, p. 314; Card. Zigliara, *Phil. mor.*, p. II, lib. II, c. I, a. 5; Costa-Rossetti, *Inst. Eth. et jur. nat.* thes. 175, 176; Hammerstein, *De Eccl. et Statu*, p. 146, 158, 181; Sauvé, *Questions religieuses et sociales*, c. 10; Cavagnis, *Inst. Jur. publ. et Eccl.*, lib. IV, c. I. *Mention must also be made* (Italics ours) of Coppola, *Sul Diritto della Chiesa in ordine al publico Insegnamento*; Riess, *Der moderne Staat und die Christliche Schule*; Jansen, *De Facultate Docendi*; Conway, *The respective rights and duties of family, state and church in regard to education*; Robiano, *De Jure Ecclesiæ in Universitates Studiorum*; and finally the anonymous work of two French priests, *L'Ecole neutre en face de la Théologie*.

To these are added the various collections of the decrees and canons of the Church, and the *schema de ecclesia* prepared for the Vatican Council, but not discussed, a large array of church historians, and, in short, the entire pædagogical literature as described in *Polybiblion* (1873-74) and elsewhere. There is no lack of authorities, therefore and of course the simple reader, who has not read all the books reviewed in *Polybiblion*, is left to believe that all those authorities converge in the opinion propounded by the learned Doctor; if he happens to have overlooked, as he is very likely to do, the incidental remark in the preface: that "he [Dr. Bouquillon] could not omit, without sacrificing completeness, certain delicate points of detail on which Catholics are not in agreement."

Now, as the reader must have remarked, the Doctor divides his authorities into two classes; one whom he "*quotes in preference*," and another of whom only "*mention must be made*." He evidently lays more stress on the former, either because they have the greater weight, or because he thinks they agree with him in his views on state education. For one or both of these reasons he does not make a single reference in his work to any of the second category of authorities; although he does not rigorously exclude others who are not mentioned on the first list.

It seems to us, therefore, that if we can show that the authorities mentioned in the first class are against, or certainly not for, Dr. Bouquillon in his main point—i. e., the special and proper right of the state to educate—his position as that of one man against so many or against all the great authorities, who have written on the subject, becomes very questionable, nay, untenable.

a. In regard to these authors, and to Catholic authors generally, it may be remarked; firstly, that they do not deny the state the right to establish schools for its own special purposes; nor in any other case in which schools are necessary or expedient for the common good, and not otherwise provided for; nor the right of procuring an education for abandoned or destitute or criminal children and youths, if not otherwise cared for; nor do they even deny the state the right to establish and support a system of public schools, particularly elementary schools, for children indiscriminately, provided the rights and just demands of parents and of the Church are respected and complied with; much less do they deny this right to the state in the case in which there is an understanding between Church and state, whether by agreement or constitutional and organic union.

b. While granting to the state the right and duty of protecting, fostering, and promoting education, they deny the *proper* and *special* right of the state to *educate* in the strict sense of the word, unless in utter default of parents (and next in kin), making this right in the natural order a strictly parental right.

c. While granting that the state in union with the Church can enforce *compulsory education* they persistently deny this right to the state as such—most particularly to the *agnostic*, or purely secular, state.

d. Over *private schools,* i.e., those that are not state schools, they allow no further state supervision than that exercised over any other place where a large number of people are wont to assemble for social or mercantile purposes; while the *family education* as such is subject to no state control more than any other department of domestic life. We shall examine Dr. Bouquillon's authorities one by one.

1. *Taparelli*,[1] one of the first authorities on natural law, lays, indeed, great stress on the rights and duties of the state *in regard to* education, insists that the state should offer all legitimate advantages for popular, scientific and technical education, and emphasizes also what he calls *civil* education, or education in the social or civic duties. But this latter education seems to consist practically, or chiefly, in the equitable discharge of the ordinary functions of civil government not in any scholastic training (cf. Saggio nn. 909-987).

Nowhere do we find a passage in this author indicating, or capable of being interpreted as justifying, the right of the state to interfere in private education, or in domestic affairs generally, except in cases of flagrant abuse or neglect, endangering the social order. He advocates the fullest freedom from state interference for all schools, also for public schools that are not strictly government or state schools. He everywhere represents education as the special, proper and exclusive right and duty of parents. He sums up the influence of civil authority on education in the following words (n. 1570).

"From the preceding considerations what should be the influence of civil society [the state] on private education? As private education belongs altogether to the department of *domestic authority* and is one of the motives of the perpetuity of marriage, if civil and political authority had the right to interfere in private education, it could be only to direct it to the common good, or to repress disorders. The first cause [the direction to the common good] cannot occur because all education conducted on the principles of morality tends of itself to the common good, to order. *Order itself demands that the right of parents in this matter be safeguarded*, since this right is *inalienable*, being at the same time a right and a duty; the exercise of this right could not be more safely confided than to the tenderness of parents. This exercise is also facilitated by the community of life and by the total natural dependence of the child [on parental aid]. *Civil power cannot therefore in normal circumstances arrogate to itself the right to direct private education*. The state, however, may open to

[1] Saggio teoretico di diritto raturale; Esame critico degli ordini representativi. Not having the original Italian at hand we quote from the French edition of the *Saggio*, published under the supervision of the author in Paris and Tournai 1857 in 4 Volumes.

youth the pure fountains of the true and the good. It may, while offering guarantees to parents [for the preservation of faith and morals] come to their aid in the work of education, *provided only it use no force in the matter.* In this affair the state may *not arrogate right, but offer assistance;* this is a laudable endeavor in a progressive society."

Taparelli vindicates this same right to the next in kin in default of parents. "In default of parents the duty of education devolves upon the next in kin; they shall have to that effect *all the rights necessary*" (n. 1575). Again (lib. viii. c. 4. prop. 3) he says: "A good government should not interfere in the *private affairs* of its citizens except to correct *disorders* that have become *notorious by infamy* or by legal denunciation [réclamation]. "Civil authority should so distribute its public functions as *not to meddle in the domestic and private affairs* of its subjects." (Ibid. prop. 4).

(Vol. iv. p. 344–345. Note 140). Taparelli puts the query: Whether the parents are free to entrust the education and instruction of their children to whomsoever they please? He answers: "There is no doubt as far as *private* and *domestic* instruction is concerned, if he in whom they place this trust has the qualities required. However public authority cannot interfere unless there is question of a *notoriously immoral or suspected person.*"

He then puts the same question in regard to *public* instruction as distinguished from what he calls *social* instruction. The former is that given to the children of several families united; the latter that which is given in the name of the state, in state schools. In the former case which corresponds to our parochial schools and all others that are not state schools, he says, "civil authority, acquires in consequence of this *material publicity* [publicité materielle] the right of supervision since the action of teaching is no longer confined within the precincts of the family, under domestic authority. But society does not contract any *obligation* to guarantee the doctrines [of such schools] by its authority as it does in the case of social [state] instruction. Therefore it has not the right, arising from such obligation, to prepare a formula [programme] for the instruction to be given by the teachers [of such schools]. The state will, therefore, be in the same condition in regard to such teachers as we have observed in our answer to the first query [in regard to strictly private schools]." "A *christian state* [société croyante] derives from the infallibility in which it believes the right to prohibit error. But a *non-Christian state* [société incrédule] cannot show any title to direct the moral teaching [of such schools], since the latter depends on conscience, to which the state has guranteed liberty. The *material publicity of such schools gives no further right to the state over them than that which it has over every other numerous gathering, in which the diversity of families united produces a similar material publicity.* Public authority, therefore, in such cases has the right to provide for peace and sanitary conditions, and respect for law as in the case of a pleasure party or an insurance company. But as in these latter cases it cannot exclude anyone *because he is unable to dance, or has not administrative abilities*, neither can it in the case of private schools attempt to exclude teachers or pupils on account of their incapacity."

Again, (Ibid. p. 347) he says: " A state which does not present any reasonable title to infallibility *cannot control the teachings, nor reject the teachers, nor, consequently, exclude from the public employments the pupils of free* [that is, public, but not state] *schools.* If the state should pretend in this matter to bind men's consciences by its ordinances, it would commit *the gravest outrage* against that liberty which it has guaranteed."

(Ibid. p. 348). Taparelli establishes and proves the following propositions: 1. " The education of youth is *strictly* (proprement) *of parental or domestic right.* 2. [Against Gioberti] Ecclesiastics can, *even of themselves alone* [i. e., without aid from seculars] sufficiently assist parents in the education of their children; and *the secular influence of civil wisdom*, as Gioberti calls it, may in the matter of education prove eminently dangerous." In connection with the second proposition he says:

" This proposition seems to us to be evident from what has been said in the text (n. 1560), and it is impossible to see how the elementary education of their children can be wrested from the hands of parents *without infringing on the rights of nature*. Even Gioberti when he advocates public education, *certainly does not wish to enforce compulsion*, but only to improve the public institutions in such a way that parents of themselves might have recourse to them for the education of their children. If it were permitted to civil authority thus to restrict parental rights, how could it be forbidden to the most perfect of societies [the Church] whose aim is spiritual, whose teaching is infallible, whose legislation is holy and universal in its extent, violently to force from infidel parents their children to bring them regenerated into the harbor of salvation? *The Church, however, reproves the imprudent zeal of those who would prevent infidel parents from educating their own children.* How, then, could we concede to civil authority, for a temporal advantage that power which is denied the religious society [the Church] for man's spiritual and eternal weal."

When we compare this teaching with that of the defenders of state education we cannot but marvel that Dr. Bouquillon could put the name of Taperelli at the head of his favorite authorities. We may add here that the passage quoted from Taparelli by Dr. Bouquillon (p. 17) of itself completely undoes the latter's position.

"Let us consider the child," says Taparelli, "at the moment when his reason puts forth its first complete and formal act. Evidently at that moment the child does not know all truth; it scarcely has any clear ideas; for a long while it will need masters to impart to it by their authority the simplest and most necessary notions. As soon as these primal ideas are proposed to it, it sees their fitness, at least, vaguely and confusedly; and if they were not proposed to it, it would remain in ignorance of them for a long time. The intention of nature is that they be proposed to it, for nature has formed intellect for the knowledge of the truth, and society to facilitate and develop such knowledge. *And so the parent has the obligation of instructing and the child the obligation of attending to the instruction, until the day when the reason of the youth is matured* (Italics ours) and he can discover for himself the principles of conduct, the laws of his moral activity. Then only, *when the reason of the child is nearly as well developed as that of the father*, the child being equally capable of knowing the truth by himself, is he bound to give to his own reason that obedience which formerly he yielded to the reason of the parent."[1] (Ibid. n. 1565-56).

If the parent has the obligation and, consequently, the right of instructing the child " until the day when the reason of youth is matured " and " the child as nearly as well developed as the father " what room is there left for state education?[2]

2. Next in order of citation is *Cardinal Zigliara*,[3] an author of the

---

[1] Translation by Dr. Bouquillon.

[2] These questions are treated more extensively in Taparelli's *Esame Critico* (Part I. c. 7).

[3] Sum. Phil. Vol. iii. pars. ii. lib. ii. c. i. a 5.

greatest weight in philosophical matters. He treats the question of education in his ethics with that fulness and conciseness that we might expect in a text-book of the dimensions of his *Summa philosophica*. Now, what is Zigliara's teaching?

He sternly rejects *state monopoly* of education, as advocated by Victor Cousin and other liberals whom he characterizes as the *public destroyers of parental authority* (publici oppressores patriae potestatis).

He grants to the state, what no one denies, the right and also the duty of *procuring suitable means of education* (procurandi media aptiora ad educationem), and of watching over education, both intellectual and moral, so as to keep it within the bounds of truth and morality (this, of course, only in as far as truth and morality comes under the external moral order).

He establishes the following thesis: *Civil authority has no right to obtrude its own teachers, and its own schools on parents* for the intellectual and moral education of their children. [1]

He does not treat *ex professo* the question of *compulsory education;* but he sufficiently expresses his disapproval of compulsion particulary by an irreligious, indifferent, or agnostic state. In solving a difficulty fetched from the supposed right of the state to impose *obligatory instruction*, he says: " I do not wish to detract in aught from the rights of the state; *but state rights are not divine rights;* they are limited rights which presuppose other rights no less, nay, even move sacred than state rights—rights which the state is bound not to destroy, but to protect. The rights of the state extend just as far as the manifest exigency of the good of the commonwealth. Now, is *compulsory instruction* really for the common good? Speaking *in the abstract :* certainly. But considering the matter *in the concrete : it is very doubtful* (res valde dubia est)—not, indeed, if we consider instruction in itself; but, if we attend to the numberless means by which minds are corrupted under the pretext of instruction, as sad experience daily teaches. But *granted* (concedamus) the state has the right to enjoin compulsory instruction; what follows thence? Nothing else, in sooth, than this—that parents might be compelled by law to instruct their own children. But the state which under the pretence of obligatory instruction imposes its *own* instruction, a so-called *secular* (laicam)

---

[1] Status civilis nullum jus habet imponendi suos magistros, suasque scholas patribus familias quoad filiorum educationem tum intellectualem tum moralem.

instruction, and, what is still worse, a *godless* (atheam) instruction, *violates the rights of parents.*

In this passage Zigliara only grants for *argument's sake* the lawfulness of compulsory instruction (not education strictly so-called, not school attendance) because he does not wish to enter upon the question, whether from prudential reasons, or because he thinks this question is outside the scope of his elementary work. But on what side of the question his sympathy is, the unbiased reader cannot fail to see. And yet, strange to say, the learned Cardinal is cited as a defender of the public school and even of compulsory education.'

3. Nothing surprised us more than to see *Costa-Rossetti* [2] cited for Dr. Bouquillon's doctrine. Of all the authors we had the pleasure of consulting none is more explicit, none more uncompromising in his defence of the rights of the family than Father Costa-Rossetti. Yet he does not neglect to give to Cæsar what is Cæsar's.

He establishes the thesis (p. 733): " Civil authority may indeed establish schools and direct schools thus established; but it cannot prohibit the citizens themselves also from erecting public schools and controlling and directing schools thus erected; yet it cannot grant *absolute liberty* of instruction." [3] Rossetti, therefore, grants the state the right to found schools without any restriction except, of course, the common good; but he denies the right of *monopoly* to the state. He maintains that the state cannot grant *absolute liberty of instruction* because it is the duty of the state to prevent or suppress irreligious, impious and immoral schools.

So much for Cæsar; but, now for the *parents*. His thesis (pp. 736) is: " In virtue of the natural law parents cannot, in justice, be *directly* (*per se*) compelled to send their children to an elementary school;

[1] For the credit of Dr. Bouquillon, however, it is just to remark that he only says : " Nor does Cardinal Zigliara dare deny that power [of compulsory instruction] to the state" (p. 27). We must acknowledge that the Doctor, though, in our opinion, he has unconsciously misconceived and misinterpreted those great authors, treats them with a modesty and consideration characteristic of a true scholar. In this regard he contrasts favorably with the author of an article in the *Independent* of June 4, 1891, who treats the same arguments and authorities from a journalistic standpotin.

[2] Philosophia Moralis (Ed. II.). Innsbruck 1886, Pars. IV. c. 2. pp. 733-47.

[3] Auctoritas civilis scholas quidem fundare et a se fundatas dirigere postest ; sed per se prohibere nequit, ne cives ipsi scholas etiam publicas erigant ; a se ipsis erectas ordinent et dirigant, quin tamen absolutam docendi libertatem concedere possit.

they may, however, be compelled *indirectly* (*per accidens*) in certain individual cases."[1] In a foot-note he remarks in explanation of this thesis:

"In the thesis we *suppose* that the schools in question are not bad, not hurtful to religion and morality; that the teachers of Catholic children are not infidels or Protestants or Jews; that in the schools neither useless matters are taught, nor such subjects as would tend to make the lower classes of society dissatisfied with their social condition; that compulsory attendance at school does not extend over many years, so that the parents are not too long deprived of the assistance of their children.[2]

We abstain from giving the clear and cogent argumentation with which Costa-Rossetti proves the first part of his thesis, since there is question here of his *authority*, not of his arguments, and his excellent work is within the reach of most of those interested in this controversy; but we shall give a few extracts from the corollaries which he appends to this thesis (pp. 744, sq.).

"From these considerations follows:—

(1). "That no sufficient title can be found to establish the right of governments to educate children *in as much as they are citizens*, or to have them instructed in public schools, *in order to make them good citizens;* although rulers should use *other means*—e. g., good government, premiums and distinctions, vigilance for the maintenance of public morality—to promote civic virtues and patriotism (i. e., love of their own native commonwealth).

(2). "That it cannot be shown that the right of *education and instruction* emanates equally *from parental and civic power;* nor that the power has been delegated by the people to the subject invested with civil authority to *teach* and to *compel attendance* at school."

(3). "That *compulsory education* has been not unjustly regarded by some as *intellectual socialism* and *communism*, from which material com-

[1] Spectata lege naturæ parentes ab auctoritate civili per se juste cogi non possunt, ut liberos in scholam elementarem mittant ; id tamen fieri potest per accidens in casibus particularibus.

[2] Costa-Rossetti denies the right of the state in the present condition of society to compel school attendance, also in the case in which children are brought up *illiterate*, provided their physical and moral education is not notably neglected, so as to make them utterly miserable. Utrum aliquando tempora futura sint, quibus homines *ideo solum* miseri evadant, quod nesciant legere et scribere, *posteri nostri dijudicent* (p 739).

munism logically follows. For, if civil authority can arbitrarily deal with the most important right of education and of the intellectual culture of its citizens, it may *a fortiori* dispose at pleasure of the right of property and of the material prosperity of its citizens, since material goods are of a lower order. Hence it is not to be wondered at that the socialists of our day are among the most zealous defenders of compulsory education—in order that the minds of men may be predisposed for the socialistic state."

(4). "Hence *compulsory education* has been justly compared with that *guardianship* (known in German by the name of *curatel*) under which certain extravagant parents, who recklessly and viciously squander their property, are, at the request of their relations, placed by the state—with this difference however: that by compulsory education *all are made wards of the state in regard to spiritual goods;* and that without any crime being proved against them."

(5). "That, if the children are to be forced from their parents to be educated *they should also be taken from them to be nursed;* for, if the mind is to be trained by the state, why not the body as well? The bodily strength and health of its citizens are of great importance for the commonwealth—that the state may have good soldiers, farmers, workmen, &c."

In explaining the second part of his thesis, Costa-Rossetti makes this admission seemingly in favor of compulsion:—"*If it is proved* that children are so treated by their parents *that they must necessarily become miserable, unless they are relieved from parental control,* civil authority, in virtue of its office of protecting the rights of its citizens, can and must make provision for their education, and, according to circumstances, must either remove them from their parents or force the latter to send them to a school. *But this can happen only in certain particular cases and accidentally.*'

Does this admission justify a *compulsory law*? No; it only vindicates for the state the right, which no one denies, of preventing or remedying flagrant abuses of parental authority and protecting so-

---

[1] Si demonstratur, liberos a parentibus ita tractari, ut miseri fieri debeant, nisi a potestate parentum eximantur, auctoritas civilis vi muneris tutelæ jurium potest et debet illos educandos curare et, prout adjuncta exigunt, aut liberos parentibus eripere, aut hos cogere, ut illos in scholam mittant. Atqui id tantum in particularibus casibus occurrit et nonnisi per accidens.

ciety from manifestly threatening evils in particular cases. These evils, however, can be remedied without inflicting on society the much greater hardship of universal compulsion. This is the teaching of Costa-Rossetti. We leave it to the reader to judge whether or not he can be cited as an advocate of state education, or compulsory schooling.

4. Fourth on the list of authorities stands the name of *Hammerstein* —a name of no small weight on this subject. A profound jurist and canonist, in his younger days the disciple and admirer of men like Haller, Ahrens, Stahl and Bluntschli, von Hammerstein has been for more than twenty years as a publicist identified with this special question. His valuable writings on this problem are scattered through the volumes of the *Stimmen aus Maria-Laach*. But in two separate works the *Schulfrage* [1] and *Kirche und Staat* [2] (the latter published also in Latin), he has given us a summary of his principles and the arguments upon which they rest. We are indebted to Rev. Father Holaind for an extended extract in excellent English translation from the second work in his prompt and able reply to Dr. Bouquillon. [3] We shall give the salient passages from Father Holaind's translation and supplement it by an extract from the *Schulfrage*:

"The parents have the *obligation of education and all the rights of education before the Church and the state*, and in this sense, that even before the existence of any state or Church the parents could and ought to educate and instruct their children, and, if need be, send them to school. Let us suppose that neither is yet existing. Should the children then born live without education until the state should arise, or until a Church should be founded? Or could any one else be designated that should educate and instruct the children?"

"The parents, therefore, have *the right of excluding the interference of all others* who might wish to educate their children, or in some way to hinder them in the performance of their duty, by *forcing on them methods* which to the parents seem inconsistent with the proper kind of education: without this privilege, their right would be a mockery. However, one condition is to be observed: parents have the right to

[1] Freiburg, Herder (II. Ed.) 1877.   [2] Freiburg, Herder 1883 (Latin 1884).
[3] *The Parent first:* an Answer to Dr. Bouquillon's Query, &c., Benziger Bros., New York.

exclude others, *unless such others can prove* that they also have some right over the education of the children."

"In our times the state is that agency which attempts to interfere in the education of the children by controlling the schools. Let us examine with what right it does this. We cannot deny that the state or commonwealth has some rights *in regard to* the schools and the education of children. It is the state's duty to *supply what is wanting* on the part of the family. Hence, in the first place, it can *offer means* to parents whereby they may better and more easily provide for their children's education. This the state does by *founding and endowing schools according to the needs and wishes of the parents*. But with regard to *endowments*, or any other form of assistance, the state has *no right to give them*, unless they contribute to the *public good*, to which they certainly do not contribute if sufficient provision has already been made for the schools in other ways, as, for instance, through the medium of religious orders."

"In the second place, the state may *supplement the family* in educating the children, if need be, *compelling negligent parents* to fulfil their obligations in this regard."

"In the third place, the state may so far supplement the family as to *take upon itself the education*, in the case of orphans, for instance or if, for any reasons, the parents themselves cannot educate their children. This, however, supposes that those also are unable to supply the education who, *next to the parents, and in preference to the state*, have the right and duty to fill the place of parents, namely, *relatives, municipal organizations*, or the *Church* (where the Church does exist)."

"In the fourth place, the question suggests itself whether, beyond the duty of supplementing the family, the state has a *direct right*, jointly with the family, of educating the children, in so far as to have the right to *compel parents* to send their children to certain appointed schools—those, for instance, under state control; or in so far as to have the *exclusive right* to establish schools; or, in a word, *to educate and to teach;* or finally, in so far as to have the right to *insist upon a certain method* of education, a certain *kind of school*, or a certain *amount of matter*, which all are bound to learn,—matter, I mean, in excess of what is *absolutely* necessary; for to omit this would, of course, be sheer negligence."

Von Hammerstein answers these queries in the negative, defends his position against the prevailing theories of state education as advocated by Trendelenburg, Stahl, Cousin and Jürgen Bona Meyer, and thus concludes.

"Those repeated and strange attempts to prove that the state owns, jointly with the parents, or even above the parents, the right to educate, and to compel the attendance of children, show clearly that the right cannot be made good, and therefore has no existence. The conclusion is that *the parents hold the right of training and instructing their children as they judge fit and through masters of their own selection, provided that they do not overstep the boundaries of reason:* should they disregard the behests of reason, then, indeed, the state, as the civil superior, may provide for the education of the children." (De ecclesia et statu, p. 181 sq.).

In the special work entitled the *Schulfrage* (p. 6–7) Father von Hammerstein establishes the following thesis which forms the gist of his argument:

"If the state, *contrary to the wishes of parents, and of the Church,* takes into its own hands the education of youth, it commits a threefold crying violation of right."

I. "A *violation of the rights of parents;* for to them, and not to the state, God has confided the children to be educated; of them, and not of the state, God will once demand an account for the souls of the children."

II. "*A violation of that positive right established by Christ;* for the Church, and not the state, has received from Christ the power to educate children and adults to Christian life."

III. "*A violation of the historic rights of the Church;* for before any of the modern states of Europe existed the Church was in the just possession of the right of education, of the elementary schools and of countless other institutions of learning established by itself; and international treaties and agreements have acknowledged and secured to her this right."

This entire work of von Hammerstein (128 octavo pages) consists of the proof and confirmation of these three propositions from reason, from revelation, from positive law, and historic facts and statistics. Any one who is even superficially acquainted with either of these works cannot but be surprised that Father von Hammerstein could ever have been cited in defence of state education.

5. We now come to an authority which Dr. Bouquillon manifestly prizes very highly—*Mons. Cavagnis*, professor of Canon Law in the papal seminary in Rome. Dr. Bouquillon certainly does not overrate this excellent canonist, and we are sincerely grateful to him for making us acquainted with this distinguished author. On examination, however, we do not find that Cavagnis differs in his doctrine on the school question from von Hammerstein, Taparelli, Costa-Rossetti and Catholic writers generally. In his Italian work: *Nozioni di diritto &c.*, published in Rome 1886, he states his doctrine very briefly (p. 220 sq.).

He attributes to the Church the *supervision over all schools*, especially over the *elementary* schools; in which *religion cannot be separated from secular instruction* (n. 362) : the right to make *religious instruction obligatory* in all schools (n. 363) as part of the course of instruction; the *right of establishing schools* and educational institutions of her own (n. 364). The pupils of such ecclesiastical schools *cannot be debarred of the civil advantages* attendant on public schools. Either such church schools must be acknowledged by the state, or at least there must be some equitable means (public test) given to such pupils to prove their fitness for the various civil offices (n. 365).

In his Latin work (Institutiones juris &c.) published in Rome 1882 in 3 vols. he devotes over 80 pages to the matter of schools. His treatment is all that could be desired—thorough, comprehensive and exact. One can see, however, in him, as in many other European authors, who treat this subject, that he is struggling with existing circumstances and trying to reconcile things as best he can; and, therefore, he makes all concessions to the civil power that he can consistently with the rights of the Church and with the Christian character of education; and hence we may easily understand Dr. Bouquillon's veneration for him. His sources, like those of all canonists are, of course, positive laws, concordats, rescripts, compromises, &c., that suppose circumstances very different from ours. Our American situation as far as the relation between Church and state is concerned, is *sui generis*, and cannot be judged in the light of any text-book of canon law, however perfect. Orthodox and excellent as is the teaching of Cavagnis, it is inapplicable to our American circumstances. Yet no part of his teaching can be interpreted in favor of Dr. Bouquillon's theory.

According to Cavagnis it is the father's (respectively the mother's) right and duty (patrisfamilias jus et officium) to instruct his children in the true Christian doctrine (Vol. III. p. 14). Schools (p. 15) are institutions *supplementary* to the family. The secular instruction of children cannot be *separated from the moral and religious*, i.e., from Catholic education (pp. 16. sq.).

This latter proposition he proves very conclusively from reason and from the authority of Leo XIII. in his epistle to the Cardinal Vicar of Rome June 26, 1878, in which His Holiness aptly compares the separation of religion from secular instruction to the division of the child in the famous *judgment of Solomon*.[1]

Cavagnis grants that a separation may be made of the religious instruction proper, from the secular as to time and place, and the person of the teacher (quoad locum, et personam docentis), but insists that the secular education should be imbued with the spirit of religion (spiritu religioso informatam); and that religion should form a part of the programme of instruction. Hence he concludes that the teacher who would not speak of God and of the duties towards Him, would impress false ideas on the minds of his pupils (falso spiritu imbueret suos discipulos). *Natural* and *non-sectarian* (institutionem christianam in genere) religion and morality are not sufficient as being *false* and *incomplete* (p. 24).

Private schools represent the authority of the parents, the *private teacher has no other authority to teach than what he received from parents* (*nullam aliam auctoritatem habet quam receptam a patribus familias*), and this holds also of *colleges* (cum filii in collegio ponuntur); while the religious instruction must in all cases be given under the authority and supervision of the Church (pp. 25–27).

Public schools, according to Cavagnis, are those that are under the direction of civil or municipal authority, which, as long *as they are free*, *retain their parental character* to some extent (p. 32). The *compulsory public school is a violation of parental right*, though the state and civil authority may coerce and discipline those parents *who neglect their duty* in educating their children (p. 33).

In *public schools*, which, of course, must comply with the lawful de-

[1] It is here that Cavagnis cites the decree of the sacred Congregation, Aug. 17, 1688, referred to by Dr Bouquillon (p. 13) in proof of the early existence of secular schools —but for a widely different purpose, viz., to prove that religious instruction must go hand in hand with secular teaching.

mands of the Church (viz., that Catholic schools should be strictly Catholic) the teachers of Christian doctrine must be approved by the Church (ibid.). The same rule holds for middle and higher schools; while clerical seminaries can in no wise be subject to civil authority (pp. 38–50).

The Church has *not the exclusive right* of establishing and conducting schools: "*No one ever denied to parents the right to educate their own children, nor to the civil state the right to establish schools*—Patribus familias facultatem suos docendi et statui civili scholas instituendi nemo unquam denigavit"[1] (p. 53).

In regard to *freedom of education* Cavagnis says: That private individuals have the right to open schools, but under the general supervision of the state; that is, the state has the right and duty (1) to see that, while individuals (or corporations) wish to aid the development of human perfection, they do not disturb the juridical relations; (2) to punish or repress in case of perturbation (of those juridical relations), or of proximate danger of such disorder; (3) in default of private individuals or corporations, to take all measures suitable for the gradual perfection of society according to its concrete circumstances. And he thus concludes: "Therefore the state establishes schools when private schools are wanting either wholly or in part (and they will always be wanting in part: since it is hardly possible, as a rule, that there should be a sufficient number established for the poor by private charity); ..... Moreover, the state will take care that in private schools there be no disturbance of the juridical order; and, if such should happen, to repress it."[2] (p. 64).

The result of this concession is, therefore, that the state can establish schools in default of private persons or corporations—a default which will often occur; and that it can prevent or repress disorder (e. g., hazing, theft, public immorality), which we all admit.

The opinion that the *office of educating* (munus docendi) *belongs to*

[1] Sauvé quotes these golden words in CAPS. The writer in the *Independent*, above referred to, quotes only the second part of the sentence in favor of the state or public school, ignoring the context of Cavagnis himself, and of Sauvé. Dr. Bouquillon himself has recourse to the same stratagem in *Rejoinder*, p. 31.

[2] Ergo scholas instituit status cum deficiunt vel ex toto vel ex parte scholæ privatorum (et ex parte semper deficient, cum pro pauperibus vix possibile sit adsint umversim charitate privatorum constitutæ): deinde invigilabit ne in scholis privatorum perturbentur relationes juridicæ et, si id fiet, reprimet." Cf. Bouquillon, p. 19.

the state (esse munus publicum) like that of *judges* (sicut illud judicum) is manifestly *false* (patet falsitas) according to Cavagnis [1] (ibid.).

"[The right of teaching] is a *private right which cannot be violated by the state*, but only moderated or, *in extraordinary cases*, limited or suspended when the public weal demands it " (ibid.).

The state can prescribe certain *preventive measures* to test the fitness of teachers; which means, however, should not be onerous, and *are not always expedient* (p. 65). The private teacher is *not a state functionary; nor can he receive his authority to teach from the state, but only the recognition of his fitness* (p. 66). Hence it follows that the Church has at least all the rights of private individuals and corporations in regard to education; nay, the Church should enjoy greater confidence than private persons on the part of the state—abstracting from ecclesiastical immunity, in virtue of which clerics have not to answer before a secular tribunal (p 68).

But the Church has also a *special right* and title to establish schools even in a *normal state of society* in virtue of her mission to teach the religion of Christ (pp. 69–72). She has also the right to open and conduct boarding schools (p. 73–74).

The Church has in our days a *still more special right and duty* of establishing her own schools in the present *abnormal state of society*, for the preservation of the faith (ibid).

As regards the *civil effects* of education the state has the right to *test the fitness* of its own public officials: also the fitness of certain professional men; as physicians, druggists, &c. (p. 78–79). The state *cannot*, however, *compel the candidates of such offices*, or professions, to frequent *its own* schools.

Such is in substance the teaching of Cavagnis. Now, from all his concessions which are, we believe, the utmost that could be made to the state, nothing follows for the main theory of Dr. Bouquillon— that the state has the *special and proper right to educate as it has to judge and to govern* by its functionaries. Nay, Cavagnis expressly teaches the contrary—that this right is not inherent in the state. The only point in which Cavagnis seems to favor Dr. Bouquillon's theory is in regard to the testing by the state of the fitness of teachers—the exercise of which right he himself acknowledges to be often inexpedient

---

[1] Dr. Bouquillon (p. 12) seems to teach the contrary. Strange that Sauvé, who, for the rest follows Cavagnis very closely, should also cling to the opposite theory.

and always unnecessary, and, therefore, vexatious in the case of Church institutions, in which the state should have full confidence. Besides, it must be borne in mind, as we have already remarked, that Cavagnis is contending with existing circumstances, not as we are, with innovations on the part of the state.

6. It was at this stage of our writting that we had the good fortune, after much trouble, to get a copy of the work of an author who evidently enjoys the highest authority with Dr. Bouquillon—we mean *Monsignor Sauvé*[1] who was papal theologian at the Vatican Council, and some time Rector of the Catholic University of Angers in France. He is a writer of genuine merit—learned, broad-minded, and wholly devoted to the interests of the Church and of religion. His orthodoxy and loyalty to the Church cannot be questioned. Had we been able to possess ourselves of this work sooner it would have saved us a great deal of trouble; it would have thrown much light on the dark points of Dr. Bouquillon's brochure—his somewhat tortuous disposition, his method, the many apparent inconsistencies, the meaning and import of most of the authorities he quotes; but we had the bad luck to find this work last of all, though it is the very first work the student of Dr. Bouquillon's pamphlet should read.

The veneration of Dr. Bouquillon for Sauvé goes to the utmost limit of literary propriety. He adopts the same division, the same method, uses the same authorities and even translates many passages almost *ad literam*—and sometimes we must confess, without due discrimination. Sauvé has the same fundamental errors, or inaccuracies, which we have pointed out in Dr. Bouquillon's teaching—the right of every individual to teach, (p. 278 sq.), the same defective definition of education (pp. 236-8), the same theory that the right of the state to teach is implied in the right to govern and judge (cf. p. 254).

The fault we have to find with Dr. Bouquillon's treatment of his revered friend Sauvé, however, is not so much for what he has taken from this excellent author, but rather for what he has omitted. Had he given us Sauvé's treatise *pur et simple*, with all the faults we have referred to, he would have conferred a favor on us and a benefit on Catholic education; but he has given us Sauvé's concessions to civil government without giving us Sauvé's demands for family and Church, without giving us Sauvé's uncompromising conditions.

[1] Questions religieuses, &c. (2 ed.). Paris, 1888. c. 10. p. 236, sq.

Lest we should be accused of unfairness to Dr. Bouquillon we shall extract a few passages that will show clearly what is Sauvé's teaching as regards the main issue.

"The *Church* has the right to establish universities, colleges, schools of every kind, in which she may teach by professors sufficiently capable, *not only in the sacred, but also in the profane sciences*" (p. 240-41).

"*One of the duties of civil legislature is to acknowledge the right of the Church* in this matter [of education], instead of hindering her exercise of that power which in the designs of God is called upon to promote it to the utmost of its power, according to the circumstances of time and place*" (p. 243).

"*Parents* have certainly the right to educate their children—a right which *the state cannot suppress or render inefficacious* at pleasure, nor control arbitrarily. Before the civil authority, *domestic authority has natural rights of which the state cannot lawfully deprive it*" (p. 423).

"The state *cannot* without flagrant injustice arbitrarily *take the place of the parents* to dispense to their children either the physical or the intellectual and moral nourishment. The Catholic Church does not permit that children be taken from their parents against their will, even in behalf of their eternal salvation, for the sake of baptizing them" (p. 245).

"Parents may not directly or indirectly *be forced to send their children to any school*, if they wish of themselves or through others to give them a suitable education. They have also the right to demand that where schools are supported at the public expense they respond to their just demands from the Catholic standpoint; or at least that the state support Catholic schools where they may send their children in all security."

"*The state has no right to teach error*, nor those truths which it is unlawful to communicate to others [e.g., Lord Byron's poems or certain parts of physiology to children] (p. 255). The state which makes a profession of *religious indifference or hostility to Catholic doctrine is not fit to educate children and youth*, since it is the will of the Creator that these stages of life should be instructed according to the divinely established order. But the instruction given by teachers who are either indifferent or hostile to the true religion, if not essentially perverse, is, at least, very dangerous, even though the teacher (a thing difficult to conceive) should altogether abstain from every attack, direct or indirect, on religion."

Mons. Sauvé (p. 257 sq.) emphatically condemns the so-called *neutral* or *mixed* or secular *schools*, and proves his position from the decrees of the Church, the letter of Pius IX. to the Archbishop of Freiburg, July 14, 1864, the Syllabus, and the Instruction to the American Bishops, June 30, 1875. He condemns state monopoly in these words:

"The government which against the rights of the Church and of the family, contrary to the lawful demands of the citizens and the interests of society itself would exercise a monopoly of the education of children and of youth would *commit an unjustifiable act of tyranny*, which can be defended only by mere sophistry" (p. 262).

"If a commonwealth, composed of different religious denominations (divisée de croyance), and without any state religion, admits freedom of worship, and if the government of such commonwealth cannot, or will not, give a Catholic education, *it must in that case abstain from teaching altogether.* The establishment of a teaching body in the name of such a government would be *irrational and unlawful;* for without unity of doctrine a body of teachers is incapable of exercising the two functions of education which consist in forming and nourishing the intellect with truth, and directing the will towards the good" (p. 264).

"The state *has not the same right to teach as the Church and the family*, both of which have a right based on *absolute duty*, while the state has but a *relative duty* to teach—*a duty which does not exist except when the education given by the Church, by parents, and by individual teachers is insufficient* from the standpoint of social interests" (p. 268).

In summing up the rights of the state in regard to education Sauvé says (p. 277):—

(1.) "The state has not the exclusive right to educate and cannot exercise this right *except in conformity with the order established by God, respecting the rights of Church, family and individual.*

(2.) The state has the right to teach all that is useful and good to communicate to others, *provided it conform to the superior laws which bind it* [among these laws one is to respect the rights of Church, family and individual].

Again, he cites and adopts the words of M. Chesnelong:

'" The state has the right for a social interest, and in the case of the insufficiency of free education [i.e. by the Church and individuals] and also the duty to give an education at the public expense under the *threefold condition*—that it offer such education to all *without forcing it on any one;* that, besides this state education *free* (and good) *education may be carried on without hinderance ;* and, finally, that the public education *respect the conscientious convictions* of the subjects " (p. 277-78).

" The state of itself can exercise *no right over schools established by the Church:* for civil power has no right over things sacred. But *the Church can grant to the state certain faculties by way of indult or concordat;* or she can *tolerate* that some of her rights are not entirely acknowledged" (p. 308).

" The state has *not* such authority over education that it can at pleasure *substitute itself* for the family in the functions of an educator, *penetrate* into the sanctuary of the household (except in the case of crime or misdemeanor) and arbitrarily *control* the education which is given in the family."

The parents have the right and duty to *give to their children either by themselves or through suitable teachers that education which may seem necessary or useful;* they have, likewise, the right to *supervise the instruction given* to their children " (p. 309).

What, then, is the teaching of Sauvé? Abstracting from the few false or inaccurate notions already noticed it is the teaching of Taparelli whom he closely follows, and frequently cites; the teaching of von Hammerstein, Costa-Rossetti and Cavagnis, whom he also quotes with approval. It is also the teaching of Dr. Bouquillon? It is; and it is not. It is Bouquillon's teaching in as much as the latter takes most of his matter and his arguments from Sauvé to establish the power of the state; it is not Dr. Bouquillon's, in as much as he sadly minimizes, or rather disregards, the rights of Church and parents so staunchly defended by Sauvé, and only seeks to magnify the civil power.

The impression we received from reading Dr. Bouquillon's pamphlet was that the essay was first written exclusively on the rights, duties and authority of the state; and that it was only on second thought that the author decided to introduce the individual, the family and the Church in order to give the work some show of completeness. When we read those stern and uncompromising conditions with which Mons. Sauvé limits the civil power; when we consider his fearless demands for the freedom of the Church and of the family, we doubt very much whether he would sanction this use of his excellent work even by his most admiring friend and disciple These were the very parts of Sauvé's valuable treatise on the right of education which would have been most timely. A plea for state rights and government interference was uncalled for.

7. There is one more authority upon which Dr. Bouquillon evidently lays great stress. This is not the authority of a single theologian, but the collective authority of the *papal theologians of the Vatican Council*. He says (p. 14-15):—

We will close this list of authorities by giving the opinion of the theologians commissioned by Pius IX. to prepare the subject matter of the discussions of the Council of the Vatican. They intended to proclaim the right of the Church to watch over the education, religious and moral, of Catholic children, but at the same time they most explicitly recognized the right of the state to educate.

Here are the words of the proposed *schema* (?) on this point : " Non negatur jus potestatis laicæ providendi institutioni in litteris ac scientiis ad suum legitimum finem et ad bonum sociale, ac proinde etiam non negatur eidem potestati laicæ jus ad directionem scholarum, quantum legitimus ille finis postulat." [The right of the civil power to make provisions for instruction in letters and in the sciences for its own legitimate purpose and for the common good is not denied [i. e. in the schema]; and, therefore, this same civil power is not denied the right to the direction of schools, as far as that legitimate purpose demands].

For the benefit of those who may not be able at once to appreciate the value of this argument we will here note: first, that this *schema Vaticanum* is not a decree, nor collection of decrees, of the Vatican council; it is only a collection of points of doctrine, &c. that were prepared by a committee of theologians appointed by the Pope, to be submitted to the council for discussion—to be accepted, rejected or modified, as the Council would deem proper. This *schema*, although of great theological value, has therefore, no special sanction of the Pope, or of the council, or of the Church, more than any collection of theses on theological matters drawn up by, and representing the teaching of, any learned body of theologians—say, the theological faculty of a university.

Secondly, the words cited by Dr. Bouquillon *are not taken from the schema itself*, but only to be found among the voluminous and elaborate notes with which the schema was accompanied (note 47). Now, what is the import of this note? This note is *merely negative* and is not intended to express any positive opinion on the matter in question. It only states what is *not proposed for definition*, but has been wisely omitted, in that passage of the schema (c. xv.) to which this note refers. The theologians in this note will only remark for the benefit of the fathers of the Council, that the question in regard to state rights in education will still remain *an open question.* Dr. Bouquillon should have made a distinction between the *schema* itself and the *note*, and should not have quoted this remark as part of the *schema*. It makes a great difference whether these words are intended by the learned theologians to be proposed for definition, or simply to express what is not intended to be defined. The reference in foot-note (p. 15) is not sufficient to prevent a misconception in the popular mind.

It might seem strange that Sauvé, who was himself one of the committee appointed to compose the *schema* and the *notes*, makes no mention of this note, which was certainly familiar to him and no longer an official secret when he published his work (1888). He evidently knew that it had no weight as an argument. To Dr. Bouquillon, it seems, is due the entire merit of bringing this brand new weapon into the field. Stretched to its utmost, however, this note would ascribe no more power to the state than is granted by Catholic theologians generally. So much on the note.

Now what does the *schema* itself teach? It rejects in the first place, in the strongest terms the errors already condemned by the *syllabus*, and other papal utterances.

" Among the violations of the most sacred rights perpetrated in our age, to infect the nations with error and currupt Christian morals amongst them, that one is the most pernicious which insiduously contends that all schools are to be submitted to the the secular power so that the authority of the Church to provide for the religious instruction and education of Christian youth may be altogether thwarted. Nay, men have gone even so far as to assert that the Catholic religion should be altogether excluded from public education and that the schools should be merely scientific. Against this curruption of sound doctrine and morals, from the very purpose of the Church founded by Christ—to lead men through salutary faith and discipline, by her teaching and her guidance, to eternal life—all must acknowledge the right and duty in virtue of which she [the Church] carefully provides (pervigilat) that the Catholic youth is rightly educated, above all in true faith and pure morals."

Those are the words which we would have expected Dr. Bouquillon to have cited for the benefit of American Catholics, not the minimizing note (47). But the Doctor in indicting his pamphlet was too jealous of the interest of the state and thought the Church would look out for herself.

The language of the *schema proper* is clear, forcible, and uncompromising. Yet there is hardly any doubt, that, if the matter had come to be discussed and defined the definition would have been still more comprehensive. This is manifest from the postulate submitted to the council by Mons. Greith, bishop of St. Gall, April 5, 1870, demanding the condemnation of the so-called *mixed school system*. This system generally known in Germany and Switzerland under the name of *simultaneous* schools, consists in this, that the pupils of different religious denominations frequent the same school, have the secular instruction in common and the religious instruction separate. These schools are manifestly, from a Christian and Catholic standpoint, preparable to our so-called non-sectarian system. And yet the Bishop in his postulate describes them as seats of moral contagion, which infect the minds of youth with the poison of impiety, or of indifferentism. [1]

Hence he concludes that the council cannot pass them over in silence, and demands: (1) that the council *condemn* mixed schools, of whatever kind or grade; (2) that it earnestly *exhort* the bishops, parish priests and parents—the *bishops*, to fight with all their power against such schools; the *parish priests*, to try to avert the Christian youth from them; the *parents* never to intrust their children to them; (3) that it *admonish the civil magistrates*, to restore to the Church the schools of Catholic foundation taken from her by violent and unjust legislation, and to grant to Catholics that freedom of instruction *which, for the rest, paternal authority can justly claim.* [2]

---

[1] Sed *nil* in eo [schemate] dictum est de *scholis mixtis*, quæ licet sicut quædam pestis puerorum mentes vel impietatis vel indifferentismi veneno inficiant, ubique locorum passim eriguntur et catervatim a catholica juventute frequentantur.

[2] (1) Scholas mixtas cujuscumque generis ac ordinis reprobare. (2) Episcopos, parachos et parentes serio adhortari; utpote *Episcopos*, ut pro posse suo contra ejusmodi

That the demands of the bishop of St. Gall were in this case altogether in keeping with the spirit of the Church and the teaching of the Holy See may be concluded from the words of Leo XIII. to the French bishops in the letter dated Feb. 8, 1884: "The Church....has always openly condemned the so-called mixed or neutral schools."[1]

These are the genuine sentiments which prevailed at the Vatican Council and which would have, doubtless been proposed in the final definition, if the question had come to a discussion and decision. But from Dr. Bouquillon's book one who knew nothing of the Vatican Council might think that the theologians were preparing, and that the fathers were ready to approve, an eloquent plea for governmental rights in education.

We dispense with the examination of the second category of authors cited by Dr. Bouquillon as such of whom only "mention must be made," and take for granted that whatever authority they have is against the Doctor. Should he, however, claim that these authors also sustain his position, we are prepared to take the trouble of examining them for the benefit of all interested in this question.

It would be an easy task to establish a *consensus* of Catholic writers on this point, if time and space permitted. For the present, however, we shall only refer the reader to Judge Dunne's learned argument in the Quigley case before the circuit court of Ohio where he gives an extensive, though by no means complete, list of authorities "in support of the proposition, that under the natural law control of the education of the child is a parental right, which the state may not arrogate to itself."[2]

IV. Dr. Bouquillon's Method.

The Doctors's introduction commends itself by its scholarly simplicity and directness. He says:—

We reduce the subject matter of our paper to the following four questions : *right* to educate, *mission* to educate, *authority* over education, *liberty* of education. Though

Scholas militent; *parochos*, ut Christianam juventutem ab eis arcere studeant; *parentes*, ne pueros suos ejusmodi scholis unquam committant. (3) *Magistratus civiles admonere:* ut scholas Catholicæ fundationis earumque facultates Catholicis iniqua vi et lege subtractas restituant, *liberamque puerorum* instructionem ipsis concedant; quam paterna utique potestas jure exigere potest.

[1] Ecclesia....semper, scholas quas appellant mixtas, vel neutras aperte damnavit.
[2] (Compulsory Education, Catholic truth Society St. Louis 1891, p. 34. sq.).

these four aspects of the educational question touch at many points, we prefer to treat them separately. This plan may force on us some repetitions, but in compensation, it will enable us to avoid the ambiguities and confusion that too often involve in darkness this important subject. We will examine these four questions from the point of view of the *individual*, the *family*, the *state*, the *Church*.[1] (Italics ours).

It was a veritable puzzle to us, however, how and why Dr. Bouquillon could pitch on such a division of his subject; and how such a disposition could contribute anything towards avoiding "ambiguities and confusion." This division seems to us to produce "confusion worse confounded." First of all, we are unable to see how the Doctor could separate *right* and *authority* and make them coördinate parts, whereas every thinkable authority is necessarily a right, though every right may not be properly termed an authority. Hence it is that the author himself has been unable to keep these two points separate though he did endeavor to draw a line of demarcation. He says (p. 11-12):—

"The right of teaching, as far as the state is concerned therein, means [the right of] establishing schools, appointing teachers, prescribing methods and programmes of study: the state teaches in the same way as it governs and judges, viz., through delegates fitted for such functions."

The *authority* over education is thus defined (p. 21):—

Authority over education, or the control of education, must not be confounded with the right to teach. The right to educate, being, as we have defined it, a moral faculty to impart to others those things which one is fit to impart licitly and usefully to the end of forming the mind and heart, belongs to whomsoever has the fitness required. Authority over education is the right of watching over, controlling, and directing education. This authority belongs to him or to those who are vested by natural or positive law with the powers required and sufficient in the premises.[2]

When we come to examine the various functions of this *authority* or control on the part of the state we find that it very nearly coincides with what has been asserted under the heading: *the Right of the state to Educate:* viz., the right of "overseeing the education" (p. 23), of

[1] Nous verrons successivement si l'Eglise, si les parents, si l'Etat, si les simples individus et les associations peuvent revendiquer ce droit, à quel titre et dans quelle mesure. Ce sera l'objet des paragraphes suivants. Sauvé, l. c. p. 238.

[2] Le pouvoir ou l'autorité sur l'enseignement ne doit pas se confondre avec le droit d'enseigner. Le droit d'enseigner, en effet, consistant dans la faculté morale d'apprendre à d'autres ce qu'on est apte à leur communiquer licitement et utilement pour former leur esprit et leur cœur, appartient naturellement à quiconque possède cette aptitude. Le pouvoir sur l'enseignement n'étant autre chose que le droit de veiller sur l'enseignement et de le diriger d'une manière normale, ne compete qu'à celui ou à ceux qui sont investis par le droit naturel ou par le droit positif d'une autorité suffisante à cet égard. Sauvé l. c. p. 288.

"testing the fitness of teachers" (pp. 24-27), of "compelling parents" to fulfil their duty in regard to their children, of prescribing a certain "standard" or "minimum" of education (pp. 27-29). Why these functions should be classified as authority or control, while "establishing schools, appointing teachers, prescribing methods and programmes of study" as above described (p. 11-12) are but rights, is not patent to the reader. We can see no reason for the adoption of this division between the right and authority of education except in the mind of the writer; who, by the way, in this point, as in many others, goes a shade too far in his literary appreciation of Mons. Sauvé, who happens, in our opinion not luckily, to have pitched on the same division.[1]

It was a bad improvement on his master, when Dr. Bouquillon headed the second part of his pamphlet; *The Mission to Educate* (Sauvé uses *devoir*); for a mission signifies a duty imposed in virtue of a positive charge or mandate. This was also bad policy from Dr. Bouquillon's standpoint; for, if education is a mission, where is the *mission* of the state to educate? The Church has a mission in virtue of her foundation; parents have a mission by nature itself, by positive divine command (Gen. i, 28), in virtue of the sacrament of matrimony, and by the laws of the Church; but where is the mission of the state?

In the subdivision of his subject Dr. Bouquillon reverses the order followed by Mons. Sauvé. The latter has the Church, the parents, the state, the individual; Dr. Bouquillon, the individual, the family, the state, the Church; The Doctor himself, however, feels the inconvenience of this division; for after the first part he dismisses the "*individual*" altogether, giving him neither *mission*, nor *authority* nor *liberty* to educate, satisfied with barely vindicating for him the *right* to educate; he treats *in globo* the last point, *Liberty of Education;* which he defines thus:—

And now were we to define in what consists true liberty of education, that liberty which is the honor of a people, worthy and capable of self-government, we should say

---

[1] Sauvé l. c. thus divides his entire subject : Art. I. Du droit d'enseigner. Art. II. Du devoir d'enseigner. Art. III. Du pouvoir ou de l'autorité sur l'enseignement. Art. IV. De l'application des vrais principes sur l'enseignement. The last article of the French Monsignore has been omitted, probably because the writer had decided not to make any practical application, or because the application did not suit his purpose; he compensates us, however, for this loss by the insertion of a section on the liberty of education.

that it consists in the absence of all useless obstacles to the communication of truth on the part of individuals, families, associations, of all those in a word, who are fit to teach. This liberty, thanks be to God, exists in the United States, nowhere so wide and sacred.

We take no exception to this definition of the liberty of education and we thank God with Dr. Bouquillon that we have this liberty in the United States. We have thus far the liberty of educating our own children according to our own convictions, because American common sense has always vindicated the principle of parental right as against state interference, whatever theorists might think, and write, and speak to the contrary; and we have little fear that America will swerve from this principle. For if Americans have inherited anything praiseworthy from those they love to call their Anglo-Saxon forefathers it is the principle that every man's home is his castle; and to the home, that is, to parental authority belongs, in the very first place, the education of the young. The idea of state education is not American; it is an exotic growth, which will hardly thrive in this country. Americans, we hope, will always be so jealous of their personal and domestic liberties that they will shrink from putting them into the hands of commissioners and superintendents of education, or of school boards and school teachers. Thus much only we would say to Dr. Bouquillon and his advisers: If this priceless boon of liberty exists in the United States, why not leave good enough alone? Why invite state interference? Why labor to establish a principle which, if once admitted, necessarily leads to educational tyranny, to state monopoly, to thraldom worse than Spartan? Let us not, however, exaggerate our freedom of education; it is not an unmixed good to have the freedom of educating our own children and the duty of paying for the education of our neighbor's children besides.

Here we would fain bring our investigation to a close, but we must still crave the indulgence of our readers and consider —

V. The Details of Dr. Bouquillon's Procedure.

1. We have already pointed out that Dr. Bouquillon proceeds from a defective definition of education which leads him to various false conclusions—e. g., that every individual or corporation has the right to educate, and, consequently, that the state has the right to educate. We have shown that his argument in favor of state education is fallacious;

we have proved that his authorities do not sustain him. We also adverted to the fact that his treatment of the rights of the family and of the Church is very deficient. Herein the Doctor most grievously fails, but more by omission than by commission. In fact, it would almost seem as though he undertook to treat the rights of parents and of the Church for the sole purpose of showing us that they are not paramount, and to take occasion to remind us that the state has also its say in the education of our children.

a. Thus (p. 10) after quoting St. Thomas, Taparelli and Leo XIII. to prove the absolute, inalienable and indefeasible right of parents to educate their own offspring as against state and even Church (in case of infidels), instead of drawing the conclusion that is evidently contained in the premises he goes on to remind us that this right of parents is not "absolute, unlimited, independent, but subjected to the control of authority, civil and religious." Now, if by this control or supervision, as far as the state is concerned, he would understand the control or supervision which the state justly exercises over other external domestic affairs we are all at one with him, and his remarks are superfluous. For as civil authority can, and ought to, protect the wife who is ill-used by her husband, so it can, and ought to, protect the child, who is evidently brought up for misery, to be a nuisance and a burden to the community. But if this right of control or supervision should imply the right to interfere in the education itself further than to offer facilities and inducements, we say that the state oversteps the limits of its power and arrogates to itself rights it cannot prove, consequently, rights which it does not possess; for a right that cannot be proved is no right.

b. To the *mission* (i. e. the duty) of parents to educate, the Doctor devotes little more than half a page of his pamphlet (p. 17). But in those few lines he makes the suicidal concession that "the mission of parents is to *form men* for the Church and the state;" and that "evidently this formation implies the development of the *physical, intellectual* and *moral* faculties" (Italics ours). From this mission, he admits, that the right of parents to educate "mainly springs." Therefore, according to the Doctor's own admission, the parents have the right and the duty to superintend the physical, intellectual and moral (i. e. the entire) education of their children. But if the parents have the right to superintend the entire education, what, then is left, to the state in normal circumstances, but to offer facilities, &c. ? Then the Doctor goes on to confirm these statements by the passage above cited from Taparelli, in which the Roman philosopher teaches that "the parent has the obligation of instructing the child and attending to his instruction *until* the day when the *reason of the youth is matured*.... *until the child is nearly as well developed as the father.*" Where, then, does the Doctor leave room for the state to step in and contribute its *quotum* to the education of the child ?

c. To *parental authority in education* the Doctor gives not quite a page of his valuable space (p. 22). But here again he admits all that is desired to prove that the parent, in normal circumstances, has the right to control the education of his child to the exclusion of all others.

Parents have authority to regulate, direct, and control the education of their children. They may teach their children themselves or get them taught by others ; they may choose the masters to whom they confide them, determine the sciences they wish to be imparted to them, the means of correcting them. Other individuals, associations, municipalities, and the state should take account of the wishes of the parents in the organization of schools ; *for the father can never lose control of the education of his child.* (Italics ours).

The Doctor, after these admissions, proceeds to administer a gentle reminder that " parental authority is subordinate " to higher authority, and quotes a long passage from Charles Perin, which only goes to show that children may " claim from the state that protection which parental authority *might fail to give ;* that *at times* they may need defence against the abuses of that very parental authority which should protect them ;" that there is a limit to paternal jurisdiction—a truth which no one denies. No one will vindicate the same right or authority to the father of the family in our day as was given to the patriarchs of old, who were invested at the same time with parental, sacerdotal and kingly power. This limitation of paternal power, however, does not regard the work of education as such, but the abuse of paternal authority or the neglect of manifest duties in regard to children. The author, therefore, again goes out of his way to impose restrictions on paternal authority, or to treat us to a mere truism.

As Charles Perin is a writer of the highest authority on social subjects, and has been repeatedly quoted by Dr. Bouquillon, we may be allowed here to give his idea of education, as it should be. We find it well expressed in the words which he adopts from the *E'tudes Re-*

ligieuses for March 1874, in the work cited by Dr. Bouquillon.[1] "The perfect order of public instruction which best corresponds to the normal state of society is the following—that the Church alone, actually and juridically, possesses the direction of instruction in all its phases. This order would require that the general supervision of elementary, intermediate and higher schools should be confided to the Church, so that dogma and morals should suffer nothing and nowhere, either in the religious instruction or in the teaching of the profane sciences. It is necessary that we should know and bear in mind that the Church shall never give her consent to renounce or to abridge that sovereign right to direct the entire education of her children, i. e. of all those who belong to her by baptism ; for, the Church, as the Vatican Council declares, has been placed by God as the mother and the teacher of the nations." The Doctor should have treated us to such passages from his favorite authors.

2. The right, mission and authority of *the Church* are dismissed in the same perfunctory manner.

a. The *Right of the Church to educate* is treated in one paragraph of moderate length (p. 16). Here we read :—

The Church, having received *directly* from God the right to teach revealed religion, is thereby *indirectly* endowed with the right to teach the sciences and letters, in so far as they are necessary or useful to the knowledge and practice of revelation. The right to teach religion comprehends the right to communicate whatever may serve religious education. We do not say that the teaching of profane sciences and letters belongs to the Church by the same title that the teaching of religion does ; much less do we say that such teaching belongs to her exclusively; what we do say is, that the right to spread the revelation entails the right to whatever is profitable to revelation. Now human sciences and letters are destined by God to be handmaidens of faith and of the chief among sciences, theology.—This right is a special right, proper to the Church, direct as to revelation, indirect as to other knowledge.—Moreover, if we consider the Church merely as a human association, we cannot refuse to her the natural right to teach the truths she is adapted and fitted to impart to men. Such right belongs, as we have seen, to associations.

In this setting forth of the Church's rights we cannot fail to discover in the distinguished author a lamentable tendency to minimize. We do not claim for the Church the direct divine mission to teach profane sciences, though we do respect the opinion of those who take that view. But we cannot, and Dr. Bouquillon cannot, overlook the *historic right* of

[1] Les lois de la société chrétienne, liv. iv. 1. 2.—Not having the original at hand, we quote from an authorized German translation, Freiburg, Herder 1876, p. 387.

the Church acknowledged by the greatest jurists. The Church, for more than 1800 years, has acted as the teacher and the educator of the nations not only in religious but also in profane sciences. She possesses, therefore, by immemorial prescription, the right to educate also in the profane sciences, not, indeed, exclusively (she never claimed the exclusive right), but free and untrammelled. And this is a *special* right which she claims against all opponents and which has been universally acknowledged at least in principle by the civil authority.

Besides, the Doctor cannot have overlooked the fact that the Church has always claimed the right to the free control of the *elementary education* of all her children, and that this right was safeguarded in all her agreements with the civil power. This is evidently something more than the *direct right* to teach revelation, and the *indirect right* to teach profane science, "in so far as they are necessary or useful to the knowledge and practice of religion." According to the Doctor's teaching the Church would be in a worse condition in regard to education than the state or the village school board ; for the state according to him, has the *special* and *proper* right to educate as it has the right to govern and to judge by its delegates (p. 12), which is certainly not an *indirect*, but a *direct right*. The same might be said in behalf of the authority of any school board or private corporation as against the Church.

b. Again on the *mission of the Church* to educate (p. 20) we are reminded that "the Church has not received the mission to make known the human sciences." "Her duty of teaching human sciences is only *indirect*, a work of *charity*, or of *necessity :* of charity when they are not sufficiently taught by *others* (?), *who have that duty* (Italics ours) ; of necessity when they are badly taught, that is, taught in a sense opposed to supernatural truth and morality." It was in this manner that bishops of old "took in hand the administration and defence of cities"—we might add, lead armies, and dictated terms of peace and war. Hence in our day "' bishops found schools, colleges, academies, universities"—" a *regretable necessity* " (Italics ours). Did the Church then, we would ask, overstep the limits of her mission when she founded and conducted such educational institutions in past ages without this " regretable necessity ?" Did not the Church found most, and conduct all the institutions of learning before the so-called Reformation ? Was this always a "regretable necessity," such as that which urged the bishops of Church to raise and support and lead armies, and defend cities and strongholds ?

In order not to seem to dismiss this subject too lightly the Doctor here gives a side thrust to those who hold that the Church has received the *direct mission* to teach human science. " To assert that the Church has received the direct mission and duty of imparting the human sciences, is to make the Church responsible for the conditions of the sciences, letters and arts among Christian nations. . . . But we think that Christian apologetics should not be handicapped by useless and dangerous assumptions." We said before that we do not hold the opinion that the Church is sent *directly*, in virtue of her supernatural mission, to teach human sciences. But we do assert that she has a *special mission* in regard to human sciences, apart from necessity or charity (for both these come to the same thing), as history shows, and the laws of nations acknowledge. We would add that there is nothing on the Church's record to make her or any of her children blush at the manner in which she has fulfilled this special calling. If we would take Dr. Bouquillon's view of the matter, we would have to admit that the Church in all ages was guilty of intolerable arrogance in assuming a duty which did not belong to her. The state, on the other hand, which, according to the Doctor's views, has the mission, as it has the right, strict and proper, to educate, would have been guilty of the most unheard of negligence in utterly failing to discharge this duty towards its subjects for more than 6000 years; for state education was a thing almost unheard of until within the last century.

c. The same distinction is kept up in defining the *authority of the Church* over education (p. 28–29): "Religious teaching comes *directly* and exclusively under her [the Church's] control, whereas secular teaching, which *directly* is under the control of the civil or domestic authority, depends on the Church *only indirectly* in the name of faith and morals." And to substantiate this teaching the Doctor again quotes the minimizing note (47) to the *schema vaticanum*—minimizing, in as much as it gives only the minimum of the Church's claims— not the *schema* itself, as might naturally be concluded from the context.

This is the doctrine as laid down in the proposed Vatican *Schema* already quoted. "Non asseritur potestati ecclesiasticæ, velut *ex divina constitutione* consequens auctoritas ad positivam directionem scholarum quatenus in iis litteræ et scientia naturales traduntur; sed vindicatur ecclesiæ auctoritas ad directionem scholarum, *quantum ipse finis Ecclesiæ postulat;* adeoque asseritur jus et officium *prospiciendi fidei et christianis moribus juventutis catholicæ* hocque ipso cavendi ne pretiosa hæc bona per ipsam institutionem in sch lis corrumpantur. Hoc jus Ecclesiæ in se spectatum non minus ad superiores quam ad inferiores scholas extenditur. . . . Cæterum per se clarum est exercitium hujus juris in applicatione ad diversos terminos necessario debere esse diversum." It is the denial of this authority of the Church which is condemned in the 45th and 47th propositions of the Syllabus.

This note (47), as we have before remarked, does not give the positive teaching of the theologians of the Council, but only assigns the limits, or the *minimum*, of the doctrine proposed for definition in the chapter of the Schema, to which it refers. This would have been the place for the Doctor to insert the teaching of the *Schema* itself. Why does he continually, as if shy of the main point, take refuge to this note? Or did he think that the 45th and 47th propositions of the Syllabus were so well known to American readers that it is sufficient barely to refer to them? To supply this omission on the part of the Doctor, we shall here insert them; and, lest some one might accuse us of minimizing, we shall add the 48th proposition.

Proposition 45. "The entire direction of the public schools in which the youth of a Christian state is educated, diocesan seminaries to a certain extent excepted, can and must be apportioned to the civil authority, and that in such a way that no other authority has the right to interfere in the discipline of the schools, the direction of the studies, the conferring of degrees, or the choice and approbation of the teachers.

Proposition 47. "The most perfect state of civil society requires that the common schools, which are open to the children of all classes of the people, and the public institutions in general, which are destined for teaching letters and the exact sciences, and educating the youth, should be exempted from the authority, direction, and interference of the Church, and be subjected to the absolute power of civil authority, at the discretion of the rulers of the state and according to the standard of prevailing public opinion."

Proposition 48. "Catholic men may approve that system of education of youth which is divorced from Catholic faith and the power of the Church, and which regards only, or at least chiefly, the natural sciences and the domain of social life on earth."

These propositions being condemned by the Church their contradictories must be true. Now, as we understand them, their contradictories may be thus summarized:

(1). The state has not absolute power over the schools: in other words, they are not and cannot be mere state institutions, under the sole direction of civil authority.

(2). There can be no legitimate plea for exempting the schools from the authority of the Church, whether they are mere elementary schools, or literary and scientific.

(3). No Catholic can connive at a system of education which has divorced itself from the authority of the Church and the Catholic faith, and has for its object, solely or mainly, natural or secular training.

This is the doctrine of the supreme teaching-office of the Church on secular public schools; from which the reader may conclude in what light those so-called Catholics are to be considered who tell us that the public schools are as good as any else, and that neither they themselves nor their children have ever taken any harm from them—who insist on eulogizing and patronizing the system of secular public schools set up in this country. Those are the things it behoved us to know, and not the *minimum* of authority which the Church must claim over education by *right divine*.

The exercise of the Church's power in various ages is again described in minimizing terms (p. 29).

In the course of ages the Church has exercised this authority more or less extensively according to circumstances. She has exacted from teachers certain guarantees of religion and piety; in this sense she has demanded a profession of faith from whomever would teach. She has also demanded guarantees of fitness in exacting the licentia docendi already spoken of. She has reminded parents of their strict duty of giving to their children sufficient instruction. She has at times taken severe measures in regard to unworthy parents. In a word she has employed, in view of the spiritual end, means analogous to those used by the State in view of the secular end of mankind.

The Church has done all this; but she has done much more. The learned Doctor here omits what is the most important claim of the Church in regard to education—i. e., the free and entire control of the *elementary schools* frequented by her children also in regard to the secular teaching. This is a right which has always been most jealously guarded by the Church and acknowledged by the civil power.. The Church has never yielded this right to any secular authority. The Doctor cannot be unacquainted with the letter of Pius IX. to the Archbishop of Freiburg, dated July 14, 1864, in which this right is clearly set forth and strenuously insisted upon.

" As common schools have been instituted *mainly for the religious education* of the people, to foster Christian piety and morality, they have, therefore, always deservedly and *with perfect right* claimed the *whole care, solicitude, and watchfulness* of the Church, above all other educational institutions. And, therefore, the designs and endeavors of excluding the Church's authority from the common schools proceed from a most hostile disposition to the Church, and from the desire of extinguishing the Divine light of holy faith in the nations. Wherefore the Church, *which first founded those schools*, has always bestowed the *greatest care and zeal* upon them, and considered them as *the most important department of her authority and jurisdiction;* and any separation of them from the Church cannot but be productive of the greatest loss to the Church and to the schools themselves. All those who would have the Church resign, or withdraw her salutary *direction of the popular schools*, demand nothing less than that the Church should act *against the behests of her Divine Founder*, and neglect the *most important charge* committed to her of procuring the salvation of men."

This is the demand of the Church in regard to elementary schools. From these demands she never receded in principle, or even in practice. This right she cannot cede because it is most intimately connected with her divine mission. We consider it a grave omission on the part of Dr. Bouquillon to have entirely overlooked this most important right of the Church, which has been always most dear to her.

3. Scant as is Dr. Bouquillon's treatment of the rights, duties and authority of parents and Church, his treatment of those of the *state* is all the more copious. On this point he brings to bear all the treasures of his extensive learning—*nova ac vetera*.

a. The Doctor opens that section entitled: *The right of the state to educate*, with the " impregnable " argument (p. 11-12) which we have above submitted to a separate examination. With this argument, as we have shown, you might prove anything, and, therefore, it proves nothing. The positive arguments which follow (pp. 13 sq.) have no more convincing force.

The Details of Dr. Bouquillon's Procedure.

We will produce facts and documents to show that all Christian nations have always held this opinion [that the state has the special and proper right to educate]. How astonished Charlemagne would have been had he been told that he had no right to found schools ; how astonished the bishops of his time had such a doctrine been put before them ! Those very bishops were the men who, in the Council of Toul, exhorted princes as well as the ordinaries of dioceses to appoint everywhere teachers of divine and human learning (p. 13).

Give us Christian princes, in a Christian state, like Charlemagne, princes who are the patrons, protectors and secular arm of the Church, and we shall gladly allow them the privilege not only of founding schools, but also of directing them, appointing teachers, albeit in agreement with the Church in all that strictly appertains to her domain; our councils will also encourage and exhort them to this laudable work; but do not preach to us that secular princes and powers generally have the same right as Christian princes in a Christian state.

According to Father Denifle, the eminent historian of the mediæval universities, we are told, four of the universities of Italy, and five of Spain, had been founded by the *civil authority alone* (ibid). Very true; but who had the direction of those universities? Who filled their chairs ? Was it mere state officials? Were those state universities, or were they ecclesiastical institutions ? Let us hear the learned historian himself on this point.

Of the University of Naples, which is cited as the first instance of a state-founded university, Father Denifle says:[1] "It has been said that the University of Naples was a *state university;* nay, that it was the first university founded by a secular prince. *Both these assertions are false.* The word state university is intended to convey the same meaning we attach to it in modern times. But in the middle ages there was no such thing as *a state in the modern sense;* we cannot, therefore, speak of *a state university in the modern sense.* It might at most be called an imperial or territorial university." In those days there was no such thing as a secular state in the modern sense; so there was no such thing as a secular state university. Christian universities, like Christian states, were governed by the combined power of Church and state, the Church, however, having the immediate control.

The foundation of a university, however, we should bear in mind,

[1] Entstehung der Universitäten. p. 452.

neither supposes nor begets, in the founder, the right or duty to *educate*, nor does it make him an educator, as is manifest from daily experience. When one of our millionaires founds a university we do not see that he possesses or acquires the right to educate, or that he deserves the name of an educator. He himself may be untutored, uncultured, ignorant, and unacquainted with even the first elements of the sciences taught in the institution that bears his name; he would make a poor educator; he would be a poor hand to govern a university; he may be intellectually and morally incapable of performing any of the numerous functions, and, therefore, also of acquiring the rights, of education. All the right he has is to the gratitude of his fellow-men. In a similar way we would judge of a sovereign, or a state, that would found a university.

A foundation *per se* neither supposes nor confers any right to educate. By the free bounty of the Church, however, founders have always enjoyed certain rights and privileges in regard to their foundations, e. g., the right to nominate, present, or appoint incumbents for such foundations, benefices, &c.,—always, however, in agreement with ecclesiastical authority; and these rights and privileges in the course of time became positive laws in regard to certain foundations. But manifestly such cases can have little application to the question as it confronts us in this age and country. What are the rights of the non-religious state in regard to the education of Christian (i. e., Catholic) subjects? So the problem presents itself to the Christian philosopher and statesman of our day? This is the question which we would have solved; but with this question Dr. Bouquillon failed to grapple.

What the Doctor relates of the communal schools of Spalatro in the seventeenth century and of the schools founded by Leo XII. in the Pontifical States (p. 13-14) is altogether irrelevant, as both cases suppose the closest union between Church and state.

The Doctor winds up with a remark to which he seems to attribute great weight. "Finally," he says, "we have yet to learn that any Pope has ever declared that the state went beyond its right in founding schools, *provided the instruction be organized in the spirit of Christianity*" (Italics Dr. Bouquillon's). Now, this assertion, which seems so very fairly made, is not altogether unobjectionable. This statement is, in one regard, too restricted: no Pope ever denied the right of secular states to found schools at all, even though, for some reason, the instruction should not be organized "in the spirit of Christianity ; no Pope and, in fact, no man will, for instance, deny the right of the British government to found schools in the East Indies for Pagan Hindoos and Parsees, nor of the Emperor of Morocco to found schools for the education of his Pagan, Mohammedan, or Jewish subjects. Nor would any one deny the right of the states of this Union, under certain restrictions, to establish and support secular schools for the education of the millions of children of its pagan inhabitants. The case is different in regard to the children of Christian subjects ; and for this case the statement of Dr. Bouquillon is vague and misleading. What is this "spirit of Christianity?" One will say unsectarian Christianity, such as the pupil may imbibe from Emerson, Carlyle and George Elliot. Another will say bible-reading without note or comment ; but Catholics must say—Catholicity with all that belongs to it, i. e., the Church must be *free not only to give the religious instruction full and entire* as an essential part of the programme, *but also to superintend the secular teaching so as to prevent all dangers to faith and morals.* But the American, who, knowing no better, reads Dr. Bouquillon's statement, will argue thus: our public schools are organized in the *spirit of Christianity* in its broadest and best sense. The Popes never objected to such schools. *Ergo* our public schools have the sanction of the Pope; and Catholics who object to them from the standpoint of Christianity would be more Christian than the Pope himself. In our humble opinion, this statement of Dr. Bouquillon is too vague to bear *italicizing* unless he would draw attention to its very broadness and vagueness.

Hereupon follows (p. 14-15) the collective testimony of a number of Dr. Bouquillon's favorite authorities—Zigliara, Costa-Rossetti, Hammerstein and the Vatican theologians. But we have already disposed of these authorities, and have shown that without a single solitary exception they reject the right *special* and *proper* of the state to *educate*.

The Doctor closes this section with the solution of some objections (p. 15). For the benefit of the reader, and to avoid even the semblance of unfairness we shall quote his words at full length.

<small>At times we have heard serious men deny to the state the right to educate under the pretext that *the state might abuse that right* (Italics ours). This is bad reasoning. The abuse that authority may make of a right cannot destroy the right. You would not deny</small>

to the state the right of making laws, of declaring war, because it may make bad laws, or lead the nation into unjust wars. Not only is such reasoning bad, it is very imprudent. It is true that to-day, more than ever, we must be careful not to attribute to the state rights to which it is not entitled; but neither should we fall into the contrary error and contest the rights to which it is entitled. That would be to deprive the state of powers it may indeed abuse at times, but also might rightly use; it would be to condemn what governments faithful to their mission have done in the past and are doing to-day.

We beg to remind the Doctor that the argument of his opponents against state education is not an argument *ex abusu*. If the state has the *inherent*, *special*, and *proper right to educate*, there is no abuse in the state's discharging this office; nay, it would be a culpable breach of duty on the part of the state to neglect to do so. The state, therefore, in Dr. Bouquillon's admission, might lawfully and *laudably* control the education of every child within its confines; it could consistently divide cities and country places into sections and districts and force every child to go to its own section or district school; it could prescribe programmes of study, qualify, appoint, dismiss, and retain teachers, contrary to the wishes and demands of parents and of the Church; for, on the one hand, the common good has the precedence over that of individuals, and, on the other hand, the Church's right is in many places not acknowledged. In short, as the state justly monopolizes the offices of judges and other public functionaries, why should it not in that case also monopolize the office of teaching to the exclusion of all others. Our argument is, therefore, not from the *abuse* but from the *licit use* of such a right in the supposition that it did exist, or is actually conceded.

We were somewhat surprised to see that the Doctor condescended to take notice of the following objection:—

It has been said that the state cannot teach, because it has no teaching to give. An absolutely false assertion. *The state has its own doctrines, and must have them* (Italics ours). How otherwise could it make laws? We must, however, admit that the state is not qualified to define and impose religious doctrines. It is from the Church the state must receive such teaching. But the state knows the natural law [?], at least in its fundamental principles, and is bound to secure the execution thereof; and the state certainly knows the rational sciences on which depend agriculture, industry and the arts.

This objection is weak, if not silly; but the answer is still weaker. We were reminded of old Homer's nod when we read it, but we were fully amazed to see that the Doctor took the trouble to copy both objection and answer almost word for word from his revered friend Sauvé.¹?

The state assuredly may have *its doctrines*, and had them before now. Sparta had its doctrines; and Louis XIV. had his doctrines; and the French directory had its doctrines; and Oliver Cromwell had his; the communists had theirs; and the anarchists, if they came to rule, would have theirs. If then, the state has its doctrines, whatever they be, and if it is moreover, the God-appointed teacher of the people, as Dr. Bouquillon will have it, who can prevent it from teaching them, and forcing them upon us, whether we will accept them or not. Dr. Bouquillon gives us no solution to this difficulty; but if he had read and copied a few lines more from Mons. Suavé, he would have found us an easy way out of it. "It goes without saying," adds that distinguished writer, "that if the state professes to have no moral or religious tenets, and if it banish religion from its schools, it thereby declares itself incapable and unworthy of teaching, as I have already said."²

The Doctor concludes this section (p. 15–16) by a paragraph limiting the right of the state. He says: "The state *cannot set up schools that are atheistic or agnostic*." But whence can he derive this limitation? If the state has the right special and proper to educate, who or what is to prevent it to set up atheistic or agnostic schools? A purely secular state, call it godless, atheistic, or agnostic, if it sets up any schools, must set up atheistic and agnostic schools. The Church has no acknowledged right against such a state, and the right of the parents must yield where the right of the state begins. Therefore if the state has the right to educate, it can not only establish atheistic and agnostic schools, but also enforce attendance of such schools. Therefore, if Dr. Bouquillon wishes to be consistent he must either simply deny the secular state the right to educate altogether with Mons. Sauvé or give it the full right of enforcing secular education.

¹ Mais, dira-t-on, l'Etat n'a pas de doctrines; et comment enseigner sans doctrines?
Je réponds: l'Etat peut et doit avoir des doctrines. Sans doute il ne lui appartient pas de déterminer infailliblement quelles sont les vraies doctrines religieuses et morales; mais il doit les recevoir de l'Eglise, et il peut les enseigner au nom et dans la dépendance de l'autorité ecclésiastique. Sauvé, l. c.

² Il va de soi que, si l'Etat fait profession de n'avoir pas de doctrines religieuses et morales, et qu'il bannisse la religion de ses écoles, il se déclare par là même incapable et indigne d'enseigner, comme je l'ai déja dit. Ibid.

If he admits the premises he should not shrink from the conclusion.

b. The weakest part of Dr. Bouquillon's brochure is that on the *Mission of the State to Educate* (pp. 18–20). There is not much to be said on the matter, as far as the state, at least, is concerned. Mons. Sauvé perceived this fact and disposed of the duties, or mission, of the Church, the state, the family and the individual in a few short paragraphs.[1] To fill out the gap, as it were, Dr. Bouquillon here treats us to an excursion on the two-fold purpose of civil power, quotes in illustration the preamble to the Constitution of the United States, and confirms his propositions on the end of civil authority—which, for the rest, no Catholic writer denies—by an extract from a small handbook on civil government by Professors W. W. and W. P. Willoughby, who, on their part, adopt the opinion of Professor Winslow Wilson as laid down in his work entitled *The State*. We are, therefore, not so much concerned with what the Professors Willoughby say as with what Professor Wilson teaches. In his work entitled *The State* we read (p. 666) "It is the object of the family to mould the individual, to form him in the period of immaturity in the practice of morality and obedience... It is the proper object of the state to *give leave to his individuality*...Family discipline must... lead the individual. *But the state must not lead ; it must create conditions, not mould individuals.*" And yet this same Professor Winslow Wilson who insists so strongly that it is the business of the family to mould the individual, and that this is not the business of the state, in the very next paragraph asserts and maintains that education (i. e., the moulding of the individual) is the proper right and duty of the state. An author who so egregiously contradicts himself on the same page, weighs little in the balance of authority. Yet it is but fair to say that Dr. Bouquillon does not quote the Johns Hopkins professors for anything they say on the rights of education, but for what they have to say on the general functions of government —and that only, we would fain suppose, to pay a compliment to the learned professors, or to give some show of importance to his rather meagre subject—the mission to educate incumbent on the state. We say so because we do not see any cause why the Doctor should make such a parade of authority to prove what everybody grants.

Having thus established the two functions of government—the primary and secondary, or the essential and accidental, or the constitu-

---

[1] Sauvé l. c. pp. 285–287.

The Details of Dr. Bouquillon's Procedure.   61

ant and ministrant, as Professor Wilson learnedly calls them, on the basis of St. Thomas, the Constitution of the United States, Mons. Cavagnis and Professors Winslow Wilson, Westel, W. Willoughby and William P. Willoughby, the Doctor proceeds to show that "the state has the mission to educate." To prove this he reverts to the "impregnable" argument which we have already examined in this paper—an argument by which he might as well endeavor to prove that the state has the mission to prescribe a certain regime, and to administer certain medicines to every man, woman, and child within its boundaries from the fact that it has the duty to promote public health. Yet, though the state has the right and duty to promote public health, the Doctor will not thence conclude that it has the duty or even the right to prescribe physic.

Here again the Doctor himself shrinks from the conclusion contained in his premises, and only concludes (p. 19) that "generally speaking, the state is bound to take measures for the diffusion of human knowledge," to which all agree under certain conditions and restrictions. "It can fulfil this glorious mission by encouraging private efforts, helping parents [that need help], establishing schools [where needed and not otherwise provided], appointing capable teachers [for its own special schools, or for other state-supported schools in agreement with parents and with the Church]."

This is modesty put by the learned Doctor. But lest he should seem to anyone unduly to limit the function of the state he closes this section by reminding us that the right of the state extends much farther than its duty or mission.

Finally, to avoid all danger of misconception, we wish to state that for civil society, as for individuals, right goes beyond duty in this matter. Therefore, while saying that the state should provide instruction, where private individuals fail to do so, we do not mean to say that the state may teach only when and where individuals fail to do their duty. The exercise of the duty of the state is allowable *whenever the state judges the exercise of this duty to be useful* (Italics ours), without being absolutely necessary.

Therefore the power of the state is, after all, arbitrary, and can go just as far as the state, or politicians, or corrupt majorities, may choose to push it. Dr. Bouquillon will say that it must be restricted by the common good, by equity, by the harmony between individual, family, state and Church. But who is to decide what is for the common good? Certainly the state, or the majority; not the family, or the Church. And where is that equity and harmony? The Doctor may contemplate it in his mental vision; but it is far from being actual; nor can it ever be actual in our circumstances. State and Church with us can only agree to differ, i. e., to live as good neighbors, and go each its own way.

c. The *authority of the state over education* as distinguished from the right to teach, is treated by the Doctor at great length (pp. 23–28). There is question here only of the authority of the state over "schools of human science founded by individuals, families, associations [the Church?]." This general control of the state over education is proved from the end of the state to promote the common good, and from the accumulated evidence of the Vatican Theologians, Cardinal Zigliara, Sauvé, Cavagnis and another Roman canonist Lucidi, who makes, it seems, the same admission as Cardinal Zigliara; or the same appropriate protest that he has no mind to abridge the rights of the state. Now, of this argument, and of these authorities we have already treated, so we dispense with further comment on them.

If the Doctor had only stated the extent of this general control of the state and told us exactly how far he would have it go, whether it is direct or indirect, whether it regards the education itself as such, or only its external aspects and its relation to public order, &c., we might express our agreement or disagreement with him. But, somehow, the Doctor is always shy of drawing lines of demarcation. Here, however, he is pleased to be somewhat more explicit than usual and, contrary to his purpose, proceeds to make "some practical applications" (p. 24).

(1). "The state," he says, "has the right to prevent the unworthy and the incapable from assuming the role of educators." Certainly; if their unworthiness is manifest from public immorality or legal denunciation; in all other cases, however, we hold with Taparelli and Catholic philosophers generally whose authority Dr. Bouquillon prizes highly, that in the case of private schools the state cannot interfere, more than it can in regard to servants, and nurses, or the officials and clerks of an insurance company, or the members and officers of an athletic club.

"But has it [the state] the power to exact from those who wish to enter into the work of education that they give evidence of worth and capability?" asks the Doctor. He answers: "We think that the state cannot be refused the power of exacting ordinary and reasonable conditions." This answer is rather timid for one who holds that the state has the proper and special right to educate. In his supposition, we would say that the state has the power not only to exact conditions, but to exact whatever conditions it deems proper, such as it exacts for the qualification of its judges and other civil functionaries—therefore, to exact that educators are trained in state schools, according to its own methods, and undergo whatever test it may think proper to require. But we deny the principle—that is, that the state has *per se* the right to educate—as arbitrary, unproved, and untrue; and, accordingly, we deny all the inferences.

We are pleased to see Father Mariana quoted with approval (p.24). But if Dr. Bouquillon thinks that Mariana would allow the teachers of Christian schools to be tested by the officials of a secular state, we must consider him unjust to the age and country in which Mariana lived, and unfair to the character of the Spanish Jesuit himself. Cavagnis, as we have shown, and as may be seen even from the words quoted by Dr. Bouquillon (p. 24), reduces this right of the state to establish a public test to a minimum. He exempts ecclesiastical institutions or schools from that burden altogether, and declares that such a test is rarely expedient. Are there no further means to prove the fitness of a teacher than a public or state examination ? Do the testimonials of teachers go for naught? Everybody knows that the recommendation of the president or principal of an educational institution is a better warrant for the efficiency of a teacher than a state examination and certificate. Why, then, should the state interfere with the appointment of the teachers of private schools, or with their retention in, or removal from, office so long as no abuse, no public crime or misdemeanor, has been charged against them ? If there is an agreement between Church and state as Cavagnis, Sauvé and others suppose, very well; this privilege on the part of the state may lawfully form an item in the agreement; but neither Cavagnis, nor Sauvé, nor any other Catholic author of name that we know of—not even Dr. Bouquillon—has dared to say in express terms that a secular state has of itself the right to examine the teachers of a private Christian school or institution. And this is precisely the question the public would have an answer to; not, what might be, in conditions which are not soon likely to be ours.

The argument fetched from the functions of the *scholasticus* of mediæval institution and from the fact that the civil authority has the right to confer *degrees* (p. 24-25) is not conclusive. First, the *scholasticus* was an ecclesiastical functionary, as Dr. Bouquillon himself admits; nor does it follow that the state can, in like manner, have its *scholasticus* in every district to examine and to grant license to teachers; for, as we hold, the state has no mission to educate, while the Church decidedly has. Secondly, *the conferring of degrees* has little in common with the office of teaching, or the work of education. For what is a degree? A degree is a testimonial certifying the possession of certain abilities and attainments in an individual. Any one who is competent to judge might give such a testimonial; but, in order that it may have legal value, it must be endorsed by public authority, ecclesiastical or civil. That the state, therefore, should give a legal certificate of proficiency in the secular sciences or letters is no more a proof of its right to examine all teachers than the fact that it can grant a license to a pilot is a proof that it has the right to test the ability of all seamen. This is all the more the case in our times when degrees (doctorate, licentiate, &c.) do not, as in ancient times, confer any authority to teach, but are simply legal certificates of proficiency.

(2). Dr. Bouquillon now comes to the question of *compulsory education* (p. 25).

The state has authority to see to it that parents fulfil their duty of educating their children, to compel them, if need be, and to substitute itself to them in the fulfilment of this duty in certain cases. In the use of this authority the state does but lend a hand to the execution of the natural law. It forces the parents to fulfil a duty that binds them most strictly, it protects the child and safeguards his future, it removes from society most serious perils.

We have little fault to find with this form of compulsion, if the Doctor would understand it to be applied only to particular cases in which flagrant abuses are manifest, when the natural law is evidently violated; and if it be not enforced by vexatious laws. To this kind of compulsion, authors generally do not object; and the words of Mariana, Taparelli and Charles Perin cited in proof do not justify further compulsory measures. Such is also the teaching of von Hammerstein, Costa-Rossetti, Sauvé, Cavagnis, Cathrein, Stöckl, Joseph Rickaby and many other Catholic authors. So far, therefore, we have no quarrel with Dr. Bouquillon, if he understands compulsory education or instruction as these authors do, but the Doctor is careful not to tell how far he would have compulsion extend. According to his principle that the state is strictly an educator he should go "as far as who goes farthest." But Dr. Bouquillon has the virtue of being illogical; or he fears the imputation of "liberalism," as would appear from a remark to his recalcitrant readers (p. 26): "We have deeply at heart to remark most emphatically right here, that the above named writers [he means Cavagnis and Sauvé, and indirectly himself] have a reputation for orthodoxy so well established that no vague and wild accusation of liberalism will avail against them." Whatever may be said of these estimable authors, we readily agree that Dr. Bouquillon for one is more orthodox than logical.

(3). On this vague and indefinite coactive power of the state, however, Dr. Bouquillon will establish the right of the state to prescribe a *standard*, or *minimum* of instruction to be imparted to children.

<small>If the state may coërce parents who neglect the education of their children, so also may it determine a minimum of instruction and make it obligatory. Who admits the former must admit the latter. The consequence seems to us logically necessary and we are surprised that all do not see it. Consider, when are parents called negligent? Evidently, when they do not give their children a minimum of education. If then you grant to the state power over cases of neglect, you at once give it power to define what is the minimum of education, and to exact that minimum by way of prevention and of general precept. A law prescribing a minimum of instruction is nothing else, it seems to us, than the application of a principal of natural law to the given circumstances of this or that country.</small>

To this we would say that to determine the *minimum* and *maximum* of instruction to be received by the child is the business, in the first place, of the parent or the person who, according to the natural law, takes the place of the parent; as it is also the right of the parent to determine the kind, quality and quantity of the child's food and clothing, and the state has no right to interfere as long as there is not flagrant neglect, cruelty, or abuse. As the parent can, on medical or other grounds, make his child abstain to a certain age from certain kinds of food or drink, or certain kinds of amusement, up to a certain age, so he can also make him abstain from learning the three R's up to a certain age, (say 8 or 10 or even 12 years) without getting a license from the state.

But what, if in the existence of such freedom, some would remain *illiterate* in a civilized community? This evil, in our opinion, is not sufficiently grave to justify the vexation of the entire population by universal state interference. If illiteracy is a great inconvenience, parents generally will be sufficiently eager to avail themselves of the educational facilities offered in a civilized state. The state has other efficacious means of encouraging and promoting education and exterminating illiteracy without infringing on the personal and domestic rights of its subjects. Such means are, for instance, to offer the best educational facilities, to exclude illiterates from certain civil rights and privileges, &c.

Imagine the state sending a programme of studies to every family in the country, containing reading, writing, arithmetic, geography, history, natural philosophy, civil government, physiology, hygiene, the effects of stimulants and narcotics on the human system, &c., &c., &c. Against a certain day before the close of the fourteenth, or sixteenth, (in the state of New York the twenty-first) year every boy and girl, from the White House down to the lowest hovel in the land, is duly summoned to present himself or herself for examination in said branches before the local school board or the representatives thereof, unless such boy or girl has gone through the course customary in our public schools. And in case the child fails in the ordeal, parent or child, or both, are to be disciplined according to law. Or such a crucial test must be gone through every year from the sixth to the fourteenth, sixteenth or twenty-first year completed. Is it any wonder that sound philosophers and statesmen should condemn such a vexatious system? Is it any wonder that free citizens should shrink from it?

And what if compulsory *school-attendance* is added? In fact, if you once admit the principle of compulsory instruction there is no reason why we should not have compulsory school attendance as well. This is the most efficacious and most convenient means of enforcing compulsory instruction, and if the state has a right to the end, it has a right to the means necessary and effectual to that end. If it has the right to prescribe a standard or plan of instruction, it has also the right to see that this plan is carried out by competent officials of its own training. Is Dr. Bouquillon ready to accept all the consequences implied in compulsory instruction? If so, why not go the whole length of state monopoly? He will find eager followers; but a compromise of this kind will satisfy neither his friends nor his opponents.

To steer safe of these inconveniences, which nothing but a union or agreement between Church and state can remedy, we deny the premises and maintain with Taparelli, von Hammerstein, Rossetti, and also with Cavagnis and Sauvé, upon whose authority Dr. Bouquillon relies most of all, that the secular state has no power to enforce upon the children of Christian parents any form of instruction or education, intellectual, moral or religious, *except in particular cases, to be proved individually, in which the parents are guilty of flagrant neglect or cruelty, or are otherwise incapacitated for the discharge of the duties of parents.*

We have strong reasons and good authorities on our side in this opinion, while we have thus far been unable to discover a single solid argument or a single authority worth considering against us. The reasons of our opponents commonly appeal only to sentiment—to false patriotism, national feeling, &c. We confess ourselves not altogether insensible to such motives; but truth goes before sentiment. We have given our reasons and have considered those of our opponents more at length elsewhere.[1]

The arguments of the editors of the *Civiltà Catolica*,[2] and of Costa-Rossetti (he might have added Taparelli and Hammerstein, who teach the very same, and his friends Cavagnis and Sauvé, who profess to follow the teaching of these authors) do not convince Bouquillon. He ex-

[1] Cf. Respective Rights, pp. 29 sq.

The most learned, complete and convincing arguments against compulsory education, at least in the English language, we take to be the pleas of Judge E. F. Dunne in the Quigley case in the courts of Ohio—First Argument, New York, *Freeman's Journal*, May 30 and June 6, 1891, Second Argument (*Compulsory Education*), Catholic Truth Society, St. Louis, Mo., 1891. The brief shortly to be filed in the Supreme Court of Ohio, in the same case will, it is expected, eclipse all the Judge's previous efforts. Whatever view the court may finally take of the Judge's arguments the unbiassed philosopher and jurist cannot fail to see that, as far as principles are concerned, right is on his side. These pleas are not merely masterpieces of forensic oratory, but specimens of the ablest philosophical and juridical argumentation; which, if we mistake not, will be read and studied long after all the pompous panegyrics of our public school compulsory system of education have been forgotten.

[2] The editors of the *Civiltà* have answered for themselves in an extended Review of Dr. Bouquillon's pamphlet (January 2d, 1892), and will probably again be heard from. They are still true to the teaching of Taparelli and Liberatore and pronounced against compulsory education, in any shape. This Review has already appeared in English translation in various Catholic papers, and has been published in separate pamphlet by Benziger Brothers, New York, under the title: *Education to whom does it belong*. Review by S. M. Brandi, S.J.

amined their reasons, he says, and found them faulty; but he does not take the trouble of refuting them. Need we say in return, that we have examined Dr. Bouquillon's arguments, and that they do not go far to convince us? His argments from reason, as we have seen, prove too much; prove so much that he himself shrinks from the logical consequences. His arguments from authority, on the other hand, prove nothing, because the authors he cites, as we have shown, are one and all against him.

Let us remark in passing that the fact that the "state can hinder parents from sending their children to labor above the strength of their age, say in the mines" (p. 26–27), is no reason why it may compel them to send their children to school or have them taught reading, writing, figuring and physiology. In the first instance, there is question of the violation of a negative precept of the natural law, while in the second case no part of the natural law can be shown to be violated. While the state may possibly forbid *all that is evil*, as far as it comes within its sphere, it can not command *all that is good*.[1]

Dr. Bouquillon (p. 27) returns again to his staple authorities to clinch his argument. He says:—

> At any rate, we are not left without respectable authorities in favor of our opinion. St. Thomas teaches that the legislator may take measures concerning " bonam disciplinam per quam cives informantur ut commune bonum justitæ et pacis conservent." Jerome de Medicis, one of the best commentators of St. Thomas, in the XVI. century, adds to the above sentence, " sicut si princeps condat legem ut adolescentes debeant litteris studere, ut hoc studio cives informentur, ut commune bonum justitæ et pacis conservent." To our forefathers compulsory education was not a bugbear. In our days, Mgr. Sauvé declares that he dares not refuse to the state the authority to make obligatory so much of elementary education as is strictly necessary or useful. Nor does Cardinal Zigliara dare deny that power to the state. Cardinal Manning acknowledges that the state has the power to punish the father who neglects to send his child to school, and this power is incontestably within the competence of the state. At times we have seen missionaries make obligatory on the faithful, not only the elementary religious, but the elementary secular instruction in reading and writing; and yet over such instruction the missionaries have only an indirect authority and control.

To begin with the Doctor's last fact, what "missionaries" can do by ecclesiastical power, the state cannot do by secular power. The question is of *state authority*, but of ecclesiastical jurisdiction. Of Cardinal Zigliara's teaching we have already treated. He grants *for argument's sake only* to the state the power to coërce parents to have

---

[1] Cf. S. Thom. I. II. q. 96. a. 3; Suarez, de leg. lib. III. c. 12. n. 11.

their children instructed. We have sought in vain for any expression of Cardinal Manning's which would commit him to compulsory education; but we did find in an article in the Ninteenth Century written by the Cardinal in 1883, entitled: *Is Christianity in England worth preserving*, the strongest expressions in condemnation of compulsory education.

First, the Cardinal endorses the following words of Bishop Grace of St. Paul, addressed to the Hon. Zachary Montgomery, approving the latter's efforts for educational reform as based on parental rights.

"If you need any words of mine to encourage you in the course you are pursuing, you have them from my heart. Every day convinces me more and more that the ground you have taken in defence of *the rights of the family against the encroachments of the state* is really the ground upon which the opposition to the state school system should have been based from the beginning. *Natural rights as involved in this question no legitimate government will infringe or allow to be infringed upon due proof. The law of majorities, the vox populi, has no weight against the claims of natural family rights.*"

Then the Cardinal goes on to comment upon the American public school as follows:—" Such is the common school system in the American Republic, over which, as yet, the Platonic and communistic theory that the children of a state belong not to their parents, but to the state has never yet exerted its malignant spell. The American commonwealth has in it too much of English and Puritan blood, its vital relation to our seventeenth century is too vivid and powerful, to endure the theory that the children belong to 'the general public,' and that the state may create them in its own image and likeness. Nevertheless, in its zeal for education, it has admitted the *false principles which legitimately lead to this conclusion.* Education that is only *secular* dooms religion to gradual extinction. Education that is *common* violates conscience. Education that is *secular, common, and compulsory violates the rights both of parents and of children.* Logically on these principles the schools are schools of the state, the children are the children of the state, and their formation is at the will of the state against all rights, parental or divine."[1]

Thus thought and wrote the illustrious Cardinal of Westminster in 1883. If he taught otherwise in his pastoral of 1872, as Dr. Bouquillon

[1] Nineteenth Century, April, 1883, Vol. xiii. p. 621.

assures us on the authority of a certain P. Pradié, he has made honorable amends in these plain and emphatic words. '

St. Thomas is evidently here quoted by the Doctor, not for his own sake, but on account of the comment of Jerôme de Medicis, in regard to whose authority we would say: first, that Dr. Bouquillon or Jerôme de Medicis could hardly sustain the thesis that compulsory education appertains to that *bona disciplina* of which the Angelic Doctor here speaks; secondly, that Jerôme de Medicis makes this remark only incidentally by way of illustration, as a point possibly appertaining to good discipline; thirdly, that it is by no means certain (nay, the contrary is very probable) that the commentator would have such law extend to all the youth, but only to certain youths by way of privilege; and therefore Sauvê, from whom the Doctor took this argument, very shrewdly makes such possible law apply only to some youths (à *des* jeunes gens). ²

Now, finally, as to Sauvé's own testimony, why has the Doctor not given us Sauvé's own words in full? Sauvé says: "I would not venture absolutely to dispute the right of the state, at least in certain circumstances of time and place, to make obligatory that elementary instruction, which is strictly useful or necessary, *on condition that such instruction were, above all, religious and moral.*" ³ And here the Monsignore

---

[1] Since the above was put in print our attention was drawn to the following words from a pastoral of the lamented Cardinal dated Lent 1872:—

"Every Christian child has a right in himself to a Christian education: every Christian parent is the guardian of that right in his child. And over the Christian parent is the authority of the Church as the guardian of the rights and the guide of the liberty both of the parent and of the child. The education of Christian children in faith and morals— and nothing less than such formation is worthy of the name of education—belongs *directly and by divine right* to the authority which in faith and morals is both the ultimate judge and supreme guide . . These principles are to you as axioms both of the natural and of the Christian law. You need not, therefore, be told that the *Civil power has received no right either by the law of nature or of Christianity, to assume to itself the formation or education of the people. A worse tyranny could not be imagined.* A people educated by a government without faith—and what government pretends to have a faith ?—a people formed to the image and likeness of an atheistic Commune or a Voltairean civil power can only grow up to scourge itself with intestine feuds, and to commit suicide as a nation." Can these be the words referred to by Pierre Pradié?

[2] Cf. Sauvé, l. c. p. 307. The passage of St. Thomas referred to is Sum. Theol. 1, 2, quest. 96 (not 95) a. 3.

[3] Je n'oserais contester *entièrement* à l'Etat le droit de rendre obligatoire, du moins

goes on to quote the opinion of von Hammerstein, who puts the same condition.

This is the "be all and the end all" of Dr. Bouquillon's argument in favor of compulsory education. Unless he would walk in a solitary path of his own, he must acknowledge with the authorities whom he "quotes in preference," *that a secular state cannot by law enforce compulsory education in any shape or form on Christian subjects.*

Perhaps Dr. Bouquillon will tell us that he holds the same opinion. We would be agreeably surprised, if he did. But, we say if the Doctor does hold this doctrine with Cavagnis, Sauvé, Taparelli, and others whose authority he professes to follow, why not say so? Why manufacture arms for those who endeavor to force upon us Catholics a system of *secular* (*neutral, mixed*) education which the Catholic Church has always wisely abhorred and condemned?

VI. CONCLUSION.

The *result* to which the learned Doctor comes, we must confess, is most unsatisfactory. He closes with the words:—

Education : to whom does it belong, is the question with which we started out. We now make answer. It belongs to the individual, physical or moral, to the family, to the state, to the Church ; to none of these solely and exclusively, but to all four combined in harmonious working, for the reason that man is not an isolated but a social being. Precisely in the harmonious combination of these four factors in education is the difficulty of practical application. Practical application is the work of the men whom God has placed at the head of the Church and the state, not ours.

We knew all this before; we knew more. We knew not only that these powers in the ideal state should be *harmoniously combined;* but we knew something about the combination and subordination of these forces. The Doctor has contributed nothing to the solution of the great problem. Nay, he has only made it more complicated for this country at least. He has unsettled in the public mind what was thus far settled, throwing before us an indigested mass of general principles, concessions, compromises, views and assumptions, based on quite different circumstances, and having little or no application to the conditions of Church and state in our Republic. Till now we have been guided in this most important matter by the intelligent zeal of our Bishops, by the national ecclesiastical legislation of three

en certains temps et lieux, l'instruction élémentaire, rigoureusement utile ou nécessaire, à la condition que cette instruction fût avant tout religieuse ou morale.

plenary councils, by the decrees and instructions of the Holy See and of the sacred congregations; we had some fixed ecclesiastical discipline in regard to parochial schools; but the layman, at least, who happens to read Dr. Bouquillon's pamphlet, will put it down with the painful impression that we have nothing fixed; and that we are, consequently, free to do as we please; that, before we come to any decided line of action in regard to parochial and public schools we must ransack the pedagogic literature from the Capitularies of Charlemagne to the works of the most recent canonist; and that on the basis of these researches our hierarchy have to build up that harmonious educational system which will give its due share to the individual, the family, the state, and the Church. Is this the outcome of the thought and activity of the first century of our American Hierarchy?

This being the only result of Dr. Bouquillon's pamphlet, we must conclude that it is most inopportune and should never have seen the light; for, as the author rightly remarks (p. 30) "No one is at liberty to teach...inopportune truth; for inopportune truth is truth accidentally injurious."

The mischief likely to follow from this publication will be all the greater, owing to the well-deserved reputation of its author for orthodoxy and true ecclesiastical spirit, as well as for solid and extensive learning; owing to the fact that it will be taken at least by outsiders to represent the teaching of the Catholic University of America; and that it purports to have been written at the request, though not at the inspiration, of ecclesiastical authorities (see preface). Now we would be sorry to detract one tittle from the well-earned renown of the learned author, or to say a single word derogatory to that promising institution of which he is a conspicuous light, or to seem in the least disrespectful to any, even the lowest, ecclesiastical superiors.

Thus much, however, we may be allowed to say : first, in regard to the author—that although his opinion may have, and certainly has, the greatest weight in other matters, yet in this matter, differing as he does from Catholic theologians and jurists generally, even from those whom he himself quotes for his views in this pamphlet, it carries with it but little authority. Besides, it is sufficiently well known, at least in learned circles, that Dr. Bouquillon does not in this question represent the teaching, or the opinion, of the Catholic

Conclusion. 73

University. And as to the fact that he has written his pamphlet at the request of ecclesiastical superiors, this adds nothing to its authority. We might truly say as much of this paper; but we would not thereby make any one but ourselves responsible for anything it contains. And, in like manner, Dr. Bouquillon would be the last to throw any responsibility for his opinions on any ecclesiastical superior. The pamphlet is, therefore, the work of an individual, and has just that authority which its author can claim in this precise field of knowledge; no more, and no less.

Moreover, the Doctor has evidently formed his ideas on education in countries and under circumstances very different from ours—in countries where there is at least a semblance of union between Church and state; where there exist different conditions of right; where the state encroaches on the rights of the Church and the family, and the Church makes concessions to the state; where, owing to the malice of men, the Church is glad to have any tolerable *modus vivendi;* while here the Church is perfectly free and independent of the state, and the state takes no cognizance of her rights more than of those of any private corporation. Manifestly those principles of law which govern education in countries where there is union, or agreement, between Church and state can have no application to our circumstances, unless in as far as they are at the same time the expression of the natural law. The natural law alone, and not positive laws and customs as based on agreements and concessions on the part of the Church, must decide the relations between state, family and individual in this country; while the Church as such can claim only the rights of its individual members. The individual has the right to practise his religion as long as it does not clash with public order; but the Church *as such* has no acknowledged right. Principles of positive canon law have, therefore, little application to this country, as far as the relation between Church and state is concerned; and it would be unsafe to make any practical applications based exclusively upon positive Church law.

But the author declines to make *practical applications* (cf. preface, and p. 31). Practical applications from a man of Dr. Bouquillon's authority would, we think, have been in order. Speculative science is for the sake of the practical; and the science in which the Doctor has distinguished himself is an eminently practical one. Practical instruction is just what was needed and expected from him; but he disappointed the public expectation also in this regard. Practically disposed Americans, however, will draw their own practical conclusions from Dr. Bouquillon's teaching; but these logical consequences, we fear, will not be beneficial to Catholic interests in this country. Statesmen will make their application: if the state has the right *to educate*, and is, therefore, the God-appointed educator of its citizens, let us control education, as is done in other countries: we have no state Church looking on as a jealous partner to thwart our endeavors. Parents will make the application, and say: if the state is the natural educator of our children, let the state have them; its education is the cheapest and, from a worldly standpoint, probably the best; and if the state has the right to educate them, it cannot be wrong to let it do so. And why should not priests, too, make their practical applications, if one of themselves, to whom they look up for enlightenment, tells them that the state has the right *to educate:* Why, then, let it educate, we are well rid of the hardships of building and supporting and conducting our parochial schools; our Bishops have been too quick to impose this superfluous burden on us. May not even some of those who have been set by the Holy Ghost to rule the Church of God also make their practical applications?

A defence of state rights in this country like that before us is, therefore, to our thinking, unwarranted and uncalled for. There is no tendency among Catholics, that we can see, unduly to abridge, or in any way to imperil, state rights. And if there were, the state is able to take care of itself, and will doubtless do so without the aid of any plea on the part of Catholics, or any other religious denomination. Such an unwarrantable plea for the rights of the state can only create the false impression among statesmen and non-Catholics —either that there is an under-current of anarchism and disloyalty among Catholics in this country, or that the over-zealous preachers of state prerogatives are guilty of servility and desirous of gaining popular favor or securing political influence.

The states of this union are, as a rule, not at all eager to meddle in our affairs; they let us mind our own business. Why should we, then, invite their interference in those matters in which no right can be proved on the part of the state? Catholics *qua* Catholics owe nothing to the state except the loyalty of good citizens, while the state owes much to them. Their schools have no material obligation towards the state; on the contrary, the state has great obligations towards them; they yearly save the state many millions of dollars. Why should the state then, arrogate rights to the control or direction of our schools which it cannot prove, and which do not exist? We take this to be very bad policy on the part of the state. Such it has proved to be in Illinois and Wisconsin. The people called a halt. Such it would doubtless prove itself elsewhere if put to the test of intelligent public opinion.

We cannot believe that the bulk of Americans have come to that pass that they are willing to have their domestic affairs controlled by state power, or that they are disposed to impose upon themselves that intolerable yoke of paternalism which the more intelligent of European nations are so eager to shake off. We can hardly think that such a tendency will prevail in America in the long run and we are of the opinion that any effort to make such a policy popular is, to say the very least, labor ill-spent. We would not, however, be understood as implying that Dr. Bouquillon is an advocate of paternalism; but so much we would say, and we believe that we have shown it to evidence in the preceding pages, that by his recent pamphlet he has been playing vigorously into the hands of paternalists.

Should such a policy of state education gain favor in this country, as we trust it never will, what safeguard would remain for the Church, the family, the individual? If public opinion is worked up to such a pitch that the state legislatures and executives of this Union consider themselves justified in taking the control of domestic affairs, insinuating themselves into the household and the sanctuary, what is to prevent them? If it is once made plausible to the country, by good or bad reasoning, by just or unjust precedent, by authorities however insignificant, provided they be popular, that the state or public authority has the inherent right, *special* and *proper*, to *educate* its citizens in the proper sense of this word, what is to prevent it from forcing all children into state or public schools against the protests of individual, family, and Church? The Church, *as such*, has no acknowledged right in this country, and the family and individual must yield to the prevailing right, or, at least to the prevailing force, of the state. Therefore we say that to vindicate to the state the right of education, particularly since such a right cannot be proved is, to use the very mildest expression, a work of questionable wisdom

—a work which is now and here highly "inopportune" and, consequently, at least, "accidentally injurious."

How strongly do the following words of instruction and warning from our illustrious Cardinal, *qui nil molitur inepte*, contrast with the general tenor of Dr. Bouquillon's pamphlet? "The religious and secular education of our children cannot be *divorced* from each other without inflicting a fatal wound upon the soul. The usual consequence of such a separation is to paralyze the moral faculties and to foment a spirit of indifference in matters of faith. Education is to the soul what food is to the body. The milk, with which the infant is nourished at its mother's breast, feeds not only its head, but permeates at the same time its heart and the other organs of the body. In like manner, the intellectual and moral growth of our children should go hand in hand; otherwise, their education is shallow and fragmentary, and often proves a curse instead of a blessing."

"Piety is not to be put on like a holiday dress, to be worn on state occasions, but it is to be exhibited in our conduct at all times. Our youth must put in practice every day the Commandments of God, as well as the rules of grammar and arithmetic. How can they familiarize themselves with these sacred duties, if they are not daily inculcated?"[1]

Doctor Bouquillon, on the other hand, has not a word to say in favor of religious education, in behalf of our parochial schools, in defence of the legislation of our Councils and the decrees of the Church concerning the little ones of the flock of Christ. He will respectfully beg us to remember that his theme is: *Education: To Whom Does it Belong;* and that he has earnestly at heart to restore to the state, in the estimation of the people at least, that *quotum* in the education of youth, of which, in his opinion, the over-zealous defenders of the rights of the family and the Church, have unjustly deprived it; but we beg reverently to submit that we here speak of the opportuneness of his pamphlet, and that our remarks are in order.

We have followed the Doctor patiently and impartially; we have studied the sources from which he gathered his materials; we have compared his references as far as it could be deemed necessary or relevant; we have carefully weighed his arguments, and have come to the conclusion that far from producing anything that could in any

[1] Our Christian Heritage, p. 493.

Conclusion. 77

way contribute to the solution of the education problem in this or any other country, he has only involved it in new difficulties, at least for this country, by putting before the public a collection of principles, partly false, partly vague and ambiguous, and altogether inapplicable to our circumstances, since they presuppose conditions entirely different from ours. We have found his argumentation to be loose and fallacious; his authorities misconceived, misinterpreted, and misapplied; his method illogical; the details of his procedure inexact and inconsistent. He has not been able to muster a single argument to prove the strict, special and proper right of the state to educate in the accepted sense of this word; with this right the whole theory of state education falls to the ground.

However we would not have the Doctor or anybody else think that we are less friendly disposed to the state than he. True patriotism, it would seem to us, does not consist in throwing ourselves and all our concerns into the all-embracing arms of the state; but in faithfully performing our duties as individual citizens. The best friend of the state, we observe, is he who gives least trouble to the state; and the most troublesome are the wards of the state. We would not have our children become wards of the state. If there is anything calculated to stamp out patriotism from the hearts of citizens, it is undue interference on the part of the state. Our American freedom consists not only in free suffrage, but also in the protection which it offers to personal and domestic rights, so that every one who comes to our shores from European states, even before partaking of the rights of a citizen, feels that the heavy burden of paternalism and bureaucracy has been lifted from his shoulders; and that he breathes more freely. Let us beware, then, of trying to impose upon our fellow-citizens that foreign and un-American yoke which we ourselves would have borne with reluctance. It would be highly unpatriotic, or, at best, mistaken patriotism, to swerve from the time-tested principle, that a man's home is his castle, and to make ourselves and our children wards of the state.

But we Catholics have no choice in this matter. According to the teaching of our Church, and according to the ecclesiastical legislation of our country, we can neither use, nor approve of, a system of education, which is divorced from religion and from the influence of the Church, and which regards only, or chiefly, the domain of profane knowledge. Any thing, therefore, that is calculated to shake this belief in the minds of the faithful, or to relax the discipline of the Church in the matter of Catholic education, cannot but prove highly detrimental to the Church in this country. We would not insinuate that the work before us was written with this intention; far be it from us; but certain it is that, however sincere the intention may have been, the book itself cannot fail to have this effect on many of its readers. It was to counteract this evil, as far as possible, that we undertook this study, and we hope to have attained our purpose, as far as depended on us. We have found not an item in Dr. Bouquillon's pamphlet that could make us swerve one tittle from the principles we have already set forth on this subject. We have travelled the whole ground anew and have only been confirmed in the convictions which had grown upon us in our first study of the question.

We hold now, as we did then, that the parents are the God-given educators of their children; that the work of education is their personal duty and their inalienable and indefeasible right, which they can neither surrender nor forfeit, except by crime or inability.

We hold that the Church, too, has her God-given educational mission, supplementing and superseding that of parents, as far as faith and morals are concerned, but not confined to the sphere of revelation. No, we maintain that the Church has not only the *indirect* right, duty, and authority to teach the profane sciences in virtue of her supernatural end; but that, like every other teaching corporation, the Church has the *direct* right and duty to teach; nay, that the Church has by immemorial prescription the inviolable *historic right* to cultivate and to teach the profane sciences, unhindered and untrammelled by any earthly power; therefore that the Church has the right and authority not only to teach the Christian doctrine in all schools and to superintend the secular teaching so as to assure herself that it contains nothing in itself or its adjuncts dangerous to faith and morals; but that she has the right to found and direct her own schools for the teaching of the profane as well as of the sacred sciences; while the elementary instruction of her children belongs *exclusively* to her.

We hold that the state *per se* i. e., of its own nature or constitution, has neither the right nor the mission, nor the authority to teach in the sense of educating, though it may and must indirectly and for its own special purposes exercise certain rights and discharge certain duties in regard to education—e. g., establish and conduct military and naval academies, establish schools where manifestly useful or necessary, and not otherwise provided for; found industrial schools for the children of the poor and abandoned classes, not otherwise cared for; encourage and promote scientific investigation and research, &c. We deny, however, that the purely secular state has the right or authority to enforce compulsory education, whether by compelling attendance at school or by prescribing a certain programme, plan of studies, or minimum of instruction, except in particular cases of utter neglect or manifest abuse of parental authority, likely to expose the child to moral ruin; which neglect or abuse, however, must be proved in each case.

The result of our study of Dr. Bouquillon's problem: (*Education: to whom does it belong?*) is, therefore, a fitting supplement to Father Holaind's reply. Father Holaind's answer was: *The Parent First;* we add—THE STATE LAST.

SUPPLEMENT.

DR. BOUQUILLON'S REJOINDER.

I. Some Features of the Rejoinder.

After having sent the foregoing pages to the press we received Dr. Bouquillon's *Rejoinder to Critics*, which is a document of 42 pages octavo written in defence of 32 pages of the same size, chiefly against the strictures of the Rev. R. I. Holaind, S.J., of whose prompt and able reply mention has been made in the preceding, and against certain comments of the Rev. E. A. Higgins, S.J., in the *Catholic News;* and also against some minor criticisms in the *American Ecclesiastical Review* and other Catholic papers not mentioned. The purport of the *Rejoinder* is briefly expressed in the opening lines.

My pamphlet on Education has provoked adverse criticism. Critics, notably Rev. R. I. Holaind, S.J., have seen in it what I did not say, and have not seen in it what I did say. I feel called on to offer some explanations that I trust, will put the truth in clearer light, end misunderstandings and dissipate prejudices.

As we have not, to our knowledge, seen in the pamphlet what the Doctor did not say, nor, as we trust, failed to see what he did say; as we allowed the Doctor to speak for himself and to say over again the most important passages of his pamphlet, and as we have not attributed any motive or purpose to him but what he himself openly declared, these words cannot subsequently be made refer to us. Besides, our treatment of the Doctor's pamphlet, as he himself will readily admit, is very different from that of any of his other critics though our opinions will be found to coincide with theirs in the main. In fact, our review was all but completed before any noteworthy criticism of the pamphlet, except Father Holaind's, had been published; nor did we deem it necessary after reading the criticisms of others, whether favorable to the Doctor or otherwise, in aught to modify our own views or statements—not even after reading the Doctor's *Rejoinder* itself.

We might, therefore, have dispensed ourselves from the task of reviewing the *Rejoinder;* but, on the one hand, we deemed it due to the Doctor and to the public to notice what he had to say in his own defence, and, on the other hand, we feared that, if we neglected to notice it, some over-zealous friends of his might give out that we too were refuted in advance by his *Rejoinder.* We, on the contrary, are of opinion that, if the Doctor had bided his time, and awaited our review of his pamphlet that he would have altogether abandoned the idea of replying, or would have replied in a very different tone and manner; and thus we might have been relieved of the delicate task of reviewing this review of the reviews of his pamphlet.

The task, however, is not so formidable after all, as it might seem at first sight. If we deduct from those 42 pages all that is personal, (whether it regards the author himself, or Father Holaind, or Father Higgins), all that is irrelevant, all that is impertinent to the subject, all that is but a repetition of the former pamphlet, and all that is directly met by us in the body of our review—but little will remain to be examined.

Personal or *irrelevant* is the greater part of the first three sections of the *Rejoinder*, justifying the Doctor's object and purpose and the authorities and quotations contained in his first pamphlet, as also the first and second of his *general observations* (pp. 1-9). We cannot, for instance, see how the Doctor, who was so chary of his words in some parts of his first pamphlet could waste almost two pages (p. 9-10) in defending himself against the charge of state-worship as implied in saying "state and Church," instead of "Church and state," while much graver accusations are brought against him. This making much of trifles is noticeable also (p. 10) where the Doctor tries to make a point out of Father Holaind's waiving certain abstract questions on the modifications of the natural law, which it would take a volume to explain. Had Father Holaind not had the phantasm of the voluminous work of Suarez so vividly before his mind, had he instead Mons. Sauvé's *Questions,* &c. on his desk, open at p. 280, as Dr. Bouquillon seems to have had when he referred (Pamph. I. p. 9) to the *" distinctions lumineuses"* [1] of Suarez (De Legib. l. ii. c. 13), he would not have

---

[1] Si ces *distinctions lumineuses* de Suarez étaient présentes aux yeux de tous les publicistes, plusieurs erreurs au sujet des droits naturels de l'homme seraient facilement évitées. Car tout droit qui n'est pas *commandé* mais seulement *accordé* par la nature,

summarily dismissed these interesting questions, to "turn to the live issues of the hour" (p. 8). The same may be said of the paragraph (p. 21) in which the Doctor tries to make capital of the kind word which Father Holaind has for those who try to vindicate to the Church the direct divine mission of teaching profane sciences. Such methods of controversy may discredit an opponent in the eyes of the vulgar, but not in the eyes of intelligent readers.[1]

Impertinent to the subject we would call, for instance, that long excursion (pp. 17–19) on the right of association, which has not the slightest bearing on the matter in hand except through the artificial and arbitrary connection established by the Doctor in trying to vindicate to the individual and to associations the right to educate. This whole discussion is exceedingly far fetched. If the Journal that brought the objection referred to (p. 17) is not worth naming the objection is not worth considering; nor is the dreaded axiom that *associations are fictitious beings, mere creations of the law*, likely to gain ground in this land of freedom of association. The whole discussion seems to have been put here to give some show of strength and importance to the Doctor's tottering position. In like manner, the learned excursion on the "natural verities" (pp. 21–23) serve at most for filling out, and do nothing towards clearing away the difficulties that beset the reader's path; nay, such overloading with impertinent matter can only divert the ordinary reader from the main issue—a consummation which seems to be rather in the interest of the learned Doctor.

II. THE STATE CHRISTIAN AND NON-CHRISTIAN.

Waiving such irrelevant and impertinent discussions we now come to a cardinal point of the Doctor's teaching (pp. 11–14).

A capital objection against me is, that in my treatment of education *I make no distinction between the state Christian and the state non-Christian* (Italics ours). Most

peut être modifié, ou même aliéné par les hommes, parce qu'il dépend de la volonté de celui qui le possède, et aussi de la volonté de l'Etat en ce qui est nécessaire ou utile au bien commun. Question religieuses et sociales, p. 280.

[1] We would have it distinctly understood that we do not undertake to defend Father Holaind or any other of Dr. Bouquillon's critics in these pages. We have no right or commission to defend them; they are all able to defend themselves. We have to deal directly with Dr. Bouquillon's *Rejoinder*, only indirectly with his critics.

assuredly I make none, and no more do I make any between the family Christian and the family non-Christian, the individual Christian and the individual non-Christian. I repeat, I make no such distinction, and this is why: Civil society and its inherent authority are in the natural order; the Church and its inherent authority are in the supernatural order. . . . (p. 11).

Here we have to deal with a lamentable confusion of ideas. This would have been the place for the Doctor to apply some of Suarez' "luminous distinctions." But here they do not serve his purpose. The Doctor's entire argumentation is based on one fallacy. He considers the civil authority (*in se*) *in the abstract*, and predicates of the state *in the concrete* (i. e., of the governing person, physical or moral) what is true only of civil authority considered in itself or in the abstract. *In the abstract* it is most true that civil authority always regards the *temporal*, the *profane* (as the Doctor rightly puts it with Webster), and is always *the same;* but, *in the concrete*, he who wields the civil power may be also invested with spiritual, supernatural power, whether *in virtue of his office* as the pope, who is lawful temporal sovereign, and in virtue of his office is at the same time supreme pontiff; or *by delegation*, as in the case of a temporal sovereign or ruler who, by agreement or usage may perform certain spiritual functions, e. g., nominate or present incumbents for ecclesiastical benefices, and invest them with the power and prerogatives thereto annexed.

This union of the natural and supernatural, of the temporal and eternal we find in every believing Christian. In every believing Christian there is intelligence, or natural knowledge, and there is faith or supernatural knowledge; while in the non-believing non-Christian there is natural intelligence without supernatural faith. So it is also in the state, Christian and non-Christian, taken in the concrete; in the latter there is civil authority simply regarding temporal and profane matters; in the former there is also, or at least there may be, a certain amount of spiritual authority attached, whether delegated, as in secular rulers, or ordinary, as when a bishop is at the same time a ruling sovereign.

Suarez in the very chapter here cited by the Doctor (De Leg. lib. iii. c. 11, n. 10) carefully makes the distinction between the civil power proper to Christian rulers and that which they have by concession of the Church or by the very fact of their being rulers of Christian subjects. Hence it is, he says, that temporal rulers can punish those vices and crimes that are specifically against the Christian religion as such, e. g., heresy, blasphemy against Christ, the Jewish rite of circumcision, &c. "Some of these acts," he says, " belong to the civil authority, not of themselves, but by concession of the ecclesiastical authority, and, as it were, by a tacit or express invocation of the secular arm."[1]

And he further adds that the civil state has the power to punish such crimes also, in as much as they are contrary to the peace of Christian subjects.[2] The Christian state, therefore, may have a more extensive power from two sources: from the concession of the Church and from the exigence of its Christian subjects. This power is spiritual, accessory to the temporal or purely civil power. But it resides, or at least may reside, in a temporal ruler. Suarez, therefore, while maintaining the essential distinction between civil and ecclesiastical authority, admits that both may reside in a temporal ruler, as natural intelligence and supernatural faith can exist in the same rational subject. We wonder that the Doctor cannot, or will not see, this distinction. This "luminous distinction" of Suarez manifestly does not suit the Doctor's purpose.

The same confusion of the concrete with the abstract goes through this whole discussion on the Christian and non-Christian state (p. 11 -14). When the Doctor asserts (p. 11, *b*) that the civil authority retains substantially the same character as under the pagan dispensation, or as it would have *in statu naturæ puræ* this is true only in the abstract. It is only in the abstract that whatever is *sacred* belongs to the spiritual and whatever is *profane* belongs to the civil power. In the concrete both these powers may be, to some extent, vested in the same subject, whether this subject be temporal or spiritual; not as if the two powers were mixed, or confused, or blended into one; no; the spiritual power remains spiritual and the temporal power remains temporal; though the former may be partially vested in a temporal subject, and the latter wholly or partly in a spiritual subject. It is

[1] Respondeo imprimis aliqua ex his non tam per se pertinere ad sæcularem potestatem, quam *ex concessione ecclesiasticæ potestatis*, et quasi per tacitam vel expressam invocationem ejus postulantis auxilium brachii secularis (Ibid).

[2] Deinde dicimus illa vitia et peccata quæ dicuntur mixti fori, eatenus puniri et cohiberi per leges civiles, quatenus supposito hoc statu reipublicæ christianæ illam perturbant, et magna nocumenta illi afferunt etiam quoad suam pacem, et externam felicitatem ac conservationem (Ibid).

only in the abstract, therefore, that state power is "everywhere *substantially the same* in infidel and protestant as well as in Catholic nations." In the abstract it is the same in China as in France; but in the concrete it is not the same in Genghis Khan as in Charlemagne. The Doctor closes his remarks on the Christian and non-Christian state with these words:

> I do not make nor admit the distinction between state and state my critics demand of me, because (1) it is unfounded, (2) *it implies that the government of the United States is not Christian, an assumption I regard as untrue in its full extent* (Italics ours). Are my critics conscious of the unenviable position to which they are driven by denying that the state has the right to educate?

That the distinction is not *unfounded*, we have sufficiently shown. Nor can we see that it throws any unfavorable light on the government of these states. Americans, to our thinking, do not wish to seem more Christian than they really are, and would only enjoy a laugh at the expense of those whose ill-timed zeal would endeavor to make them seem more Christian than they actually wish to be. We cannot see the connection of the question—whether the government of the United States is Christian or non-Christian—with the subject on hand; unless it is this, that Dr. Bouquillon would like to sound his opponents on this delicate matter. Well, we shall try to give a solution according to the Doctor's own admissions.

a. " That the government of the United States is not Christian " is " an assumption I regard as *untrue in its full extent*" (Italics ours, p. 14, l. 11–12).

b. "As to this country, it may be said truly that it is Christian *in a certain sense*" (Italics Dr. Bouquillon's, p. 13, l. 9–10).

c. " The acceptation by the state of the divine law . . . has two aspects, *negative* and *positive* (Italics ours). The negative is the obligation on the part of the state to make no enactments contrary to spiritual interests. The positive . . . is the active concurrence of the state with the Church in procuring and furthering spiritual interests" (p. 12 foot). Now these distinctions are well taken with Suarez and the Vatican theologians (Schema note 45). A state in the latter sense is *positively* Christian, and in the former sense is *negatively* Christian. The American states do bind themselves not to enact any laws contrary to religion or to spiritual interests, as long as these do not conflict with public order and morality; but they do not actively concur with the Church in procuring spiritual interests. Therefore according to Dr. Bouquillon the American states are *negatively Christian.*

But does the Doctor not see that our states are *negatively* Jewish, Mohammedan, Theosophian, Ingersollian, Christian-scientist, as well? Their respective governments assume the same negative obligations to all those sects as towards Christianity, so long as their public worship does not clash with public order. In his reference to Webster's eloquent plea for the Christianity of our government the Doctor should have informed the reader that the court, on that occasion, decided against Webster.

The Doctor has, therefore, made a weak point for the Christianity of our government. We think that a more successful plea might be made for the Christian character of our national and state constitutions. The Doctor, therefore, does well to refer the reader to Aug. Carlier's *République Américaine;* else he himself might be driven to that "unenviable position" against which he cautions his opponents.

The United States government, or the American state, therefore, may be Christian or non-Christian, as far as Dr. Bouquillon's argument is concerned. But what shall we say of the American *public school?* There's the rub. The Doctor will hardly assert that the American public school is Christian. We have read a voluminous and elaborate digest of the laws and regulations that govern public schools in some thirty-eight states of this Union,[1] and we have not found that any cognizance was taken of the Christian religion and of Christian morals as part of the programme of studies. There we found under the heading *Morals* and *Manners*, "truthfulness," "kindness to animals," and even "love to God and man," but nothing specifically Christian; we found in some places "opening with prayer and Bible-reading without note or comment;" which, for the rest is no more Christian than it is Jewish; but all this has been since then in most states declared unconstitutional by the courts.[2] The non-Christian character of the schools is no mere theory; the principle is practically acted upon. We could name an American High School—we believe one of the best in the country—, for whose teachers we have the highest esteem, as an illustration of the non-Christian character of the public school.

[1] Cf. Report of the Commissioner of Education, 1870.
[2] Cf. Bardeen School. Law pp. 50 sq.

As we have been credibly informed, in a meeting of the faculty of said High School, it was suggested *bona fide* by a distinguished member that the name of Christ should not be used in the customary prayers, as being offensive to the Jews, who frequented the institution. The suggestion was favorably entertained and, as we have been given to understand, subsequently acted upon. We do not mention this fact as derogatory to the American public school, nor in any way discreditable to the faculty of the High School referred to. If we have any fault to find, it is that in said High School prayer was not abolished altogether. This, we think, would have been more consistent with the present laws and usages regulating our public schools. We would only illustrate the fact that, although our government may in some sense, be called Christian, yet our public schools are decidedly non-Christian; and "all the water of Neptune's great ocean" will not wash them clean of this "damned spot."

Suppose we did grant Dr. Bouquillon that there was no distinction between the Christian and the non-Christian state, between the state *in statu naturæ lapsæ et reparatæ,* and the state *in statu naturæ puræ,* what then? All the worse for Dr. Bouquillon. The Doctor knows as well as we do that moral philosophers treat this question independently of all positive religion; and yet the Doctor knows by this time that the entire school of Catholic philosophers denies the state the *right to educate* in the proper sense of this word. Moreover, the Doctor's "impregnable" argument is taken from the standpoint of pure nature; but we have shown that the "impregnable" argument proves nothing. Whether or not, therefore, the Doctor grants greater power to the Christian than to the non-Christian ruler, his position is untenable. By his present unmistakable attitude in regard to the Christian state the Doctor has only weakened his position.

III. EDUCATION AND INSTRUCTION.

Dr. Bouquillon persists in the *synonymous use of education and instruction* (p. 14, ll. 15-28).

I am blamed for confusing *Teaching* with *Education*, and urging in favor of the right to educate arguments that avail only for the right to teach. The answer is easy and very clear.

The words Teaching, Education, may be used in a strict or in a loose sense. In the strict sense, education is the formation of the heart, the will, the interior dispositions of the soul; it is the imparting of virtuous habits. Teaching in the strict sense is the formation of the mind, the communication of truth. In a loose sense education and teaching equally mean the complete formation of man in general, or of man in any special avocation, of the Christian, the priest, the soldier, and the like. But it is ordinarily in regard to the special work done in schools that the terms *teaching* and *education* are used; and in reference to this they are commonly employed almost indiscriminately.

We must confess that we have little fault to find with the Doctor for this indiscriminate use of the terms, since the official language (it might more properly be called jargon) of state pedagogics would have it so. In the vocabulary of state school politics we find *education, instruction, teaching; Erziehung, Unterricht; éducation, instruction, enseignement; educazione, istruzione, insegnamento,* &c., &c., used indiscriminately. In a scientific treatise, however, education in its stricter sense should be distinguished from education in its wider sense, education as a complex process from education or instruction as a special function. What we chiefly objected to the Doctor (supra p. 12 sq.) was that he takes education in the vague sense, not merely of instruction, but in the meaning of incidental communication of ideas, and applies what may be said of education in this loose sense to education strictly so-called—applies to education as such what may be affirmed only of a very subordinate function in education. This is a fallacy, which the Doctor, consciously or unconsciously, made use of to prove the right of the individual to teach, i. e., to educate.

It is strange that the reverend Doctor cannot even now prevail upon himself to adopt a correct definition of education. Instead of conceiving *education* as the entire complex process of the training, development, formation of all the human faculties—physical, intellectual, moral—the direction of the child or youth on the way that he should go, in relation to his Creator and last end, to his neighbor, and to himself; instead of making teaching, or instruction, a subordinate function or means, he falls into the new error of making education and instruction co-ordinate functions; and that without proof or precedent, that we could discover. We have, we may say without boasting, read considerably in this field of literature, and we do not recollect to have met a single author worthy of notice who takes this view of education. We have quoted Cardinal Gibbons' definition which is certainly the result of careful thought and collation of the best authors. We might cite Herbert Spencer from the agnostic camp, who takes substantially the same view of education. We treated the subject ourselves in two different publications. We may be allowed to place here our view of the nature of education as briefly laid down in the *Rights of Our Little Ones* (questions, 1, 4, 10).

Q. 1. "What is education?

"Education, which, according to the meaning of the word, signifies a bringing out, is such a harmonious development of the faculties of man by external training as to facilitate for him the attainment of his end in this life and in the life to come.

Q. 4. "Which are the chief functions of education?

"The chief functions of education are four, viz.:

a. The *physical*, or that appertaining to the development and perfection of the body and bodily faculties.

b. "The *mental*, or that appertaining to the development and culture of the mind.

c. "The *moral*, or that appertaining to the formation and discipline of the will and affections.

d. "The *religious*, which, though essentially belonging to the mental and moral development of man, has for its special object to fit man for the attainment of his last end.

"Hence we speak of physical, intellectual, moral and religious education as distinct, though not always different, much less separate functions.

Q. 10. "Can a moral and mental education be imparted without religion?

"A moral and mental education cannot be imparted without religion:

a. "Because morality or virtue, especially Christian virtue, cannot exist without being based on religious truths and motives, fostered by religious practices, and sustained by supernatural aid, which can only be obtained by acts of religion.

b. "Because the mind of man cannot be perfected according to the intent of the Creator while the most momentous truths—the truths of religion—are withheld from it."

For the very reason that education is a complex process, an organic development consisting of various inseparable functions—physical, intellectual, moral and religious—we always maintained that the state *per se* has no right to educate. The intellectual, moral and religious education are inseparable from one another. We cannot,

The Right of Individuals and Associations.

therefore, leave one to the state, another to the parent, and a third to the Church. "The religious side of education" as the Doctor rightly remarks (p. 15, l. 11) "is not within the province of the state." Therefore neither is the moral side of education; for as the Doctor again truly remarks (p. 23, l. 11–12) *"it is impossible to separate morality from religion";* and, we would add, it is impossible to separate morality *and* religion from the careful training, formation and instruction of the intellect, much less from *education* taken in its entirety. Hence we conclude that the instruction of childhood and youth is not and cannot be within the competence of the state. The Doctor, therefore, speaks volumes against himself when he says (p. 15).

Having carefully shown that *the religious side of education is not within the province of the state* (Italics ours), I proved that the state has a right to found schools, "to provide education in the letters, sciences, and arts," to inculcate the moral principles of the natural law,—in a word, to provide and to exercise authority over all that part of education which concerns the temporal welfare of human society.

It will be borne in mind that we do not deny the state the right "to found schools, to provide education in letters, sciences and arts" for its own legitimate purposes, and in certain cases which we have stated more than once. The state may "inculcate the moral principles of the natural law" in its own way and within its own sphere by legislation and the administration of justice, but not directly by school instruction or education properly so-called, except in default of those upon whom nature imposes this duty, and to whom it vindicates this right. Whatever construction, therefore, may be put on the Doctor's words—whether instruction or education—it is equally false *that the state has the right special and proper to educate.*

IV. THE RIGHT OF INDIVIDUALS AND ASSOCIATIONS.

The Doctor insists on his argument that *the individual, physical or moral, and, consequently, the state has the right to educate* (p. 15, sq.). We feared that we were doing an injustice to him by supposing (supra p. 15), that he seriously wished to defend this, as an argument. But we now find that we were none too severe in our judgment. He says (p. 15–16):—

I am met with the plea that the argument may be admitted for teaching, but not for educating in the strict sense of the term (F. Holaind, p. 6).—I answer: there is no essential difference between the formation of the mind and that of the heart, if the point under consideration be the right to effect that formation. But let us exchange words and see what kind of argument we get. What is education? The formation of charac ter, the inculcation of virtue, the correction of faults and defects. But every man has the right to inculcate virtue on his neighbor, to correct his neighbor's faults. Among the *works of spiritual mercy*, we find not only the *teaching of the ignorant*, but also the *correction of sinners* (Italics ours), and if you should want to know what that implies, I refer you to Valentia, 2-2, disp. 3, quæst. 10. Correction is " qualiscunque sermo quo quis vel monendo, vel reprehendendo, vel hortando, vel rogando, vel quippiam indicando, vel alia hujusmodi ratione nitatur proximum a peccato revocare et ad officium virtutemque traducere?" Is education anything else? Therefore [!] every individual has the right to educate.

Here, in our humble opinion, Father Holaind was much too lenient to the learned Doctor. If we are to understand by instruction or teaching the formation of the mind or any kind of "methodical and continuous" communication of knowledge, as Dr. Bouquillon (pamph. I, p. 8) defines education with Mons. Sauvé, we deny that any individual may exercise such a function towards any other individual without that individual's consent, or towards any child without the consent of such child's parent, or of the person who takes the place of parent in regard to such child—except in the case in which charity or mercy demands it. The spiritual works of mercy, the Doctor should know, can be exercised only towards the *miserable*, who alone are objects of mercy. But the right of aiding the miserable does not confer the right to teach in the scholastic sense.

This argument [of Father Holaind, quoth the Doctor] reveals a sad confusion, about *right* and the *exercise of a right*. I have the right to practice medicine, but I may not and cannot be a physician except to those who will put themselves under my care. Just so I have the right to teach and to educate; but I can exercise the right only on those who have the goodness to take me as master. *If the client I solicit is sui juris, his consent suffices to give effect to my right:* thus the founder of a religious community gets his right made practical, the right, namely, to give a religious education to those who associate with him, by their consent. *If my would-be client is a child, I must needs get the consent of his parents* (Italics ours). Is my position plain? Must I say in so many words, that when I assert for every individual the right to teach, I do not assert the right to take pupils by the collar and teach them willy nilly? *My right to teach does not imply a right to force myself on others* (Italics ours), but does imply an obligation on the part of others not to hinder my giving education to those who are willing to accept my services as a teacher (p. 16).

There is no confusion here between right and the exercise of a right; for the simple reason that here no *right* exists, as we have shown (supra p. 13) unless a *negative right*, such as I have to dispose of my neighbor's property—i. e., no one has the right to prevent me from justly acquiring it, if my neighbor is ready to part with it. We wonder the Doctor did not perceive that the concessions here made completely undermines his position. A right which can in all cases be lawfully frustrated is no right; but the right of the individual to teach, as the Doctor now admits, is confined to those who "are willing to accept his services as a teacher"; and, "if his client is a child he must get the consent of his parents." Therefore the parents can justly and efficaciously frustrate the right of all individuals either to teach or to educate their children, as long as these are minors; and the pupil himself, if he is *sui juris* can do the same. Consequently, the individual has no right to educate except what he receives from parents, or pupils. And as the Doctor bases the right of corporations on the rights of individuals these too must receive their rights from parents and pupils. Again, since the right of the state to educate is based by the Doctor on the right of corporations, it follows with the same logical necessity that the state cannot educate without the consent of parents, or of pupils, if these are *sui juris*. Consequently, the state has no inherent right to educate, or to force any system, plan or programme of education, on parents or pupils. But if we add, with Leo XIII., that the right of parents to educate their children is inalienable, and indefeasible, that it can neither be extinguished, nor absorbed by the state,[1] what becomes of the right of the state to educate? Verily, the Doctor has here made easy work for his opponents.

We dismiss the long discussion of the rights of corporations tacked on to this argument (pp. 17-19) as impertinent to the subject.

V. RIGHT AND DUTY OF PARENTS AND CHURCH.

In the following two sections on the *Right, Mission (duty), and Authority of parents and of the Church* the Doctor does little more than repeat what he said in his first pamphlet, giving greater emphasis to some passages, and trying to show the unfair dealing of his critics.

1. Here, as in his first pamphlet, in treating of the right of parents, the Doctor supplies an invincible argument that the *state has not the right to educate;* but he has not the heart to draw the inevitable conclusion contained in his premises. He admits that "the rights of parents are sacred and must be respected"; that the duty of parents is "paramount"; that parents "can never lose" their authority (p. 19 —20); but, instead of concluding: *therefore* the state cannot arrogate

[1] Officio sanctissimo. 22. Dec. 1887: Rerum novarum, May 15, 1891.

to itself the right to educate, he feels justified only in asserting that, " if the state establishes public schools, it is bound to take account of the reasonable wishes of parents; and allow them a legitimate share in the carrying on of such schools." He also expresses his preference for municipal schools "as in this country." We fear the Doctor is but poorly informed on the nature of the public school system of this country; else he would not have implied that the municipal system is prevalent in these states. But what if the majority of the municipality itself is agnostic, or indifferent, or even hostile to religion? Have Christian parents any guarantee for the moral and religious education of their children by such municipality, more than by the state or federal government? To these questions the Doctor has no answer.

2. The Doctor (p. 20–21) offers the following apology for his scant treatment of the right, duty and authority of the Church in his first pamphlet:

When I came to treat this part, I found that I had either to spread over many pages, if I wished to be complete, or confine myself to the mere statement of general principles and indication of principal proofs. This latter alternative was imposed on me by the very nature of my work.

Does this justify the omissions we pointed out (supra pp. 8, 47, 49, 51, 53, sq.)? May these objections be disposed of by the remark: *Quod abundat non vitiat?* We leave this to the judgment of the reader.

The discussion of the principles of the natural law and of the relation of Church and state to these fundamental moral truths (pp. 22–23) we have characterized as impertinent to the subject, yet we cannot refrain from drawing the attention of the reader to some of those principles which are directly opposed to the Doctor's main thesis. Thus, for instance, (p. 22 *b*.):—

The precepts of the natural law may be known naturally by the very light of reason, as St. Paul teaches in his epistle to the Romans. But they are known more fully and perfectly by the light of revelation; for *revelation is necessary in order that these precepts should be known by all, easily, certainly, and without any mixture of error* (Italics ours): *ut ab omnibus expedite, firma certitudine et nullo admixto errore cognosci possint.* (Conc. Vat.).

Therefore the precepts of the moral law cannot be known by all with certainty, etc., except through the teaching of the Church, the infallible expounder of revelation. Now, if God embodied those natural truths in His revelation, and instituted an infallible teaching office to explain them, it is certainly not His will that they should be further taught by a fallible and erring school of ministers, comissioners, or superintendents of education.

In passing let us note the ambiguity of the following proposition (p. 22 *e.*):—

The state, which is bound to sanction the principles of moral law, *is* consequently *bound to inculcate* them on the members of society; the Church has a similar duty, but of a higher order, in regard to the faithful; for *these two authorities have both the mission to procure the moral education of men*, though each one at a different point of view (Italics ours).

That the state is bound to "sanction the principles of the moral law" by rewards and punishments we grant; but that it is bound directly to inculcate these principles, otherwise than by laws and judgments, we deny. That the state has any direct mission to procure the "moral education of men" as we understand it in the question on hand, is false; for as the reverend Doctor " was taught by his regretted master, Cardinal Franzelin, in his treatise *de divina traditione et scriptura* (ed. I., p. 110) " " the supernatural moral order comprehends the natural moral order" (Rejoinder pp. 21–22). Therefore in the supernatural order in which by divine goodness, we exist, it is the business of the Church (and, of course, of parents by commission of the Church) to teach this supernatural order. Hence we must conclude that in the supernatural order the state's "occupation's gone," as far as the teaching of morality is concerned, unless we admit a " morale civique " or " independente," or a merely secular or natural morality—which the Doctor as well as ourselves repudiates. For *merely* natural morality, which abstracts from the supernatural end of man, is according to the words of Leo XIII. (*Humanum genus* cited by the Doctor, footnote p. 23), "*civic, free* and *independent*" morality. [1]

Moreover, we draw attention to the following words of Dr. Bouquillon which lead to the same conclusion: " *It is impossible to separate* either politics from morality or *morality from religion* " (p. 23 *f*).

---

[1] Mundi enim opifex idemque providus gubernator Deus: lex æterna naturalem ordinem conservari jubens, perturbari vetans; *ultimus hominum finis multo excelsior rebus humanis extra hæc mundana hospitia constitutus: hi fontes, hæc principia sunt totius justitiæ et honestatis*.... Et sane disciplina morum, quæ Massonum familiæ probatur unice, et qua informari adolescentium ætatem contendunt oportere, ea est quam *civicam* nomniant et *solutam* ac *liberam; scilicet in qua opinio nulla sit religionis inclusa*.

Finally we may be permitted to say that the Doctor might have spared the "final remark" (p. 23, ll. 14-20). His opponents have given some thought to all those bearings of the "natural moral truths"—upon traditionalism and upon the salvation of the heathen.

VI. DR. BOUQUILLON'S ATTITUDE TOWARDS NEUTRAL SCHOOLS.

Here we may be allowed a remark which strikes us as in justice due to Dr. Bouquillon particularly after reading his second pamphlet. It has been asserted by some critics of the Doctor's first pamphlet, that that publication was intended as a plea for the American secular public school. There is nothing, we believe, farther from the truth. No word of the Doctor's can be interpreted in favor of *secular*, *neutral* or *mixed* education. In his second pamphlet he emphatically repudiates this construction of his teaching, and it is but fair to give him credit for it. He says (p. 4):—

> Neither was it my purpose to speak *ex professo* and at length of the obligation of parents to entrust their children to worthy masters and support good schools. Such obligation is of the domain of practical morals, and has been so often defined by competent authority that I might be dispensed from passing my opinion on it. And notwithstanding, have I not expressed my conviction on this very point most unmistakably, since more than once I have asserted in the pamphlet (pp. 10, 20) that *parents have not the right to give to their children an education detrimental to faith and morals, that in the presence of a system of education indifferent to religion the Church has the duty of establishing Christian schools* (Italics ours) ?

Again (p. 20):—

> I have asserted and proved (pp. 10, 16) that it is the duty of parents to give their children education, not education of an indifferent, vague kind, but a civic and *Catholic education*, that will make the children into good citizens and *good Christians ; that this parental duty is strict and paramount* (Italics ours), though by no means a duty of commutative justice,[1] as Father Holaind would hold (p. 10, line 35). Why, then, does he [Father Holaind] quote against me (p. 16), the decree of the Holy See and the American Hierarchy on neutral schools ?[2] Where is the word of mine contrary to those decrees ?

The same is implied (page 34) where the Doctor admits that "the *neutral school* is condemned on principle." There he also makes the admission that "the non-Christian state is not qualified to exercise over Christians its rights in the matter of education," supposing, of

---

[1] We should like to see the Doctor's proof against Father Holaind, that the duty of parents to give the necessary education to their children is not one of *commutative justice*.

[2] "The decrees of the Holy See and the American Hierachy" were quoted by Father Holaind, *not against* the Doctor, but, as by ourselves, to supply a grave omission in the Doctor's pamphlet.

course, all the time that the state has the proper right to educate. And again (p. 34-35):—

Let it be understood that I am here speaking of the *establishment of schools* by the state, *not of the use of such schools by the parents* (Italics ours). Be the state reprehensible or not in establishing schools negatively indifferent, more or less dangerous, the duties of Catholic parents remain those indicated in the Third Council of Baltimore, n. 198, and in the *Instruction* given by the Holy See, 24 Nov., 1875.

The Doctor then goes on to quote the *Instruction* of the Holy See to the American hierarchy. We wish to put this on record not only for the sake of Dr. Bouquillon's opponents and in fairness to Dr. Bouquillon himself, but chiefly for the sake of his friends. These have no right to cite him in favor of neutral schools in any shape or form, or for any kind of state education which is not Catholic to the fullest extent. His friends have, therefore, been more cruel to Dr. Bouquillon than have been his adversaries; and they have done him real and deep injustice by invoking his authority in favor of any system, or plan, or compromise, that would in any way interfere with the fully Catholic character of the school.

We cannot, therefore, conceal our astonishment at the fact that, while the Doctor so keenly resents what he considers unfairness on the part of his opponents, he is so patient of this injustice done to him by his friends. We sincerely hope that his next *rejoinder* will be directed not against his opponents, but against those who abuse his authority in their endeavors to secularize our Catholic parochial schools: *ab inimicis meis libera me!*

VII. THE IMPREGNABLE ARGUMENT.

In reasserting the right of the state to educate (p. 24 sq.) the Doctor defends, first, his "impregnable," argument, and, secondly, his authorities, we have treated these two points so fully in the body of our essay that we might well be excused from further noticing them here.

"Father Holaind (p. 15) criticizes the major, the minor [of the Doctor's "impregnable" argument] and finds that the conclusion does not follow from the premises." So do we (supra p.15 sq.); and we come to the same conclusion; so do numerous other critics; and all find the argument faulty. Major, minor and conclusion, as we have seen, must be considerably modified. The Doctor says he made the necessary qualifications and printed them in *Italics* in various parts of his pamphlet. Very true; but why did the Doctor not make the necessary qualifications here (pamphlet I. p. 12), where they were needed to prevent the false conclusion: that *the state had the right to teach, i. e., to educate*. And why does the Doctor shift his position now? His position was that the state has the right *special and proper to educate*, i. e., *the right of establishing schools, appointing teachers, prescribing methods and programmes of study, in the same way as it governs and judges, viz.: through delegates fitted for such functions*. He now takes his stand with Prof. Moulart, who has not a single word to justify the assumption, that he attributes to the state the right to educate.

Meanwhile, I maintain what I have said on this point, and I repeat it, making my own words of Prof. Moulart, of the University of Louvain. "Civil instruction, after religious instruction, is the first means of civilizing a people. The first duty of the public power is to *favor and propagate knowledge*. The state is bound to *promote* scientific, literary, technical or industrial training, to *safeguard* its subjects against fraud and injustice by *providing means* (preceding Italics ours) whereby they can know *persons* and *things*, and know the laws that regulate *relations* between persons, the *enjoyment* and *use* of things and the *exercise* of rights." (p. 26).

Is there a word in this extract from Prof. Moulart to imply that *education strict and proper* by the state is a legitimate means of procuring the common good, or that education is an inherent right of the state? The Professor does insist on "civil instruction" but not necessarily by the state; he does insist on the duty of the state to "favor," "propagate," "promote," "safeguard," "provide means" for the diffusion of useful knowledge; but where is the *right to educate?*

In fact Dr. Bouquillon himself no longer insists, in his conclusion, on the *right of the state to educate;* but only on the right of "giving voluntary aid to teachers" and "establishing schools," if it "thinks necessary the establishment of schools." But he immediately submits that this implies "education" as well as "teaching"; and proves this by the authority of St. Thomas and Suarez (ibid.).

But, insists the Rev. Father, this proves at most that the state can give teaching, but not education. Excuse me, *it proves both* (Italics ours). Morality is not less necessary than knowledge. Does not St. Thomas teach that there is no virtue the acts of which the state may not prescribe, and Suarez, that "the end of civil law is the temporal happiness of the commonwealth, which cannot be obtained without the observance of all the moral virtues; hence, the civil law may prescribe in the domain of all the moral virtues."[1]

[1] I.-II q. 96, a. 3. "Nulla est virtus de cujus actibus lex præcipere non possit." *De*

Now, we beg the Rev. Doctor, to excuse us. This argument of his *proves neither* the right of *teaching* nor the right of *educating*. We have already shown from the Doctor's own teaching that the state cannot *teach* morality. St. Thomas and Suarez in the passages cited do not speak of teaching but of law, precept and punishment. They assert that the civil power can legislate and, of course, also judge and punish in the matter of all the moral virtues (e. g., punish drunkenness, theft and public disorder, enforce military service, if necessary, &c.). Both these authors, however, take very good care to add, that the civil power cannot enforce all acts of all virtues, as, for instance, virginity and other acts of perfection that are only of council.¹ Whence the Doctor should have concluded, that the state has no right to educate or to enforce any certain kind of education.

And immediately, after thus confounding teaching with governing, legislating and judging once more, the Doctor rates Father Holaind for noticing such a trifling mistake in his first pamphlet.

To this argument [that is, the "impregnable"] I added a cursory remark of minor importance, that the state necessarily teaches, if not in schools, at least in its laws and juridical verdicts. The Rev. Father answers that legislating and judging are not quite the same thing as holding school. I knew that. In order that no one might impute to me so childish a *naiveté*, I wrote, p. 12, "that the civil power does necessarily teach *in one way or another*" when it legislates and judges. The Rev. Father might very well have passed so secondary an observation, but he is wrong in calling it *metaphorical*. It is not in a metaphorical, but in a very proper sense, that divine law in Scripture is called *Lux, Lucerna, Lumen*, and that St. Basil says, *Lex doctrix et magistra* (p. 26-27).

Here the Doctor clears himself of one "childish *naiveté*" and falls into another, by maintaining that education as applied to governing and judging is not *metaphorical*, and that the examples alleged by him are not metaphorical but employed in their proper sense. When the Doctor exclaims (p. 42): "Was the *light* [i. e., of his first pamphlet] so dazzling that it hurt the eyes of some [of his opponents]?" Does he understand *light* in its proper, not in a metaphorical, sense? If

---

Leg., lib. III., c. 12, n. 8. "Finis juris civilis est felicitas vera naturalis politicæ civitatis; hæc autem obtineri non potest sine observantia omnium virtutum moralium; ergo in omnibus potest præcipere jus civile."

¹ Non tamen de omnibus actibus omnium virtutum lex humana præcipit, sed solum de illis qui ordinabiles sunt ad bonum commune.—S. Thom. Ibid.

Dicendum est leges civiles non posse fieri de omnibus actibus omnium et singularum virtutum..... Non enim potest præcipi virginitas, etiamsi optimus actus virtutis sit, et idem est de aliis actibus, qui proprie dicuntur consiliorum. Suarez, Ibid. n. 11.

so, we must furthermore consult, not the divine, but the oculist. (Cf. supra p. 18).

VIII. FACTS AND DOCUMENTS.

The historical arguments adduced (pp. 27-29) prove nothing, as we have shown (supra p. 55 sq.), because they suppose a union, or agreement, between Church and state. The same may be said of the appeal to the German Centre party (p. 5-6). We have had a fair opportunity of observing the policy of the German Catholic Centre for the last twenty years, and we have followed events in Germany with some interest. Now, if we rightly understand the tendency of this illustrious Catholic party, it is this: *to secure to the Church that freedom which is guaranteed by the constitution.* But, according to the constitutions of the various German states there is an understanding between Church and state regulated by concordats, or agreements, which grant to the state the right to the control of schools, while they secure to the Church the fullest liberty to superintend the education in her own schools. In Germany each denomination has its own separate schools, established and supported by the government. Compulsory education, like many other paternal provisions of German legislation, is a *fait accompli*, and does not lie within the programme of the Centre party. For the present they are satisfied with freedom of education as guaranteed by the constitution; and, as we hold with von Hammerstein and other Catholic authors, compulsory education, if enforced with the consent of the parents and of the Church, contains nothing objectionable. For the rest, the policy of the Centre party has been strictly in accord with the principles of eminent German Catholic publicists, as represented by von Hammerstein, Stökl, Cathrein, Lehmkuhl and others; who are all the most staunch defenders of parental right against state aggression.

We must protest against the insinuation (p. 27 text and foot-note) that Father Holaind attributes any further virtue to the "oil that shone on Charlemagne's brow" than that it was symbolic of the union of Church and state and of the sacredness of the charge entrusted to kings—not to speak of the general effects of the sacramentals of the Church. All Father Holaind says is that "the brow of Charlemagne is glossy with the sacred oil." But the Doctor has already proved himself a bad exponent of metaphors. The learned foot-note (p. 27) we must, therefore, regard as altogether superfluous and uncalled for.

The Doctor appeals to the letter of Leo XIII to the Cardinal vicar June 26, 1878. But to no purpose. The Pope here deals with existing facts. If instead of *neutral* schools the municipal government of Rome had established Catholic elementary schools and put them under the direction of the Church, who would deny its right to do so? This, as we often repeated, would not imply the exercise of the right of education, but only the right and duty of aiding and promoting education. But to establish neutral schools for so-called civic education and to control these to the exclusion of the influence of the Church and of the parents interested, implies the right to educate. This is precisely what the Pope condemned in that very letter—the establishment of schools in which religion and Christian morality are separated from secular teaching (v. supra p. 33). Therefore the Pope implicitly denies the right of the municipality of Rome, as then and now constituted, to *educate* the Catholic children of Rome; whereas if said municipality were Christian and, in accord with the Church, founded and conducted Christian schools, the Pope would probably have sanctioned and lauded its efforts, though it was but the creation of a band of robbers.

We must likewise protest against the construction put on the Pope's teaching in the Encyclical *Immortale Dei* (p. 29 ll. 15–22).

In the Encyclical *Immortale Dei*, Leo XIII makes a strong appeal to Catholics to take an active part in the politics of their country, even where the constitution is rationalistic, and does not recognize the Church. He advises them especially not to neglect municipal politics. Now, why? *Please attend: because schools are of the jurisdiction of municipalities* (Italics ours), and Catholics should not neglect this most powerful means of assuring to their offspring a good education.

The passage referred to literally translated is this: "It is also of importance for the public welfare, prudently to devote attention to the administration of municipal affairs and herein to use the greatest care and endeavor that provision be made on the part of the municipality (publice) for the religious and moral instruction of the youth in a manner becoming Christians."[1] Here there is not a word to

---

[1] "Illud etiam publicæ salutis interest, ad rerum urbanarum administrationem conferre sapienter operam, in eaque studere maxime et efficere, ut adolescentibus ad religionem, ad probos mores informandis ea ratione, qua æquum est Christianis, publice consultum sit."

imply that "*schools are of the jurisdiction of municipalities.*" But Christian men are exhorted (since the municipal governments actually in most places do control the schools) to see that such provisions are made as may save the Christian character of the schools. To this the reader will "please attend."

Finally, the concordat of August 18, 1886, with the Prince of Montenegro, proves what all concordats prove, that the Church may cede some of her rights, in regard to education and similar departments of her jurisdiction, to the temporal power, whether the latter be vested in a Catholic, Protestant, schismatic, or infidel.

IX. Dr. Bouquillon's Authorities Once More.

Having thus endeavored to defend his "impregnable" argument and the historical reasons by which he tried to back it up, the Doctor comes to the defence of his authorities. He says (p. 29-30):—

Finally, I brought (p. 14) to the support of my thesis the authority of some serious publicists of the day. I selected from Austria and Germany two Jesuits, Costa-Rossetti and Hammerstein; from France, Mgr. Sauvé, who, for his knowledge of the positive science, and for the accuracy of his judgment, is recognized as a man of the first order; from Italy, I chose Cardinal Zigliara, a Dominican. I might have added others; I regret, especially, the omission of the illustrious Bishop of Mayence, Mgr. Ketteler. But these were surely sufficient.

We have put the teaching of these "serious publicists" before our readers at full length, even at the risk of trespassing on their patience and on the kindness of our publishers, giving not only those passages which were manifestly against the Doctor's position, but also those that seem to favor him. Now we have only to refer the reader to those extracts (supra pp. 18-43).

The Doctor regrets the omission of the late Mons. von Ketteler on the list of his authorities. As we have taken the liberty of supplying in these pages much graver omissions of the reverend Doctor we shall also cheerfully make up for this rather pardonable oversight on his part.

First, Monsignor von Ketteler most forcibly emphasizes and uncompromisingly insists upon the inalienable and inviolable rights of parents and of the Church. Secondly, Monsignor von Ketteler strongly insists on the organic union of Church and state, and considers everything that would in any way loosen this union as destructive and dangerous. These rights safeguarded, and this union supposed, Monsignor von Ketteler, in accordance with the positive law of Germany, and in accordance with the opinion of the positive German law school (he cites Stahl, who is refuted by Hammerstein, Cathrein, Rossetti, Th. Meyer, &c.), grants the state the right to enforce compulsory education, or prescribe a minimum of elementary instruction.[1] Under such conditions, we believe that few Catholic writers would object to a reasonable and moderate provision for enforcing a limited amount of instruction.

Such is the doctrine of Ketteler. It practically differs very little from that of Hammerstein and others, although Ketteler bases his opinions on the teaching of a school of jurists which Hammerstein and Catholic writers generally reject.

The practical question for us in America, however, as I have repeated more than once, is not whether the state considered in itself can enforce compulsory education or not; or whether a given state with the consent of parents and of the Church can do so; but whether a *purely secular* state like ours (call it Christian or non-Christian), can impose a system of compulsory education, or enjoin a certain plan, programme, minimum, or standard, of obligatory instruction on the children of Christian parents. We have been unable to find a solution for this problem in the works of Mons. von Ketteler, all excellent though they be. Mons. von Ketteler was an eminently practical as well as learned man. He wrote German for Germans, as Mon. Suavé writes French for Frenchmen; and we should endeavor to write American for Americans.

For the rest, what Bishop Ketteler thought of the existing system of compulsory education in Germany, which has been of late emphatically commended by pronounced admirers of Dr. Bouquillon,[2] may be concluded from the following words: " A system of education such as modern liberalism seeks to establish, as an independent state institution, divorced from family and Church— with *direct compulsion in the elementary schools, and indirect compulsion in the higher schools*, in as much as the attendance of state schools is necessary as a qualification

---

[1] Cf. Freiheit, Auctoritat und Kirche, 4 ed. Maniz 1862 pp. 182-219.

[2] Cf. *Northwestern Chronicle* January 1, 1892, letter dated Berlin (?). The *Church Progress* of St. Louis positively asserts that said letter was concocted in Baltimore, for the secular press—manifestly in the interest of the cause which Dr. Bouquillon champions. See *Progress* January 16, 1892.

for public offices—*is the most destructive and degrading intellectual and moral thraldom.* . . . The conduct of the emperor [Julian the Apostate] is a gentle persecution compared with that which is planned by modern liberalism against Christianity; for at that time *compulsory education* had not yet been heard of. Julian would only deprive the Christians of higher education; but the state school in the sense of modern liberalism is an intellectual prison, into which the children of Christian parents are cast, to rob them of their Christian faith."[1]

We can, therefore, safely say, after examining every single authority the Doctor has produced that not one of them sustains him in his main thesis *that the state has the right to teach, i. e., to educate.* And yet the Doctor grows wroth with those critics who but insinuate what we have proved to evidence. He says:—

Father Holaind slyly insinuates (p. 4) that these references deserve a relative confidence. Father E. A. Higgins, S.J., is bolder; he plainly tells the readers of the *Catholic News* that he has carefully looked up my references, and that of all the writers quoted by me not one gives to the state the right of education as I have formulated it, that is, the right to establish schools, pay teachers, prescribe programmes; not a single one even holds my opinion to be probable. Evidently some one does not know how to read, or is lying to the public [! ! !]. That some one is either Father E. A. Higgins, S.J., or Dr. Bouquillon. As no one is judge in his own cause, I produce the documents and appeal to the public. Let its verdict be Father Higgins' punishment or mine (p. 30).

Father Higgins, who is the chief object of the Doctor's resentment, has promptly been heard from in his own defence. In an open letter to the Doctor printed in the *Catholic News* Jan. 21, 1892, he says:—

"You complain that my criticism was unfair. My dear Doctor, I do not admit that charge. It was not unfair to show some of the weak points of your argument. That was all I did. I did not pretend to do more. I did not misrepresent your argument. An impartial reader would not say so. You object that I will not allow as upholding your thesis a single one of the authorities you so ostentatiously array on your side. You resent that sort of criticism. Well, dear Doctor, it is a question of fact. The best of these publicists, such as Jansen, Hammerstein, Costa-Rossetti, Zigliara and Taparelli, have already been quoted against you, as denying to the state in itself the right to educate. I ventured to say that, so far as I could

[1] L. c. p. 215-216.

discover, not one of your authorities directly supports the thesis that the *state has the right to educate.* I say so still."

" I have a right to insist that you use the word *educate* in the ordinary acceptation of the term. I have a right to insist that you continue to use it in the same meaning wherever it occurs: in the same meaning in your *Rejoinder* as in your first pamphlet. If you are pleased to change its meaning now, and to take the word in a loose sense for '*organizing schools, paying teachers, prescribing programmes*,' which can all be done by delegated authority, why did you not so define yourself in your pamphlet? You spoke there of authority *in se;* of state authority over all schools. You cite authors to prove that the state can provide instruction and schools according to the wishes and needs of the people, as Hammerstein puts it. Who denies that? Does that prove your thesis that the state in itself has primarily and by its own authority *the right to educate?* Are you to have the privilege of playing fast and loose with the most important terms? And if you choose to shift your ground, why should I be guilty of the same confusion? I challenged the assertion that the great publicists you named, sustained you in the thesis that the state in itself, of its own authority, has *the right to educate.* Those I have named above do not maintain that thesis. You have not proved that they do. You have proved a different thing, which was not in question. They admit that the state can aid parents in the work of education by providing instruction and schools and managing the same according to the wishes and needs of the parents. No one denies that. But that was not your thesis."

Dr. Bouquillon, however, completely refutes himself in the succeeding paragraph. While endeavoring to prove to the public that it is Father E. A. Higgins, S.J., who "does not know how to read, or is lying to the public," he manages to establish with perplexing evidence that it is somebody else who "does not know how to read, or is lying to the public." We cite his argument in full, to avoid even the possibility of unfairness, adding our own Italics to his.

I have quoted Costa-Rossetti, Hammerstein, Sauvé, Zigliara. Here are the texts. Costa-Rossetti, *Inst. Eth. et juris nat.*, th. 175, p. 691, 1st ed.: "Auctoritas civilis quidem *scholas fundare et a se fundatas dirigere potest;* sed per se prohibere nequit ne cives ipsi scholas etiam publicas erigant, ab ipsis erectas ordinent et dirigant, quin tamen absolutam docendi libertatem concedere possit."—Hammerstein, *De Ecclesia et Statu*, 1st ed., ii, 2, p. 98: " Concedimus ipsius (status) esse *scholas fundare, si opus*

Supplement.—Dr. Bouquillon's Rejoinder.

sit, ut parentes meliorem nanciscantur opportunitatem ad liberos instruendos;" item iii. 3, p. 146: *Scholæ publicæ* tum ab Ecclesia tum a potestate civili *institui possunt ;*" again, iii, p. 182: "Negare non potest, statui jura quædam *circa* liberorum educationem et scholas competere. Ipsius enim est, supplere familiam. Hinc primo parentibus *media offere* potest, ut melius et efficacius educationi provideant. Quod facit *scholas fundando et dotando* secundum parentum necessitates et vota."—Sauvé, *Questions Sociales*, c. 10, p. 269-271 : L'Etat a de lui-même *le droit d'enseigner* . . . ce qu'il est licite de communiquer à d'autres. Oui, l'état a *le droit d'ouvrir des écoles*, qui, sans préjudicier aux droits de l'Eglise, à ceux des familles et des individus, peuvent être *nécessaires ou utiles* au bien social, dont l'état est juge. . . . *Entendu de la sorte*, [i. e., ouvrir des écoles . . . necessaires ou utiles. . .] le droit d'enseigner peut-il être raisonnablement dénié à l'état ? Ne serait-ce pas lui refuser le droit de communiquer à d'autres ce qui est bon et utile, et même d'accomplir ce qui peut être pour lui un devoir ? . . . Ma thèse est donc celle-ci: Le pouvoir civil a été investi par Dieu du droit de procurer le bien cummun temporel, et par là même de *favoriser et d'ouvrir au besoin des écoles* qui contribuent à ce bien. . . . La thèse opposée à la nôtre qui refuserait à l'état tout droit d'enseigner [i. e., de favoriser et d'ouvrir au besoin des écoles] ne nous paraît pas probable."—Zigliara, *Phil. Mor.*, lib. ii, c. 1, a. 5, n. 7: "Statui jus simul et officium inesse *procurandi media aptiora ad educationem* tum *intellectualem* tum *moralem*, negat profecto nemo. Cum enim in societatem civilem formandam familiæ conveniant, ut auxilia a communitate habeant, quæ solæ aut nullo modo aut nonnisi imperfecte in prompto habere possunt, necesse est ut de jure et officio socialis auctoritatis sit *illa media aptiora suppeditare.*"—Cavagnis, *Instit. jur. publ. eccl.*, iii, n. 89, p. 59 : "Facultatem statui civili *scholas instituendi* nemo unquam denegavit."

Let the reader compare these extracts which have been carefully culled by the Doctor and taken out of their context to support his thesis with the same as we have rendered them in translation, carefully noting the context and supplying those passages of these authors, in which they expressly or implicitly deny the state the right to educate; and then let him judge between Dr. Bouquillon and Father Higgins. For the rest, we have only to read those extracts themselves to perceive that not a single one of the authors cited attributes to the *state the right to educate*. They do vindicate to the state the right to *found schools*, where useful or necessary; they attribute to the state certain rights *in regard to* education,—*to offer suitable means*, or the right to *teach* in the sense of *communicating lawful knowledge, opening and favoring schools* (Sauvé). But not a single passage is to be found in all these authors to imply that the state has the *right to educate* in the common acceptation of this term.

And yet Dr. Bouquillon, after reviewing this array of authorities, who are all against him, goes on to vent his wrath on Father Higgins (p. 31).

Is comment needed? Let not Father E. A. Higgins say that those writers mean *teaching*, not *education*: they speak of *schools* and, therefore, of [the means of] education, as well as teaching, and at any rate they use expressly the word *education* [does this imply the right to educate?]. Let not Father Higgins say that those writers allow no probability to my thesis; it is to his they give no value whatsoever! Hammerstein and Costa-Rossetti did not even deign to discuss his opinion [!!]; Sauvé expressly says it is not probable [!!"]; Cavagnis and Zigliara assert that nobody ever taught it [i. e., that the state has not the right to establish schools, and supply suitable means]. Let not Father Higgins hereafter say what he has said. But let me say that Father E. A. Higgins has given to the world an instance of audacious negation in the face of truth [!] such as I have never met with. To break down my thesis he would make me a forger [!!]. I resent it.

This specimen of controversy is not very creditable to the learned professor. This wriggling and shifting and juggling plainly show the weakness of the Doctor's position, as does also his bad temper.

This is the outcome of that great array of authorities quoted by Dr Bouquillon for the theory *that the state has the right to educate*. They have vanished into thin air, and not one of them is found to support him in the moment of trial. And these are the very same authorities that formed the stock in trade of the panegyrists of state education in some portions of the so-called Catholic press of this country for the last twelve months and more. These, together with the theologian of the Vatican, are the authorities which were paraded in the New York *Independent* of June 4, 1891, to prove to the American non-Catholic world a *concensus* of Catholic theologians in favor of state education as against the parochial school system enjoined on the Catholics of this country not only by the divine law, but also by the decrees of the Holy See, and by their own national conciliar legislation. We were then solicited to examine and expose this fallacy We did examine the authorities; but we persistently refused to publish the result of our investigation, until it became an imperative duty to do so. It seems to have been the disposition of a special providence that this entire arsenal should explode, not peacemeal in the hands of retailing newspaper writers, but altogether upon the head of the chief manufacturer.¹

¹ Strange conjectures have been expressed on this phenomenal literary performance of Dr. Bouquillon. The freest and boldest that we have seen in print is that of the reviewer in the Civiltà Cattolica (Jan. 2, 1892) who ventures to doubt the genuineness of the work, owing to the enormous difference between it and the Doctor's previous publications. "Infine," says the reviewer, " ci sia lecito di espremere un dubbio che molte volte ci è venuto alla mente nel leggere questo opuscolo. È esso *genuina* opera di quell

What, then, shall we say of the learned Doctor, who as he tells us (p. 41), has thus "taken his stand in the serene regions of science?" Shall we judge him in his own words, and say: either he "does not know how to read, or is lying to the public?" No; far be that from us! There is a *mean;* but the Doctor in the heat of his resentment did not see it. Dr. Bouquillon is not "lying to the public;" Dr. Bouquillon "does know how to read;" but Dr. Bouquillon *did not* read the meaning of those authors, but rather read his own views *into them.*

X. A Fresh Onset.

But the vials of the Doctor's wrath are not yet empty. Before we give him the floor against Father Higgins again, however, we shall submit to the reader the cause of his resentment in Father Higgins' own words, which run as follows:

"Let us turn for a moment to the author's argument. Dr. Bouquillon is bound to prove that "the state has the right to educate." And this is how he proves it: 'Every individual,' he says, 'has by nature the right to teach. Now, an association or society has the same rights as an individual. Therefore the state, which is a civil society or association, has the right to educate.'"

"To anyone acquainted with the rules of correct reasoning, this pretended argument must appear like a caricature. It sounds like a bad joke perpetrated upon the dull members of a class in logic. Why, Mr. Editor, even if the premises were true, the conclusion of this argument would not follow. The right *to teach,* even when it is established and acknowledged, does not imply or include the right *to educate.* The two things are entirely different. The learned Doctor

stesso teologo moralista, la di cui *Theologia moralis fundamentalis* lodammo nel nostro primo quaderno del passato Agosto? Si così è, bisogna pur che esclamiamo: "*Quantum mutatus ab illo!*"

Whoever the author or authors be, Dr. Bouquillon has undoubtedly made it his own by putting his name to it, and he is responsible for whatever it contains, and, in our opinion, also for most of the weapons which have been used in the campaign for the secularization of our Catholic schools long before the pamphlet : *Education: to whom does it belong* was given to the public. Let the curious reader carefully compare the letter in the *Independent* referred to with Doctor Bouquillon's pamphlet, and then let him read Mons. Sauvé's *Questions, etc.,* c. 10, from which most of the raw material is borrowed; and let him judge whether or not "there is method in this madness." Cf. Bouquillon, Theol. mor. fund. Ed. II. p. 408, footnote 5 and p. 410, footnote 1.

knows that the function of *teaching* or *instructing* is only a small element in the work of *education*, and parents may be justified in employing as *teachers* or *instructors* certain persons, to whom they would not intrust the duty of *educating* their children. This then is the first blot in the argument. The conclusion does not follow from the premises.

" But in the second place, the premises themselves are not true. It is not true that 'every individual has by nature the right to teach.' Nature gives no such right. There are many qualities requisite in the one who claims the right to teach. Some of these qualities are intellectual, some are moral; some pertain to knowledge, others to character, to tact, to virtue and to skill. Now, it is plain that nature does not bestow these on every individual. Doubtless every one has a right to qualify himself, if he can, to become a teacher; but this is quite a different thing from saying that 'every one has by nature the right to teach.' The first premise of Dr. Bouquillon's argument, then, is false.

" The second proposition, 'Every society or association has the same right as the individual' is so transparently untrue as to require no refutation. Individual rights are perfectly distinct from those of the family, the state and every other sort of organization. Individuals, as such, have many rights which societies have not, and in the nature of things cannot have. The usurpation by the state of the individual's rights constitutes tyranny or state despotism. To argue from the rights of the individuals to the rights of the state is to argue in favor of the most unlimited state absolutism. The propositions, therefore, that attribute to the state the rights of the individual, is not only false but pernicious."

"Both premises, then, being false, the argument of Dr. Bouquillon falls to the ground. And what shall we say of the logic which is capable of constructing an argument on two false premises? Yet this is the foundation on which Dr. Bouquillon attempts to build up his thesis, namely, a conclusion that is not contained in the premises and a pair of premises which are themselves untrue. And this seems to be the best he can do to sustain, in behalf of the state, a right which every prominent American jurist has invariably attributed to the parent as among his natural and inalienable rights."

Father Higgins criticizes the Doctor's argument as we do, as numerous other critics do, and points out the fallacy. We do not see that he treats the Doctor discourteously; he does not bid him " go to school," as the Doctor asserts; he does not imply that he is untruthful or deceitful; he does not say that this is the Doctor's only argument; but he does insinuate that the argument is a fundamental one in the Doctor's theory. The latter, instead of answering his objection, as became a writer who was solely concerned for the truth of his doctrine, indulges in a strain of invective eloquence, which does little honor to him as a scholar and a controversialist. He says (p. 32-33):—

Before entering upon the study of the right of the state to teach, page 11 of my pamphlet, I threw out a previous consideration in these words : "We ask if the state has the special and proper right of teaching human knowledge. We say *special and proper* right, for there can be no question of a vague and general right; it were unreasonable to refuse to the state that which is granted to every legitimate association." Thereupon the Rev. Father E. A. Higgins, S.J., actually says that this previous remark is all the argument I have for the state's right, he puts this pretended argument in form, declares it a caricature and bids me go to school to learn logic.

He has set up a man of straw and knocks him down. Again I appeal to the fair minded reader and beg him to give verdict. I have gone to school many years ago, to the school of Franzelin, Patrizzi, and Ballerini, S.J., to that same school I go as often as I can. But Father Higgins' school! No, I hie me not thither, it is a school of deceit. And now shall I tarry to justify—not my argument, I have done that just now in answering Father Holaind's objections to my syllogism—but a simple preliminary observation made by the way in one line [We beg to remind the reader that Father Higgins' objection is directed not against this simple "observation," but against a theory to the defence of which the Doctor devotes many pages of his first pamphlet and of his *rejoinder*—i. e., that every individual, whether single or corporate, has the right to educate] ? I will merely say that I am not the first who has made this observation, and that it has been advanced in favor of the Church, especially in lands where the Church is not recognized as a perfect society. Father E. A. Higgins, S.J., whose name is attached to no great scientific work that I know, may apply to Mgr. Sauvé, author of first class works, the epithets with which he has honored me, may bid him go back to school! Here I drop the Rev. Father. May the reader excuse me for wasting on him so much of his and my time. I should not have stopped to answer his unfair criticism had it not been signed with a name, the religious affixes of which attached to the criticism credit in the eyes of Catholics.

We shall let Father Higgins answer for himself. He says in the open letter already referred to:—

"You are angry because I summarized a fundamental argument of yours and presented it in such a manner as to show its flimsiness. It looked so easy to prove by a bit of philosophizing and generalizing that the state has the right to educate. Borrowing a sentiment of Mgr. Sauvé's to the effect that *everyone who has the ability* has a natural right to teach those who may choose to listen to him, you changed it into the general proposition that *everybody* has a natural right to teach. Now an association or society (you went on to say) has the same rights as an individual; and the state which is a moral person can fit itself to impart instruction as well a physical person. Therefore (you concluded) the state has the the *right to educate*, which is your conclusion, not Mgr. Sauvé's. This was substantially your argument. I did not change it. I said it sounded like a caricature of reasoning. Here was a conclusion not contained in the premises. Even granting the premise true, this conclusion would not follow from them. And then, dear Doctor, I went on to show that the premises themselves as you stated them, as you changed them from the careful wording of Mgr. Sauvé into your own general propositions, were not true. Now if you were satisfied that the premises furnished you by Mgr. Sauvé were true, why did not you limit your conclusion to the same terms and say, 'Therefore the state has the right *to teach*'? Why? Because your thesis required you to say 'Therefore the state has the right *to educate;*' and you said it, though in saying it you introduced a fourth term into your syllogism. I ventured to call that manner of argument a caricature. A syllogism with four terms is not generally regarded in the schools of logic as a creditable performance. Does it become respectable in the school of Dr. Bouquillon? You grow angry over it as if I had constructed the false syllogism and palmed it off on you. The argument was not mine, it was yours. You were guilty of it, not I."

"And now, dear Doctor, in your *Rejoinder*, how do you explain away this choice specimen of reasoning? You fall back on the words of Mgr. Suavé, which you now quote in full with the saving clauses that make them essentially different from the propositions in your first pamphlet. But you take very good care to leave out altogether the obnoxious conclusion "Therefore the state has *the right to educate.*" Why do you leave it out in the Rejoinder? Because you see now how absurd it would be. And with this *subterfuge* before our eyes, you talk of *a school of deceit*. My dear Doctor, if there is *a school of deceit* in this matter, whose is it? Mine, which fairly stated your illogical argument in full? Or yours, which slyly omits in the *Rejoinder* the offensive and illegitimate conclusion? If there is *a school of deceit*, whose is it? Yours, which practised the sophistry? Or mine, which simply exposed it? If there is *a school of deceit* I know not where to look for it, unless it be where there is a constant juggling with the words *teach, instruct, organize schools,* and *educate,* as if the last were perfectly equivalent to the others, whereas it stands for something essentially different. The right to educate implies jurisdiction. It involves authority and power to compel obedience and to impose the obligation of receiving instruction and training. That power belongs primarily by natural law and divine law to the parents. It cannot be taken from the parent except by usurpation and tyranny. To surrender that right or power to the state is the betrayal of the most sacred right of parents."

This is the case as between Dr. Bouquillon and Father Higgins; and it may be said to be the case between Dr. Bouquillon and ourselves, as we have raised the same objections to his argument. We have put both sides before the public. Let the reader judge for himself. Father Higgins needs no defence on our part. He is not unknown to the American reading public. He treated educational and other social problems on the rostrum and in print, long before the name of Dr. Bouquillon was heard of on this side of the Atlantic; and if " his name is not attached to any great scientific work," as the Doctor takes care to remind us, this is no proof that, if he did write a scientific work, it would not be a good one; as the fact that a man has written one or more learned works is no sure guarantee that he may not sometime be guilty of writing a bad book. We could point to a distinguished author, who has written most meritorious works; and that same learned author consented " at the request of ecclesiastical superiors," to write a book on education, which is admitted by the better and more intelligent class of Catholics of this country to be of very questionable merit. And the same learned author has defended this book by a second work entitled a *Rejoinder to Critics*, which added little to his reputation. [1]

XI. Dangerous Tactics.

We shall only deal with one other point which Dr. Bouquillon endeavored to make against his critics. In his first pamphlet (p. 23)

---

[1] The most singular performance in connection with this controversy, that has come to our notice, is the attempt of the Rev. Thomas O'Gorman, D.D., of the Catholic University, in a letter to the *Michigan Catholic*, January 28, 1892, to reconcile the teaching of Father Higgins with that of Dr. Bouquillon. He might as well try to bridge chaos.

Dangerous Tactics.

the Doctor, to prove *the authority of the state over education*, made the following argument:—

We affirm that the state has authority over education. This authority is included in that general authority with which the state is invested for promoting the common good, for guaranteeing to each man his rights, for preventing abuses. Education, well-directed or ill-directed, is one of the great means of good or of evil to the social body. It is on the education he receives that the future of the child depends; and the child needs protection all the more that he is weak and at the mercy of others. There is no need that we should insist on this motive, it seems to us self-evident.

This argument we dismissed as another form of the "impregnable" argument, which we said might prove anything, or nothing. Father Holaind also (p. 17) finds that it proves too much. Now, the Doctor has discovered that this identical argument has been used by Pope Leo XIII in his Encyclical on the *Condition of Labor;* and he triumphs in this discovery. Well he might, if it were so. We shall give the Doctor's statement of his discovery in full (Rejoinder, p. 38-39):—

The argument *ab absurdo* is a weapon of little effect at times, of very careful handling, of some danger to the fencer. If Father Holaind has read the Encyclical *Rerum Novarum* since he wrote that hasty pamphlet of his, he must be sorry that he tried to fence with that treacherous weapon. Let us examine the reasoning of Leo XIII in the question of labor. *Major:* "Eis qui imperant videndum ut communitatem ejusque partes tueantur." *Minor:* "Atqui int.rest salutis cum publicæ tum privatæ....validos adolescere cives, juvandæ tutandæque, si res postulat, civitati idoneos." *Conclusion :* "Quamobrem.... si valetudini noceatur opere immodico, nec ad sexum ætatemve accomodato, plane adhibenda, *certos intra fines*, vis et actoritas legum." I have reasoned in the question of education exactly on the same line as the Pope in the question of labor. If the culinary objection of Father Holaind has any force, it hits the Holy Father more directly than it hits me; for good victuals are surely of the highest importance to the health of the growing citizen. But I hasten to assure Father Holaind that he is guilty of no irreverence, because his objection is of no account, and Leo XIII has quietly brushed it aside with three little words, *certos intra fines*, which I take the liberty of italicising in the quotation. He explains the three little words thus : "quos fines eadem, quæ legum poscit opem, causa determinat, videlicet, non plura suscipienda legibus, nec ultra progrediendum quam incommodorum sanatio, vel periculi depulsio requirat." I had made precisely the same observation : we may grant to the state what is reasonable and possible without granting to it what is unreasonable and impossible. At any rate does not the state busy itself within reasonable limits with the material welfare of the citizens ? Does it not inspect food, meats, drinks, the sanitary conditions of homes, the justness of weights and measures and a thousand other matters? Why then give out exclamations of holy horror when you are told that this same authority, that does all those things without a protest from you, can protect the intellectual and moral life of the children of the people by imposing a minimum of instruction !

If we examine the Encyclical itself we find that the discovery is for the Doctor not such a happy one after all. First, the Pope carefully warns his readers that the right of the individual and family should not be absorbed by the state; and that both the individual and family should be allowed freedom of action as far as this is possible without prejudice to the common good or to the rights of others.¹ These two conditions are supposed in the Pope's argument. And even then legislation, or coaction, must be restricted to certain limits (*certos intra fines*). If the learned Doctor will take the trouble to examine the Pope's argument once more, he will find that in all the cases he enumerates there is an evident violation of right and positive detriment to the common good implied.² But we would ask the Doctor what right is violated or wherein is the common good prejudiced by the fact that parents are allowed to educate their own children, without let or hinderance or interference on the part of public authority, so long as no flagrant breach of duty can be imputed to them. The Doctor says he "made precisely the same observation as the Pope." He made the observations contained in his argument, which we have given in full, and no more. The Doctor, it seems to us, has in this place had recourse to " a weapon of *less* effect, of *more* careful handling, and of *more* danger to the fencer " than Father Holaind's argument *ab absurdo*. If the Doctor has had the misfortune unwittingly to use a fallacious argument, he should endeavor to father the fallacy on the Pope.

The Pope's argument should not be distorted from its proper use and meaning. The Pope teaches exactly the contrary of the Doctor's thesis in the Encyclical *Sapientiæ Christianæ*: "Parents have by nature the strict right (jus suum) to educate their own offspring; and

¹ Non civem, ut diximus, non familiam absorberi a republica rectum est: suam utrique facultatem agendi cum libertate permittere æquum est, quantum incolumi bono communi et sine cuiusquam injuria potest.

² Quamobrem, si quando fiat, ut quippiam turbarum impendeat ob secessionem opificum, aut intermissas ex composito operas, ut naturalia familiæ nexa apud proletarios relaxentur: ut religio in opificibus violetur non satis impertiendo commodi ad officia pietatis: si periculum in officiis integritati morum aut ingruat a sexu promiscuo, aliisve perniciosis invitamentis peccandi: aut opificum ordinem herilis ordo iniquis prematoneribus, vel alienis a persona ac dignitate humana conditionibus affligat; si valetudini noceatur opere immodico, nec ad sexum ætatemve accommodato, *his in causis* plane adhibend.. *certos intra fines*, vis et auctoritas legum.

to this right is added the duty of directing the education and instruction of their children to that end for which God has blessed them with issue. *Therefore parents must use every effort and endeavor to ward off all unjust interference in this matter, and by all means effect that the education of their children is under their own control, as is meet in accordance with Christian usage."* [1]

Here we take leave of Dr. Bouquillon. We have followed him with that attention and interest, which the work of so eminent an author seemed to demand. In so doing we considered fairness a serious duty which we owed to him, to the public, and to ourselves; and we trust that we have succeeded in giving an impartial estimate of the works we have undertaken to review. We were forced to point out not a few grave errors or misconceptions. We have done so frankly, but without ill will. And we sincerely hope that, while we have succeeded in proving to the reader that Dr. Bouquillon's views on education are in themselves unsound and dangerous, and prejudicial to Catholic education in this country, we have detracted nothing from his true merits as an author and a scholar.

NOTE.—Since we sent this *Supplement* to the press various other contributions have been added to the literature on the school question. Among the most remarkable that came to our notice, apart from the criticisms of Father Holaind, Father Higgins and of the *Civiltà Cattolica* already noticed, is an article on *Secular Education* by Rt. Rev. Bishop Becker in the *American Cath. Quarterly*, January 1892, articles in the *American Ecclesiastical Review* by Rt. Rev. Bishop Chatard, by Rt. Rev. Dr. Messmer, Bishop-elect, by Rev. Dr. Laughlin, Chancellor of the Archdiocese of Philadelphia, and by Rev. H. J. Heuser, editor of said *Review*, all bearing on this controversy, and all unanimous in their condemnation of Dr. Bouquillon's teaching. We understand that Judge E. F. Dunne has already filed his third Argument on *Compulsory Education* in the Supreme Court of Ohio,

[1] Natura parentes habent jus suum instituendi, quos procrearint; hoc adjuncto officio, ut cum fine, cujus gratia sobolem Dei beneficio susceperunt, ipsa educatio conveniat et doctrina puerilis. *Igitur parentibus est necessarium eniti et contendere, ut omnem in hoc genere propulsent injuriam; omninoque pervincant, ut sua in potestate sit educare liberos, uti par est more Christiano.*

which together with his previous Arguments, to which we have already referred, will soon be before the public in book form. A new edition of Rt. Rev. Bishop McQuaid's publications on the school question is likewise in requisition, and will, as we understand, soon be forthcoming. In referring to the most recent literature on this momentous question we cannot omit to mention the gallant work done by some of our Catholic editors, particularly by Dr. Condé B. Pallen of the *Church Progress*, St. Louis, and the Rev. Dr Michael Walsh of the *Catholic Herald*, New York, and the Rev. E. J. McCabe of the *Catholic Youth*, Brooklyn. On the other side, we have not thus far met with even a serious attempt at a defence of Dr. Bouquillon's teaching in any reputable Catholic paper or magazine.

THE END.

CORRIGENDA.

p. 26, line 5 from foot (note), for *standpotin* read *standpoint*.
p. 34, line 10, for *denigavit* read *denegavit*.
p. 68, line 3 from foot, for *is* read *is not*.

THE TEMPORAL SOVEREIGNTY

— OF —

THE HOLY SEE.

BY

REV. JOHN MING, S. J.

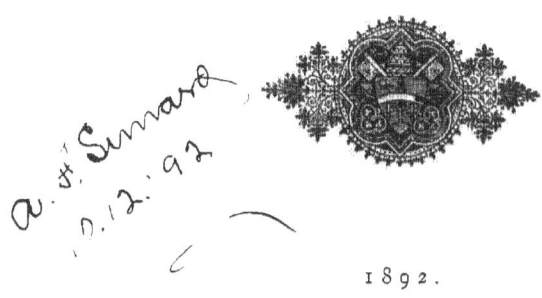

1892.

FR. PUSTET,
Printer to the Holy See and the S. Congregation of Rites.

FR. PUSTET & CO.,
NEW YORK AND CINCINNATI.

Imprimatur.

✠ MICHAEL AUGUSTINE,

Archbishop of New York.

Aug. 3, 1892.

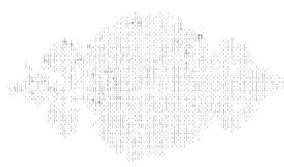

COPYRIGHT, 1892,
E. STEINBACK.
FIRM FR. PUSTET & CO.

PREFACE.

The following pages may be looked on by not a few as an untimely publication. It has been said that the Roman question needs no further discussion, that time itself has solved it and that the intelligent portion of the Church has fully acquiesced in the solution.

Liberal sentiments may have suggested this view. Deeper reflection leads others to quite a different conviction. Matters bound up with religion, with public justice and morality, do not allow themselves to be disposed of by main force and state-craft. If any attempt is made to deal with them in this way, the result, according to the nature of things, can be no other than general discontent, social disorders and convulsions. In the face of this truth, evident to reason and amply confirmed by the history of all ages, the question, whether the Roman States ought to be subject or not to the civil rule of the Pope, must be regarded even in our day, yet as little solved as it was twenty-two years ago when the troops of Victor Emmanuel poured into the Eternal City. For the Roman Pontiff claimed sacred and incontestible rights to the sovereignty over his old dominions, and this sovereignty, far from being of merely political importance, is inseparably connected with the spiritual welfare of the Church and the moral health of human society. His opponents, however, have thus far resorted against him to no other means than violence and intrigues.

It is the object of this pamphlet to throw some light on this struggle now carried on during a quarter of a century, to set forth, on the one hand, the sacred interests of justice and religion involved in the cause which the Pope defends, and, on the other hand, the wrongs committed and the evils threatened by his assailants.

THE AUTHOR.

Prairie du Chien, Wis., June 16, 1892.

CONTENTS.

	PAGE.
Preface..	3
I. The Historical Rights of the Holy See...................	7
II. The Recent Occupation of the Roman States..............	14
III. The Teaching of the Church concerning the Temporal Power of the Pope.....................................	21
IV. Independence a Prerogative of the Holy See.............	31
V. The Pope not Independent unless a Sovereign............	38
VI. Reconciliation with the Italian Government Impossible....	45

'11

The Temporal Sovereignty of the Holy See.

I.

The Historical Rights of the Holy See.

Human society is based on justice. Without this basis, however rich its material resources, however high its intellectual culture may be, it must necessarily collapse and be succeeded by universal confusion. It is, therefore, chiefly by inquiring into right and wrong that we ought to form our judgment on all matters touching the social order. In the light of this axiomatic truth we should study the Roman Question, which recent events have again made the subject of much public discussion. For it is a question which pre-eminently bears on society at large. The temporal sovereignty of the Pope over the Roman States, since it concerns two hundred and fifty millions of Catholics spread all over the earth and is bound up with the dearest interests they have in common, cannot remain suppressed or be restored without far-reaching consequences for the universal peace.

But if we have to judge in this matter from the standpoint of justice, we must first of all search into the right of the Pope to the Roman States. If such a right, certain and undeniable, exists, the late occupation of Rome by the Italian government must be condemned as an enormous wrong, and as a redress the restoration of the ancient royal-pontifical throne is demanded by the strictest of all duties. The American mind being known for its strongly-developed sense of justice, the Roman Question may well be presented to it under this aspect.

But has the Pope a clear and inviolable right to govern Rome as its civil ruler?

To show to evidence the legitimacy of the titles on which his temporal sovereignty is founded, it is necessary to trace them back to their origin in an early period of the Christian era.[1] I must, therefore, take the reader back to the times consequent on the downfall of the Western Roman Empire. Barbarians had descended from the East and North of Europe and, after conquering the once victorious Roman legions, established new empires in Gaul, Spain, and Italy. In 533 Justinian I., emperor of Constantinople, through his valiant General Narses defeated the Ostrogoths in the Apennine peninsula and overthrew their kingdom. Considering the country he had wrested from them as his own by right both of inheritance and of conquest, he reduced the greater part of Northern and Central Italy into a dependency of the Eastern Empire. In 568 an imperial governor or exarch, vested with absolute power, was sent over by Justin II. and took up his residence in Ravenna.

But the hold which the emperors had laid on Italy was weak. When as early as 568 the Lombards poured down from the Alps, the exarch was unable to resist their inroads. During the long-protracted war which ensued, one portion of the exarchate after the other revolted or fell a prey to the invaders, until in 752 the entire domain was irretrievably lost. No less unsuccessful was the internal administration of Italy. The East was at this time convulsed by political revolutions and ecclesiastical heresies, which were generally supported by the imperial government. The exarchs, powerless against the Lombards, persecuted the Italian Catholics and in particular the Popes who condemned the heretical doctrines. It was during this period that S. Martin I. was sent into exile, that the lives of several Pontiffs were imperilled, and that many ecclesiastical possessions were confiscated. Especially violent was the persecution which was carried on by the Iconoclastic Emperor Leo the Isaurian, during the pontificates of Gregory II. (715-731) and Gregory III. (731-741). A policy of this kind could not but render the emperors, as well as the exarchs odious and ruin their authority.

During this long period of universal distress, incessantly harassed by the Lombards and unjustly persecuted by the imperial officers, the people could find protection nowhere but in Rome at the hands of the Pontiffs. And the arm that protected them was by no means weak.

[1] *On the origin of the Papal States see M. Gosselin,* The Power of the Popes during the Middle Ages, *translated by Rev. M. Kelly, Vol. I.*

From the time of Constantine the Great, the Catholic bishops were not only exempted in many regards from civil jurisdiction, but even shared, to a considerable extent, the judicial power and the administration of the state. It stands to reason that a prominent share was granted to the Roman Pontiff.

Moreover the see of Rome possessed a very large amount of landed property offered, in the course of time, as patrimony of St. Peter by the piety of the faithful. These estates were situated not only in and around the Eternal City, but also in other parts of Italy, in Sicily, Northern Africa, Sardinia, Corsica, and Dalmatia, and are estimated to have covered eighty-five geographical square miles. The large revenues derived from them were employed by the Popes to assist the poor and afflicted, to support Christian schools for the education of youth and the preservation of the ancient civilization, often also to defray the expenses of the government, and to furnish the necessary means for the defence of the country. By their spiritual authority, the Roman Pontiffs settled doctrinal controversies, restored peace to the Church, and not unfrequently also to the state, reconciled political factions, exhorted the people to obedience and submission, and the rulers to justice. They often negotiated with the emperors on civil matters, and concluded peace with the invaders, thus saving the Eternal City from pillage and destruction. In this way the Popes exercised also in civil affairs a powerful and beneficial influence, which increased in proportion as that of the much-hated ministers of the emperor diminished.

At last, during the reign of the Iconoclasts, when the exarchs, utterly defeated by the Lombard kings, persecuted Pope Gregory II. and even sought his life, the duchy of Rome [1] in 726 threw off their rule, as did also other districts, and promised civil obedience to the Roman Pontiffs. The imperial authority was, nominally at least, still recognized but owing merely to Pope Gregory's intervention; for the people on their part were determined to renounce allegiance to the emperor. And when the cities of the exarchate, one after the other,

---

[1] *Certain districts into which the exarchate was divided were called duchies, and their governors dukes. The duchy of Rome included a part of Etruria with Sabina and a part of Umbria and Campagnia, a territory nearly coextensive with what is now called the patrimony of St. Peter and a part of Umbria and Campagnia di Roma, or with the dominion subject to Pius IX. from 1860-1870.*

were conquered by the Lombards, they regarded their new conquerors as oppressors, and mostly submitted to the Roman Pontiff as their protector and political head.

After the destruction of the exarchate, the duchy of Rome, subject to the Pope, represented the old Roman Commonwealth, being then the only remnant of it in the West still independent and unconquered by the immigrating barbarians. But its fall, too, seemed near at hand. Astolf, King of the Lombards, was approaching Rome after having taken several of the neighboring cities. Pope Stephen asked the emperor Constantine V. for assistance, which, however, was not sent. As a last resort, he crossed the Alps in 753, to implore the protection of Pepin, King of the Franks. Twice the latter descended into Italy with an army and defeated the Lombards. The second time, in 755, he wrested from them the exarchate of Ravenna, [1] restored it together with several cities which had likewise placed themselves under pontifical protection, to the Holy See and the Roman Commonwealth, and forced Astolf to do the same. The keys of the cities and the deed of donation, as the restoration was called, [2] were laid on the tomb of St. Peter, to testify that the grant was made to the See of the Apostle and out of love and reverence for it. The territory restored to the Pope comprised twenty-two cities, and was bounded on the North and West respectively by the Po and the Tanaro, on the West by the Apennines, and on the East by the Adriatic Sea. Some years later, Desiderius, King of the Lombards, added the cities of Faënza, Imola, Ferrara, Ancona, Osino, and Umana.

Peace being now restored, the Emperor Constantine demanded from Pepin the exarchate of Ravenna. But the emperor's right to a province which he himself had abandoned, was looked upon as extinct. [3] And the conqueror declared that he would never tolerate that province to be wrested from the Roman Church, protesting under oath that he had not been impelled by any human consideration to make his expeditions into Italy, but solely by the love of St. Peter and the hope of obtaining the remission of his sins.

From that time the Popes reigned over Rome and the above-mentioned cities as sovereigns independent of the Eastern Empire and

[1] *The exarchate of Ravenna in its more restricted sense, or as it was bounded in its last years of existence, corresponds nearly to the modern Romagna.*
[2] *Gosselin, p. I. § 40.*   [3] *Ibid. §§ 42 and 43.*

ot Pepin, who as Roman patrician was but their protector.[1] Charlemagne, in 774, solemnly confirmed his father's donation and promised to add some new territories, which promise, however, unforeseen circumstances prevented him from fulfilling. Crowned emperor by Pope Leo III. in 800, he did not obtain more than the protectorship of the Holy See; and of the Church, for the new dignity was created only for the purpose of consolidating the Pope's sovereignty and securing his independence of any political power both in the East and in the West.[2]

This is, in short, the origin of the Ecclesiastical States, and, at the same time, a clear evidence of the legitimate titles to sovereignty over them by the Roman Pontiffs. For by that very same right by which the Popes first attained possession of them, they ruled over them for eleven hundred years down to our days. They never renounced their claims established in the eighth century, not even when residing in Avignon (1306–1376); nor were they ever divested of them. For, though often forced to leave the Eternal City, they were always led back to it, their absence being considered as an exile into which they were driven by sheer violence. No event has ever extinguished or weakened their titles; neither an empire nor a meeting of Powers has ever looked on them as void or forfeited; even as late as 1814, when the international Congress of Vienna was held, they were regarded as valid. Indeed the right of the Holy See to sovereignty, founded on the historical facts stated above, is altogether certain and undeniable. The civil supremacy over Rome and the exarchate of Ravenna was lost by the Eastern Emperor and in full justice transferred to the Roman Pontiffs. The emperors no longer had a claim to a country which for a considerable length of time they were unable and, of late, even unwilling, to defend and to govern in peace and justice. The Roman people urged the Pope to take the government of the commonwealth into his hands. For more than a century he had been their only protector and the only support of order, and now there was nobody else powerful enough to rule and defend them. Under the circumstances the Pontiff alone could be their sovereign.

A right thus established is as certain and incontestable as any on earth can be. This is the conviction not of Catholics alone. Even

[1] *Gosselin, p* 1, §§ 36 *and* 66.   [2] *Ibid.* §§ 45 *and* 69.

Gibbon defends the temporal dominion of the Popes and considers as their noblest title to it the free choice of a people whom they had redeemed from slavery.[1] This right of the Popes is not only certain and undeniable, but also sacred. The sovereignty over the Roman States was conferred, or rather urged on them by the people out of respect for their spiritual authority, and out of gratitude for the benefits which they also in temporal affairs derived from the same, and it was restored to them, in part at least, by King Pepin out of reverence of St. Peter and his See in Rome. It was thus bestowed to the Holy See and to the Church, and in consequence was consecrated to God.

The right of the Popes was furthermore divine, because their sovereignty was evidently established and preserved by a special dispensation of Divine Providence. It sprang from the spiritual supremacy of the Roman Pontiffs on the one hand, and the migration of the Teutonic nations on the other, both which causes have to be traced back to God. The supremacy of St. Peter was instituted by Christ, and was by the death of the Apostle attached to the See of Rome.[2] The migration of the Northern nations and their descent into the Roman Empire was intended by God, in order to destroy the degenerate heathens of the West, to people Europe with new races and to engraft Christianity on them. And both these causes necessarily resulted in the Papal sovereignty. From the downfall of the Western Empire things took such a course that the Roman Pontiffs, true to their office, naturally became the sovereigns of Rome and the territory around it. No less evident was God's intervention in the preservation of the temporal power of the Popes. A hundred and seventy-one times[3] were they despoiled of their dominions by kings, emperors, or powerful factions. But it could never be done, as Cardinal Manning remarks[4] without a disturbance of political affairs throughout Europe. And every time were the Popes, by an example unheard of in the history of any dynasty, re-established on their throne. If we see a phenomenon recur regularly, we do not doubt but that it was produced by a force acting according to some fixed law. If we cannot

[1] The Decline and Fall of the R. Empire, *Ch. xlix.*
[2] *See Mgr. J. Schroeder*, American Catholics and the Roman Question, *pp.* 29-31.
[3] La Verità nella Soluzione della Questione Romana, *C. vi.*
[4] *Independence of the Holy See*, 1877.

separate things or change their relations without causing disturbances, we understand what order and connection is required by nature itself. Should we, then, not likewise recognize the operation and design of a higher power in the preservation and repeated restoration of the temporal sovereignty of the Popes, in spite of all human efforts to destroy it? Should we not infer that it enters the providential order as a factor necessary for the peace and welfare of the Christian nations?

II.

The Recent Occupation of the Roman States.

If the Papal sovereignty was thus founded on a right certain, sacred, and divine, how could it be suddenly abolished in the second half of the nineteenth century? Have events occurred which annulled its ancient titles? Has a new order of things sprung into existence with the progress of our age and lawfully done away with all former claims, however just, however respectable for their antiquity? Or have, on the contrary, crime and injustice prevailed and succeeded in shattering the very foundations of society? Let us in brief review the causes that led to the dethroning of the Pope. They must be still fresh in the memory of many a reader.

Ever since the beginning of this century, Italy was undermined by secret societies professing anti-Christian principles, and pursuing the ends of the French Revolution, ends which consisted in nothing less than the overthrow of the Church and of any civil government resting on a Christian basis. After many unsuccessful attempts they were at last, in the beginning of the Pontificate of Pius IX., ready to carry out a deep-laid plan. Italy, they gave out, heretofore divided into numerous principalities, some of which were ruled by foreigners, was to be united into one body-politic. The project was undoubtedly patriotic and could not but flatter the hopes of the whole nation and meet with hearty co-operation. But as the new movement towards national union was started by the secret societies, so it was also to be controlled by them and to be directed to such an issue as would establish their universal sway. Victor Emmanuel was to be proclaimed king of the united Italy, yet with the understanding that he should obey their orders and be nothing more than a tool in their hands. Anxious as he was to increase the splendor of his house, he was willing under any condition to further their plans by all means in his power. Louis Napoleon, raised to the throne of France by the Revolution, and in his turn bound to promote the same, was pledged to drive the Austrians from the peninsula, formally to recognize the new kingdom, and to ward off from it foreign intervention in favor of the deposed dynasties, and particularly of the Holy See.

The war between France and Austria broke out in the spring of 1859. At the same time an insurrection was stirred up in Tuscany and the Papal provinces of the Romagna, and supported by money and weapons from Piedmont. After the war was brought to a close, the integrity of the Pontifical States was guaranteed by the belligerents in the treaties of Villa Franca and Zurich, but notwithstanding this, the revolting provinces were occupied by the Piedmontese troops, and soon after a plebiscit was obtained for their annexation to the subalpine monarchy. The following year, under the pretext of restoring order, the Piedmontese troops occupied the Marches and Ancona, which had likewise been incited to rebellion. The Pontifical army under La Moricière was crushed, at Castel Fidardo and Ancona, by a sudden and treacherous attack contrary to the usages of civilized nations, whilst Louis Napoleon assured the Pope that no invasion of the Roman States would be tolerated. Another plebiscit followed, as also the annexation of these provinces to Piedmont. In 1861, after Naples and Sicily had been conquered in a like manner, the new kingdom of Italy was formed and officially recognized in Paris, Rome being proclaimed its capital. The next object in view was the occupation of the Eternal City.

But here hostilities suddenly came to a standstill. The French Catholics, by their energetic protests, forced the emperor to desist from open persecution of the Holy See. A convention was in consequence concluded on the 15th of September, 1864, in which Louis Napoleon agreed to withdraw his troops from Rome, and the Piedmontese government guaranteed the integrity of the Papal dominions. Italy, it was said, was henceforward to rely only on moral means to carry into effect her plan of national union. These moral means consisted in inciting the Roman population to insurrection, and the Pontifical army to treason. When such methods would not avail, Garibaldi, in 1867, again took up arms and, with a body of desperadoes attached to his person and some royal soldiers, attacked the Roman troops, whose ranks were then composed chiefly of heroic youths gathered from all parts of the Church. This time, however, he was defeated and shamefully put to flight.

Then came the Franco-Prussian war. After the rest of the French troops had been withdrawn from Rome, Prince Bismarck, in order to prevent Italy from carrying assistance to France, instigated the Italian radicals to demand from their government the occupation of Rome under circumstances so favorable; and Count Arnim, the Prussian minister at the Vatican, displayed extraordinary activity in furthering the scheme. Accordingly Victor Emmanuel, in a letter full of protestations of filial love and zeal for the Holy See, demanded from the Pope the surrender of the remaining Ecclesiastical dominions; but without awaiting an answer and making a formal declaration of war, sent an army of 60,000 men and a train of 150 pieces of artillery, to make an attack on the Eternal City, and, after a bombardment of five hours, gained possession of it on the 20th of September, 1870. Again the suffrages were taken for a plebiscit, and then Rome was made the seat of the Italian government. The Pope was deprived of all his possessions except the Vatican. As a compensation an annual income, the sacredness and inviolability of his person, and the prerogatives of a sovereign were guaranteed to him by an act of Parliament, yet with no security that this enactment would be carried out with more faithfulness than the solemn treaties had hitherto been kept.

By what right was all this done? Had those who dispossessed the Roman Pontiff any superior claims which invalidated his? Had Victor Emmanuel as King of Piedmont, or as head of the house of Savoy, acquired a title to the Papal States? He did not even pretend to have one. Had the secret societies any real claims, because they were the representatives of the Revolution, the negation of Christianity? Who might dare to say so? Could the plebiscit divest the Pope of his royalty? The plebiscit taken was not the voice of the people. The voters were the Revolutionists, strangers drawn into the cities, the rabble bribed and excited. The better classes, the conscientious Catholics, who formed the majority of the citizens, did not vote at all, just as nowadays they refrain from taking any part in the elections and shun any participation in the new government or in legislation. The votes were taken after the cities had been occupied by the Piedmontese troops and thus all freedom was precluded. Voting for the Pope was impossible, as up to this hour every manifestation in his favor is violently suppressed. '

See the Roman Question by the Bishop of Salford, (1889), *Chap. vi.*

And even had the plebiscit been the genuine expression of the popular will, it could not have abolished the Pope's right to sovereignty. No such power is inherent in the will of the subjects. They are not the ultimate source of civil power. Nor is it true that power is conferred *only* through the will of the people. It may be conferred by God Himself. And the sovereignty over the Roman States has evidently been bestowed upon the Popes by a special dispensation of His Providence. But even when the people may rightfully choose their rulers, they cannot depose them. Their consent to be ruled by a family or a certain succession of persons is irrevocable as long as the dynasty has not evidently become unable to carry on the government either by itself or through competent ministers, and as long as it abides by the fundamental laws agreed upon. For it is by such a consent that the state is constituted and organized, the dynasty being made its head, and the subjects its members. But the state is and must be of itself imperishable; else there would be no peace and tranquillity, no security, no steadiness in our social relations. When, a few years ago, the Southern States wished to secede, was the withdrawal of their consent to form a Union with the North respected? Were they not prevented from permanent secession by a bloody war? and that for the very reason that the Union was by its nature indissoluble? Still a political union does not imply in its idea indissolubility so evidently and so necessarily as the state or commonwealth. [1]

What has been said of the misrule of the Popes, in order thereby to prove their inability for political government, rests on the wilful exaggerations and misrepresentations of the Revolutionists. Enough has been said and written to disprove this accusation against the Papacy. [2]

There are complaints in all countries, and a host of them in the new Kingdom of Italy. Those which were heard in the former Papal States have been traced back by the most careful students, not to the Ecclesiastical government, but to the national defects of the Italians, and to the pernicious working of the secret societies. It

[1] *Mgr. J. Schroeder*, The American Catholics and the Rom. Question, pp. 47–56.
[2] *See F. Maguire,* Rome, its Ruler, and its Institutions, *and particularly in the Appendix the report of the Count de Rayneval to the French minister of Foreign Affairs;* Card. Hergenröther, Der Kirchenstaat.

would, indeed, be a most singular phenomenon, if the Popes, called to govern the whole Church and to exercise a world-wide influence, were unable to rule over a state of so small dimensions as the Papal dominions. In fact, on no throne on the face of the earth ever sat so much integrity and justice, and such profound statesmanship as on the See of Rome. Nothing but rank hatred or blind prejudice could suggest the thought that the Roman Pontiffs are an effete or disabled dynasty.

Lastly, has the right to political union, claimed by the whole of Italy, superseded the particular right of the Sovereign of Rome? Italy is not entitled to unite in contravention to rights already existing, or to an order of things lawfully and justly established; nor will a union contrary to justice ever be prosperous in the long run. It is moreover a false supposition that the interests of Italy are by their nature more universal than those of the Holy See. Italy is but a particular country, whereas the Roman See governs the Catholic, that is, the universal Church. Italy's national and political relations regard only the temporal prosperity of one people, whilst the rights and affairs of the Church, ruled by the Bishop of Rome, regard the spiritual welfare of all the nations of the globe. But shall Italy be deprived of the possibility of uniting politically, because the Holy See is within its boundaries? By no means. She can unite without dethroning the Pope. She may unite into a confederacy of states, the Papal territory being one of them, or the Pope being entrusted with the presidency, as in fact the proposal has been made. She will by doing so not risk her national greatness. Italy has no greater benefactors, no greater promoters of knowledge, arts, and civilization than the Popes, no power commanding more respect, no attraction more forcibly drawing other nations to her than the Holy See. Without it Rome would be of no importance, and without Papal Rome Italy will at most be a power of the second rank, whilst with it she may be second to no other nation.

The most careful inquiry, then, shows that the Italian government has no right whatsoever to the Roman States. The occupation of Rome, therefore, was an evident wrong, and open violation of justice. Wrong, too, were the means employed in accomplishing that unjust act; for they consisted in conspiracy, insurrection, treachery, untruthfulness, and the premeditated breach of compacts and of usages established by international laws. And the higher and the more sacred the right of the Pope is, the greater was the wrong in violating them. The usurpation of the Papal territory was the suppression of a sovereignty, the highest of all civil rights. It was the murderous destruction of a commonwealth. It was a robbery committed against the Church of God, and hence a sacrilege, an act which even the ancient heathens would have abhorred. It was the disturbance of the order established in human society and wonderfully upheld through many centuries by Divine Providence. It was a crime which the whole human race ought to detest and to avenge. For if the oldest throne in the civilized world, based on undeniable, sacred, and divine rights, a throne occupied by so many distinguished rulers, a throne resplendent with the sanctity of religion, a throne that had been the source of civilization and the support of peace for all European nations, if such a throne can be overturned with impunity, by open violence and injustice, by treason and conspiracy, by the infraction of the most solemn treaties almost at the moment when they were concluded: what government can still rest on a solid basis? what order of right and justice is still sure and steadfast? what assurance of tranquillity is yet left to human society?

The usurpation of the Pope's temporal sovereignty is a wrong to which the Church can never be reconciled, and which she must resist by all means in her power, even now after more than twenty years have elapsed since its perpetration. The faithful all over the world see the head of the Church despoiled of the lawful means by which he has to carry on the ecclesiastical administration, and thrown either upon the charity of his subjects or the mercy of his enemies in the discharge of his divine office. They see their father, the Vicar of Christ, injured, afflicted, imprisoned, and insulted, and feel themselves injured in him, until the wrong is redressed.

The Pope himself can never acquiesce in his deprivation of sovereignty. This is not a personal right of his which he may renounce at pleasure. It belongs to the Holy See, to which it is given in trust by Divine Providence. He can never resign it, especially since he has promised under oath, when he received the Cardinal's purple and when he ascended the Pontifical throne, to assert and maintain the temporal dominion of the Roman Church. Any Roman Pontiff, if solicited to surrender it, must act like Pius VII. When Radet, a

General of Napoleon I., came to him and said: "Holy Father, by command of the emperor, I must call upon you to abdicate your temporal dominion or go with me to prison," the Pope replied: "We have not the power to renounce that which does not belong to ourselves, neither are we ourselves otherwise than the administrators of the Roman Church and of her temporal dominion. This dominion, the emperor, even though he cut our body in pieces, will never obtain from us."

III.

The Teaching of the Church concerning the Temporal Power of the Pope.

There are evils which, however grievous they may be, it is better to bear with resignation, than to resist with obstinacy, not merely because they cannot be overcome by any human effort, but chiefly because they are in the providential order of God turned into plentiful sources of blessings. Death and destruction are seen everywhere in the universe, and yet nature does not perish, but always rises to new life and always reasserts its wonderful harmony. In the moral world individuals, as well as society, are stimulated to heroic deeds by unavoidable suffering. The Church of God, in particular, has attained to the fulness of her strength by enduring cruel persecutions. Ought not Catholics, then, to moderate their complaints with regard to the material losses which religion suffered by the French Revolution, and especially with regard to the deprivation of the temporal power which the Holy See had to suffer in consequence of the recent union of Italy? Is it not possible for the Pope to reconcile himself with his present condition in Rome and, submitting to the necessity in which he is, to resign his territorial sovereignty? Should he not be all the more inclined to do so, because he has not received from Christ any temporal dominion, and because the Church, spiritual as she is, has by the very despoliation of her earthly possessions, ever been but renewed and invigorated?

To answer these and similar questions which at present are not unfrequently agitated, we must enter into the design of Divine Providence and inquire into the purpose for which the temporal has been joined with the spiritual power in the Roman See. We must determine whether the two powers have been united only provisionally and incidentally, or, on the contrary, have been made inseparable by an intimate and, as it were, natural union, the one being necessary for the operation of the other. This problem is not solved by the simple remark that the spiritual should not be mixed up with the material and temporal. On this earth the material and the immaterial do not stand apart, but are not unfrequently closely knit together. Thus in man, soul and body are so united that the action of the former, though spiritual, is in a measure dependent on that of the latter. If in a like manner also the spiritual authority of the Vicar of Christ has been blended with temporal power by God's Providence, they cannot be separated again by human policy without disadvantage to religion. "What God has joined together, let no man put asunder."

This is in fact the view taken in this matter, not merely by ultramontane theologians, but by the Church herself. She distinctly and definitely teaches that the temporal sovereignty over the Roman States has been conferred on the Pope by a special dispensation of Divine Providence as a necessary safeguard for the free and unimpeded exercise of his spiritual supremacy. We are, therefore, compelled to regard the same not as a temporary or superabundant, but as an indispensable provision for the freedom of the Holy See and the welfare of the Christian flock.

Ever since their foundation the Church considered the Papal States as highly important for her well-being. This we must conclude from the extreme penalties which she inflicted on those who ventured to usurp or invade them, and from the care which she took to defend and preserve them and render them practically inalienable. Already in the first Ecumenical Council in the West, in that of the Lateran in 1123, the sentence of excommunication was pronounced against those who dare invade or plunder the possessions of the Roman Church. The Council of Trent[1] confirmed this penal law, and Pontifical bulls have, up to this day, kept it in full force.[2] The Council of Lyons, held in 1245 under Pope Innocent IV., excommunicated Emperor Frederick II. for seizing upon the Ecclesiastical States. The Council of Constance, in 1414, thought it necessary to use all its power to preserve the Papal dominion intact and undiminished during the vacancy of the Holy See. What the Popes undertook in order to guard their states, or to recover them when wrested from their hands, what they preferred to endure rather than to resign their sovereign rights, it is not necessary to mention here; the

---

[1] *Sess. XXII. De Reformatione, C. ii.*
[2] *Constitutio Sedis Apostolicæ, Series I.* § 12, *published by Pius IX. n.* 1869.

sufferings, the exile, and the captivity of Pius VI., Pius VII., and Pius IX. are still fresh in the memory of the present age.

In 1567 the sainted Pope Pius V. published the bull *Admonet Nos*, afterwards confirmed by several of his successors and also by Pius IX.,[1] by which under the penalty of excommunication he inhibited designing, advising or consenting to the alienation of the Pontifical States or any portion of them, even under the pretext of evident expediency. The observation and maintenance respectively of this law is promised under oath by the Cardinals when receiving the purple, or previous to going into Conclave, and by the Pope when acceding to the Pontifical throne.

The end for which the Papal dominions were thought to be of such high importance was marked out already by Pope Nicholas I. (858-867). In one of his letters[2] he maintains that the Roman Empire had been established as a protection of the temporal sovereignty of the Holy See in behalf of the freedom and supremacy of the Roman Church. We find the same idea more fully developed in the renowned bull *Fundamenta Militantis Ecclesiæ* issued by Pope Nicholas III. in 1278 and embodied in the Canon Law.[3] By this constitution it is provided that no king, marquis, duke, count, or baron be elected or named Roman Senator or Ruler. The avowed object of the provision is that the See of St. Peter, established in Rome on its own soil, should enjoy full liberty in all its actions and deliberations, and the election of the Roman Pontiff and the creation of Cardinals should be perfectly free.[4]

With the fullest clearness and with such force and authority as must remove all doubts from the Catholic mind the necessity of the temporal power for the free exercise of the spiritual has been taught in our century, when no longer the ambition of individual rulers, but the anti-Christian Revolution, unsettling the whole civilized world, makes war on the Holy See with the intent to overthrow Christianity. For it always so happens that, when more light is needed on a religious question, either on account of rising heresies or of peculiarly embarrassing circumstances, the Church expounds the deposit of divine truth committed to her more forcibly, definitely, and explicitly.

[1] *Constitutio Sedis Apostolicæ, Series II.*, § 13.   [2] *Epistola LXXX.*
[3] *Sext. Decret. lib. I., tit. VI. De electione et electi potest.*
[4] *See the Roman pamphlet* La verità nella Soluzione della questione Romana, *C. III.*

Never since the reign of the Revolution in Italy have Pius IX. and his Holiness Leo XIII. ceased to inculcate in their consistorial* addresses and Apostolical Letters the necessity of the temporal sovereignty of the Holy See for the freedom and independence of the supreme spiritual authority. There are no less than six Apostolical Letters and thirteen Allocutions, in which they have solemnly spoken of this subject.[1] Pope Pius IX. in the Encyclical Letter *Qui nuper*, June 18, 1859, says:

"We openly declare that, in order to exercise without any impediment its sacred power for the good of religion, the temporal power is necessary for the Holy See."

In the Apostolical Letter *Cum catholica Ecclesia* of 26th of the following March he more fully develops his views:

"Since the Catholic Church, founded and instituted by Christ our Lord to take care of the eternal welfare of men, has by virtue of her divine institution the nature of a perfect society, she must enjoy freedom to such an extent as not to be subject to any civil power in the discharge of her ministry. And since for proper freedom of action she needed such safeguards as are conformable to the condition and wants of the times, it came to pass by a special dispensation of God's Providence that, when the Roman Empire collapsed and was

---

[1] The following are the Apostolical Letters and Allocutions referred to:

APOSTOLICAL LETTERS.

A. OF PIUS IX.

Qui nuper, June 18, 1859. *Cum catholica Ecclesia*, March 26, 1860.
Nullis certe verbis, Jan. 19, 1860. *Intimo mœrore*, Sept. 10, 1860.
Respicientes, Nov. 1, 1870.

B. OF LEO XIII.
Inscrutabili, April 21, 1878.

ALLOCUTIONS.

A. OF PIUS IX.

Quibus Quantisque, April 20, 1849. *Quibus notum*, July 13, 1860.
Si semper antea, May 20, 1850. *Novos et ante hunc diem*, Sept. 28, 1860.
Ad gravissimum, June 20, 1859. *Jamdudum*, March 18, 1861.
Maximi animi nostri, Sept. 26, 1859. *Maxima quidem*, June 9, 1862.
Luctuosis exagitati, March 12, 1877.

B. OF LEO XIII.

Ubi primum, March 28, 1878. *Post excitatos*, March 24, 1884.
Convocare ad nos, Aug. 4, 1881. *Tempestivum quoddam*, Dec. 30, 1889.

divided into many states, the Roman Pontiff, whom Christ appointed the head and the centre of the whole Church, obtained a civil princedom. In this way has God Himself with great wisdom provided that in the midst of so many and diverse temporal rulers the Sovereign Pontiff should have that political liberty which is so necessary for him, to exercise his spiritual power, authority, and jurisdiction without any impediment all over the world." [1]

No sooner had his Holiness Pope Leo XIII. acceded to the pontifical throne, than he demanded in his first Encyclical Letter *Inscrutabili*, of April 21, 1878, the restoration of the Roman States to the Holy See, and alleged as a reason for this demand that the civil principality was necessary to preserve and defend the unlimited freedom of his spiritual power.

But did the Sovereign Pontiffs in these utterances make use of their teaching authority, and had they the outspoken intention of binding all the faithful by them? The answer to this question we may infer from two Pontifical documents. In the Encyclical Letter *Quanta cura*, of Dec. 8, 1864, Pope Pius IX. declares that by virtue of his apostolic ministry he has condemned the errors of our times in several of his Apostolical and Encyclical Letters and Allocutions, and among them he expressly mentions the Allocution *Maxima quidem* of June 9, 1862. Accordingly the Encyclical Letter was, by his order, accompanied by the Syllabus, which exhibits the diverse erroneous propositions condemned by the pontifical acts. Now what does the Syllabus show? It first states as condemned the propositions which assert the incompatibility of the temporal with the spiritual power, and maintain that the abolition of the temporal dominion of the Holy See would contribute to the liberty and welfare of

---

[1] *Cum catholica Ecclesia a Christo Domino fundata et instituta, ad sempiternam hominum salutem curandam, perfectæ societatis formam vi divinæ suæ institutionis obtinuerit, ea proinde libertate pollere debet, ut in sacro suo ministerio obeundo nulli civili potestati subjaceat. Et quoniam ad libere, ut par erat, agendum, iis indigebat præsidiis, quæ temporum conditioni ac necessitati congruerent, idcirco singulari prorsus divinæ providentiæ consilio factum est, ut cum Romanum corruit imperium et in plura fuit regna divisum, Romanus Pontifex, quem Christus totius Ecclesiæ suæ caput centrumque constituit, civilem assequeretur principatum. Quo sane a Deo ipso sapientissime consultum est, ut in tanta temporalium principum multitudine ac varietate Summus Pontifex illa frueretur politica libertate, quæ tantopere necessaria est ad spiritualem suam potestatem, auctoritatem et jurisdictionem toto orbe absque ullo impedimento exercendam.*

the Church. Then it goes on to remark that besides these errors noted explicitly, there are several others condemned by implication, because at variance with the doctrine laid down concerning the civil princedom of the Roman Pontiff and most firmly to be adhered to by all the faithful.[1] As documents in which this doctrine was clearly set forth, it points out the Apostolical Letter *Cum catholica Ecclesia* and five different Allocutions, all of them asserting the necessity of the Pope's temporal sovereignty. These then, at least, are evidently acts which contain authoritative teaching and lay all Catholics under obligation.

Nor did the Roman Pontiffs alone raise their voices. When on the occasion of the canonization of the Japanese Martyrs, in 1862, Pope Pius IX. had convened the Catholic hierarchy from all parts of the world, and two hundred and sixty-five Cardinals and bishops had assembled around his august throne, he, in the Allocution *Maxima quidem* on the 9th of June, gave expression to the great joy he felt over the unanimity with which the entire episcopacy had both in letters to him and in their charges to their flocks set forth the providential establishing of the temporal sovereignty of the Holy See and the necessity of the same for the freedom of the supreme spiritual authority.

"It gives us pleasure," said he, "to mention the wonderful unanimity with which you, together with all the bishops of the entire Catholic world, our venerable brothers, both in letters written to us and in your charges to the faithful, have never ceased. . . . to teach that the civil princedom of the Holy See has been bestowed on the Roman Pontiff by a special dispensation of Divine Providence, and that the same is necessary to the end that he, exempt from subjection to any prince or civil government, may, with the fullest freedom, exercise throughout the whole Church the supreme power and authority of feeding and ruling the Lord's flock conferred on him by Christ, and

---

[1] *Præter hos errores explicite notatos, alii complures implicite reprobantur, proposita et asserta doctrina quam Catholici omnes firmissime tenere debent, de civili Romani Pontificis principatu.* (*Ejusmodi doctrina luculenter traditur in Alloc. Quibus quantisque*, 20 *April*, 1849; *in Alloc. Si semper antea*, 20 *Maji*, 1850; *in Litteris apost. Cum catholica Ecclesia*, 26 *Mart.* 1860; *in Alloc. Novos*, 28 *Sept.* 1860; *in Alloc. Jamdudum*, 18 *Mart.*, 1861; *in Alloc. Maxima quidem* 9 *Junii*, 1862.) *Syllabus*, § 9.

provide for the greater good, the welfare, and the needs of the Church and the faithful." [1]

Then again the bishops in an address, read by the Dean of the Sacred College and signed by all present, expressed their belief concerning this point.

"We acknowledge the civil principality of the Holy See as necessary and as evidently founded by God's providence, and we do not hesitate to declare that in the present order of human society the same principality is by all means required for the good and free government of the Church and of souls. For the Roman Pontiff, the head of the Church, ought not to be subject, nor even the guest, of any ruler, but residing in his own dominion and realm, he should be independent and guard and defend the Catholic faith and govern the whole Christian community with a noble, august and tranquil liberty." [2]

In reply to this address the Pontiff said that he regarded the sentiment expressed as a proof of the bond of charity that closely united the bishops not only with one another, but also with the Holy See, the Chair of truth. [3]

Five hundred and thirty-five prelates prevented from going to Rome sent in by letter their adhesion to the address read in the

[1] *Juvat potius hac de re commemorare miram prorsus consensionem, qua vos ipsi una cum aliis Venerabilibus Fratribus universi catholici orbis sacrorum Antistitibus, nunquam intermisistis et epistolis ad nos datis et pastoralibus litteris ad fideles scriptis hujusmodi fallacias detegere, refutare ac simul docere, hunc civilem Sanctæ Sedis principatum Romano Pontifici fuisse singulari divinæ providentiæ consilio datum, illumque necessarium esse, ut idem Romanus Pontifex, nulli unquam principi aut civili potestati subjectus, supremam universi gregis dominici pascendi regendique potestatem auctoritatemque ab ipso Christo Domino divinitus acceptam per universam Ecclesiam plenissima libertate exercere ac majori ejusdem Ecclesiæ ac fidelium bono, utilitati et indigentiæ consulere possit. Collectio Lacensis Tom. VI. p.* 881.

[2] *Civilem Sanctæ Sedis principatum ceu quiddam necessarium ac providente Deo manifeste institutum agnoscimus, nec declarare dubitamus, in præsenti rerum humanarum statu hunc ipsum principatum civilem pro bono ac libero Ecclesiæ animarumve regimine omnino requiri. Oportebat sane totius Ecclesiæ Caput, Romanum Pontificem, nulli principi esse subjectum, imo nullius hospitem, sed in proprio dominio ac regno sedentem suimet juris esse, et in nobili, tranquilla et alma libertate catholicam fidem tueri ac propugnare totamque regere ac gubernare Christianam republicam.* Collect. Lacensis, Ibid. *p.* 884.

[3] *Collectio Lacensis, Tom. VI. p.* 890.

consistory.[1] Eight hundred bishops have thus with one voice solemnly and explicitly asserted the necessity of the temporal sovereignty of the Holy See.

The same doctrine was embodied in the decrees of several Provincial Councils, held subsequently both in Europe and in America. The Fathers of the Second Plenary Council of Baltimore expound it in the very words of Pius IX. drawn from his official acts.[2] The Fathers of the Fourth Provincial Council of Quebec enacted the following declaration concerning the Pope's temporal sovereignty:

"In agreement with all the bishops of the Catholic world and all writers truly worthy of the Catholic name, we acknowledge and openly assert that this temporal power is not only legitimate and in full accordance with the institution of Christ and the teaching of the gospel, but also necessary to the Holy See, in order to exercise its apostolic power with greater liberty and safety all over the earth."[3]

The voice of the episcopacy re-echoed in the hearts of all Catholics, who signed numerous protests against the usurpation of the Papal provinces by the Piedmontese government, and henceforth supported the Holy See in every possible way, by the enthusiastic assurances of their love and obedience, by pecuniary means, nay, by the sacrifice of their lives.

Now a doctrine authoritatively enjoined by the Holy See and, in submission to the same, solemnly professed and officially set forth by the whole body of the Catholic bishops, is not only binding on all the faithful, but also infallibly true. For the entire episcopacy of the Church, succeeding to the body of the Apostles, is in its authoritative teaching rendered infallible by the supernatural assistance of the Holy Ghost. The necessity, therefore, of the temporal sovereignty of the Holy See is no more an open question; it has been decided by the highest tribunal on earth and must be regarded as a certain and infallible truth.[4]

[1] *See* La Sovranità temporale dei Romani Pontifici propugnata dal suffragio dell' orbe cattolico, *Parte VII.*   [2] *Titul. II. Cap. I., n.* 47.

[3] *Omnibus episcopis orbis Catholici, omnibusque scriptoribus Catholico nomine vere dignis assentientes, agnoscimus et palam asserimus, istam potestatem temporalem non tantum legitimam ac institutioni Christi et evangelicæ doctrinæ admodum consentaneam, sed et necessariam esse Sedi Apostolicæ, quo liberior et tutior potestatem Apostolicam toto orbe terrarum exerceat. Tit. V.*

[4] *See* Stimmen aus Maria Laach *vol.* 36, *pp.* 529–533; D. Palmieri S.J. de Romano

We must, however, still more exactly determine the nature and the object of this decision. Above all we ought to understand that the teaching of the Church, though infallible, does in our case not settle a question of *divine faith*. The necessity of the Pope's temporal power is not and never has been considered a Catholic dogma, a truth revealed by God Himself. It is neither contained in Scripture or Tradition, nor is it essential to the primacy of the Holy See, which is altogether spiritual. Still it is closely connected with the latter. The supreme spiritual power of the Sovereign Pontiff is by its very nature, and therefore by divine right, endowed with perfect freedom. But this freedom is as to its enjoyment necessarily dependent on certain conditions agreeing with the respective state of human society. To define these without any error lies within the province of the teaching authority of the Church. For she is empowered by Christ not only to preach and expound His teachings, but also to decide any point of doctrine necessarily connected with the revealed truths, or with the belief in them. And the decisions made by her on any such point are binding on all the faithful, and must be adhered to with firm assent.[1] Accordingly the doctrine of the necessity of the Pope's temporal sovereignty, though not one contained in divine revelation or resting *immediately on God's authority*, is nevertheless to be regarded as undoubtedly true, resting on the *infallible teaching authority of the Church* as its basis.

The necessity itself, moreover, is not an *absolute*, but a *relative* one. This is clearly understood from the official acts themselves, in which it is taught. Temporal sovereignty is not absolutely necessary for the Holy See, it is necessary only for the *free exercise* of its essential power, the spiritual supremacy. Nor has it been declared to be absolutely necessary even for this end; for it is not required under all circumstances, and for every, even the least degree of freedom, but only in the *present order of human society*, and for *the full and altogether unimpeded* freedom in the *universal* discharge of the apostolic ministry. Consequently we must infer that it is likewise not necessary for the existence of the Church, but for her well-being, inasmuch as without it she could not discharge the mission entrusted to her in its

Pontificc, *p.* 506; *Mgr. J. Schroeder*, American Catholics and the Rom. Quest. *p.* 35; La Verità nella Soluzione della Questione Romana, *C. III.*

[1] *Encycl.* Quanta Cura, *Dec.* 8, 1864.

full extent all over the world. Such relative necessity, therefore, of the temporal sovereignty of the Holy See is maintained by the teaching authority of the Church and can no longer be called into question by any loyal Catholic.

IV.

Independence a Prerogative of the Holy See.

Does the necessity of the Pope's temporal power rest on authority alone? Are there no reasons founded on the nature of things that support it? Or are we, obliged as we are to submit to the decision of the Church, not allowed to inquire into them? Yes, there are such reasons, and it is lawful to search into them. The Church herself invites us to do so, for she has expounded them in her own official acts with admirable clearness. So strong and plain are they in themselves, apart from any ecclesiastical teaching, that, convinced by them, not only theologians, but also statesmen, not only Catholics, but also Protestants and unbelieving historians and philosophers have asserted and do still assert the necessity of the Pope's territorial sovereignty. The gist of all these reasons is, that independence is a necessary prerogative of the Holy See, and that temporal sovereignty is a necessary safeguard of its independence.

To start with correct and well-defined ideas, we must distinguish a twofold independence of the Sovereign Pontiff, the one official, and the other personal. The former is his independence of any earthly power in the exercise of his spiritual supremacy over the universal Church; the latter, his independence of any king or magistrate, also in things temporal and political. The necessity of the Pope's official independence cannot be questioned. His authority is not derived from the state. He has received it from the Son of God Himself, who said to St. Peter: "*Feed my lambs, feed my sheep,*"[1] and, "*I say to thee: thou art Peter; and upon this rock I will build my Church, and the gates of hell shall not prevail against it. And I will give thee the keys of the kingdom of heaven: and whatsoever thou shalt loose on earth, it shall be loosed in heaven.*"[2] Thus entrusted by God Himself to St. Peter and his successors, the supreme power over the Church is beyond

---

[1] *St. John, xxi., 15-18.* [2] *St. Matthew, xvi., 18-20.*

the domain of state jurisdiction. It is more universal than the latter, not restricted to any particular country, having the whole world subject to itself. It does not need resources procured by the civil society; for being absolute and unlimited, it involves all the means necessary to achieve its end. It has for its object not the temporal prosperity of one nation, but the eternal salvation of mankind. Being spiritual, the authority of the Holy See is not only distinct from any civil jurisdiction, but also superior to it by so much as the immaterial transcends the material, and the eternal the temporal.

The papal authority, therefore, descending from God, is *by right and by its own nature* free and independent. It must, moreover, under all circumstances, be free also *in fact*. Indeed, were it, while actually exercised, subject to any earthly influence, it would be degraded and would fail to work out the salvation of mankind. For it would then no longer be directed by the will and the law of God, but by merely human views, and would not aim at truth and holiness, but at worldly interests. Hence it is of peremptory necessity that in the actual discharge of his high office the Sovereign Pontiff be exempt from any control by the civil power, and be beyond the reach of any temporal sway. Were he to submit to the secular rule, he would betray his own dignity, as well as the eternal welfare of men.

From the nature of the primacy of St. Peter and the freedom necessary for its exercise there follows with necessity also the personal independence of the Pope. He being the Vicar of Christ, entrusted with His mission upon earth, and the spiritual ruler and father of all the faithful, teaching them God's truth, sanctifying their souls and performing for them the highest mysteries, can ever a Christian with decency be competent to keep him subject in earthly affairs, or to exact obedience from him, and if this be refused, to constrain and punish him? And if for Christians such a right is not befitting, could it with less impropriety be conceded to those who are outside the kingdom of God? Certain it is, no civil magistrate could force the Sovereign Pontiff to obedience without shocking the feelings of every Christian heart, and without disturbing the peace and tranquillity of the entire Church. Undoubtedly a right so unbecoming has not been established by divine wisdom.

Then, to advance a still more convincing proof, a dignity or power confers on the person in whom it is vested all its rights and prerogatives, being, as it were, embodied in him. The majesty of the civil rulers is an illustration of this axiom. Consequently the person of the Pope must be endowed with all the prerogatives inherent in his supreme authority over the Church. But this authority is, as was said above, not only distinct from the civil power, but also superior to the same. It is the continuation of the mission which Christ had upon earth, and therefore partakes of the sublimity and majesty peculiar to the King of kings. Because it is spiritual, it refers immediately to eternal salvation and hence is instituted to order also the things of the state, not directly by interfering with them as far as they regard merely temporal prosperity, but indirectly, by rendering them subservient to man's ultimate end. This is no exaggeration. Christ commissioned the Church and her supreme head to preach the gospel also to kings and rulers, and to introduce the moral law revealed by Him not only into private, but also into public life. For He said to His Apostles: "*Teach ye all nations.... Go ye into the whole world and preach the gospel to every creature.*"

This we must infer also from the object to which the apostolic authority of the Pope refers. He has, as the head of the Church, received the keys of the kingdom of heaven, that is, he has to lead men to their ultimate and supreme end. Now to this end everything must be subordinate; all human actions must tend to it, all human relations must be in harmony with it; every power must move and operate in its direction. Is the Pope, then, not the judge also of the morality of civil and political actions? Is he, as the bearer of the keys of the kingdom of heaven, not the ruler of rulers, because he is bound to forbid them what is contrary, and to enjoin on them what is necessary, to man's salvation? Is he, as the head of the Church and the father of the faithful, not empowered to warn and to guide the civil magistrates that are within his fold (for he does not judge those without, according to the teaching of the Apostle (I. Cor., v, 12) and to oblige them to abstain from whatsoever is detrimental to their own souls or injurious to the flock of Christ? Led by such considerations we must conclude that the person of the Pope is in no respect, not even in civil matters, subject to the state, that, on the contrary, he stands above it, and by a higher power raises it to a sublimer order and directs it to a nobler end.

Should temporal rulers ever attempt to exact obedience from him, though only in civil affairs, he could in the fulness of his authority and with a view to the welfare of the Church, annul their injunctions and ordain his own civil independence. And, if he did so, nobody could appeal to a higher tribunal against him, on the score that he had overstepped the limits of his power. For whatever he binds on earth, is bound also in heaven, and whatever he looses upon earth is loosed also in heaven.

There is no doubt whatever among Catholic canonists and jurisconsults about the civil independence of the Pope. They all agree that it is due to him by divine right, because it grows out of the spiritual supremacy conferred on him by Christ.[1] Catholic princes, too, during the ages of faith, never regarded the Roman Pontiff otherwise than as their father, and tendered him by solemn acts their submission and reverence. He had precedence before them all; he was their arbitrator in their differences, and their censor when they did wrong; he admonished them conscientiously to administer justice, in the same way as he exhorted their subjects to obedience. Nor have kings and emperors on this account lowered their majesty. Their crowns only shone with a brighter lustre, reflected on them from above, and their dominions were united in more perfect peace and harmony. Those times have passed away. Still, even in our days, when Christianity is, as it were, banished from political life, the states which guarantee religious liberty cannot ignore the Pope's civil independence. For if liberty is guaranteed to the Catholic Church, everything that is necessarily implied in her nature and her constitution must be granted to her and be left intact. Protestant denominations cannot complain as if thus a privileged position were demanded by us. We must demand the independence of the Pope consistently with our religious convictions, but they cannot claim independence for their prelates, because they acknowledge no supreme jurisdiction in them.

It might seem, however, that all the conclusions thus far reached might be granted, and yet the Pope's sovereignty be safely denied. Let his civil independence be a prerogative ever so undoubted, is it necessary for him always to assert and to enjoy it? The question is, indeed, not an idle one. A right or a prerogative is one thing, and its actual enjoyment another. The Church has in her concordats

---

[1] See Aug. Lehmkuhl. S. J. Theologia Moralis. Vol. I. n. 139.

with Catholic governments, for weighty reasons, resigned many a right undoubtedly inherent in her. Bishops and priests nowadays in most countries enjoy no personal immunity, though in former days they did, and, as the Council of Trent says, by divine and ecclesiastical law.[1] Christ Himself, whilst on earth, did not make use of all His rights. Though the King of kings, He condescended to obey the civil government and to pay tribute to Cæsar. May the Pope not likewise resign his civil independence?

The answer must be given decidedly in the negative. The reason is that the loss of his personal independence must, to a great extent entail the loss also of his official independence. Civil dependence and spiritual supremacy to be exercised with full freedom are, in the present state of affairs, irreconcilable in one and the self-same human person. It is true, they were not so in Christ. But He visibly governed the Church when she as yet consisted of few persons, whereas His Vicar rules her when spread all over the world. He is God, His Godhead shining forth by numberless miracles. His Vicar is but man. And in a merely human being any dignity, though supernatural and divine in its origin, exists and operates after the manner of human nature, whose faculties it employs, and therefore also partakes, to a certain extent, of human weakness. Hence it is, that if its bearer be punished or corrected, it will lose its prestige, and will no more be duly respected, and that if the person in whom it is vested be brought into subjection, its exercise, too, will become more or less dependent. As a man obnoxious to human passions, the spiritual head of the Church will, if civilly subject, at times lack sufficient strength to resist the influence exercised on him by those in higher power; he will be open to the fear of losses or the hope of temporal advantages; he cannot without danger and great difficulty censure his own ruler when he does wrong or oppresses the Church; he can scarcely reject offers made, in order to induce him to enact laws or to make appointments which rather serve political purposes, than promote the spiritual welfare of Christendom.

If fear and hope cannot cloud his intellect or bias his will, he may at any time be prevented by force from exercising his jurisdiction both within and without the state of which he is a citizen. He must in any case be a Pontiff displeasing any other Power than that to

[1] *Sess. xxv. de Reform. c.* 20.

which he owes allegiance, because he will always be suspected of having been elected to his office by the influence of his monarch, or of being swayed by the same in the government of the Church. His laws and decrees will, therefore, be mistrusted by foreign nations and often be refused, particularly at the time of international animosities. These are not mere imaginations, but tangible realities. For whilst the Popes are not free from human infirmities, the temporal rulers, whether monarchic or republican, are, on the whole, extremely jealous of power and most eager to extend their sway. Consulting history, we observe nearly in every one of its periods and in every country, in England, in Germany, in France, in Italy, in the East, a tendency in the secular power to gain the ascendant over the spiritual and to rise on its subserviency to unlimited absolutism. And such attempts were mostly but too successful, as long as the struggle was carried on with dependent prelates. Does not this fact prove that the Pope at least must be civilly independent? Does it not show to evidence that, whilst the evils resulting from the dependence of the bishops may be remedied by him, the consequences of his lack of freedom are irretrievable?

On the strength of such considerations not only canonists, but also the statesmen of nearly every civilized nation aver that the Pope's actual independence is necessary. Nor is this astonishing. In whatever state the Catholic religion is professed, there the government is highly interested in the perfect freedom of the Roman Pontiff, who, by his teaching and his laws, exercises an unbounded intellectual and moral influence on the Catholic subjects. For this reason the Italian government guaranteed to the Pope all the prerogatives of a sovereign by an act of Parliament, and through its ministers at all the European courts acknowledged its duty, and professed its intention, to uphold the perfect independence of the Holy See. The sincerity of these declarations must, for very good reasons, be doubted, but they show at least how the Italian politicians felt themselves compelled to deal with the Roman Question in the face of Europe. In reality, in their diplomatic answers the Powers all insisted on the Pope's personal independence.[1]

In the light, then, of both faith and reason, the Sovereign Pontiff, the Vicar of Christ, is in every respect officially and personally in-

[1] *See* The Roman Question *by the Bishop of Salford, p.* 12.

dependent of any earthly power, he is so not by any human law, but by the nature of his spiritual supremacy, and therefore by the will of Christ, and must be so during all the ages in which he governs the Church of God on earth.

V.

The Pope not Independent unless a Sovereign.

One point still remains to be discussed. The Pope's independence, official and personal, granted, is there but one way of realizing it? Is a civil princedom necessary to establish it, or are other means sufficient? The Italian government, in 1870 at least, pretended to render the Pope independent, though deprived of his states, and many Catholics, misled by the liberal views, entertained hopes that the project was feasible. But the hopes of the latter prove just as vain as the pretensions of the former are deceitful.

Whatever the abstract possibilities may be, practically this independence is in the present order of things not secured, unless the Holy See has a temporal dominion of a moderate size. Of this a few reflections will convince us. We have to demand full freedom and independence not only for the Pope himself, but also for his court and his functionaries and ministers, who form one official person with him. He cannot by himself govern the Church, spread all over the surface of the earth, he needs organs, and indeed a great many, tribunals and offices, through which he acts and speaks, gathers information, administers justice, and renders decisions. Were these subject to a government distinct from that of the Sovereign Pontiff, the exercise of the papal authority would, in effect, be dependent on the civil power, since it could at any moment be interfered with, impeded, and biased by political considerations. Would the government of the United States be free and unobstructed, if freedom were granted to the president alone, but his secretaries and their assistants and clerks were subject to the laws of a particular state and could be swayed by its policy?

Moreover the Pope is in need of a regular income, to keep up his dignity in a befitting manner, to defray the expenses of his administration, and to promote the interests of the Church. If he draws revenues from a civil power, he becomes by this very fact dependent on it; if he receives contributions from the faithful, he is in a kind of dependence on them, which does not become his exalted position, and imperils the intregrity of his officials. A regular and safe income sufficient for his needs can, without any disadvantage to his freedom, be derived only from a temporal dominion; and a vast multitude of functionaries, exempt from any danger of being politically influenced in their actions, can subsist only in a territory over which the Pope is the sovereign.

Then, if the Roman Pontiff has no territorial sovereignty, he is unprotected from the covetousness of the potentates and the oppression of unchristian governments. Whenever their longing for absolute power is no longer refrained by conscience, or their hatred of Christianity is no longer checked by external restraints, the civil rulers may and will rob the Pope living within their territory, insult and attack him, put him in prison or intercept his communication with the universal Church; they may by threats and promises exercise any pressure they like, if not on the Pope personally, on account of his sublime virtues, at least on his officials; and lastly they may without difficulty meddle with the election of a successor after his death. It would be childish to think that in our age of unbelief, events of this kind are impossible; they are now more than ever to be dreaded. We hear it said that acts of violence might be prevented by an international treaty. But would not the Pope thus become dependent, not on one Power alone, but on several? And how could the working of such an agreement be ensured? Does not the fulfilment of compacts between the supreme rulers depend altogether on the good will of those who conclude them, just as the value of guarantees depends on those who give them? Besides, since in our days nearly all states have constitutional governments with elective representation and full freedom for political parties, princes cannot for a considerable length of time be surety for their own acts. Much less could they hinder the waves of political agitation from reaching that city of their empire which is the seat of the Pope, and from disturbing and perplexing the ecclesiastical administration.

Hence there is practically no difference between the Pope who is the subject of a ruler and the Pope who has no territory over which he reigns. The state to which he is subject is no greater danger for his freedom, than the state which nominally grants him exemption, but is free to exert its influence on his administration by force as well as policy. We know from history how often the Roman Pontiff was exiled or imprisoned by temporal rulers; we have heard complaints that his ministers in their official acts, and the Cardinals, when in the Conclave, have not been free from undue influence and selfish views. What would happen, if the Pope were not a reigning sovereign, and if the government of the Church were carried on within the reach of a civil power? After an experience of seven years after the occupation of Rome, Pius IX., though by law declared independent, was obliged to say to the Cardinals in a Consistory:

"In Rome he (the Pope) must be either a sovereign or a captive; and never will there be peace, security, and tranquillity throughout the Catholic Church as long as the exercise of the supreme apostolic ministry is left exposed to the agitation of parties, to the arbitrary power of rulers, to the vicissitudes of political elections, to the designs and actions of men, who prefer their own interest to what is just."[1]

It is in the nature of things that every Pope who is not a prince will be compelled to make the same experience and to repeat the same complaint.

The conclusion, therefore, stands that the Pope's freedom and independence will never rest on a solid basis, and will never be permanently established, unless he is at the same time a spiritual and a temporal sovereign. Of course, God may direct the rulers and animate them with love for justice and religion, for their hearts are in His hands, or He may frustrate their iniquitous onslaughts, and inspire the Pope and his ministers with such lofty sentiments as will always raise them above temporal or merely human views. But a divine interference of this kind is altogether preternatural and does not lie within the usual providential order. According to His wisdom which we know from His works, God always employs proportionate means for the attainment of His purposes, and founds permanent institutions for ends permanently to be achieved, without obstructing the operation or diminishing the freedom of His creatures. Accordingly, we must expect the independence of the Holy See to be secured by a permanent arrangement of society, and such an arrangement, we maintain, must, in the present order of things, consist in providing a civil princedom for the spiritual head of the Church.

[1] *Allocution* Luctuosis exagitati *of March* 12*th*, 1877.

Many statesmen, and many authors, who differ from us in religion, fully agree with the Catholic view on this point. Some of them show a friendly or at least fair disposition towards the Church, and therefore demand for the Holy See the possession of the Roman States not only as a matter of justice, but also as a condition necessary for its free and unimpeded action. Thus acted, for instance, the Lords Liverpool, Eldon, Castlereagh, Sidmouth, Melville, Brougham, Landsdowne, Ellensborough, Normandy,[1] the English historian Alison,[2] Thiers,[3] and Guizot.[4] Others assume a hostile attitude towards the Papacy, but are compelled by the evidence of truth to plead for its temporal dominion, as were, for instance, Gregorovius[5] and La Guerronière;[6] or they see in the downfall of the civil power the imminent ruin of the Church herself, as did King Frederick II.[7] and Count Cavour.[8]

A few reflections on ecclesiastical history are yet needed, because this has been alleged as disproving the necessity of the temporal sovereignty. The Pope, it is said, was repeatedly and even for a considerable length of time without a princedom, and nevertheless wielded his full spiritual authority. During the first centuries of the Christian era the Roman Pontiffs were not only not princes, but were persecuted by the Roman emperors, or were at least subject to them; and yet did not the Church at that very time develop a marvellous strength, and spread over the whole earth? This is undoubtedly a historical truth. But is persecution the state in which the Church is intended by God to remain? Could she, if it were so, fulfil the task imposed on her by Christ Himself, which consists in teaching all nations, in fermenting, as it were, the whole rational creation with her moral principles, and in ordering human life, both private and public, to a supernatural ultimate end? Destined as she is to be the mountain of the house of the Lord to which all nations flow (Is. xxii.), she

[1] *See* The Roman Question *by the Bishop of Salford, page* 10.—*Card. Manning,* The Independence of the Holy See, *Preface.*
[2] *History of Europe,* 1789-1815, *vol. III. ch.* 57.
[3] *In a speech delivered in the Legislative Assembly in Paris, April* 13, 1865.
[4] *L'église et la société, page* 77.
[5] *History of the City of Rome, vol. III., page* 5., *and vol. IV., page* 386.
[6] *The Pope and the Congress, page* 7, 1859.
[7] *In a letter to Voltaire, Corresp. II.,* 99.
[8] *Diplomatic Documents presented to the Chambers, page* 95. Turin. 1859.

cannot always remain concealed in the catacombs, but must, freed from all shackles, hold a position commanding reverence and submission. Then, who will deny that in the condition in which she was during those centuries, she was in many ways greatly injured, that the supreme pastor was prevented from exercising his universal office and the bishops from preaching the gospel and governing their flocks? God permitted those persecutions in order to manifest the supernatural origin of the Church, and in the absence of ordinary means, supported her by preternatural intervention which tended to corroborate the Christian faith. But miracles cannot always take the place of the ordinary means of subsistence. During the following four centuries, from Constantine the Great to King Pepin, the Holy See was in part subject to the Roman emperors, in part free. Its freedom was continually growing, until it finally developed into perfect independence, not by ambitious intrigues, but by the natural course of events. Its subjection was in one respect less harmful than it would be now, inasmuch as the Roman Empire then comprised all civilized nations, a circumstance which rendered an international position of the Papacy less necessary. Still the civil dependence in which the Popes then were, was attended with many disadvantages for their freedom, as will easily be understood from the cruel death to which some of them were put, from the exile into which others were driven, and from the pressure exercised on them by heretical emperors.

From the time of King Pepin down to our days the Popes were sovereigns of the Roman States, though not unfrequently political factions in Rome and tyrannical kings and emperors interfered with their rule and forced them to leave their princedom. Yet all such attacks on them greatly disturbed the peace and tranquillity of Europe. It was at this period of history that the Papacy reached together with the fulness of its freedom, also the fulness of its might and authority, and it was then that it bestowed the greatest benefits on human society by civilizing, pacifying and uniting all nations. In the fourteenth century the Popes took up their residence in the city of Avignon, remaining sovereigns, yet being exposed to the influence of the French court. It is known how strained the relations between the Holy See and Germany became in consequence, and how utterly impossible it was to bring about a reconciliation. Concerning England at this time the historian Green writes: " The English scorned a French Pope and threatened his legates with stoning when they landed."¹ The abode of the Roman Pontiffs resulted in the great Western schism, in which first two and later three Popes were elected. In the nineteenth century Napoleon I. devised a scheme to remove the head of the Church from Rome to Paris. And what was the object he had in view? To rule the religious as well as the political world, after he had brought the Pope into subjection by depriving him of his temporal power.² When the project failed, the emperor made him a prisoner and precluded him from communication with the Church.

Finally in our own days the Pope lost Rome and its provinces by the usurpation of the Piedmontese government, and the secret working of the Revolution. But it is claimed that complete independence with ample revenues are guaranteed to him, and that, though he did not accept the guarantees, his spiritual authority is as great and as highly respected as ever. I shall presently show that with regard to Italy the Pope has not so much freedom as is due to him in his capacity of the bishop of Rome, nor as much as is granted to the bishop of any diocese in a free country. With regard to the rest of the world, he maintains his authority in no other way than by not submitting to the Italian government, by refusing its offers, and by constantly protesting against its usurpation. But a struggle between him and the country in which he lives cannot last forever; it must sooner or later end, either in the bloody triumph of the Revolution, or the restoration of the Roman States to the Holy See.

History, studied without prejudice, on the one hand convinces us of the necessity of the temporal power of the Pope for the freedom of his apostolic ministry, on the other, reveals to us a special dispensation of Divine Providence in connecting with the Roman See a civil principality at an early period of the Christian era, in preserving the same in the course of time in spite of so many obstacles, and in thus providing the spiritual head of the Church with all the means required for the free exercise of his authority.³

The necessity of the Pope's temporal power for his unimpeded

---

¹ A Short History of the English People, *p.* 229.
² *Alison*, History of Europe, 1789–1815, *vol. III, Ch. lvii.*
³ *See F. Dupanloup, Bishop of Orleans*, The Papal Sovereignty, *Ch. vii.*

freedom being thus placed beyond any reasonable doubt, the usurpation of his dominions must be considered as an attack on his spiritual authority, and consequently as detrimental to the welfare of the whole Church. What is of greater importance for any society than an efficient government? Wherever this is obstructed, the life of the social organism must be impaired, if not altogether extinguished. How can particularly the Church prosper, if the Sovereign Pontiff is mistrusted and disobeyed, if he is no longer free to teach, to condemn the prevalent errors, to remove the dangers for the purity of morals, to settle controversies and reconcile opponents, to appoint bishops, to superintend the education of youth, and especially the training of the clergy, and to promote the propagation of the faith in heathen countries? Must not her vitality be lowered, her strength and efficacy be weakened, the faith of many be imperilled, and the bonds of union be loosed? And what shall become of religion, if the Church, in which it is embodied, is thus enfeebled in her head and her members? True, the Church will not perish, though the despoliation of the Roman Pontiff should last for a longer period. For Christ has foretold her existence to the end of time. Yet it is evident that but for a special protection of God she is bound to lack that degree of unity, holiness and efficacy, with which the divine Founder wished her to be endowed.

VI.
Reconciliation with the Italian Government Impossible.

If disastrous consequences must at any time attend the suppression of the Papal sovereignty, they will of necessity most plentifully result from the persecution now raging against the Holy See. The Revolution, which united Italy and now governs it, takes no care to avoid or to mitigate the evils connected with the changes it brought about.* On the contrary, it purposes them; it endeavors to intensify them; for its avowed object is the overthrow of the Holy See and the extermination of Christianity. The leaders of the Revolutionary movement have not concealed their intentions. Victor Emmanuel in the letter in which, in 1870, he demanded from Pius IX. the surrender of the yet remaining Papal dominions, says:

"A tempest of peril is threatening Europe. Under the cover of the war which is desolating the centre· of the continent, the party of the Cosmopolitan Revolution is increasing its hardihood and audacity, and is preparing especially in the provinces governed by your Holiness, to give the last blows to the Monarchy and the Papacy."

To this statement of the king let me add the sayings of some Italian premiers. Count Cavour at the Congress at Paris in 1856 presented a formal document to the plenipotentiaries of France and England, which was described as "a manifesto of war against the temporal and spiritual power of the Papacy," and in preparing this war he said on one occasion that "the temporal power was so closely connected with the spiritual that the one could not be separated from the other without the prospect of the destruction of both." De Pretis said in an address to his constituents: "Italy of to-day, if it has not written an immortal book, has written an immortal decree, that is, the suppression of political clericalism, the liberation of civil Christianity, the emancipation of religious thought and the free worship of humanity." Cairoli said: "The catechism is an immoral book, which should be banished from our homes." Signor Crispi,.

once an intimate friend and companion of Mazzini and Garibaldi, a freemason of the thirty-third degree, and an avowed atheist, believes that the Italian people is called to destroy Catholicism, and that between the revolutionists and the Pope there can be no truce. Some years ago he declared that the Catholic Church must be overthrown, and not long ago he expressed his intention of reducing the Pope to the condition of a simple bishop of Rome. Guiseppe Ferrari, one of the most prominent revolutionary leaders, said: "The Italian Revolution represents Italy risen against Christian Europe—against the system of Christianity." [1]

What these men have proclaimed as their programme they have carried out to the best of their power. No sooner had the Piedmontese government in 1859 and 1860 taken possession of the Papal provinces under pretext of restoring order, than it promoted the diffusion and cultivation of every false doctrine, relaxed the restraints of lust and impiety, inflicted undeserved penalties on Catholic bishops and ecclesiastics of every grade, threw them into prison and allowed them to be harassed with public insults whilst it granted impunity to their persecutors and to the assailants of the dignity of the Roman Pontiff. [2]

The Italian Parliament once opened, the enactment of laws most hostile to the Church commenced. Schools and Colleges, and of late also the beneficent institutions, were wrested from her and delivered up to her most embittered enemies. Civil marriage was forced on the people. All the clergy without exception, bishops included, were declared subject to military conscription; wherefore many a priest was since compelled to serve in the Italian army. The religious orders were suppressed and banished. Numberless sacred buildings, which for centuries had been held in veneration by the entire Catholic world, were torn down or profaned. The property of the Church, not excepting that of the Propaganda, notwithstanding her sacred and inviolable rights, was mostly confiscated. At last a penal code was sanctioned and put in force, which makes it absolutely impossible for priests and bishops, and even the highest ecclesiastical authorities, to condemn or oppose any order, disposition, or decree of the govern-

[1] *See* Card. *Manning*, Independence of the Holy See, *Preface ; The Bishop of Salford*, the Roman Question ; La Verità nella Soluzione della Questione Romana.

[2] *Encycl. letter*, Respicientes *of Pius IX.*, *Nov.* 1, 1870.

ment, however injurious to the Church, to enforce any ecclesiastical law colliding with those of the state, to publish or commend any letter of the Roman Pontiff containing a censure of a governmental act, or to raise their voice in any way for the restoration of the Pope's temporal sovereignty. The new code completely enslaves the Church to the state.

The most outspoken hostility against Christian religion was manifested, when on the feast of Pentecost, 1889, the statue of Giordano Bruno was unveiled with great pomp in presence of a numerous assembly, in which were seen a hundred and eighteen deputies and seventeen senators of the Italian Parliament. The extraordinary honors which were rendered to a man disgraced by shameful immorality, cowardice, inconstancy, and hypocrisy, fallen away from a religious order, from the priesthood, and from the Christian religion, plunged into the ignominious errors of pantheism and atheism, condemned at last by the Church and publicly executed in Rome in 1600 for his heinous crimes and his obstinacy in heresy and infidelity, could mean nothing else than an insult to the Holy See and a solemn and public profession of unbelief and hatred against the Christian religion. That this was the real purpose was but too manifest from the banners of Satan which were displayed in the procession, and from the discourses held and the writings published on this occasion, in which the holiest things were turned into ridicule, and absolute freedom of thought was exalted.[1]

In this state of affairs the question can no more be seriously put whether or not the Pope should reconcile himself with united Italy by resigning his temporal power and accepting instead of it the guarantees offered for his independence. There is on the part of the Italian statesmen no desire of reconciliation, no intention of protecting his freedom. They have but one object in view which they pursue with ingrained hatred—the overthrow of the Papacy. Before they have reached this end, their hostility will not abate. And even were this not their avowed purpose, and were their promises sincere, they could never by laws or by treaties establish the independence of the Holy See on a solid basis; they could only subvert it and thus damage the supreme spiritual authority of the Church.

[1] *Allocution* Quod nuper *of Leo XIII.*, June 30, 1889.

The Holy Father, therefore, must again and again protest against the usurpation of his states; he must on all occasions claim his rights and his restoration to them, in order not to create a prejudice against them by his silence; he must set forth his legitimate titles and dwell on the injustice committed by the usurpers; he must condemn those who have perpetrated so enormous a wrong against the See of St. Peter, and deter others from participation in their crime; he must assert and defend the possessions entrusted to him by God's special providence as means altogether necessary for the free exercise of his apostolic ministry and for the welfare of the Church.

Placed on the apostolic rock he cannot give way, but is bound to resist the tempest which now rages against Christian religion. Seated on the Chair of St. Peter, he is obliged to lift up his voice like a prophet and unceasingly to recall to the minds of men the true knowledge of right and justice, to bear witness before the whole world to the truth of God, to point out to human society the impending dangers, and to counteract by word and deed the machinations openly and secretly directed against the foundations of the Church.

Not the Pope alone, however, the great Leo XIII., must fight the good fight. We are his children. How could we leave him alone in his struggle and affliction and not raise our voice with his against the enormous wrong done to the Holy See and the still greater evils that threaten it? We form the Church militant, whose divinely-appointed and courageous leader he is. We are obliged to follow him into the brunt of the battle which is fought for the kingdom of God. At stake there is the freedom of the See of St. Peter, the freedom of the spouse of Christ who has given life to us, the freedom of the mystical body of which we are members. In the very age in which we live the love of political freedom has seized the nations, and in particular the people of our beloved country, and has given them a marvellous strength to perform heroic deeds. What enthusiasm then should Catholics not show, and what sacrifices should they not be willing to make for the much sublimer freedom of the Church purchased by the blood of Christ?

www.ingramcontent.com/pod-product-compliance
Lightning Source LLC
Chambersburg PA
CBHW031947290426
44108CB00011B/706